Never Give Up

Volume 1

TOKYOPOP®

HAMBURG // LONDON // LOS ANGELES // TOKYO

Never Give Up Vol. 1
created by Hiromu Muto

Translation - Mike Kiefl
English Adaptation - Jodi Bryson
Associate Editor - Peter Ahlstrom
Retouch and Lettering - Bowen Park
Production Artist - Alyson Stetz
Cover Design- Jorge Negrete

Editor - Julie Taylor
Digital Imaging Manager - Chris Buford
Production Managers - Jennifer Miller and Mutsumi Miyazaki
Managing Editor - Lindsey Johnston
VP of Production - Ron Klamert
Publisher and E.I.C. - Mike Kiley
President and C.O.O. - John Parker
C.E.O. and Chief Creative Officer - Stuart Levy

A  Manga

TOKYOPOP Inc.
5900 Wilshire Blvd. Suite 2000
Los Angeles, CA 90036

E-mail: info@TOKYOPOP.com
Come visit us online at www.TOKYOPOP.com

ISBN: 1-59816-165-2

First TOKYOPOP printing: March 2006
10 9 8 7 6 5 4 3 2
Printed in the USA

Never Give Up™

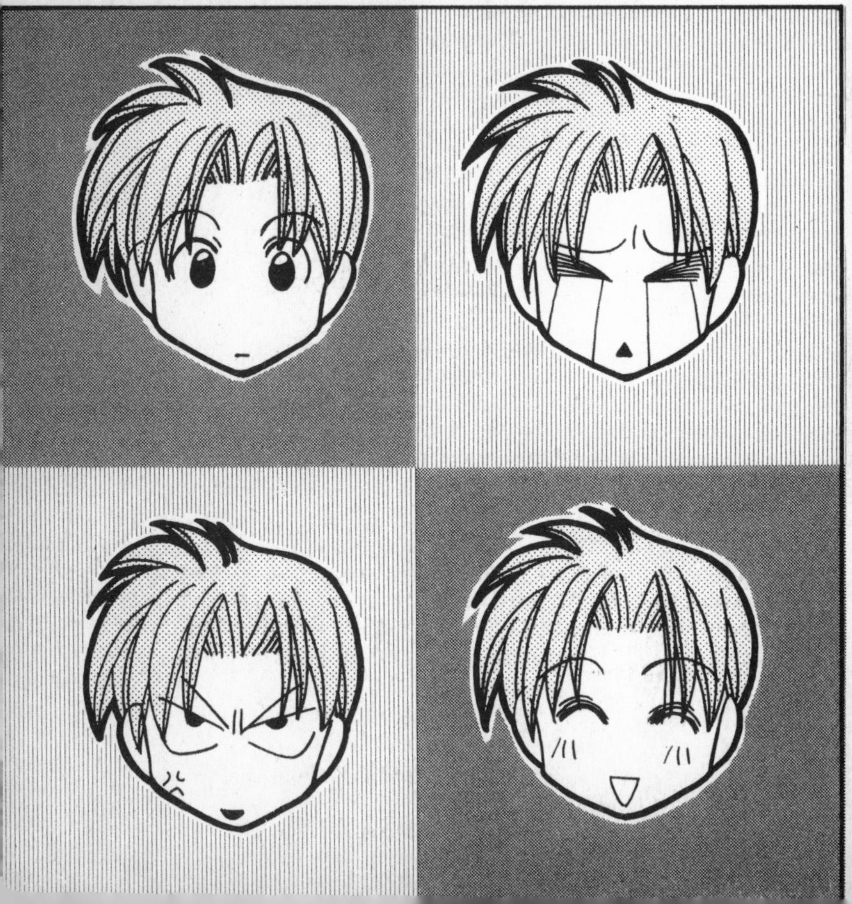

Contents

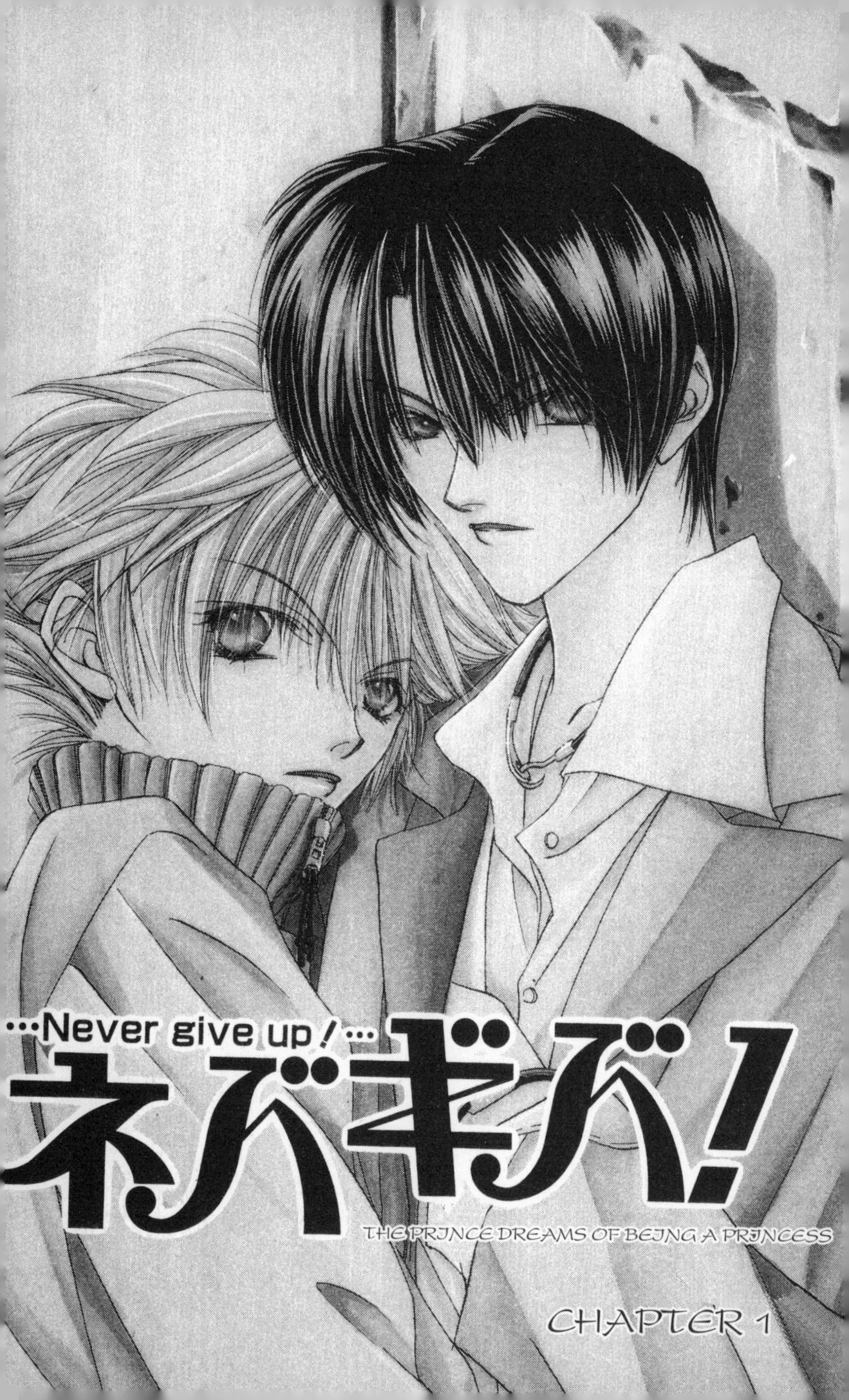
…Never give up!…
ネバギバ!
THE PRINCE DREAMS OF BEING A PRINCESS
CHAPTER 1

Prologue

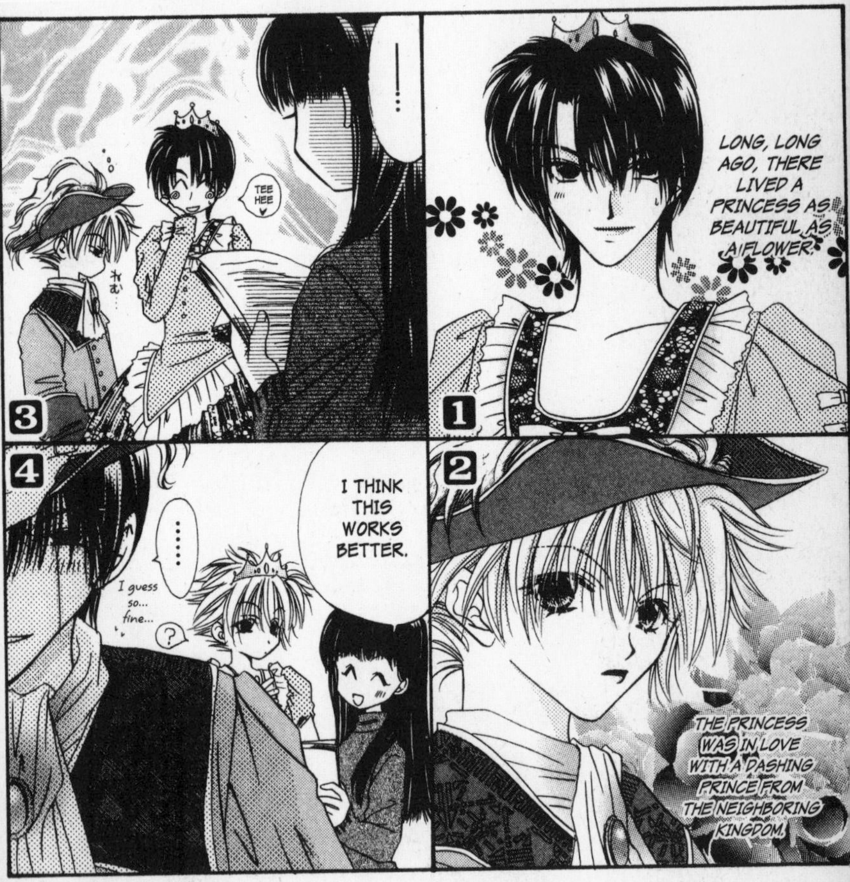

1
LONG, LONG AGO, THERE LIVED A PRINCESS AS BEAUTIFUL AS A FLOWER.
2
THE PRINCESS WAS IN LOVE WITH A DASHING PRINCE FROM THE NEIGHBORING KINGDOM.
3
!...
TEE HEE
4
I THINK THIS WORKS BETTER.
......
I guess so... fine...
?

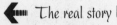

The real story begins on the next page!

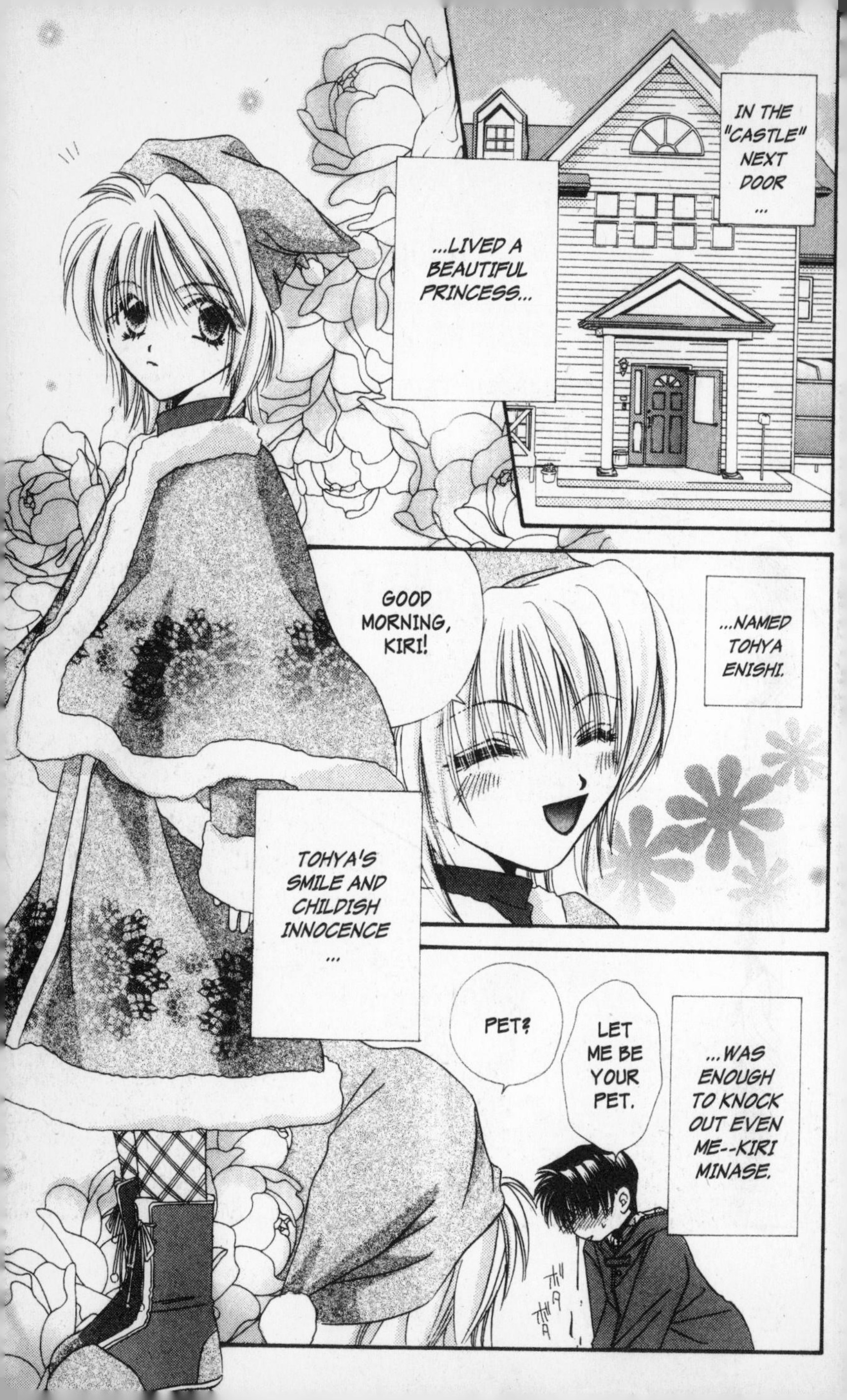
IN THE "CASTLE" NEXT DOOR ...
...LIVED A BEAUTIFUL PRINCESS...
...NAMED TOHYA ENISHI.
GOOD MORNING, KIRI!
TOHYA'S SMILE AND CHILDISH INNOCENCE ...
...WAS ENOUGH TO KNOCK OUT EVEN ME--KIRI MINASE.
LET ME BE YOUR PET.
PET?
ボタ
ボタ

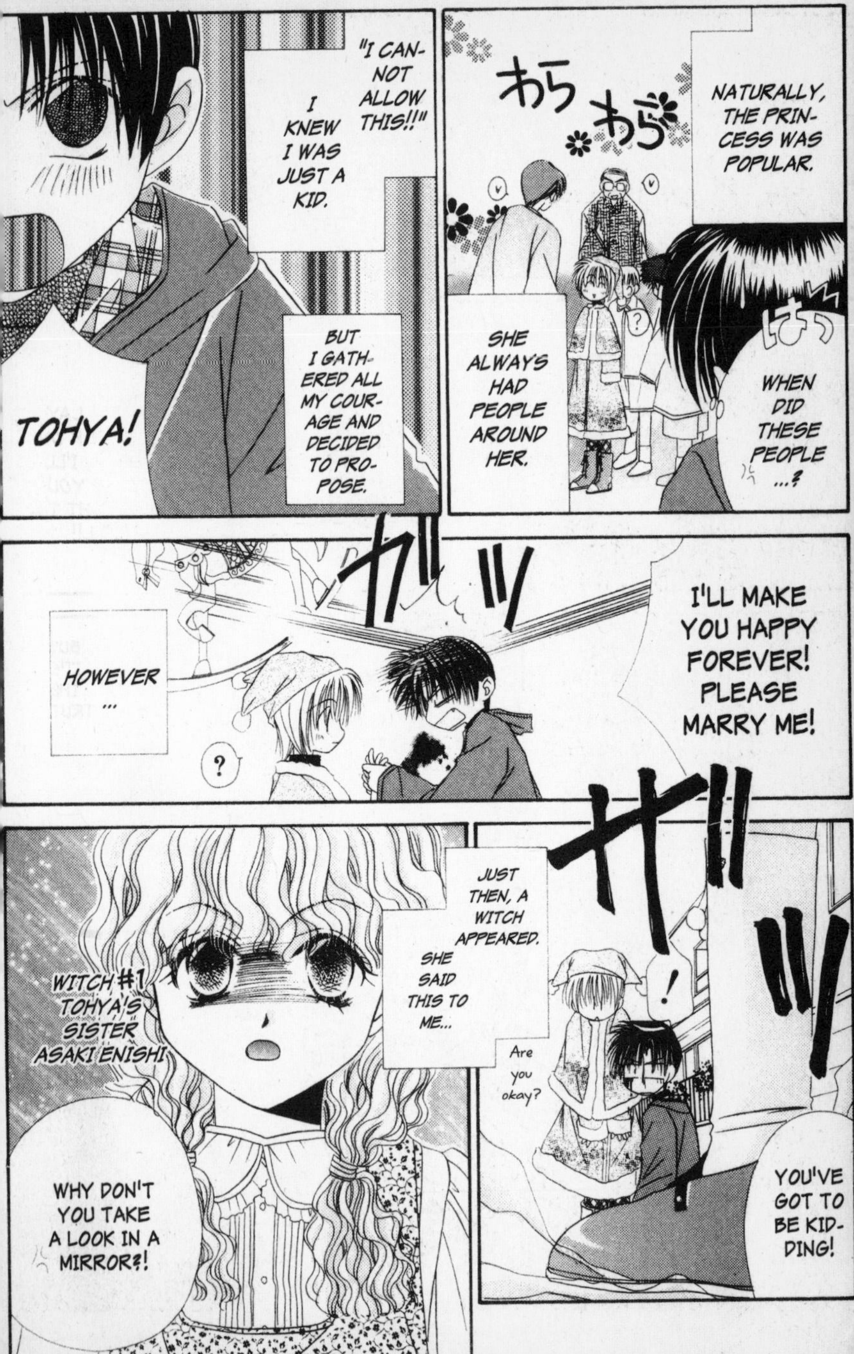

NATURALLY, THE PRINCESS WAS POPULAR.
わら わら
SHE ALWAYS HAD PEOPLE AROUND HER.
はっ
WHEN DID THESE PEOPLE ...?
"I CANNOT ALLOW THIS!!"
I KNEW I WAS JUST A KID.
BUT I GATHERED ALL MY COURAGE AND DECIDED TO PROPOSE.
TOHYA!
I'LL MAKE YOU HAPPY FOREVER! PLEASE MARRY ME!
HOWEVER ...
?
JUST THEN, A WITCH APPEARED.
SHE SAID THIS TO ME...
!
Are you okay?
YOU'VE GOT TO BE KIDDING!
WITCH #1 TOHYA'S SISTER ASAKI ENISHI
WHY DON'T YOU TAKE A LOOK IN A MIRROR?!

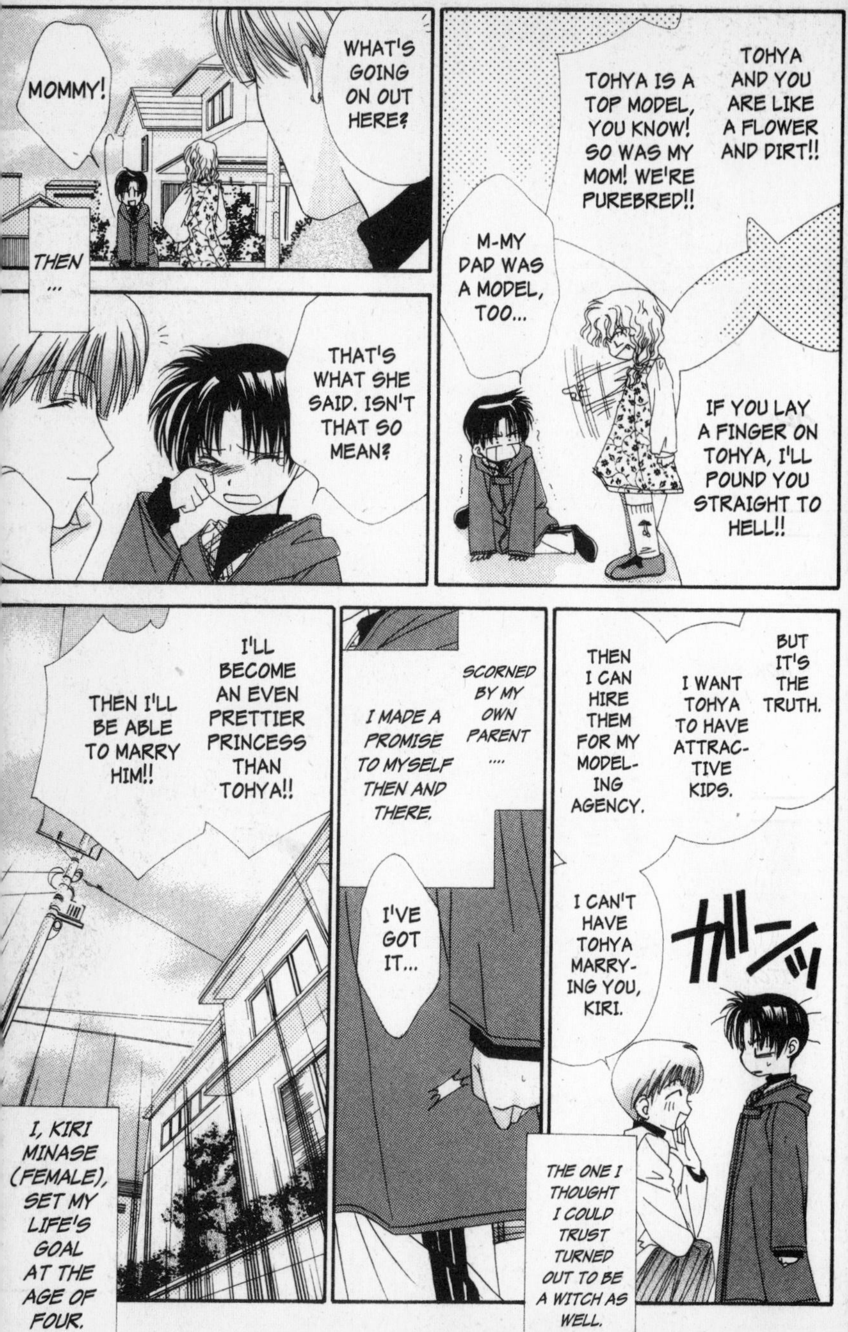
TOHYA AND YOU ARE LIKE A FLOWER AND DIRT!!
TOHYA IS A TOP MODEL, YOU KNOW! SO WAS MY MOM! WE'RE PUREBRED!!
M-MY DAD WAS A MODEL, TOO...
IF YOU LAY A FINGER ON TOHYA, I'LL POUND YOU STRAIGHT TO HELL!!
WHAT'S GOING ON OUT HERE?
MOMMY!
THEN ...
THAT'S WHAT SHE SAID. ISN'T THAT SO MEAN?
BUT IT'S THE TRUTH.
I WANT TOHYA TO HAVE ATTRACTIVE KIDS.
THEN I CAN HIRE THEM FOR MY MODELING AGENCY.
I CAN'T HAVE TOHYA MARRYING YOU, KIRI.
ガーンッ
THE ONE I THOUGHT I COULD TRUST TURNED OUT TO BE A WITCH AS WELL.
SCORNED BY MY OWN PARENT ....
I MADE A PROMISE TO MYSELF THEN AND THERE.
I'VE GOT IT...
I'LL BECOME AN EVEN PRETTIER PRINCESS THAN TOHYA!!
THEN I'LL BE ABLE TO MARRY HIM!!
I, KIRI MINASE (FEMALE), SET MY LIFE'S GOAL AT THE AGE OF FOUR.

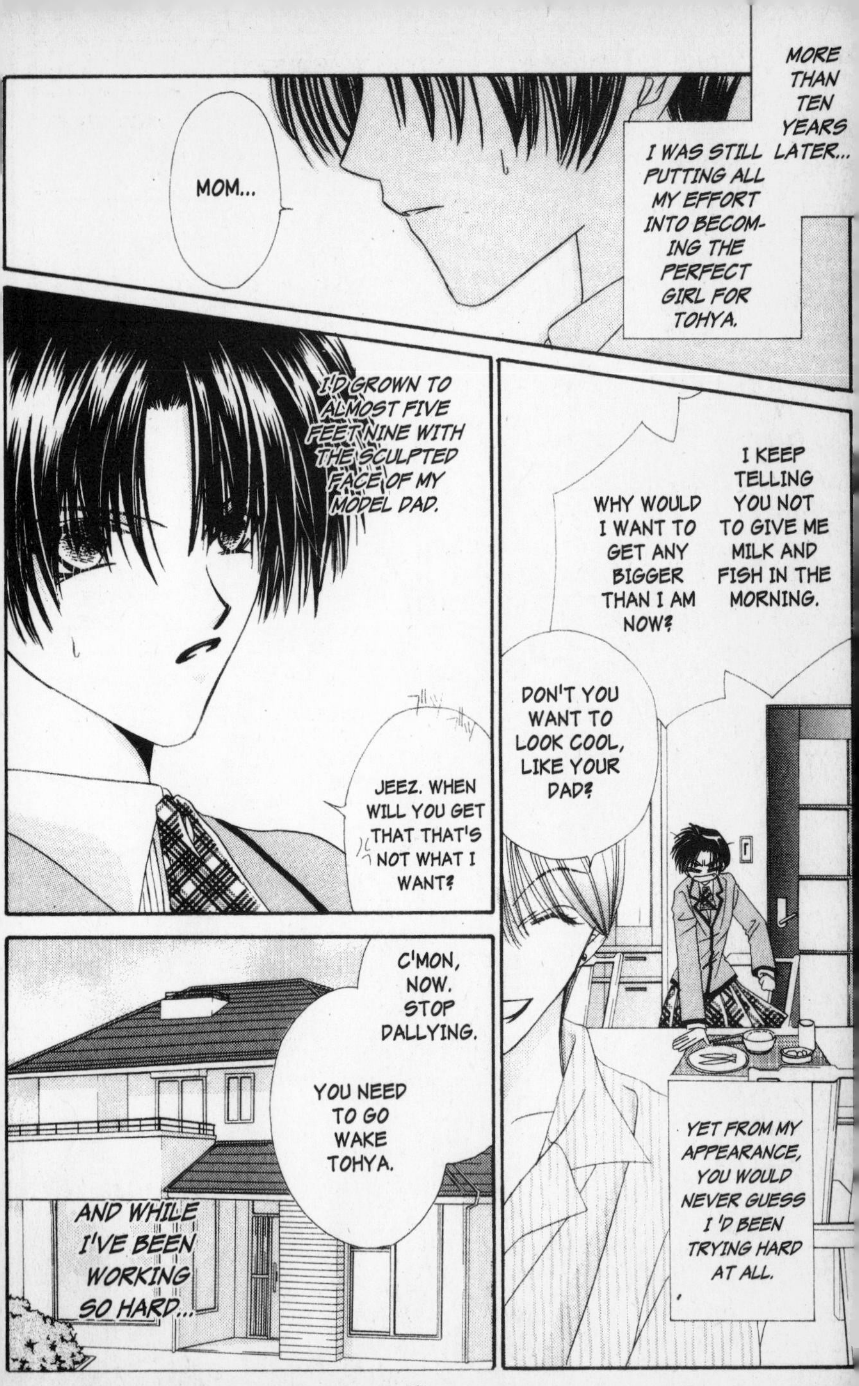
MORE THAN TEN YEARS LATER...
I WAS STILL PUTTING ALL MY EFFORT INTO BECOM-ING THE PERFECT GIRL FOR TOHYA.
MOM...
I KEEP TELLING YOU NOT TO GIVE ME MILK AND FISH IN THE MORNING.
WHY WOULD I WANT TO GET ANY BIGGER THAN I AM NOW?
DON'T YOU WANT TO LOOK COOL, LIKE YOUR DAD?
YET FROM MY APPEARANCE, YOU WOULD NEVER GUESS I'D BEEN TRYING HARD AT ALL.
I'D GROWN TO ALMOST FIVE FEET NINE WITH THE SCULPTED FACE OF MY MODEL DAD.
JEEZ. WHEN WILL YOU GET THAT THAT'S NOT WHAT I WANT?
C'MON, NOW. STOP DALLYING.
YOU NEED TO GO WAKE TOHYA.
AND WHILE I'VE BEEN WORKING SO HARD...

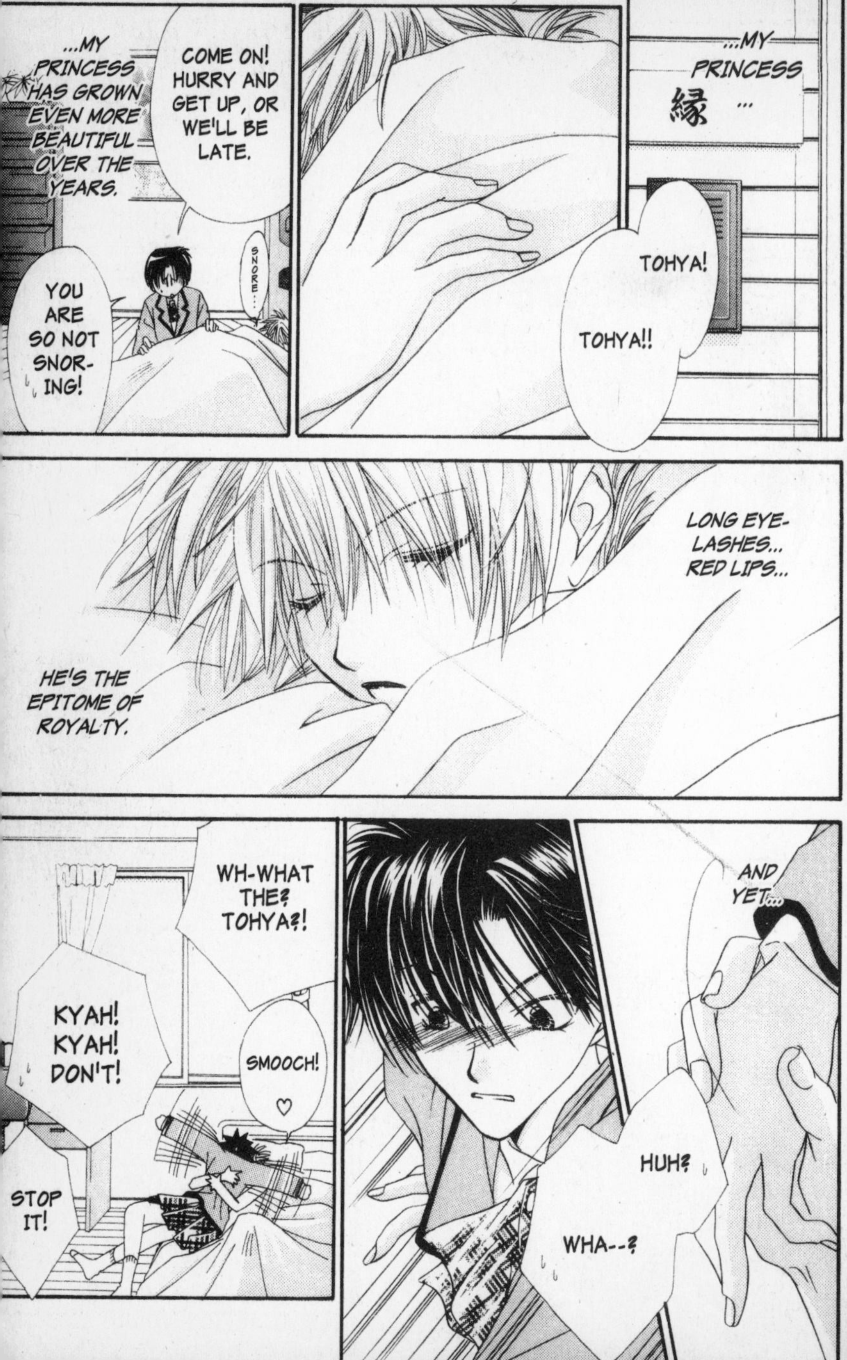
...MY PRINCESS 縁 ...
TOHYA!
TOHYA!!
COME ON! HURRY AND GET UP, OR WE'LL BE LATE.
...MY PRINCESS HAS GROWN EVEN MORE BEAUTIFUL OVER THE YEARS.
SNORE...
YOU ARE SO NOT SNORING!
LONG EYE-LASHES... RED LIPS...
HE'S THE EPITOME OF ROYALTY.
AND YET...
HUH?
WHA--?
WH-WHAT THE? TOHYA?!
SMOOCH! ♡
KYAH! KYAH! DON'T!
STOP IT!

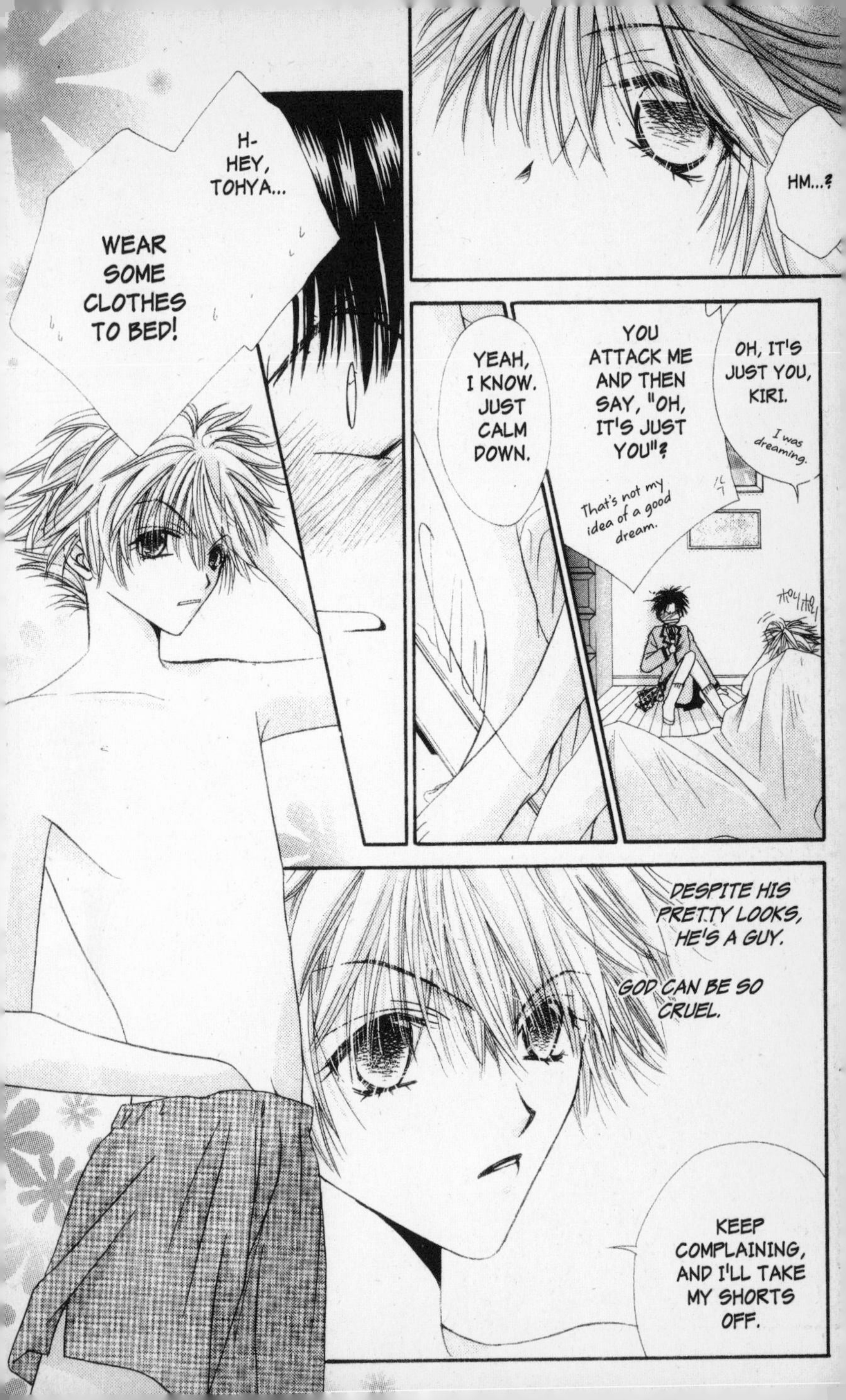
HM...?
OH, IT'S JUST YOU, KIRI.
I was dreaming.
YOU ATTACK ME AND THEN SAY, "OH, IT'S JUST YOU"?
That's not my idea of a good dream.
YEAH, I KNOW. JUST CALM DOWN.
DESPITE HIS PRETTY LOOKS, HE'S A GUY.
GOD CAN BE SO CRUEL.
KEEP COMPLAINING, AND I'LL TAKE MY SHORTS OFF.
H- HEY, TOHYA...
WEAR SOME CLOTHES TO BED!

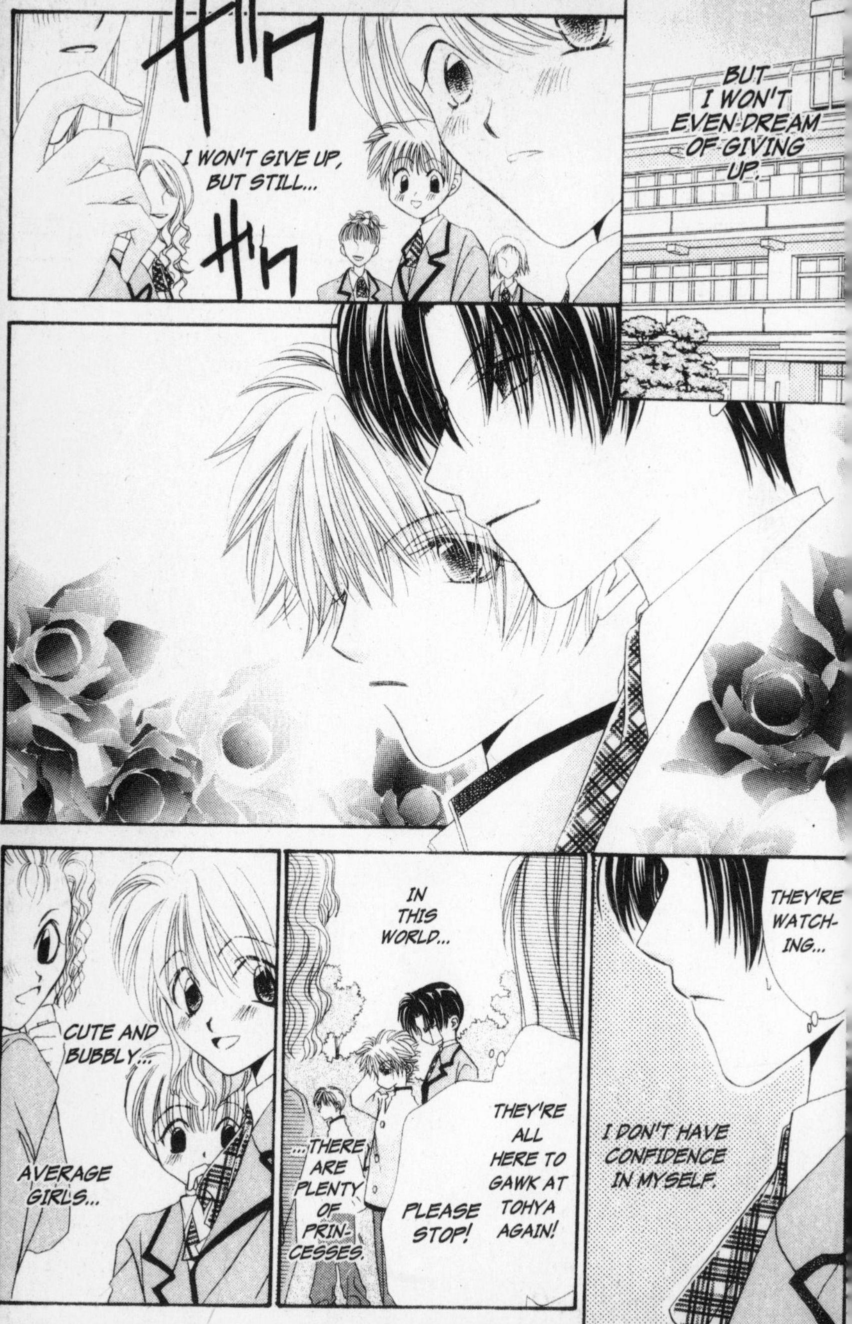
BUT I WON'T EVEN DREAM OF GIVING UP.
I WON'T GIVE UP, BUT STILL...
THEY'RE WATCHING-ING...
I DON'T HAVE CONFIDENCE IN MYSELF.
IN THIS WORLD...
THEY'RE ALL HERE TO GAWK AT TOHYA AGAIN!
PLEASE STOP!
...THERE ARE PLENTY OF PRIN-CESSES.
CUTE AND BUBBLY...
AVERAGE GIRLS...

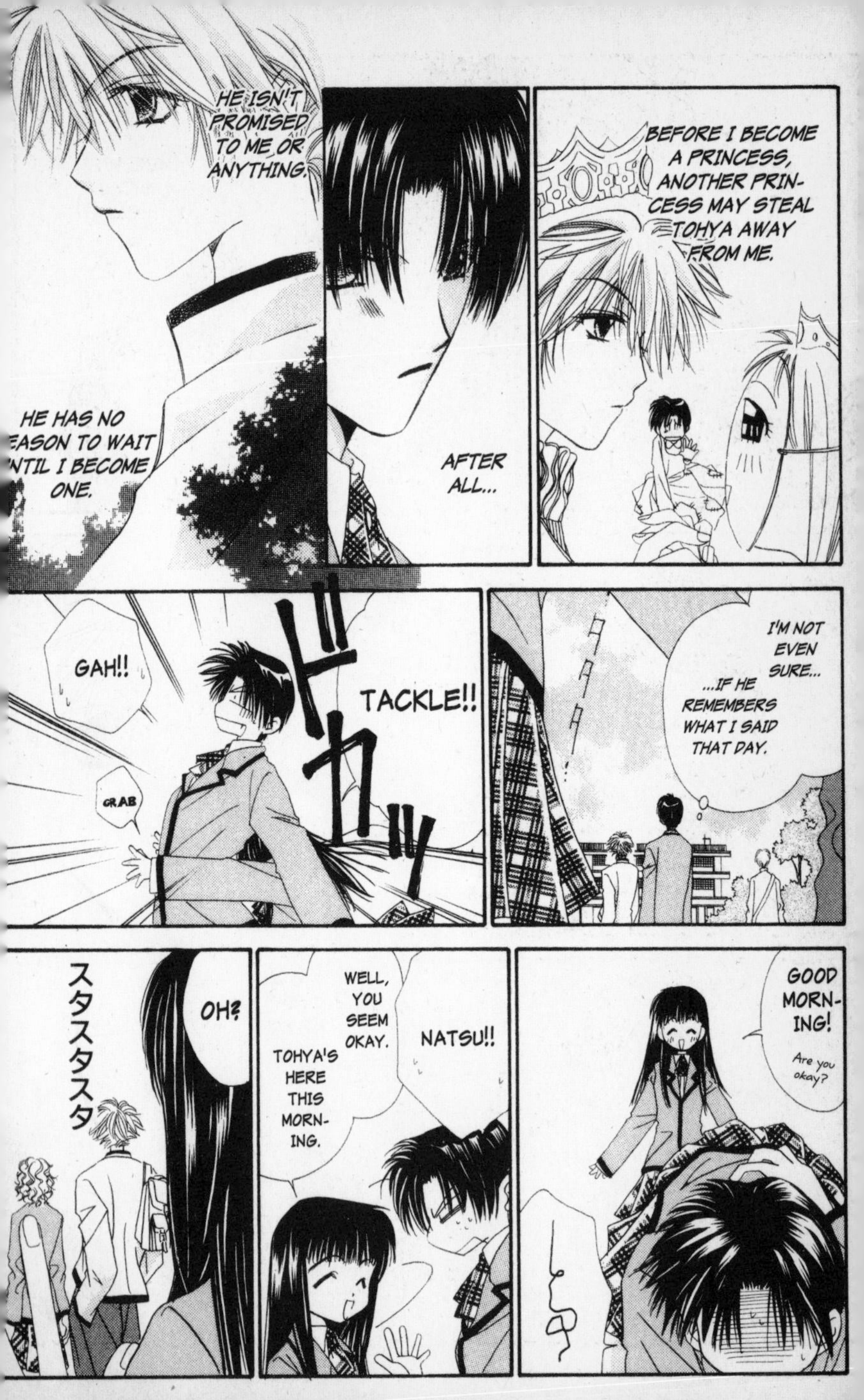
BEFORE I BECOME A PRINCESS, ANOTHER PRIN-CESS MAY STEAL TOHYA AWAY FROM ME.
AFTER ALL...
HE ISN'T PROMISED TO ME OR ANYTHING.
HE HAS NO EASON TO WAIT NTIL I BECOME ONE.
I'M NOT EVEN SURE...
...IF HE REMEMBERS WHAT I SAID THAT DAY.
ドカッ
TACKLE!!
GAH!!
GRAB
GOOD MORN-ING!
Are you okay?
NATSU!!
WELL, YOU SEEM OKAY.
TOHYA'S HERE THIS MORN-ING.
OH?
スタスタスタ

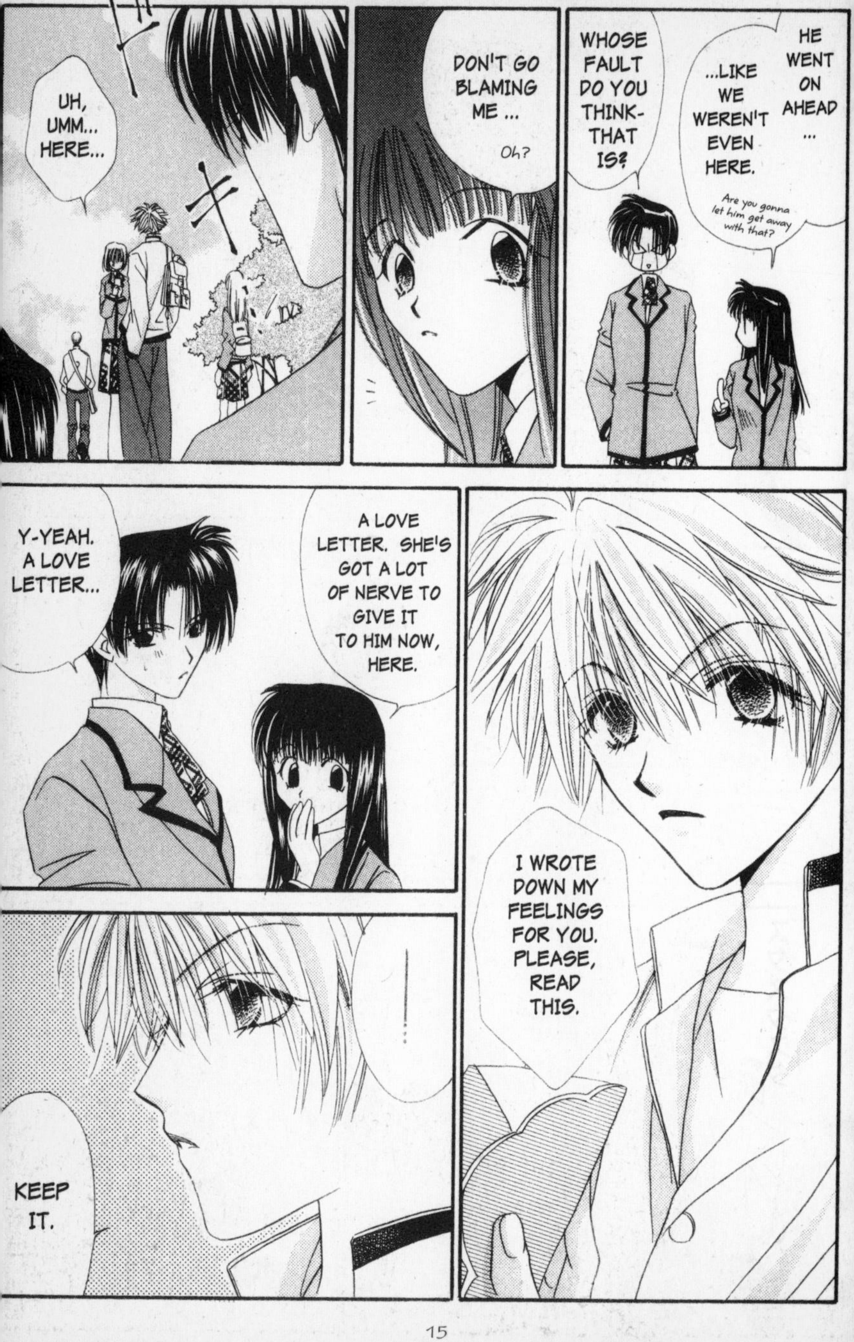
HE WENT ON AHEAD ...
...LIKE WE WEREN'T EVEN HERE.
WHOSE FAULT DO YOU THINK THAT IS?
Are you gonna let him get away with that?
DON'T GO BLAMING ME ...
Oh?
UH, UMM... HERE...
I WROTE DOWN MY FEELINGS FOR YOU. PLEASE, READ THIS.
A LOVE LETTER. SHE'S GOT A LOT OF NERVE TO GIVE IT TO HIM NOW, HERE.
Y-YEAH. A LOVE LETTER...
KEEP IT.

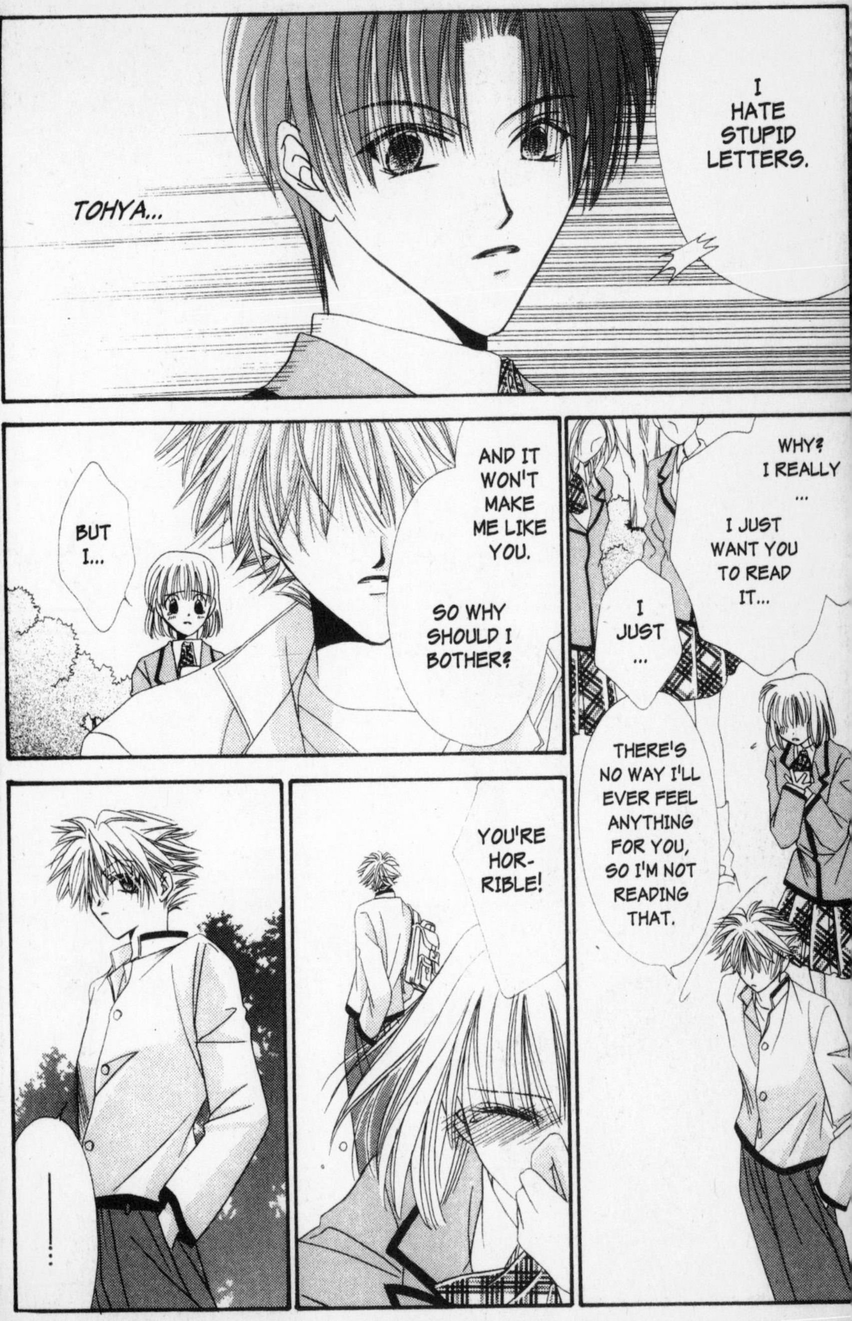
I HATE STUPID LETTERS.
TOHYA...
WHY? I REALLY ...
I JUST WANT YOU TO READ IT...
I JUST ...
THERE'S NO WAY I'LL EVER FEEL ANYTHING FOR YOU, SO I'M NOT READING THAT.
AND IT WON'T MAKE ME LIKE YOU.
SO WHY SHOULD I BOTHER?
BUT I...
YOU'RE HOR-RIBLE!
......

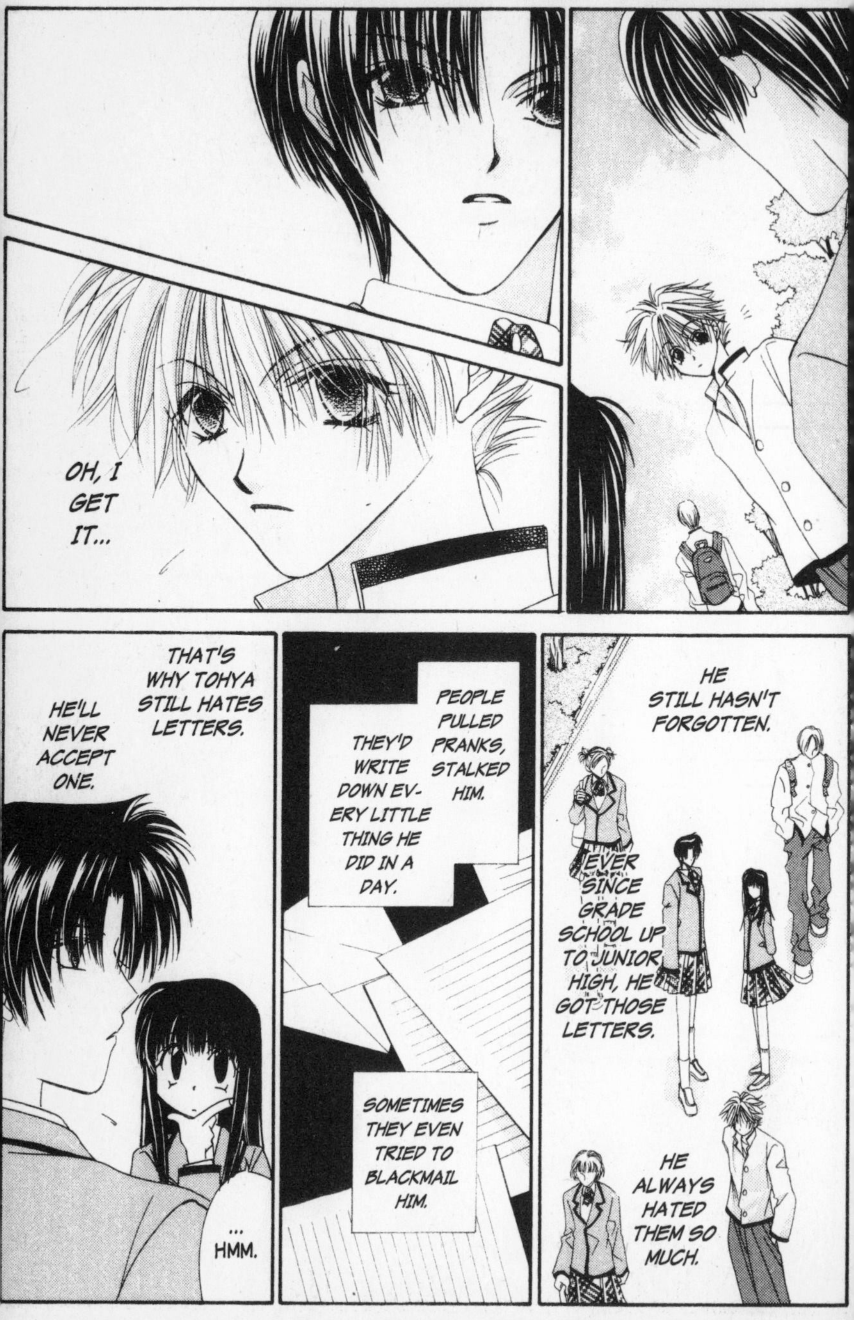
OH, I GET IT...
HE STILL HASN'T FORGOTTEN.
EVER SINCE GRADE SCHOOL UP TO JUNIOR HIGH, HE GOT THOSE LETTERS.
HE ALWAYS HATED THEM SO MUCH.
PEOPLE PULLED PRANKS, STALKED HIM.
THEY'D WRITE DOWN EVERY LITTLE THING HE DID IN A DAY.
SOMETIMES THEY EVEN TRIED TO BLACKMAIL HIM.
THAT'S WHY TOHYA STILL HATES LETTERS.
HE'LL NEVER ACCEPT ONE.
... HMM.

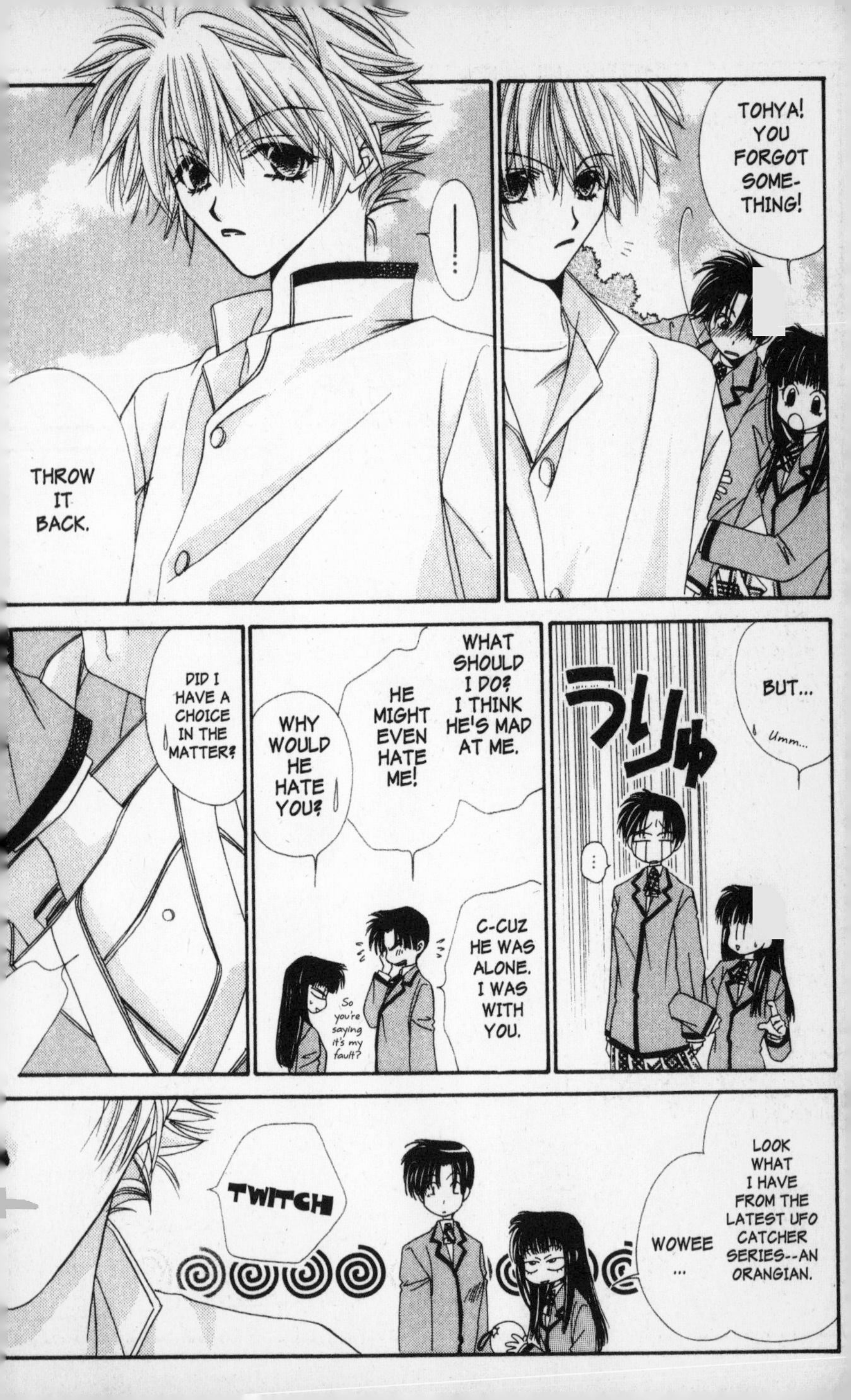
TOHYA! YOU FORGOT SOME-THING!
!
THROW IT BACK.
BUT...
Umm...
うりゅ
...
WHAT SHOULD I DO? I THINK HE'S MAD AT ME.
HE MIGHT EVEN HATE ME!
WHY WOULD HE HATE YOU?
C-CUZ HE WAS ALONE. I WAS WITH YOU.
So you're saying it's my fault?
DID I HAVE A CHOICE IN THE MATTER?
LOOK WHAT I HAVE FROM THE LATEST UFO CATCHER SERIES--AN ORANGIAN.
WOWEE ...
TWITCH

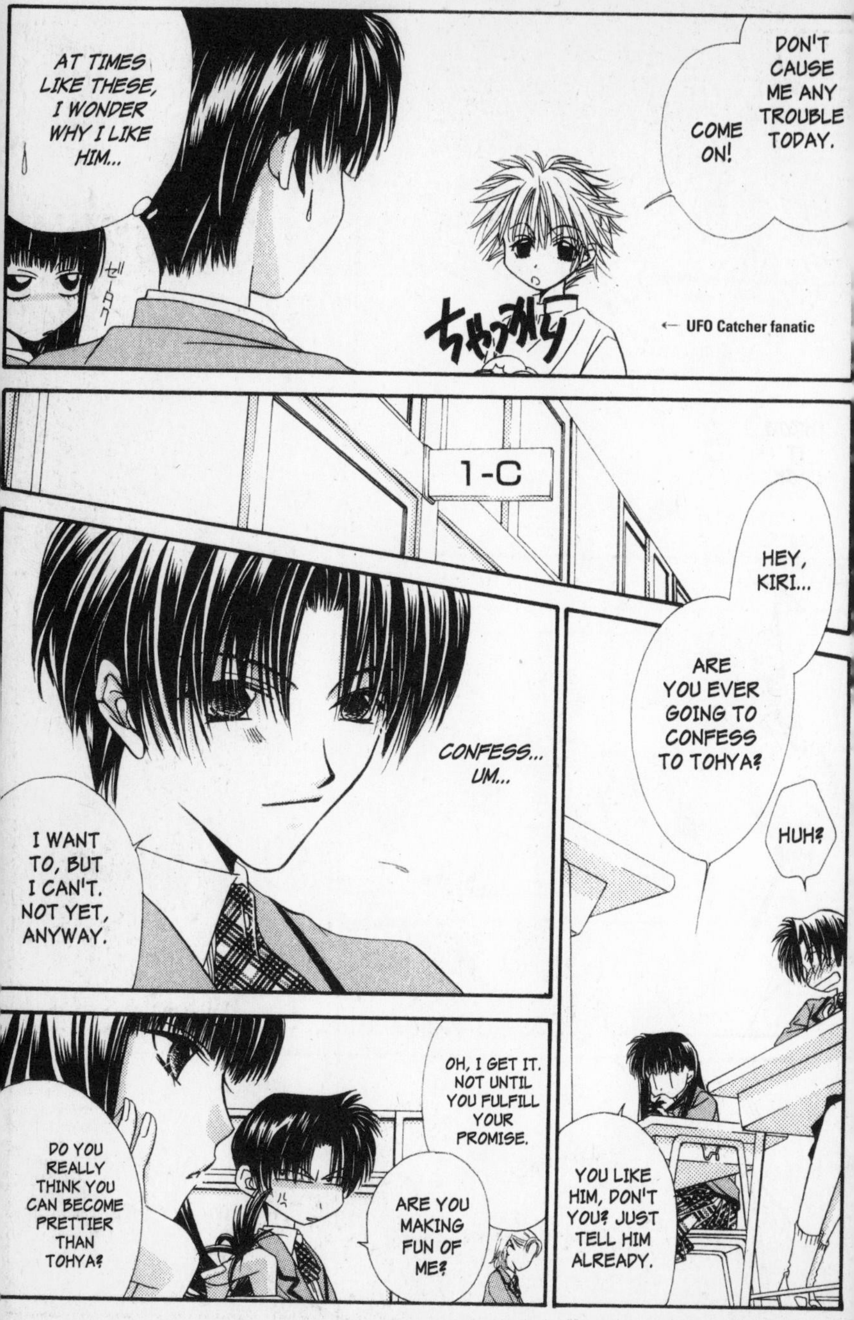
DON'T CAUSE ME ANY TROUBLE TODAY.
COME ON!
AT TIMES LIKE THESE, I WONDER WHY I LIKE HIM...
ゼータク
ちゃっかり
← UFO Catcher fanatic
1-C
HEY, KIRI...
ARE YOU EVER GOING TO CONFESS TO TOHYA?
HUH?
YOU LIKE HIM, DON'T YOU? JUST TELL HIM ALREADY.
CONFESS... UM...
I WANT TO, BUT I CAN'T. NOT YET, ANYWAY.
OH, I GET IT. NOT UNTIL YOU FULFILL YOUR PROMISE.
ARE YOU MAKING FUN OF ME?
DO YOU REALLY THINK YOU CAN BECOME PRETTIER THAN TOHYA?

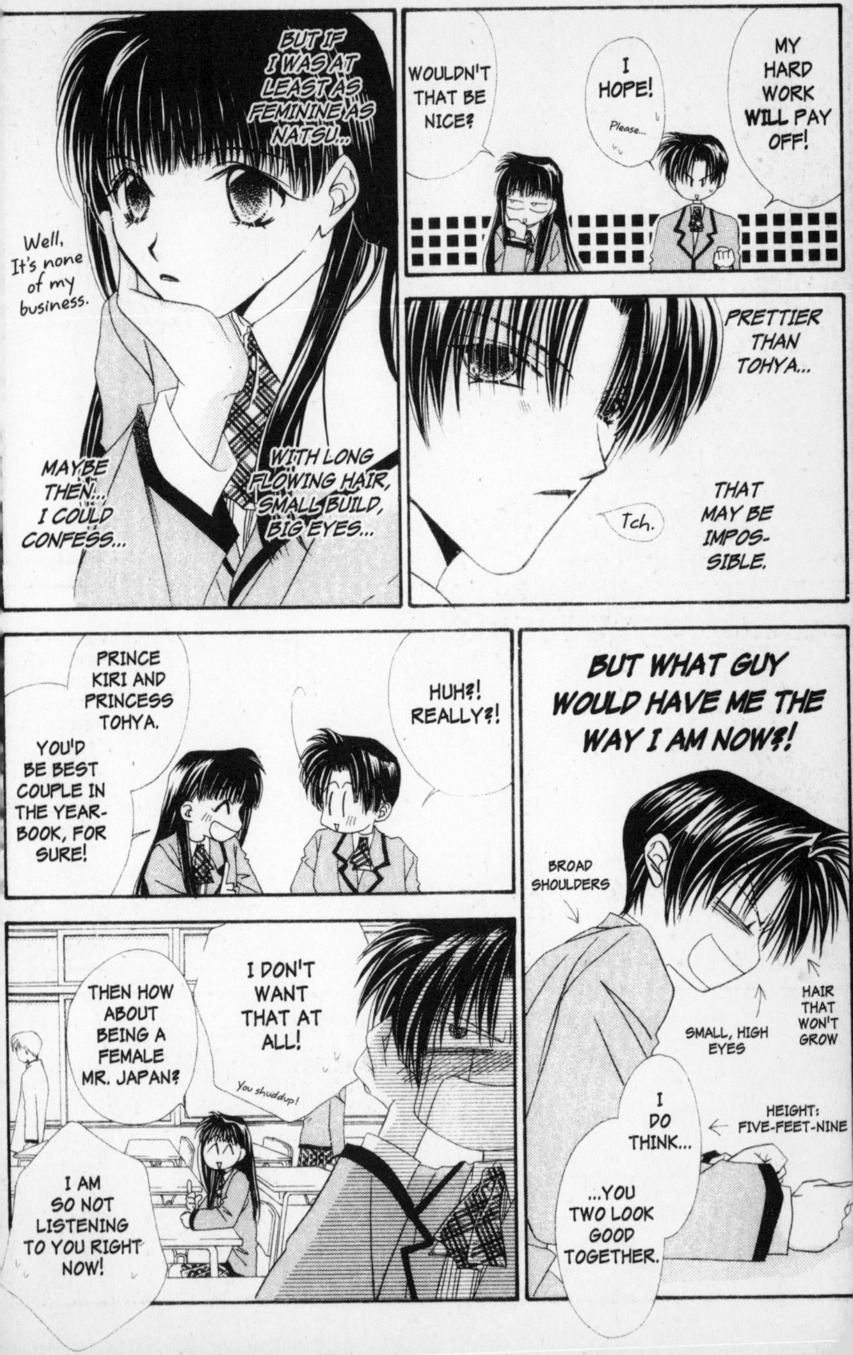
MY HARD WORK WILL PAY OFF!
I HOPE!
Please...
WOULDN'T THAT BE NICE?
PRETTIER THAN TOHYA...
THAT MAY BE IMPOSSIBLE.
Tch.
BUT IF I WAS AT LEAST AS FEMININE AS NATSU...
WITH LONG FLOWING HAIR, SMALL BUILD, BIG EYES...
MAYBE THEN... I COULD CONFESS...
Well, It's none of my business.
BUT WHAT GUY WOULD HAVE ME THE WAY I AM NOW?!
HAIR THAT WON'T GROW
SMALL, HIGH EYES
BROAD SHOULDERS
HEIGHT: FIVE-FEET-NINE
I DO THINK...
...YOU TWO LOOK GOOD TOGETHER.
HUH?! REALLY?!
PRINCE KIRI AND PRINCESS TOHYA.
YOU'D BE BEST COUPLE IN THE YEAR-BOOK, FOR SURE!
I DON'T WANT THAT AT ALL!
You shuddup!
THEN HOW ABOUT BEING A FEMALE MR. JAPAN?
I AM SO NOT LISTENING TO YOU RIGHT NOW!

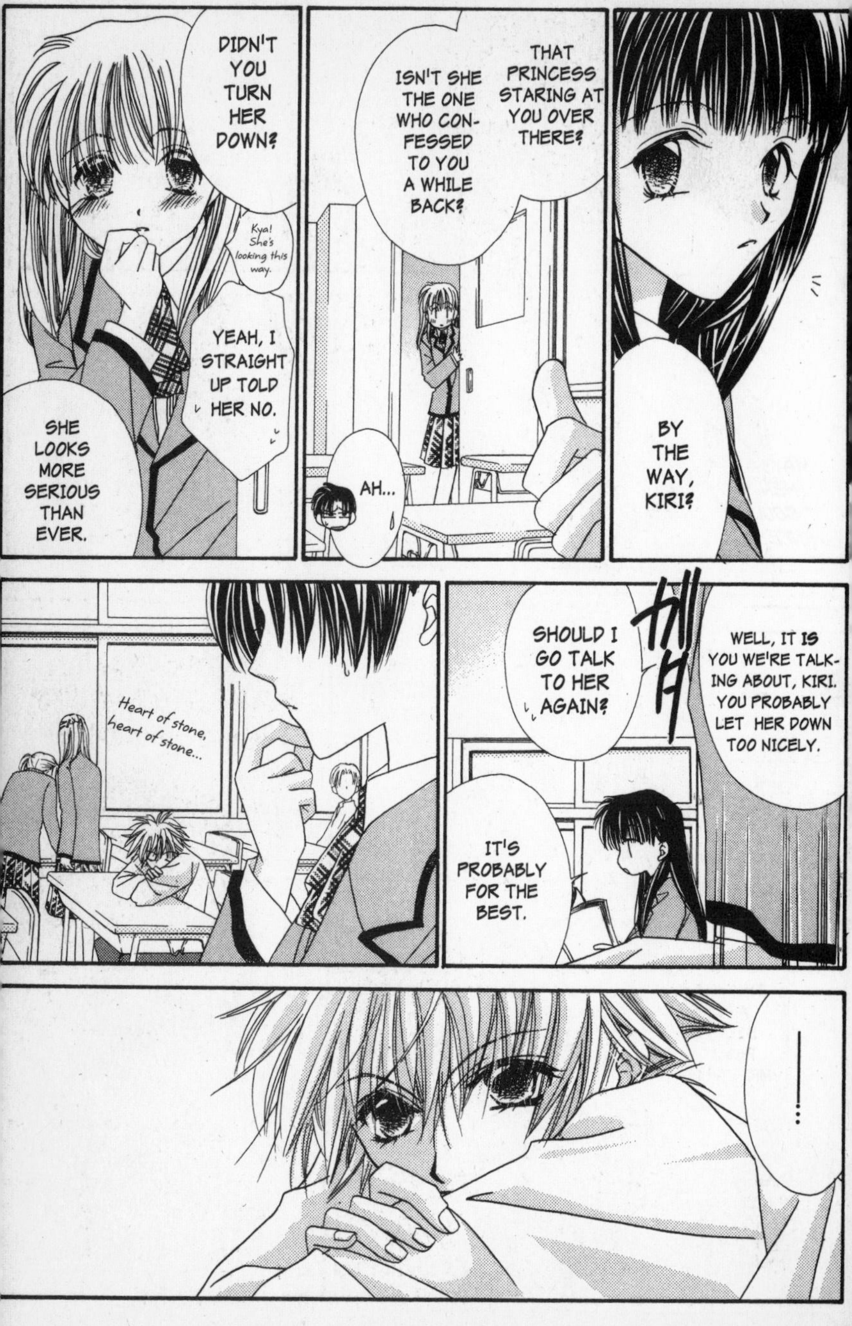
BY THE WAY, KIRI?
THAT PRINCESS STARING AT YOU OVER THERE?
ISN'T SHE THE ONE WHO CON-FESSED TO YOU A WHILE BACK?
AH...
DIDN'T YOU TURN HER DOWN?
Kya! She's looking this way.
YEAH, I STRAIGHT UP TOLD HER NO.
SHE LOOKS MORE SERIOUS THAN EVER.
WELL, IT IS YOU WE'RE TALK-ING ABOUT, KIRI. YOU PROBABLY LET HER DOWN TOO NICELY.
SHOULD I GO TALK TO HER AGAIN?
IT'S PROBABLY FOR THE BEST.
Heart of stone, heart of stone...
......

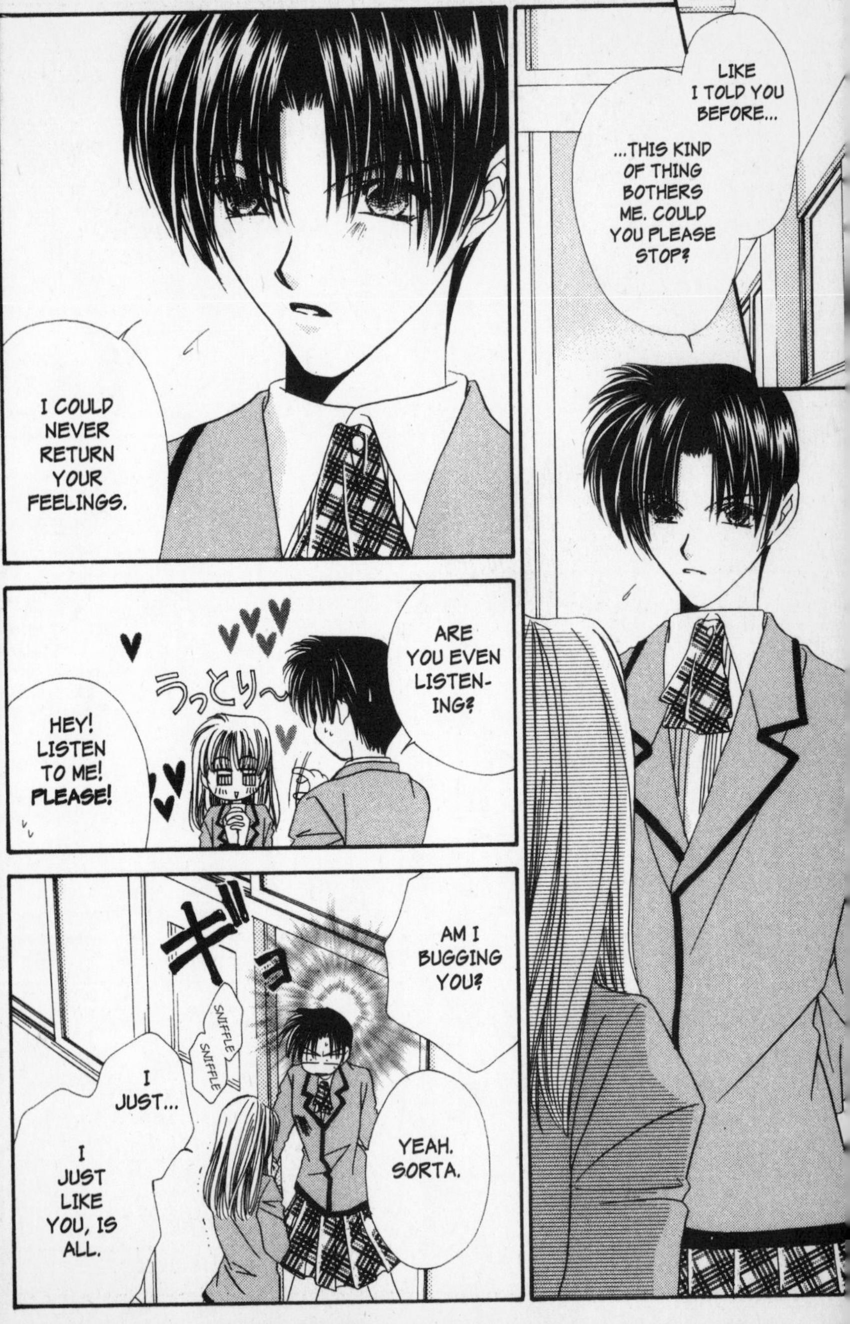
LIKE I TOLD YOU BEFORE...
...THIS KIND OF THING BOTHERS ME. COULD YOU PLEASE STOP?
I COULD NEVER RETURN YOUR FEELINGS.
ARE YOU EVEN LISTEN-ING?
うっとり～
HEY! LISTEN TO ME! PLEASE!
AM I BUGGING YOU?
YEAH. SORTA.
SNIFFLE SNIFFLE
I JUST...
I JUST LIKE YOU, IS ALL.

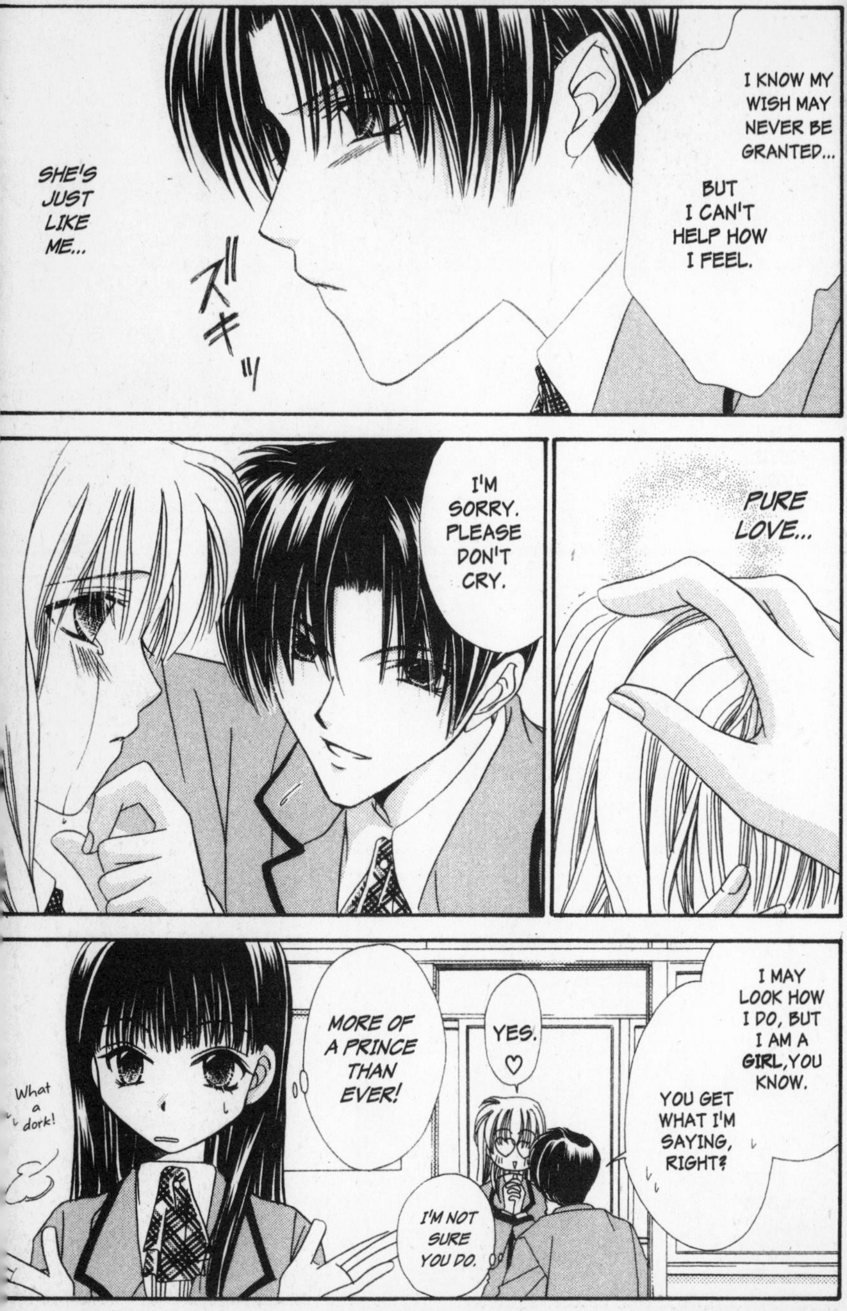
I KNOW MY WISH MAY NEVER BE GRANTED...
BUT I CAN'T HELP HOW I FEEL.
ズキッ
SHE'S JUST LIKE ME...
PURE LOVE...
I'M SORRY. PLEASE DON'T CRY.
I MAY LOOK HOW I DO, BUT I AM A GIRL, YOU KNOW.
YOU GET WHAT I'M SAYING, RIGHT?
YES. ♡
I'M NOT SURE YOU DO.
MORE OF A PRINCE THAN EVER!
What a dork!

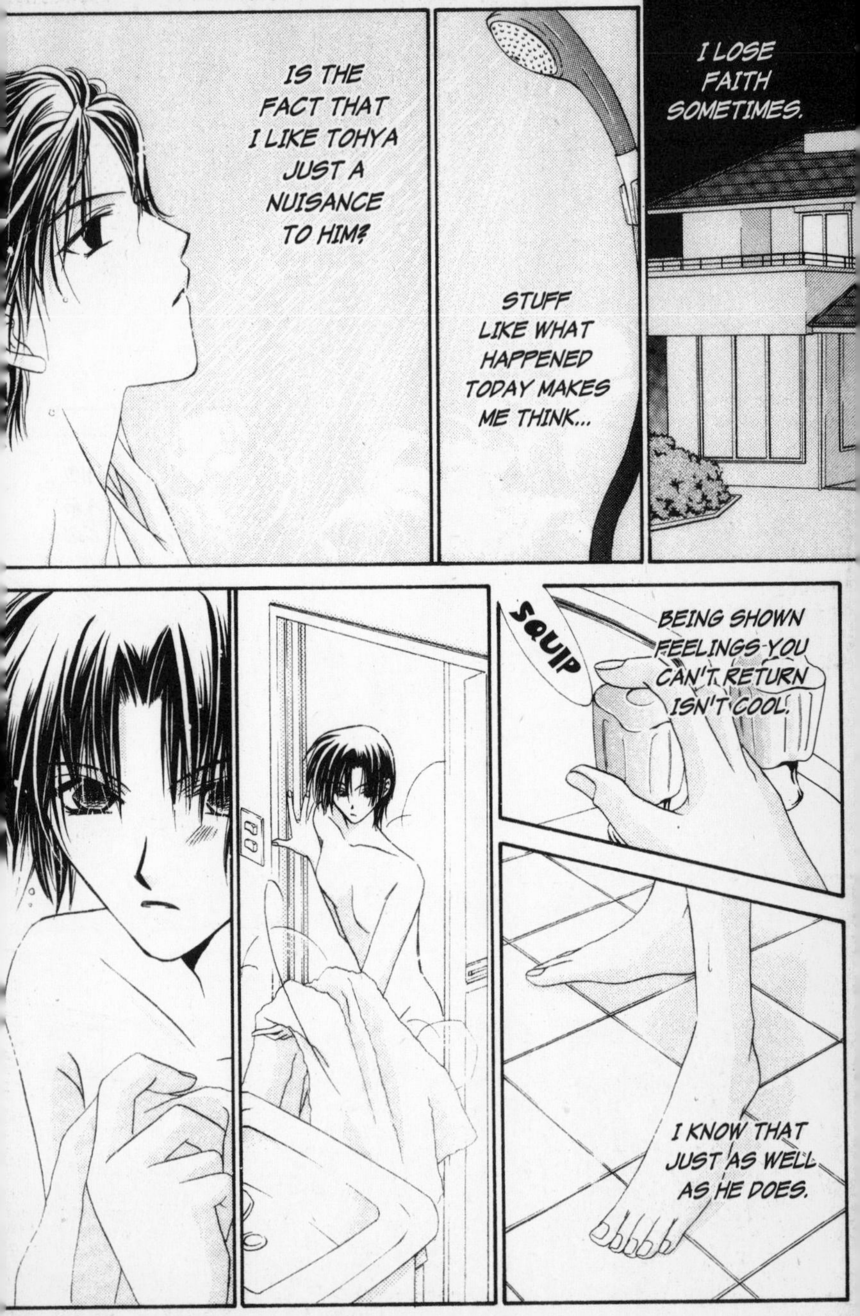
I LOSE FAITH SOMETIMES.
STUFF LIKE WHAT HAPPENED TODAY MAKES ME THINK...
IS THE FACT THAT I LIKE TOHYA JUST A NUISANCE TO HIM?
SQUIP
BEING SHOWN FEELINGS YOU CAN'T RETURN ISN'T COOL.
I KNOW THAT JUST AS WELL AS HE DOES.

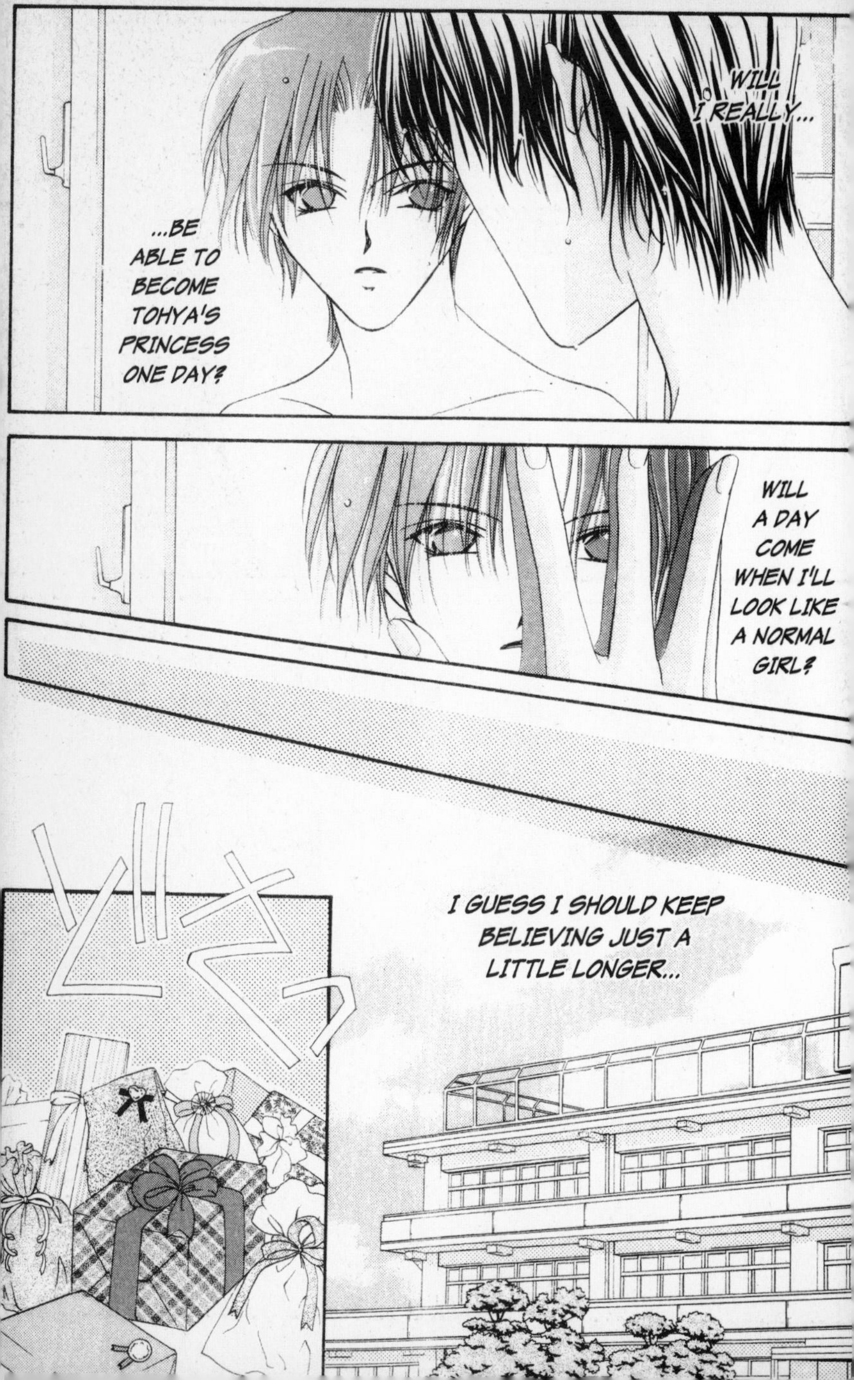
WILL I REALLY...
...BE ABLE TO BECOME TOHYA'S PRINCESS ONE DAY?
WILL A DAY COME WHEN I'LL LOOK LIKE A NORMAL GIRL?
I GUESS I SHOULD KEEP BELIEVING JUST A LITTLE LONGER...
どさっ

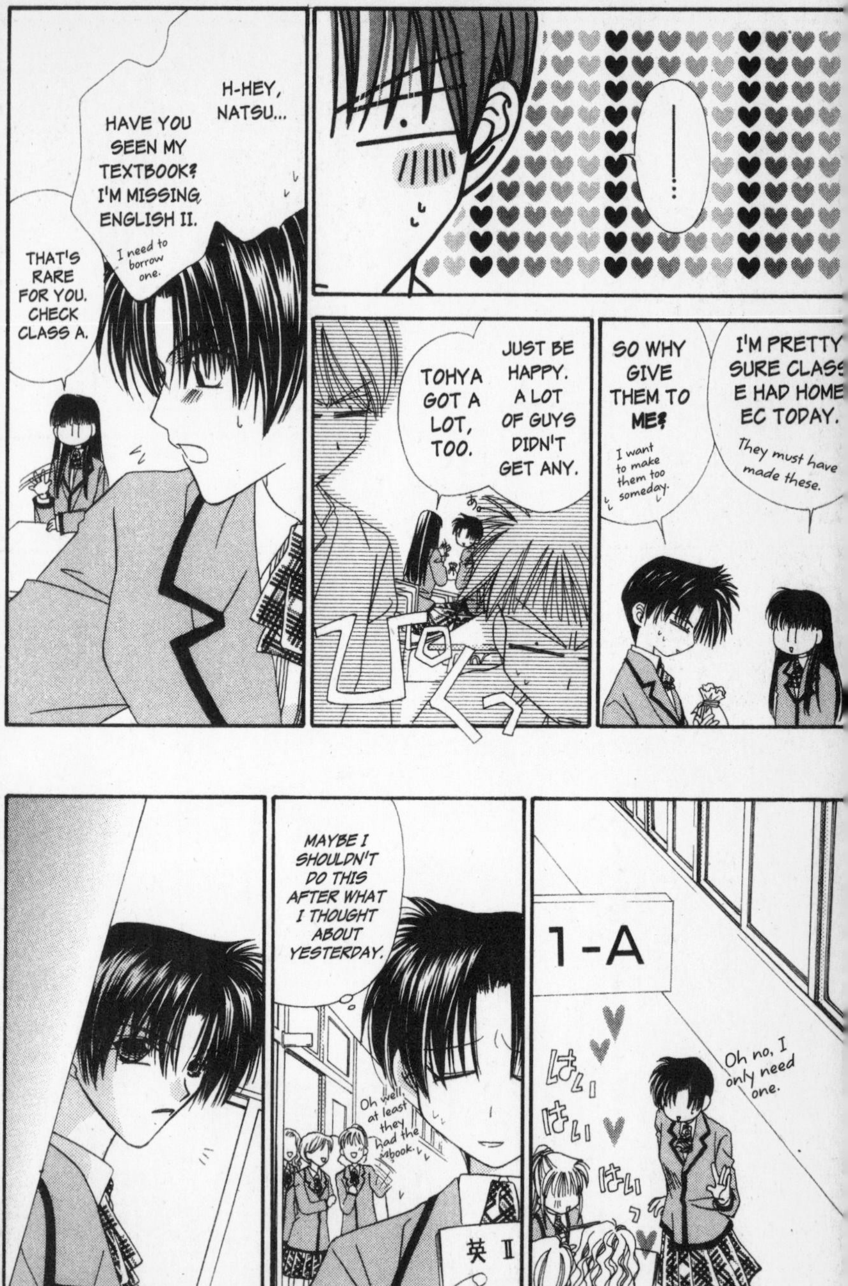
...!
I'M PRETTY SURE CLASS E HAD HOME EC TODAY.
They must have made these.
SO WHY GIVE THEM TO ME?
I want to make them too someday.
JUST BE HAPPY. A LOT OF GUYS DIDN'T GET ANY.
TOHYA GOT A LOT, TOO.
H-HEY, NATSU...
HAVE YOU SEEN MY TEXTBOOK? I'M MISSING ENGLISH II.
I need to borrow one.
THAT'S RARE FOR YOU. CHECK CLASS A.
1-A
はい
はい
はい
Oh no, I only need one.
MAYBE I SHOULDN'T DO THIS AFTER WHAT I THOUGHT ABOUT YESTERDAY.
Oh well, at least they had the book.
英 II

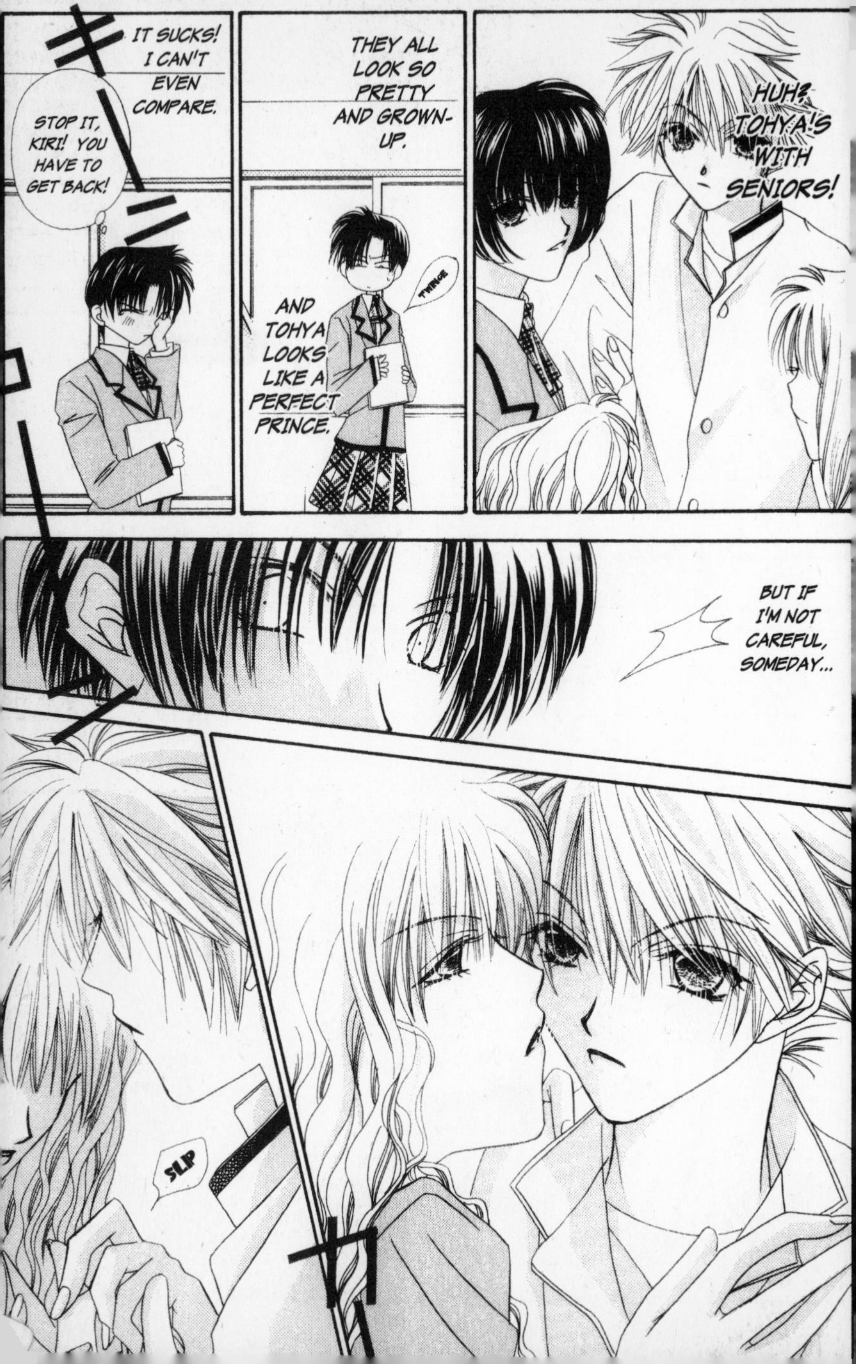
HUH? TOHYA'S WITH SENIORS!
THEY ALL LOOK SO PRETTY AND GROWN-UP.
TWINGE
AND TOHYA LOOKS LIKE A PERFECT PRINCE.
IT SUCKS! I CAN'T EVEN COMPARE.
STOP IT, KIRI! YOU HAVE TO GET BACK!
BUT IF I'M NOT CAREFUL, SOMEDAY...
SLIP

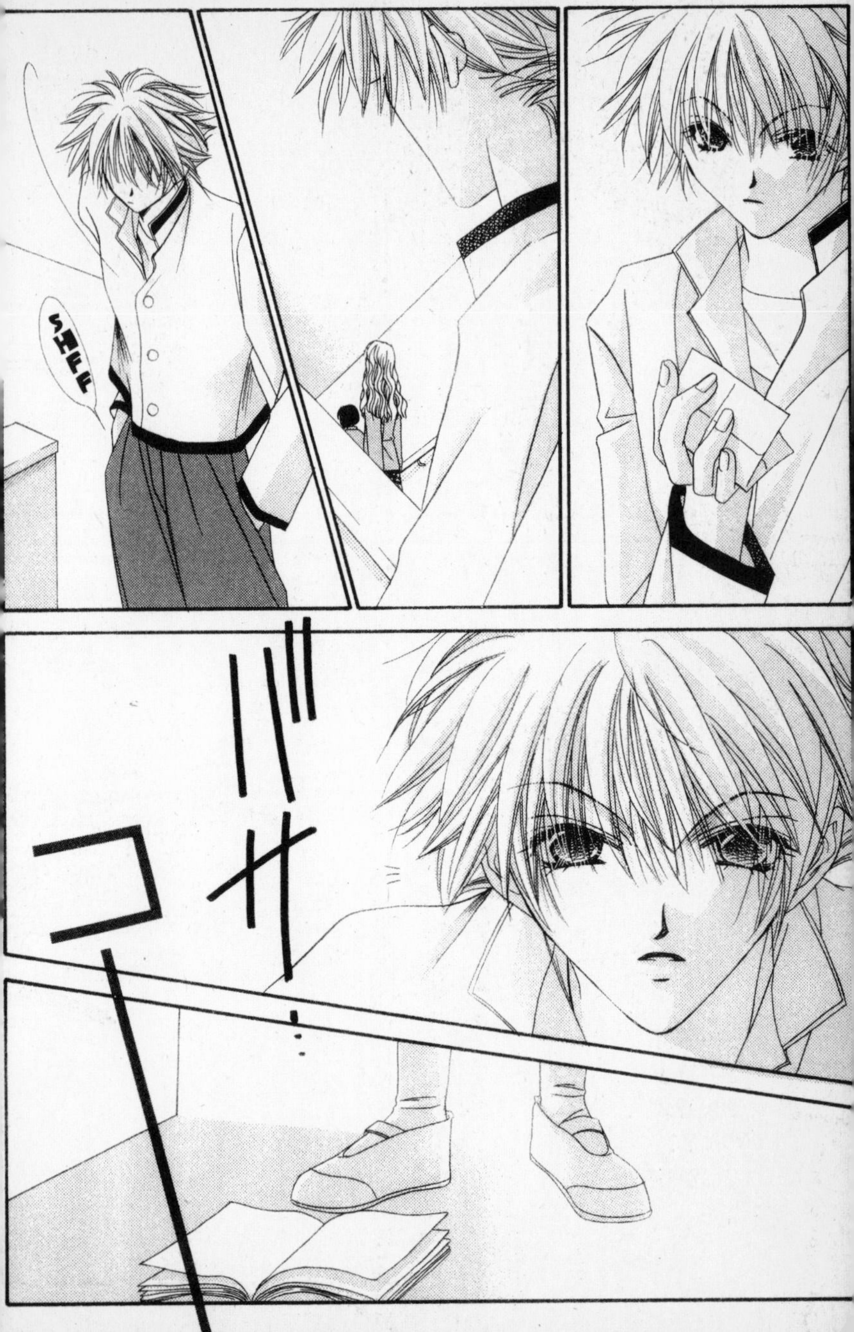

SHFF
バサッ

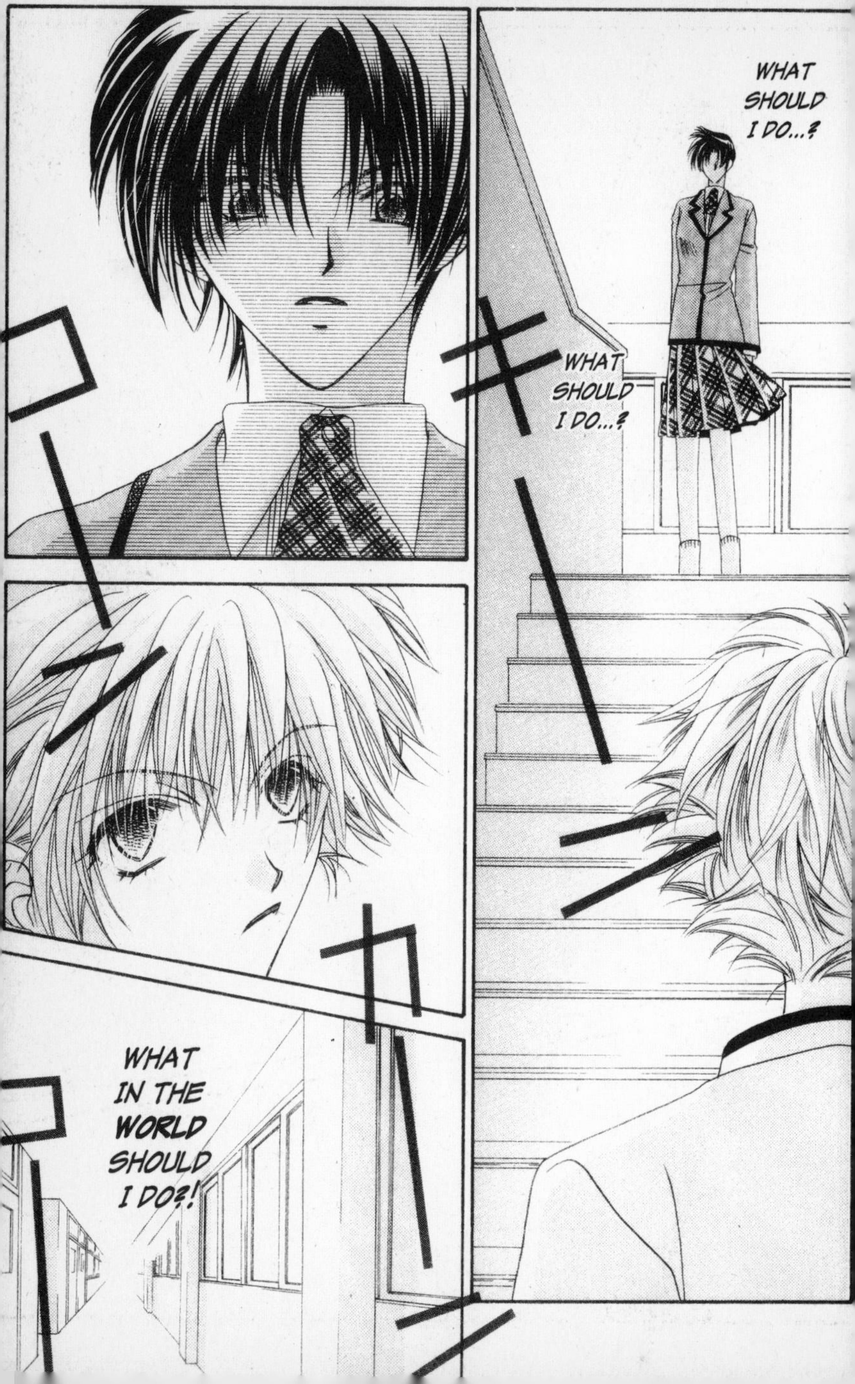
WHAT SHOULD I DO...?
WHAT SHOULD I DO...?
WHAT IN THE WORLD SHOULD I DO?!

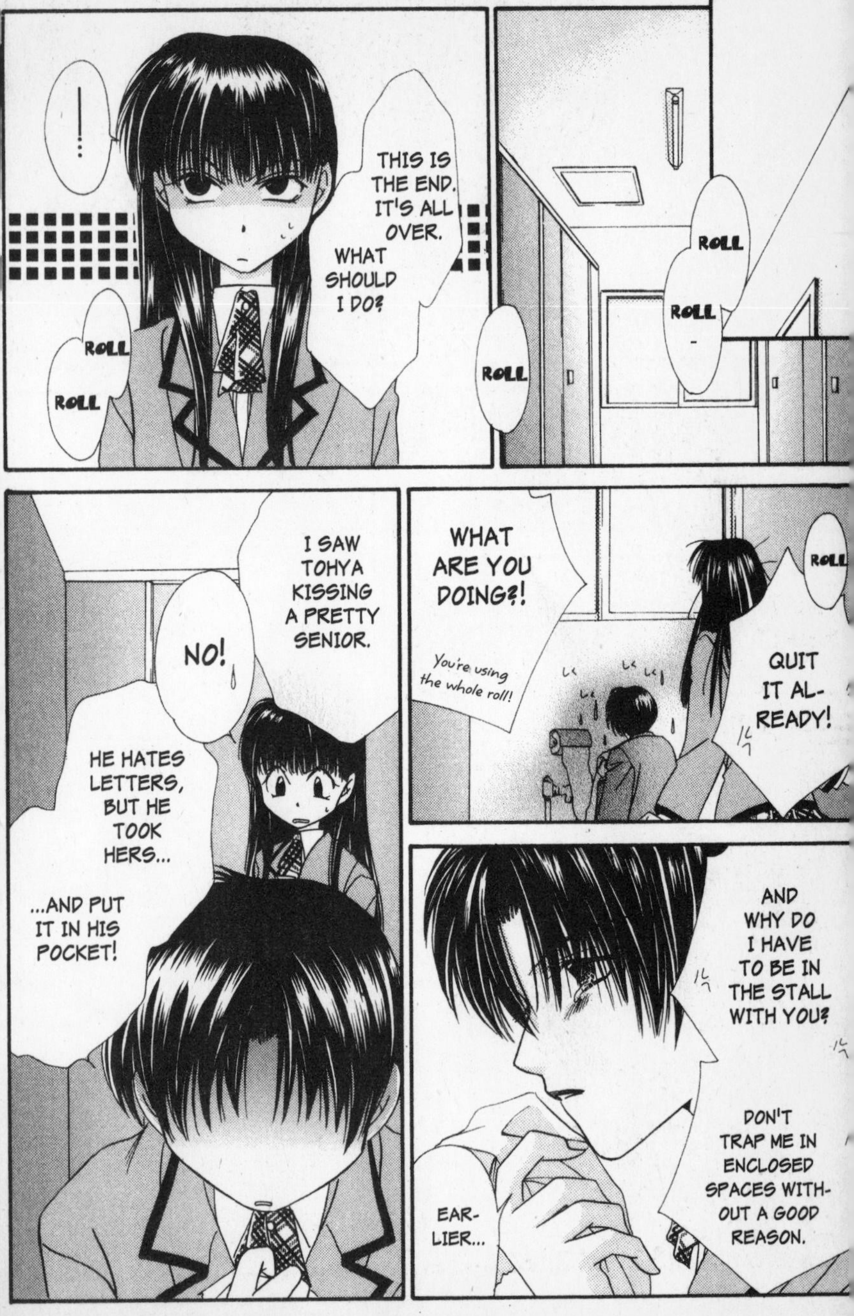
ROLL
ROLL
ROLL
!...
THIS IS THE END. IT'S ALL OVER.
WHAT SHOULD I DO?
ROLL
ROLL
ROLL
QUIT IT AL-READY!
WHAT ARE YOU DOING?!
You're using the whole roll!
AND WHY DO I HAVE TO BE IN THE STALL WITH YOU?
DON'T TRAP ME IN ENCLOSED SPACES WITH-OUT A GOOD REASON.
EAR-LIER...
I SAW TOHYA KISSING A PRETTY SENIOR.
NO!
HE HATES LETTERS, BUT HE TOOK HERS...
...AND PUT IT IN HIS POCKET!

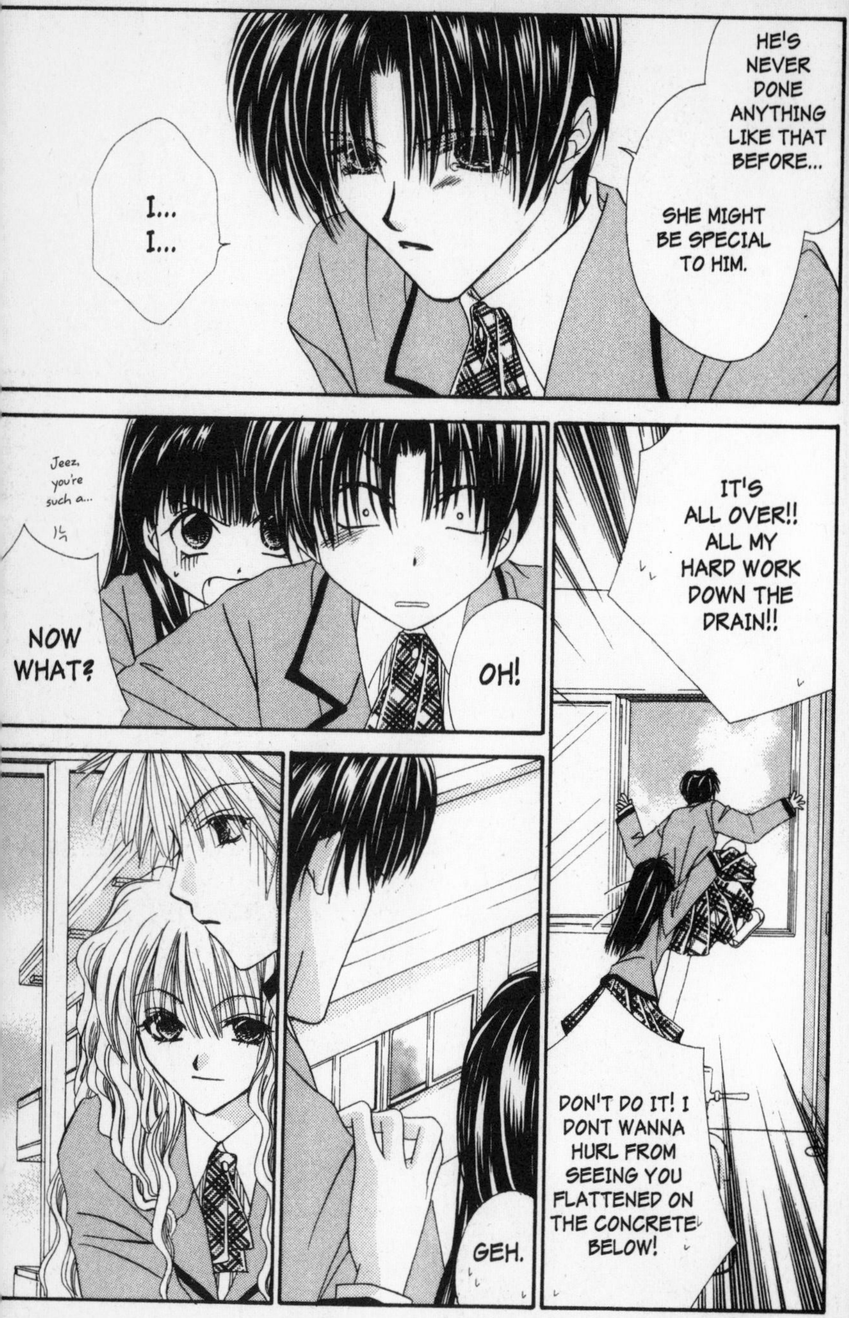
HE'S NEVER DONE ANYTHING LIKE THAT BEFORE...
SHE MIGHT BE SPECIAL TO HIM.
I... I...
IT'S ALL OVER!! ALL MY HARD WORK DOWN THE DRAIN!!
DON'T DO IT! I DONT WANNA HURL FROM SEEING YOU FLATTENED ON THE CONCRETE BELOW!
OH!
Jeez, you're such a...
NOW WHAT?
GEH.

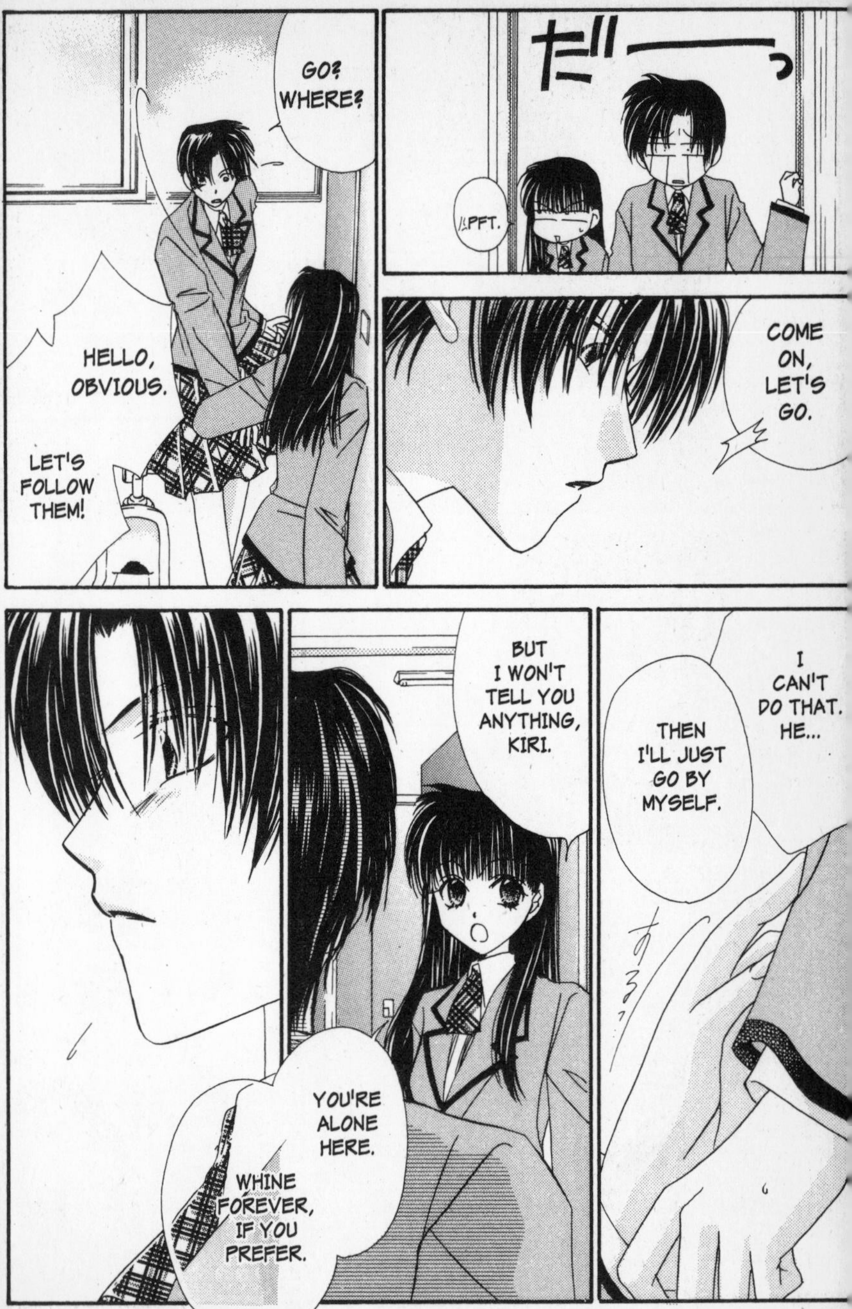
だーっ
PFT.
COME ON, LET'S GO.
GO? WHERE?
HELLO, OBVIOUS.
LET'S FOLLOW THEM!
I CAN'T DO THAT. HE...
THEN I'LL JUST GO BY MYSELF.
BUT I WON'T TELL YOU ANYTHING, KIRI.
YOU'RE ALONE HERE.
WHINE FOREVER, IF YOU PREFER.

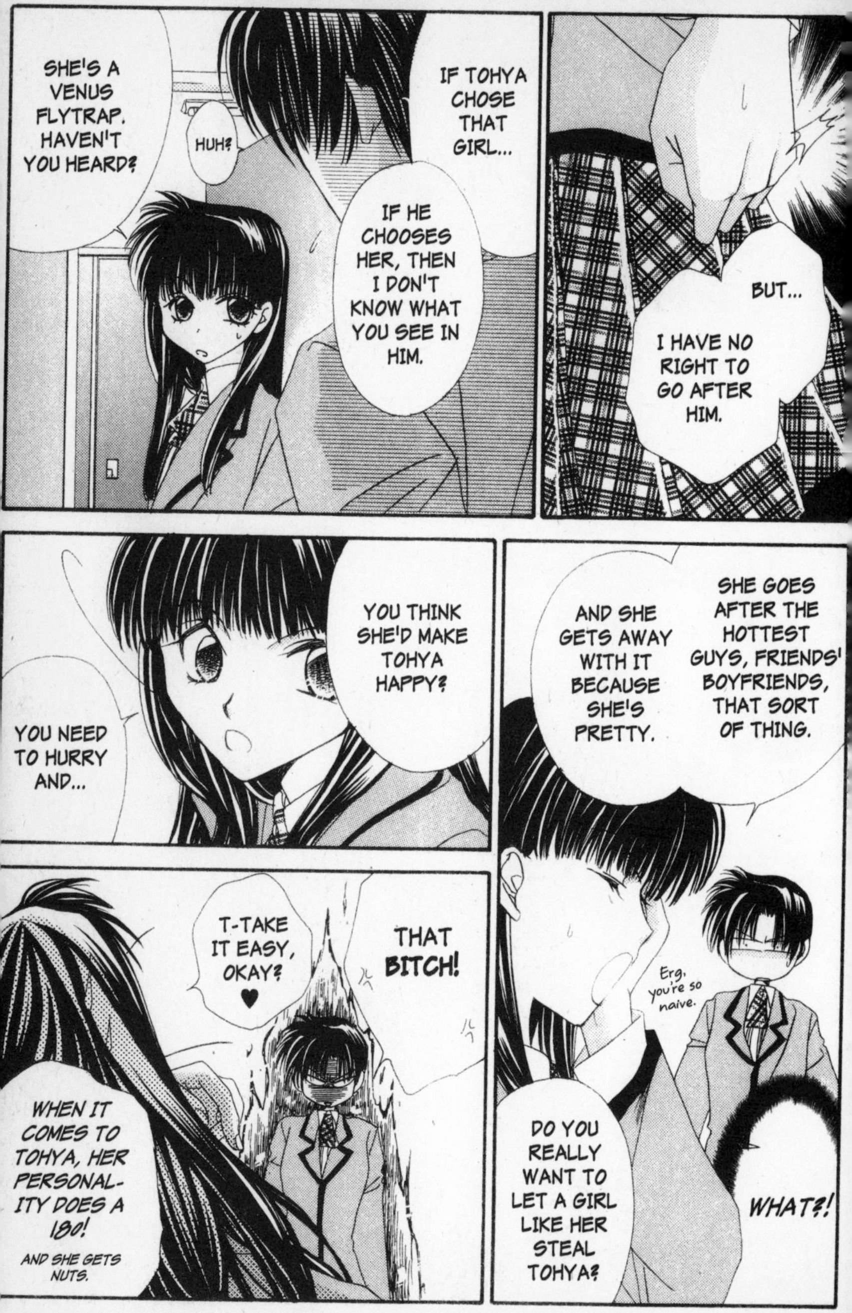
BUT...
I HAVE NO RIGHT TO GO AFTER HIM.
IF TOHYA CHOSE THAT GIRL...
IF HE CHOOSES HER, THEN I DON'T KNOW WHAT YOU SEE IN HIM.
HUH?
SHE'S A VENUS FLYTRAP. HAVEN'T YOU HEARD?
SHE GOES AFTER THE HOTTEST GUYS, FRIENDS' BOYFRIENDS, THAT SORT OF THING.
AND SHE GETS AWAY WITH IT BECAUSE SHE'S PRETTY.
Erg, you're so naive.
DO YOU REALLY WANT TO LET A GIRL LIKE HER STEAL TOHYA?
WHAT?!
YOU THINK SHE'D MAKE TOHYA HAPPY?
YOU NEED TO HURRY AND...
THAT BITCH!
T-TAKE IT EASY, OKAY? ♥
WHEN IT COMES TO TOHYA, HER PERSONAL-ITY DOES A 180!
AND SHE GETS NUTS.

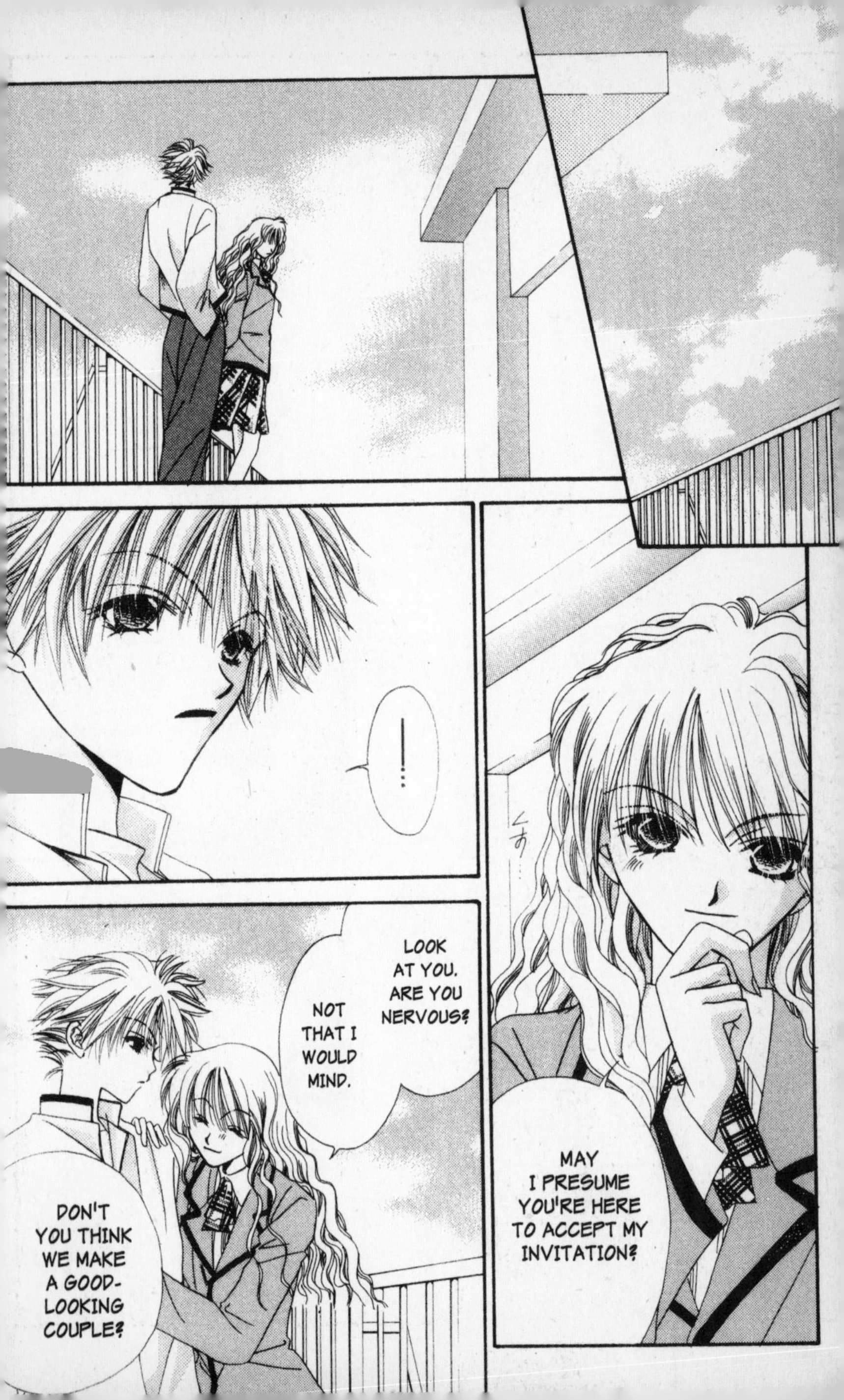
MAY I PRESUME YOU'RE HERE TO ACCEPT MY INVITATION?
!...
LOOK AT YOU. ARE YOU NERVOUS?
NOT THAT I WOULD MIND.
DON'T YOU THINK WE MAKE A GOOD-LOOKING COUPLE?

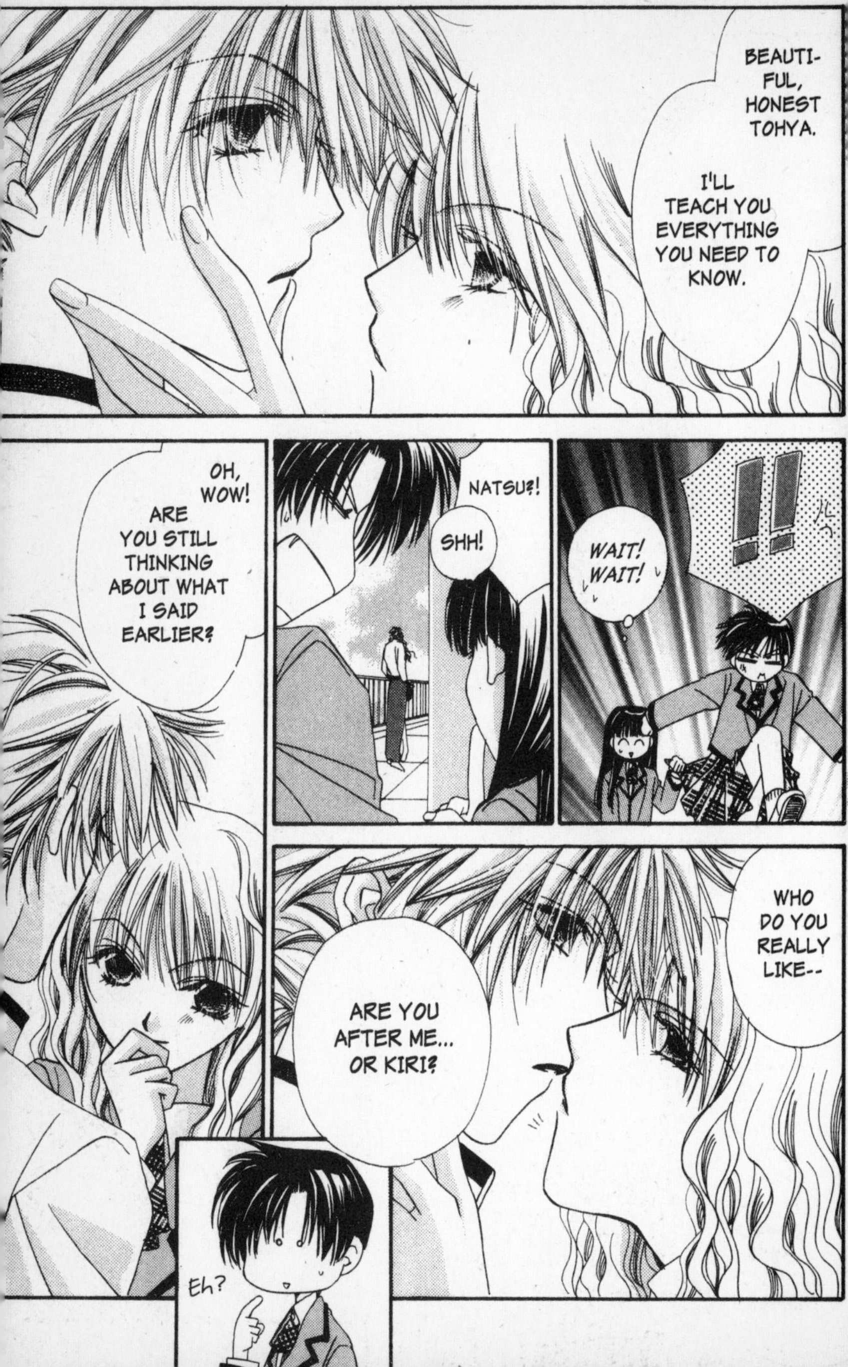
BEAUTIFUL, HONEST TOHYA.
I'LL TEACH YOU EVERYTHING YOU NEED TO KNOW.
WAIT! WAIT!
NATSU?!
SHH!
WHO DO YOU REALLY LIKE--
ARE YOU AFTER ME... OR KIRI?
Eh?
OH, WOW! ARE YOU STILL THINKING ABOUT WHAT I SAID EARLIER?

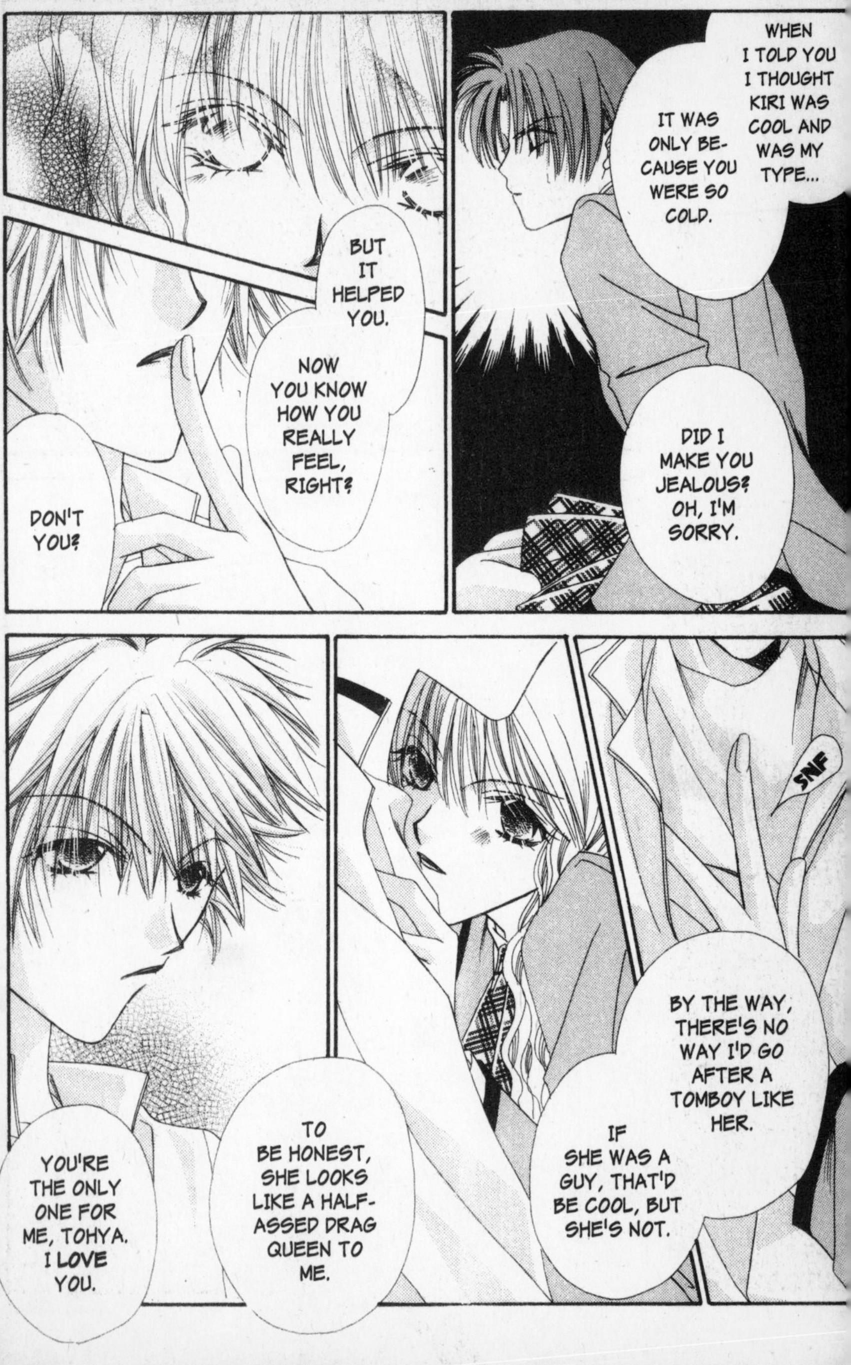
WHEN I TOLD YOU I THOUGHT KIRI WAS COOL AND WAS MY TYPE...
IT WAS ONLY BE-CAUSE YOU WERE SO COLD.
DID I MAKE YOU JEALOUS? OH, I'M SORRY.
BUT IT HELPED YOU.
NOW YOU KNOW HOW YOU REALLY FEEL, RIGHT?
DON'T YOU?
SNF
BY THE WAY, THERE'S NO WAY I'D GO AFTER A TOMBOY LIKE HER.
IF SHE WAS A GUY, THAT'D BE COOL, BUT SHE'S NOT.
TO BE HONEST, SHE LOOKS LIKE A HALF-ASSED DRAG QUEEN TO ME.
YOU'RE THE ONLY ONE FOR ME, TOHYA. I LOVE YOU.

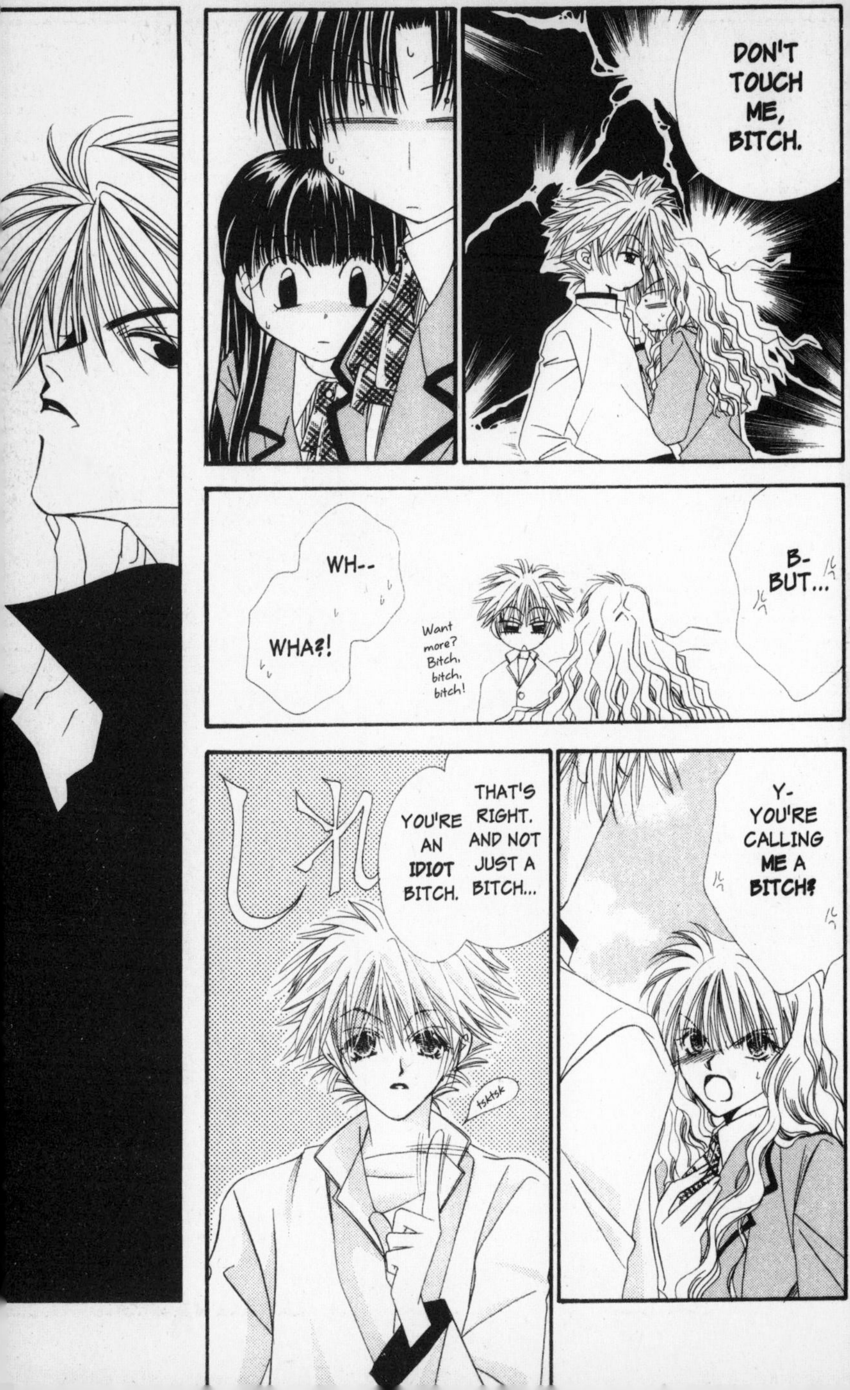
DON'T TOUCH ME, BITCH.
B-BUT...
Want more? Bitch, bitch, bitch!
WH--
WHA?!
Y-YOU'RE CALLING ME A BITCH?
THAT'S RIGHT. AND NOT JUST A BITCH...
YOU'RE AN IDIOT BITCH.
しれ
tsktsk

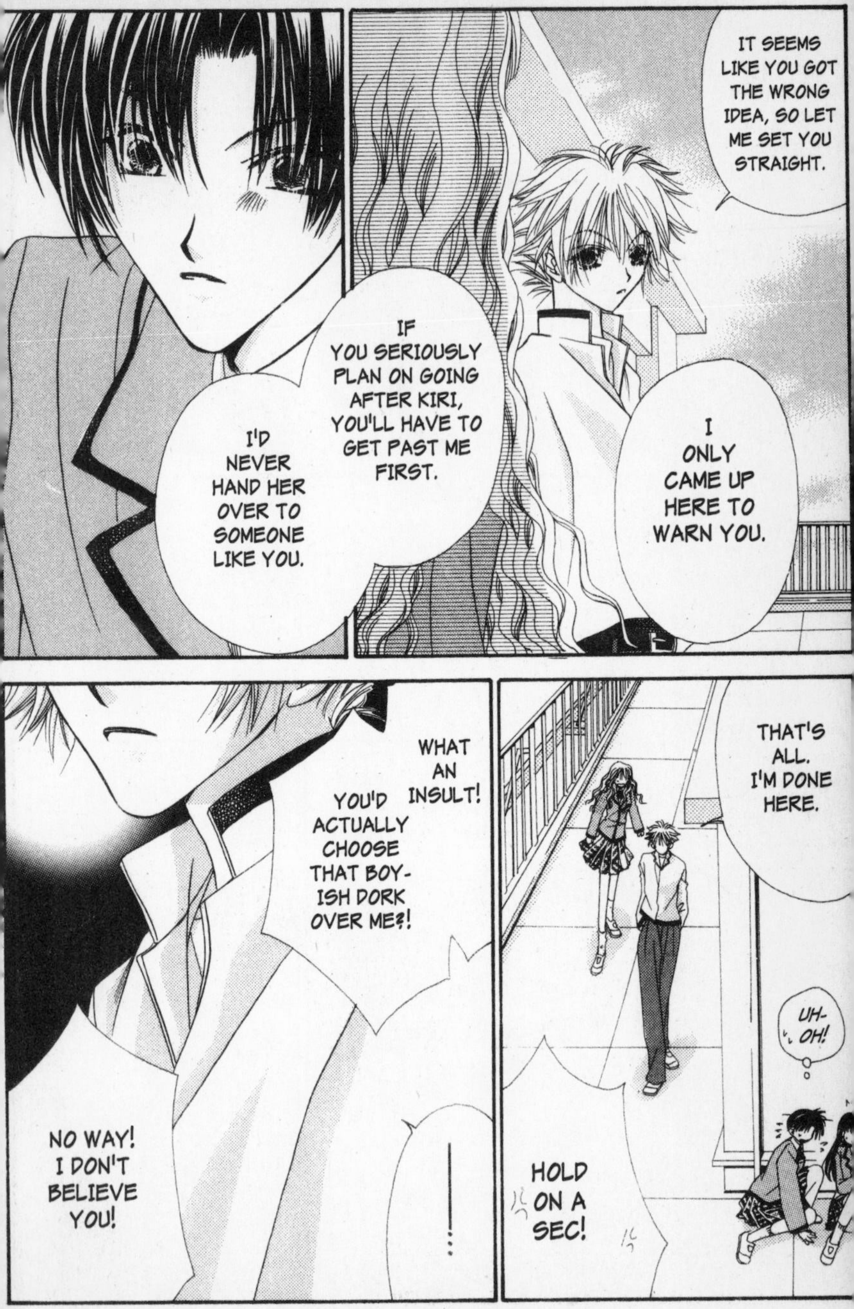
IT SEEMS LIKE YOU GOT THE WRONG IDEA, SO LET ME SET YOU STRAIGHT.
I ONLY CAME UP HERE TO WARN YOU.
IF YOU SERIOUSLY PLAN ON GOING AFTER KIRI, YOU'LL HAVE TO GET PAST ME FIRST.
I'D NEVER HAND HER OVER TO SOMEONE LIKE YOU.
THAT'S ALL. I'M DONE HERE.
UH-OH!
HOLD ON A SEC!
WHAT AN INSULT!
YOU'D ACTUALLY CHOOSE THAT BOY-ISH DORK OVER ME?!
......
NO WAY! I DON'T BELIEVE YOU!

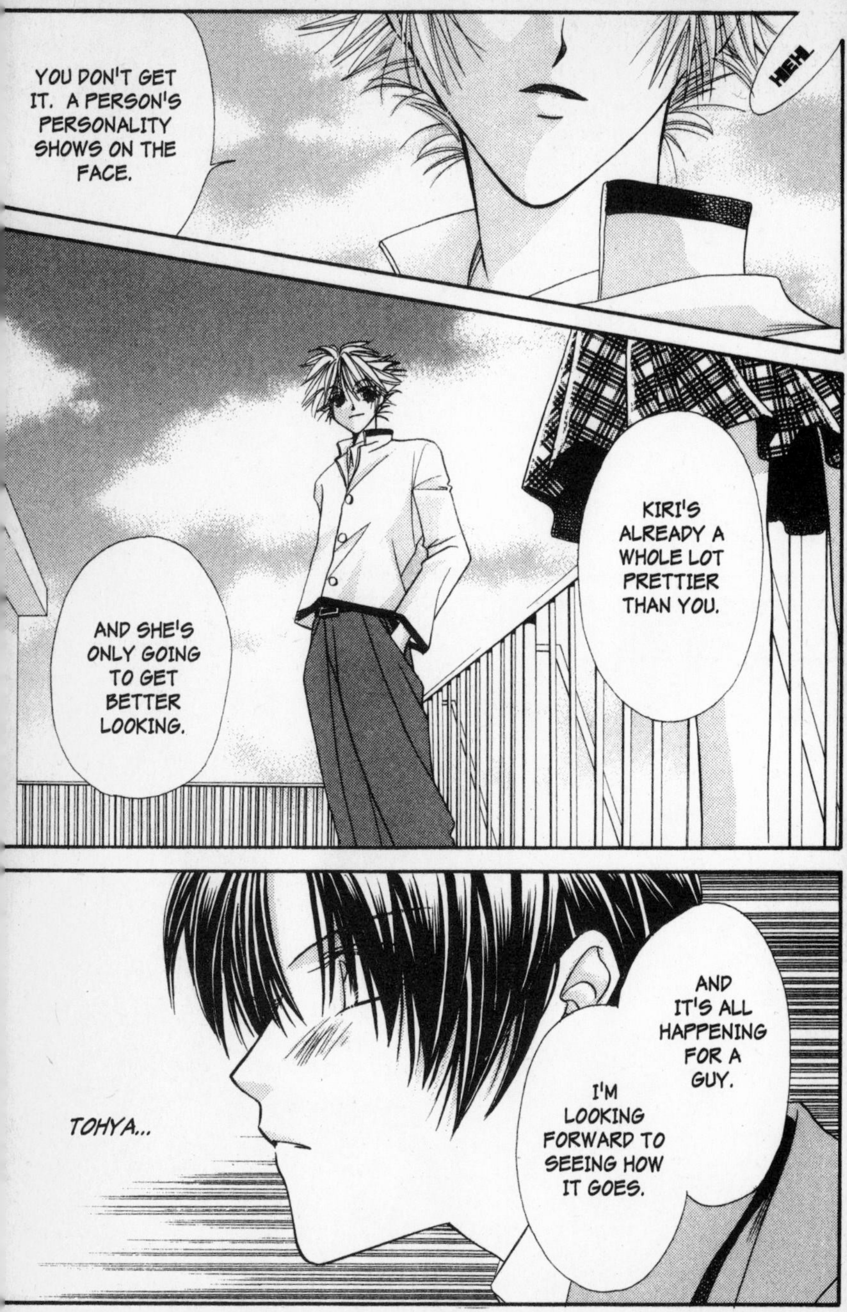
HEH.
YOU DON'T GET IT. A PERSON'S PERSONALITY SHOWS ON THE FACE.
KIRI'S ALREADY A WHOLE LOT PRETTIER THAN YOU.
AND SHE'S ONLY GOING TO GET BETTER LOOKING.
AND IT'S ALL HAPPENING FOR A GUY.
I'M LOOKING FORWARD TO SEEING HOW IT GOES.
TOHYA...

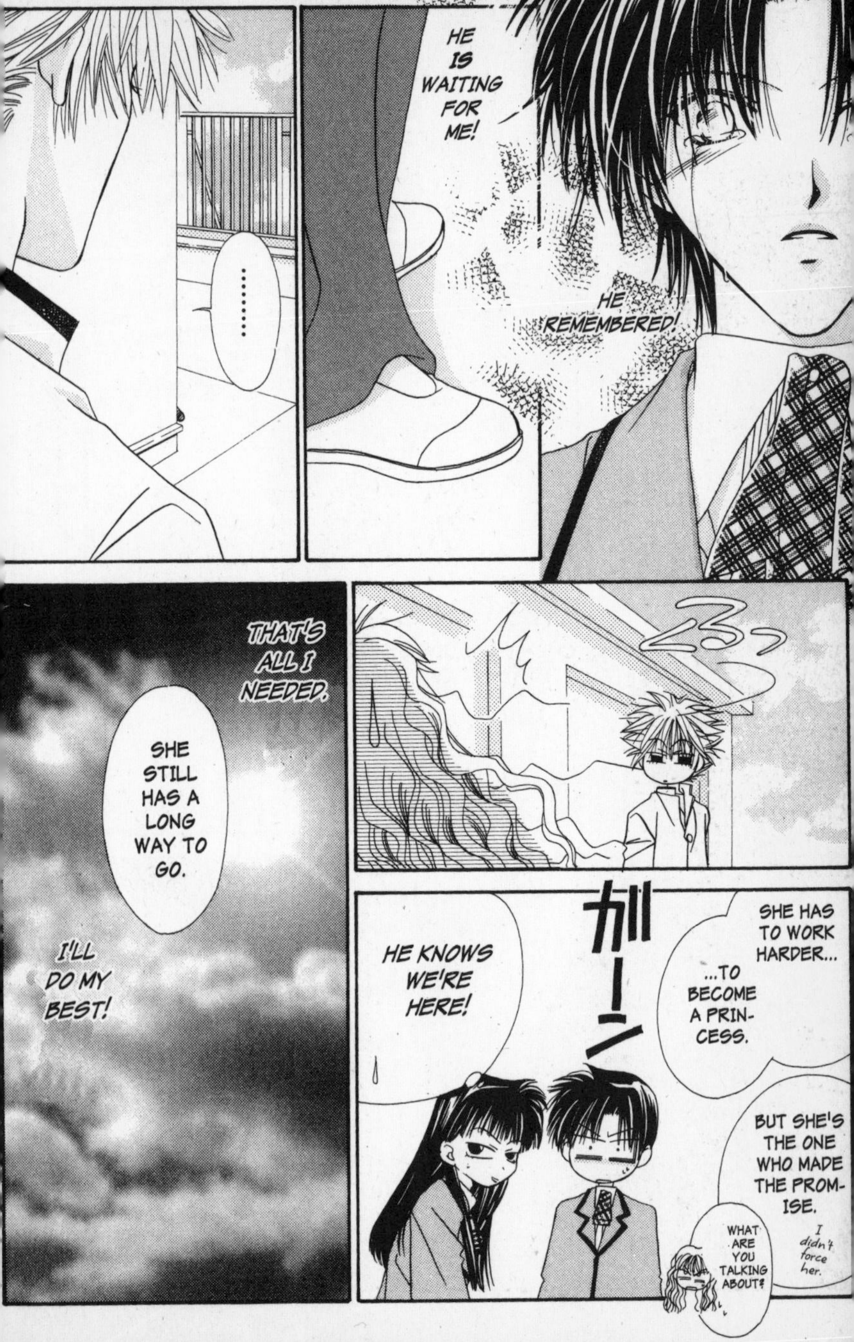
HE REMEMBERED!
HE IS WAITING FOR ME!
......
くるっ
SHE HAS TO WORK HARDER...
...TO BECOME A PRINCESS.
BUT SHE'S THE ONE WHO MADE THE PROMISE.
I didn't force her.
ガーン
HE KNOWS WE'RE HERE!
WHAT ARE YOU TALKING ABOUT?
THAT'S ALL I NEEDED.
SHE STILL HAS A LONG WAY TO GO.
I'LL DO MY BEST!

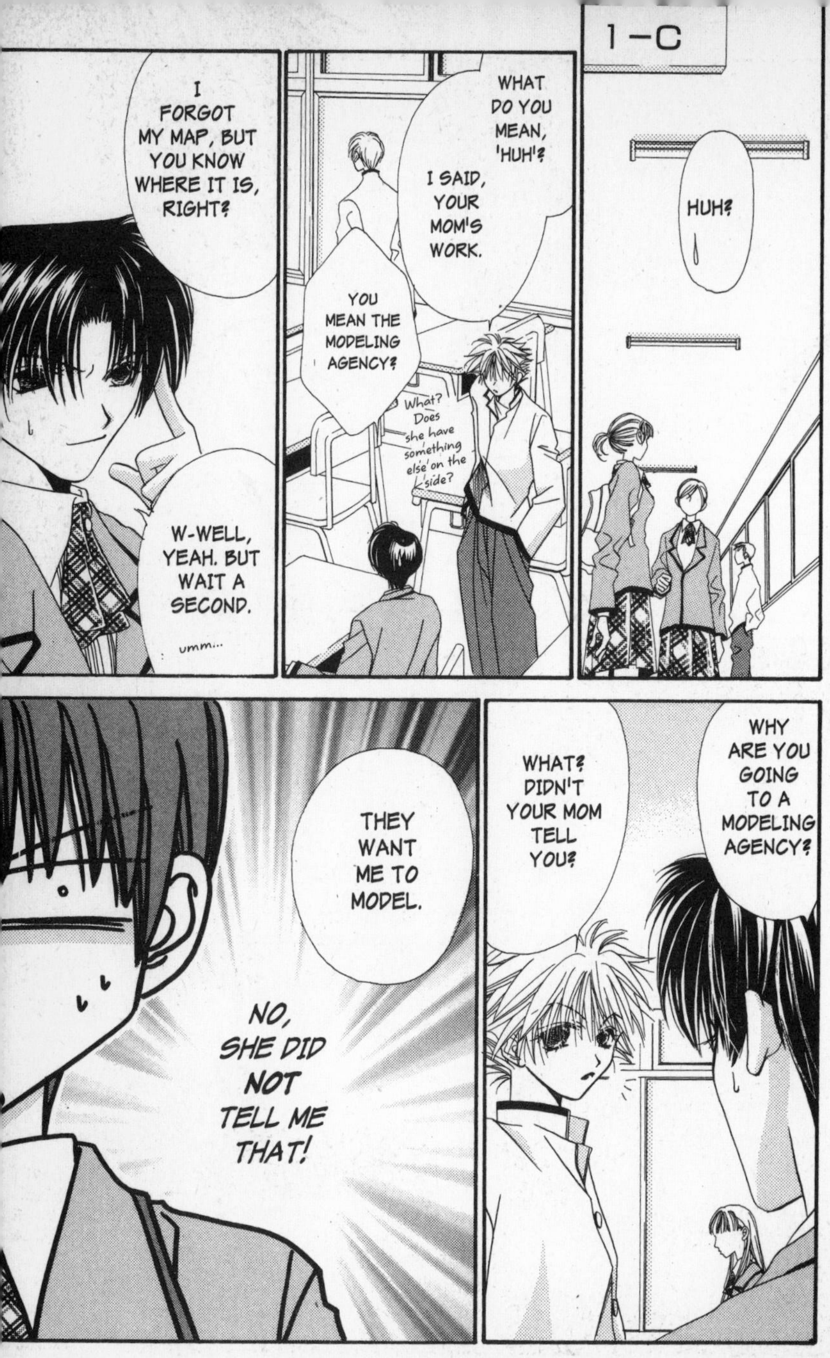
1-C
HUH?
WHAT DO YOU MEAN, 'HUH'?
I SAID, YOUR MOM'S WORK.
YOU MEAN THE MODELING AGENCY?
What? Does she have something else on the side?
I FORGOT MY MAP, BUT YOU KNOW WHERE IT IS, RIGHT?
W-WELL, YEAH. BUT WAIT A SECOND.
umm...
WHY ARE YOU GOING TO A MODELING AGENCY?
WHAT? DIDN'T YOUR MOM TELL YOU?
THEY WANT ME TO MODEL.
NO, SHE DID NOT TELL ME THAT!

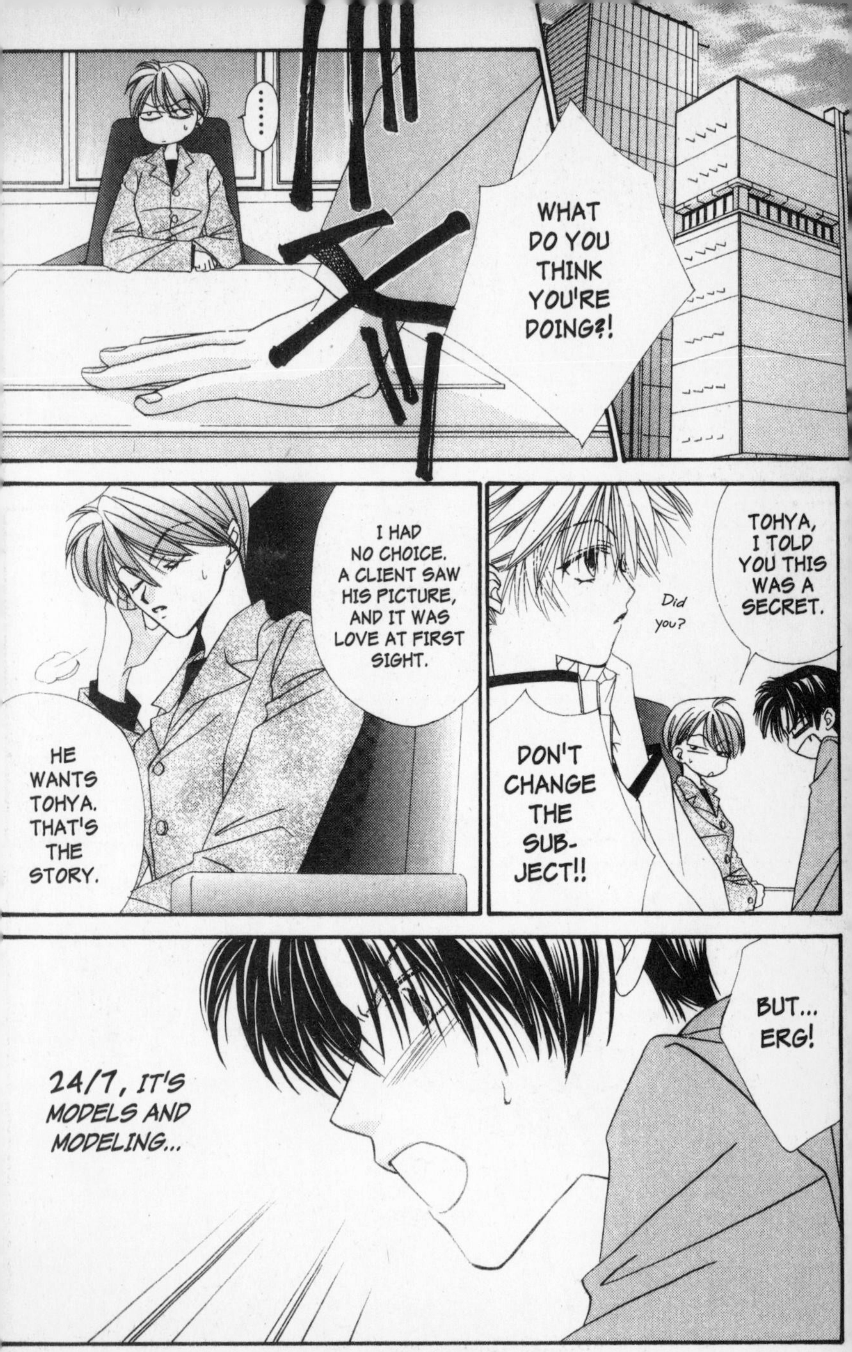

WHAT DO YOU THINK YOU'RE DOING?!
......
TOHYA, I TOLD YOU THIS WAS A SECRET.
Did you?
DON'T CHANGE THE SUB-JECT!!
I HAD NO CHOICE. A CLIENT SAW HIS PICTURE, AND IT WAS LOVE AT FIRST SIGHT.
HE WANTS TOHYA. THAT'S THE STORY.
BUT... ERG!
24/7, IT'S MODELS AND MODELING...

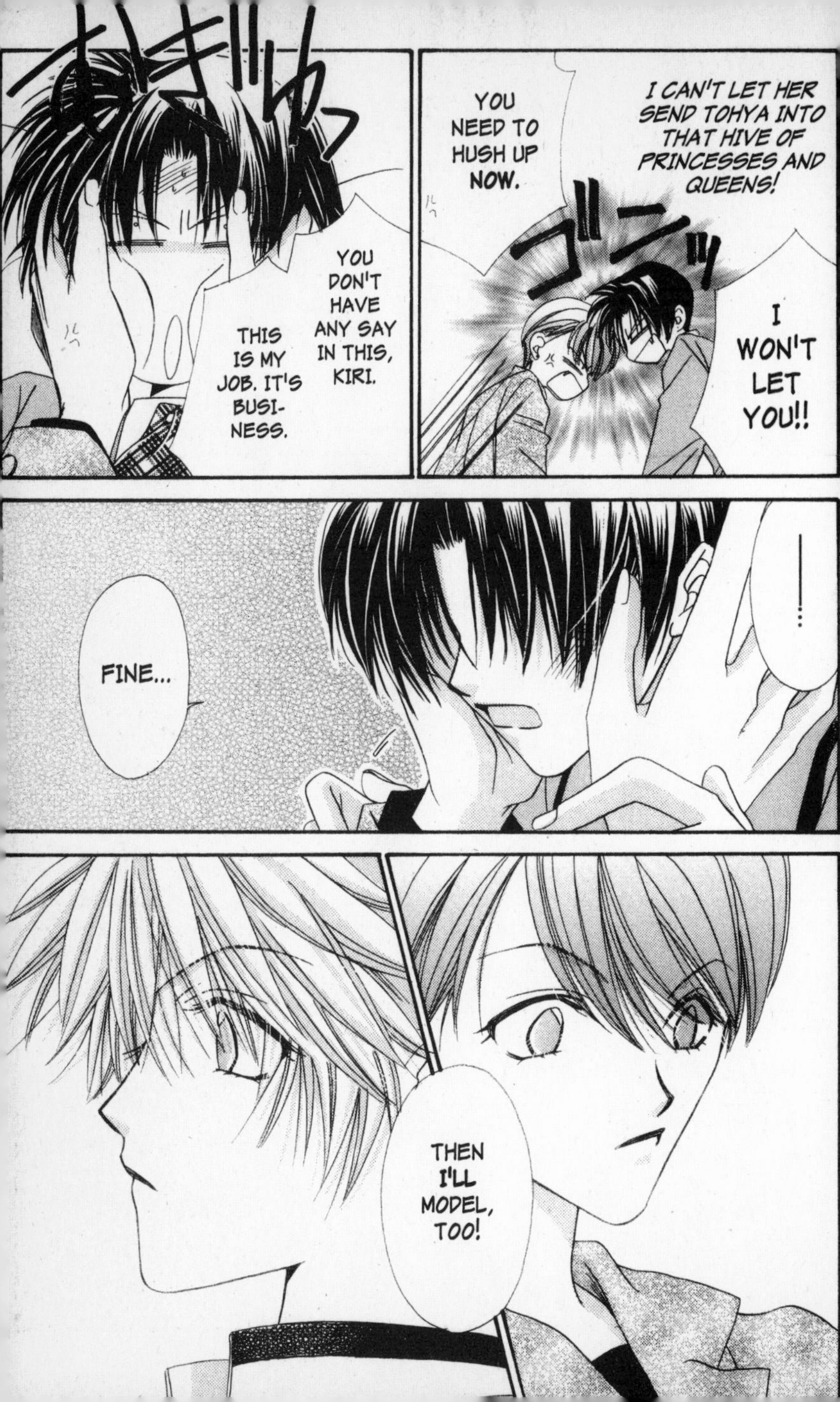
I CAN'T LET HER SEND TOHYA INTO THAT HIVE OF PRINCESSES AND QUEENS!
I WON'T LET YOU!!
YOU NEED TO HUSH UP NOW.
YOU DON'T HAVE ANY SAY IN THIS, KIRI.
THIS IS MY JOB. IT'S BUSINESS.
......
FINE...
THEN I'LL MODEL, TOO!

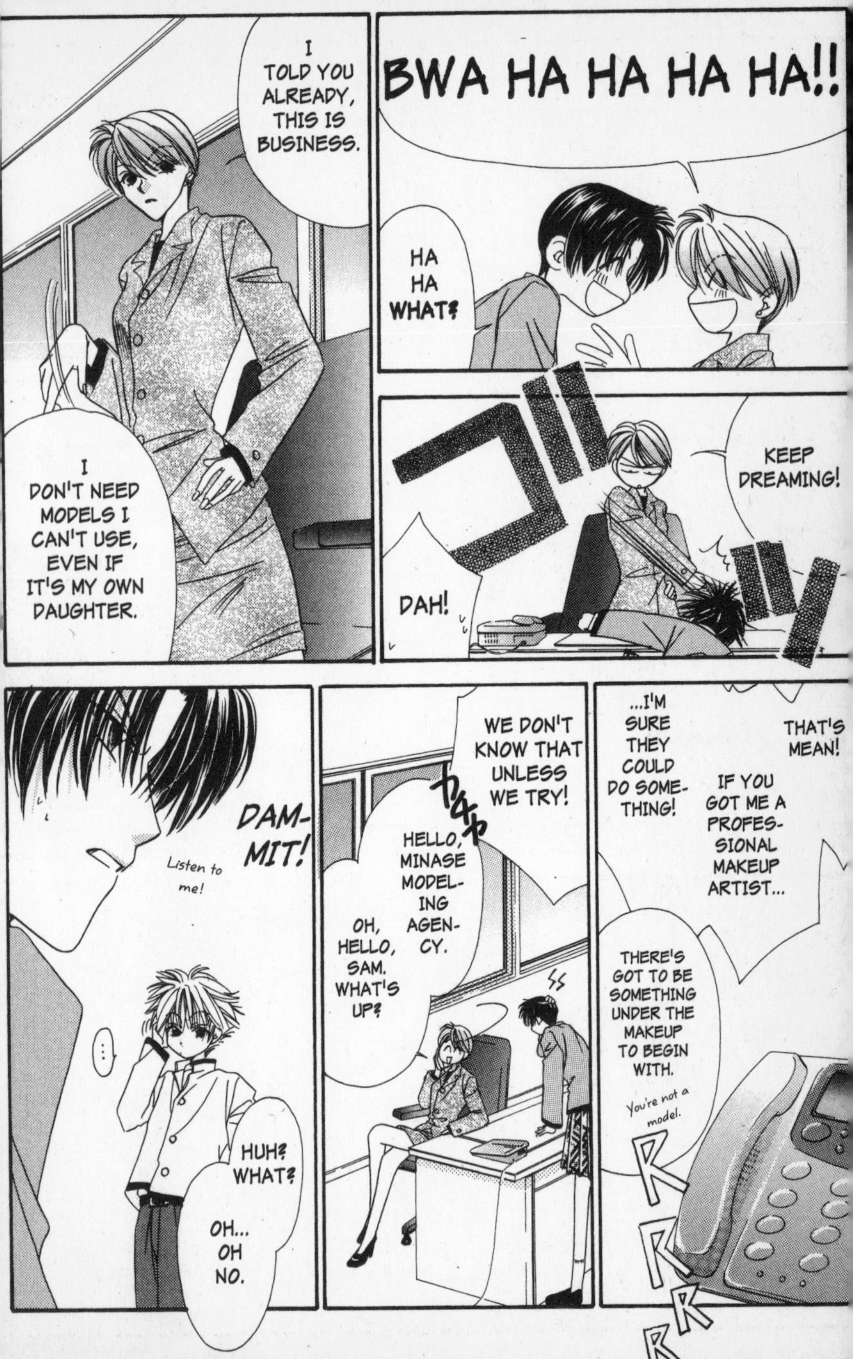
BWA HA HA HA HA!!
HA HA WHAT?
KEEP DREAMING!
DAH!
I TOLD YOU ALREADY, THIS IS BUSINESS.
I DON'T NEED MODELS I CAN'T USE, EVEN IF IT'S MY OWN DAUGHTER.
THAT'S MEAN!
...I'M SURE THEY COULD DO SOME-THING!
IF YOU GOT ME A PROFES-SIONAL MAKEUP ARTIST...
THERE'S GOT TO BE SOMETHING UNDER THE MAKEUP TO BEGIN WITH.
You're not a model.
RRRR
WE DON'T KNOW THAT UNLESS WE TRY!
HELLO, MINASE MODEL-ING AGEN-CY.
OH, HELLO, SAM. WHAT'S UP?
DAM-MIT!
Listen to me!
...
HUH? WHAT?
OH... OH NO.

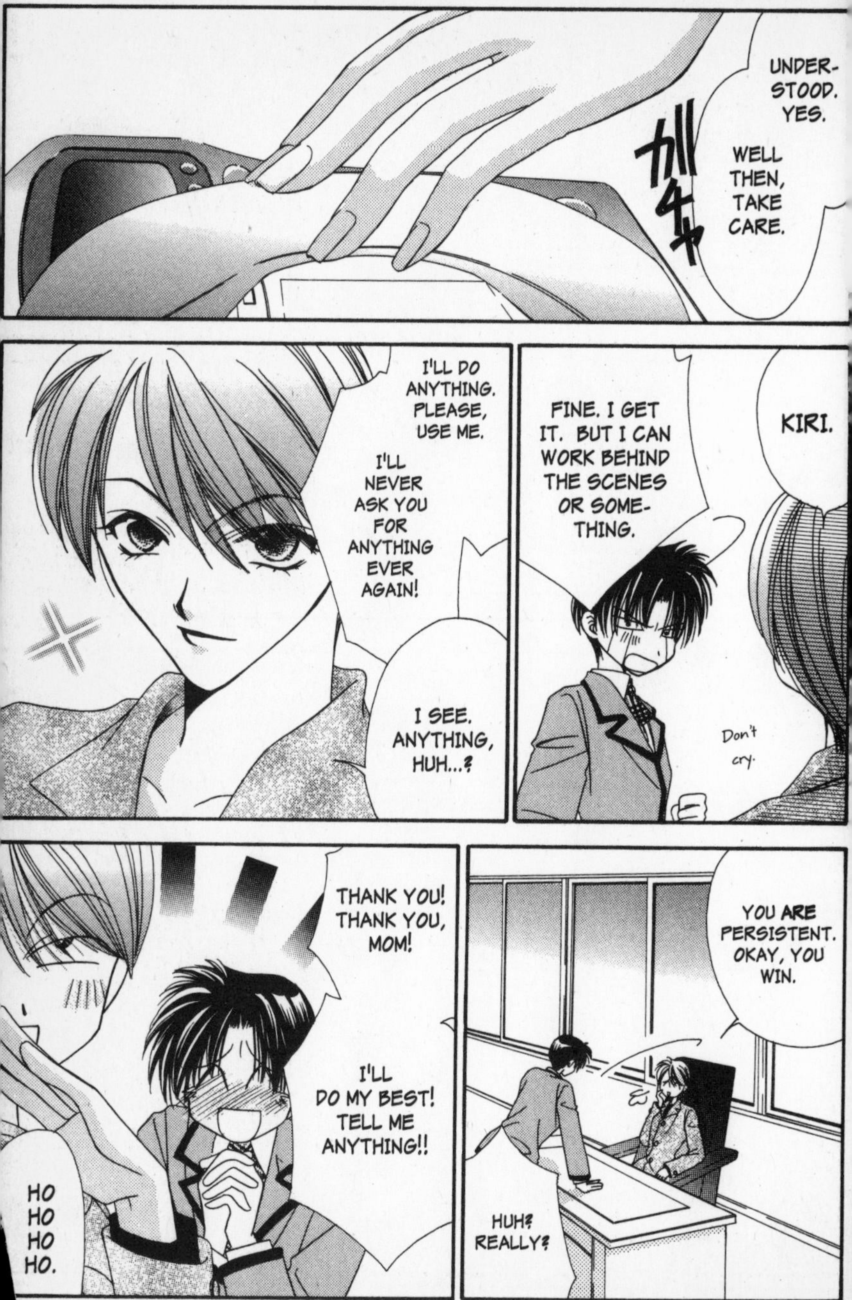
UNDER-STOOD. YES.
WELL THEN, TAKE CARE.
KIRI.
FINE. I GET IT. BUT I CAN WORK BEHIND THE SCENES OR SOME-THING.
Don't cry.
I'LL DO ANYTHING. PLEASE, USE ME.
I'LL NEVER ASK YOU FOR ANYTHING EVER AGAIN!
I SEE. ANYTHING, HUH...?
YOU ARE PERSISTENT. OKAY, YOU WIN.
HUH? REALLY?
THANK YOU! THANK YOU, MOM!
I'LL DO MY BEST! TELL ME ANYTHING!!
HO HO HO HO HO.

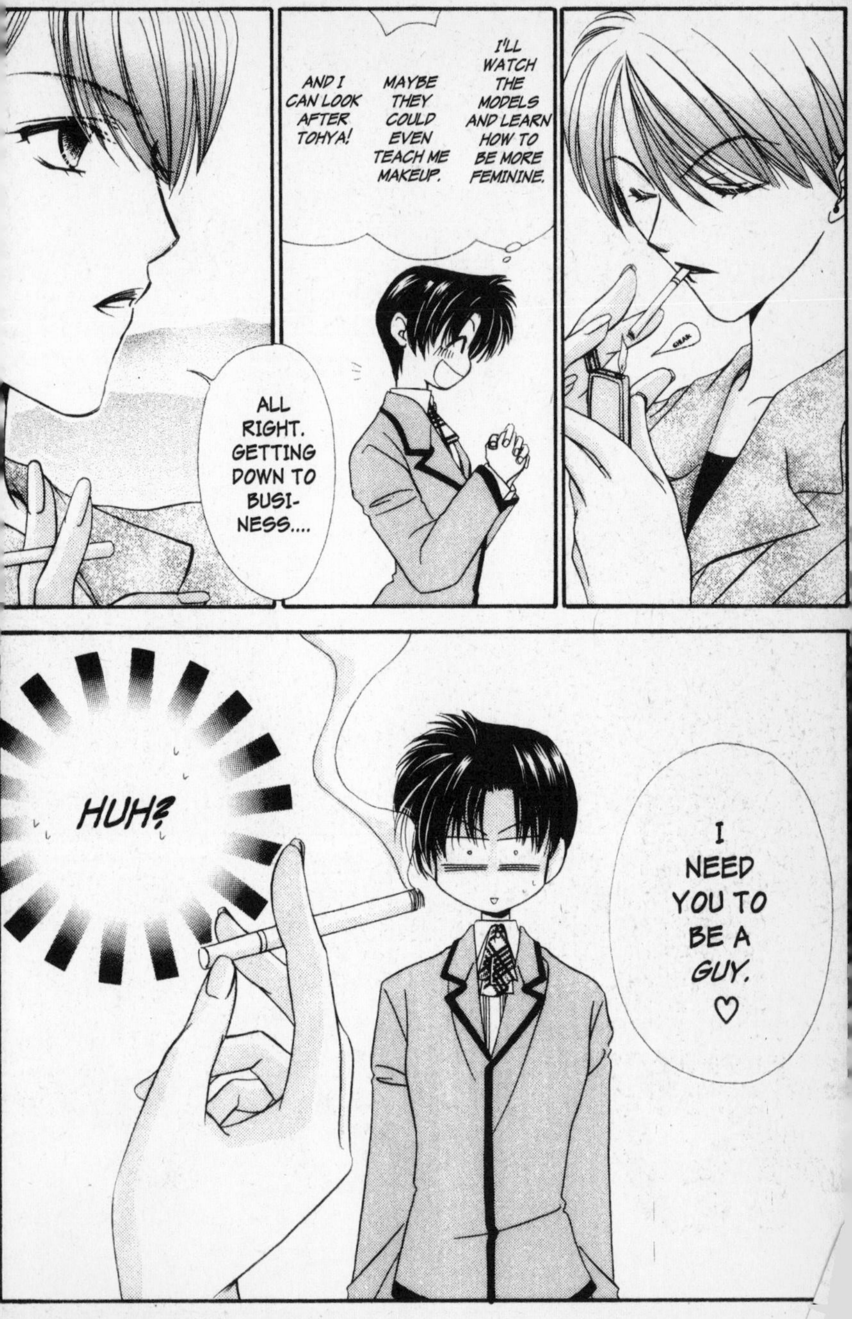
I'LL WATCH THE MODELS AND LEARN HOW TO BE MORE FEMININE.
MAYBE THEY COULD EVEN TEACH ME MAKEUP.
AND I CAN LOOK AFTER TOHYA!
ALL RIGHT. GETTING DOWN TO BUSI-NESS....
I NEED YOU TO BE A GUY. ♡
HUH?

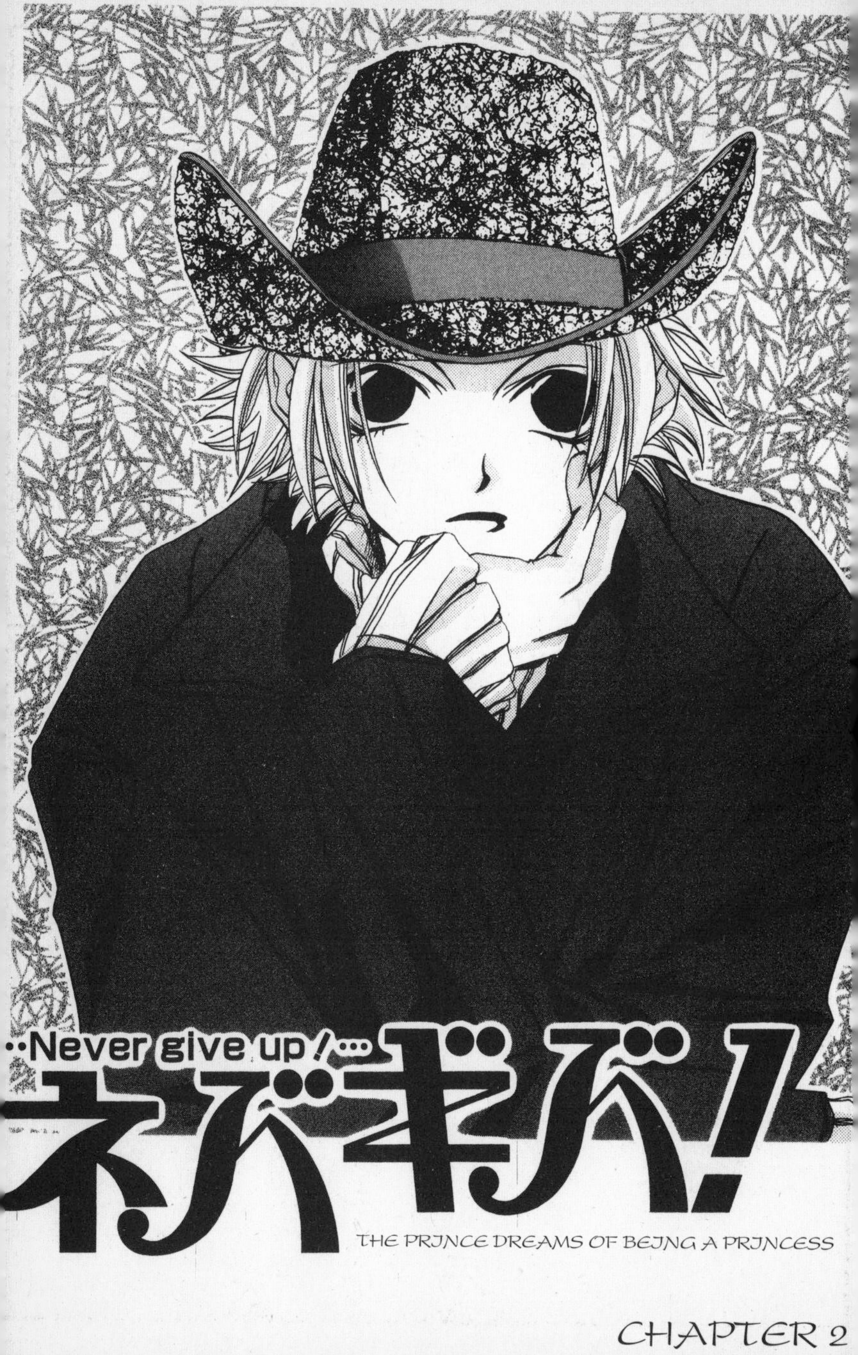

··Never give up!··· ネバギバ!

THE PRINCE DREAMS OF BEING A PRINCESS

CHAPTER 2

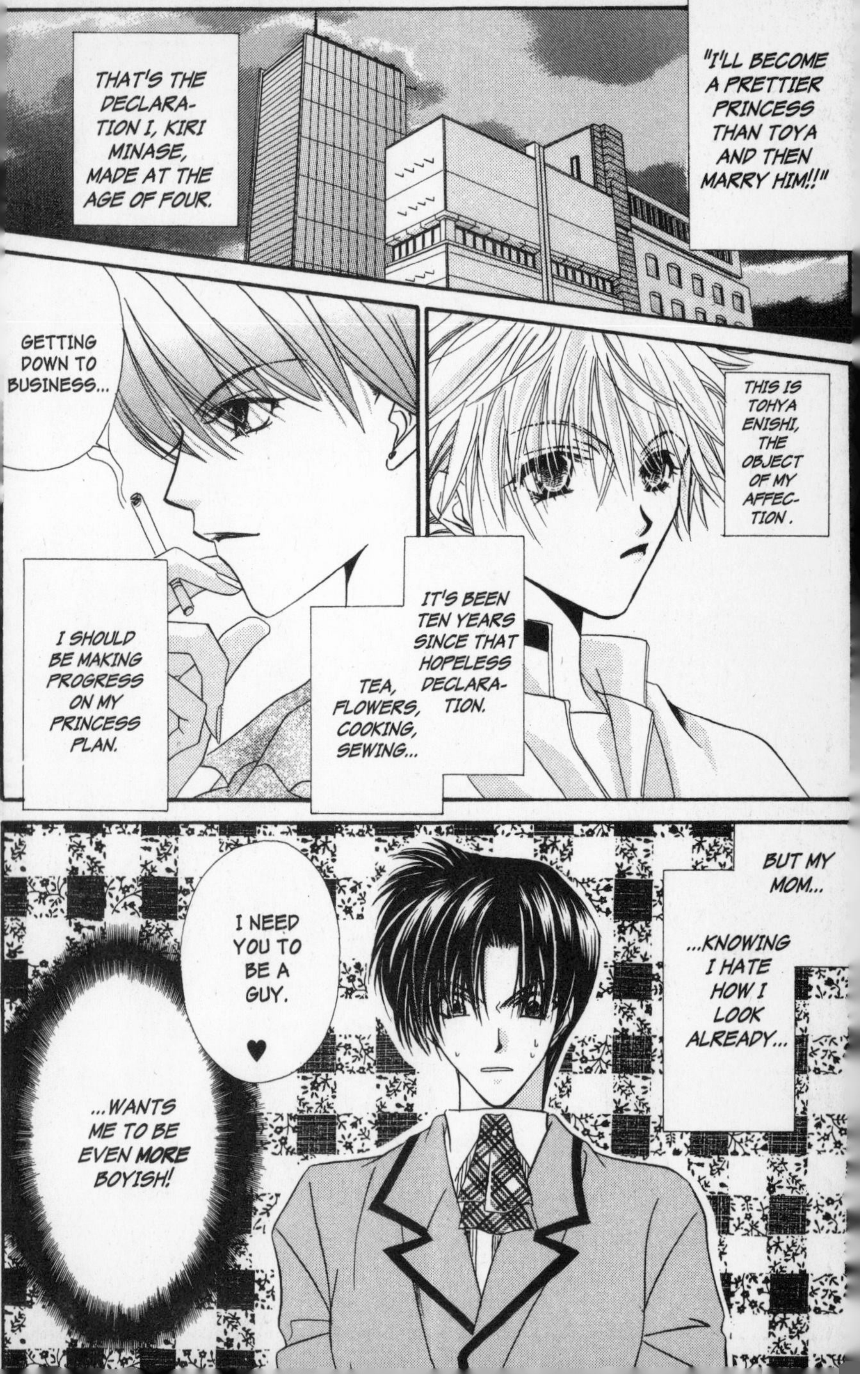
"I'LL BECOME A PRETTIER PRINCESS THAN TOYA AND THEN MARRY HIM!!"
THAT'S THE DECLARATION I, KIRI MINASE, MADE AT THE AGE OF FOUR.
THIS IS TOHYA ENISHI, THE OBJECT OF MY AFFECTION.
IT'S BEEN TEN YEARS SINCE THAT HOPELESS DECLARATION.
GETTING DOWN TO BUSINESS...
TEA, FLOWERS, COOKING, SEWING...
I SHOULD BE MAKING PROGRESS ON MY PRINCESS PLAN.
BUT MY MOM...
...KNOWING I HATE HOW I LOOK ALREADY...
I NEED YOU TO BE A GUY. ♥
...WANTS ME TO BE EVEN MORE BOYISH!

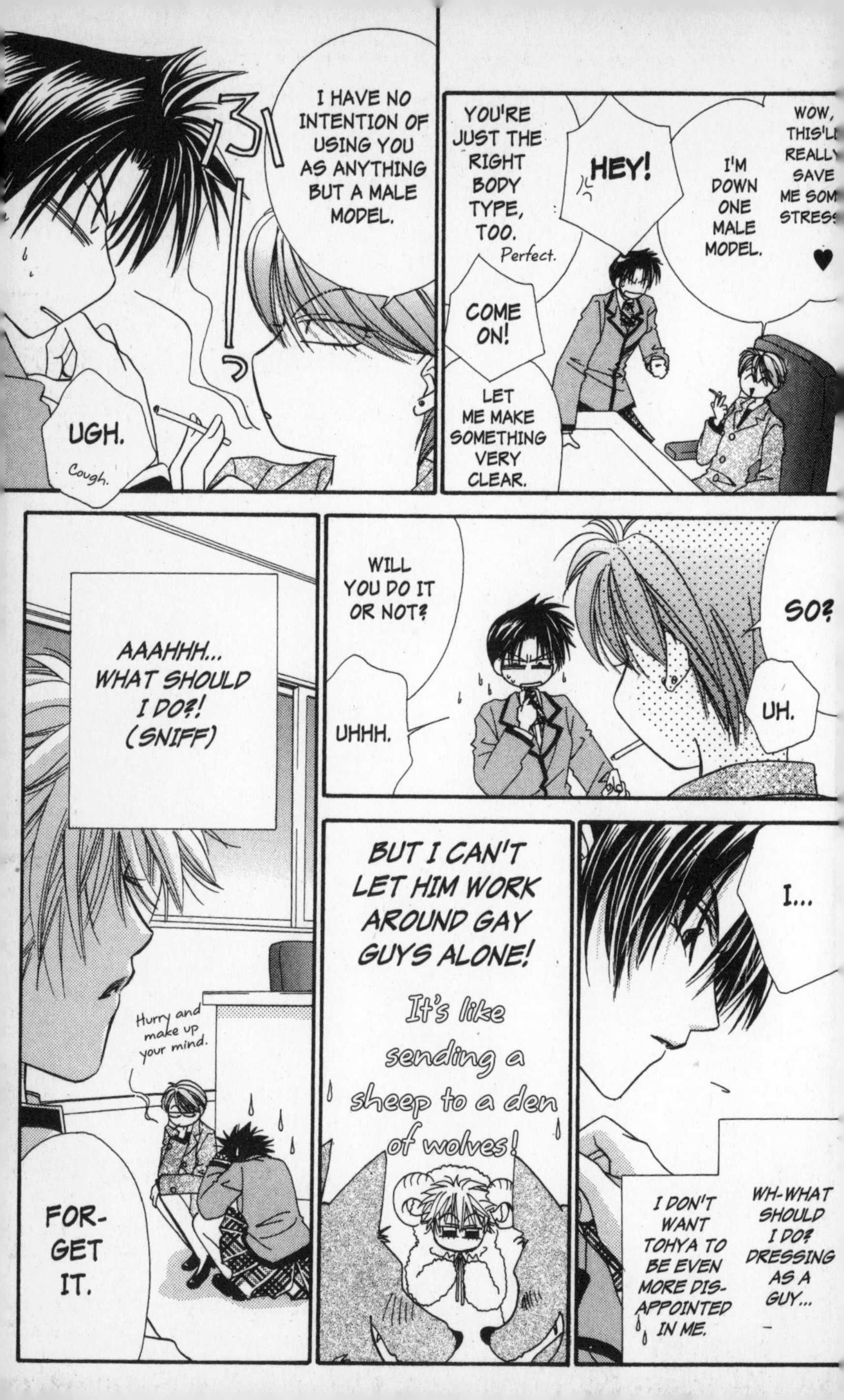
WOW, THIS'L REALLY SAVE ME SOM STRES
I'M DOWN ONE MALE MODEL.
HEY!
YOU'RE JUST THE RIGHT BODY TYPE, TOO.
Perfect.
COME ON!
LET ME MAKE SOMETHING VERY CLEAR.
I HAVE NO INTENTION OF USING YOU AS ANYTHING BUT A MALE MODEL.
UGH.
Cough.
SO?
UH.
WILL YOU DO IT OR NOT?
UHHH.
I...
WH-WHAT SHOULD I DO? DRESSING AS A GUY...
I DON'T WANT TOHYA TO BE EVEN MORE DIS-APPOINTED IN ME.
BUT I CAN'T LET HIM WORK AROUND GAY GUYS ALONE!
It's like sending a sheep to a den of wolves!
AAAHHH... WHAT SHOULD I DO?! (SNIFF)
Hurry and make up your mind.
FOR-GET IT.

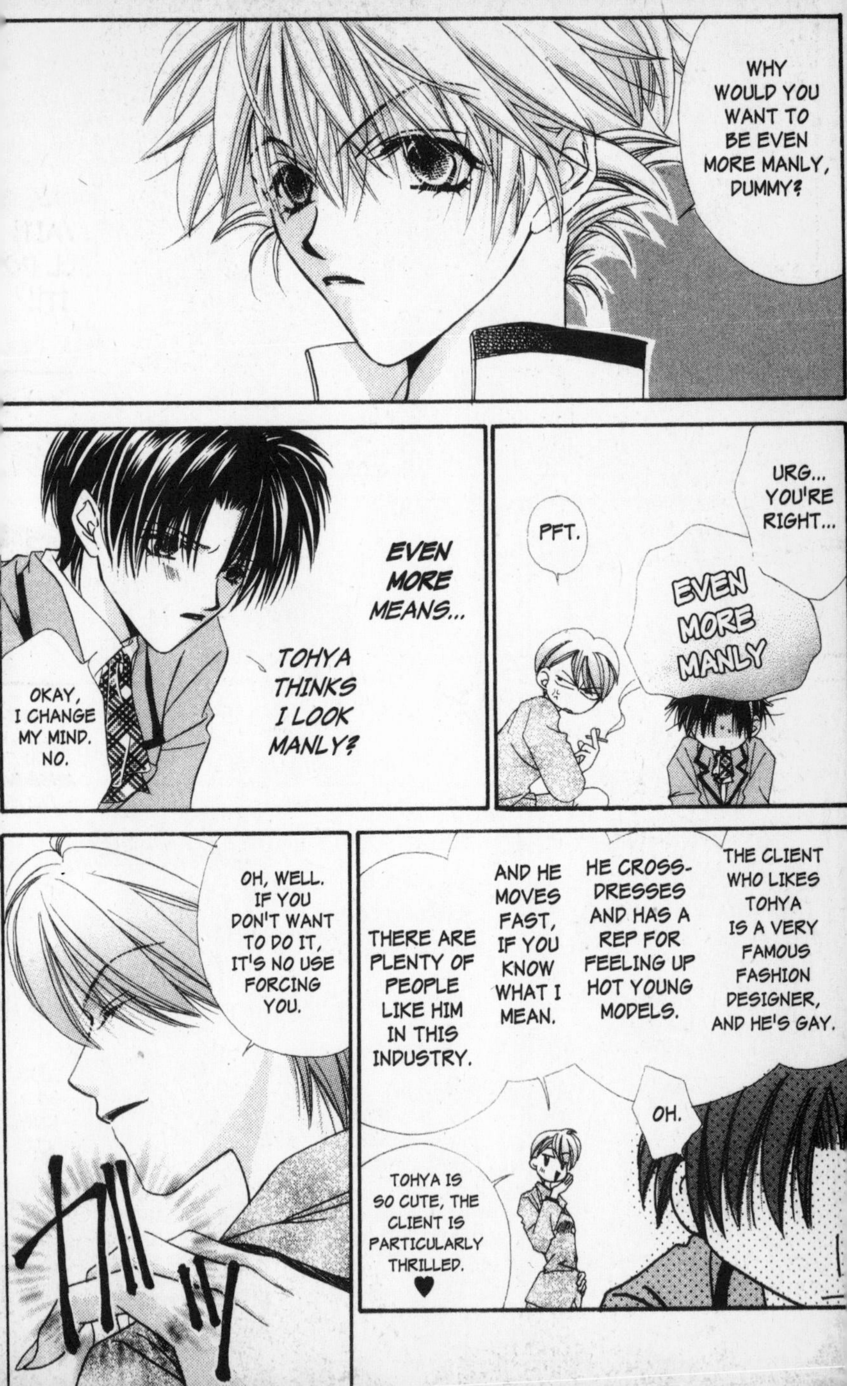
WHY WOULD YOU WANT TO BE EVEN MORE MANLY, DUMMY?
URG... YOU'RE RIGHT...
PFT.
EVEN MORE MANLY
EVEN MORE MEANS...
TOHYA THINKS I LOOK MANLY?
OKAY, I CHANGE MY MIND. NO.
THE CLIENT WHO LIKES TOHYA IS A VERY FAMOUS FASHION DESIGNER, AND HE'S GAY.
HE CROSS-DRESSES AND HAS A REP FOR FEELING UP HOT YOUNG MODELS.
AND HE MOVES FAST, IF YOU KNOW WHAT I MEAN.
THERE ARE PLENTY OF PEOPLE LIKE HIM IN THIS INDUSTRY.
OH.
TOHYA IS SO CUTE, THE CLIENT IS PARTICULARLY THRILLED. ♥
OH, WELL. IF YOU DON'T WANT TO DO IT, IT'S NO USE FORCING YOU.

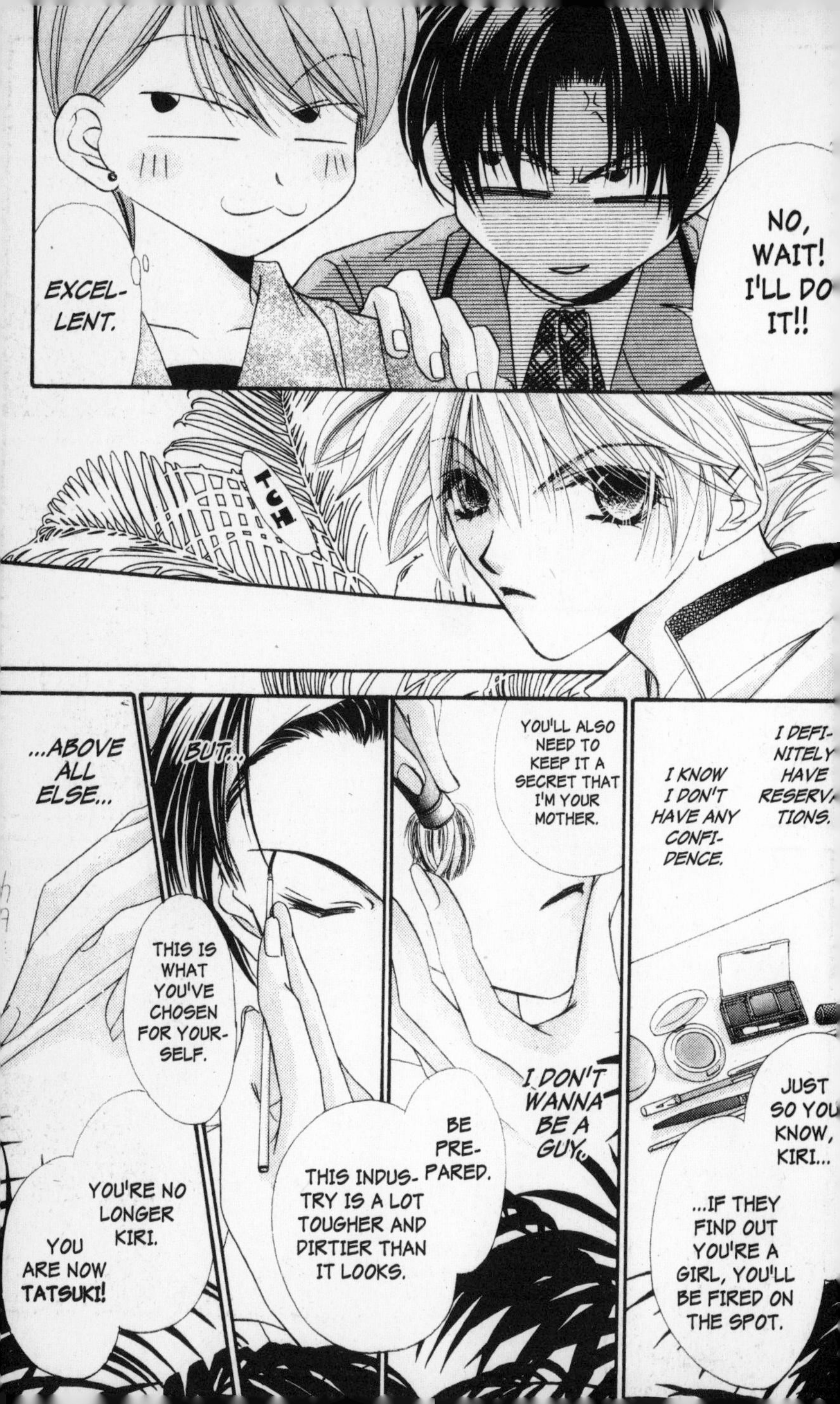
NO, WAIT! I'LL DO IT!!
EXCEL-LENT.
TCH
I DEFI-NITELY HAVE RESERVA-TIONS.
I KNOW I DON'T HAVE ANY CONFI-DENCE.
JUST SO YOU KNOW, KIRI...
...IF THEY FIND OUT YOU'RE A GIRL, YOU'LL BE FIRED ON THE SPOT.
YOU'LL ALSO NEED TO KEEP IT A SECRET THAT I'M YOUR MOTHER.
I DON'T WANNA BE A GUY.
BE PRE-PARED.
THIS INDUS-TRY IS A LOT TOUGHER AND DIRTIER THAN IT LOOKS.
BUT...
...ABOVE ALL ELSE...
THIS IS WHAT YOU'VE CHOSEN FOR YOUR-SELF.
YOU'RE NO LONGER KIRI.
YOU ARE NOW TATSUKI!

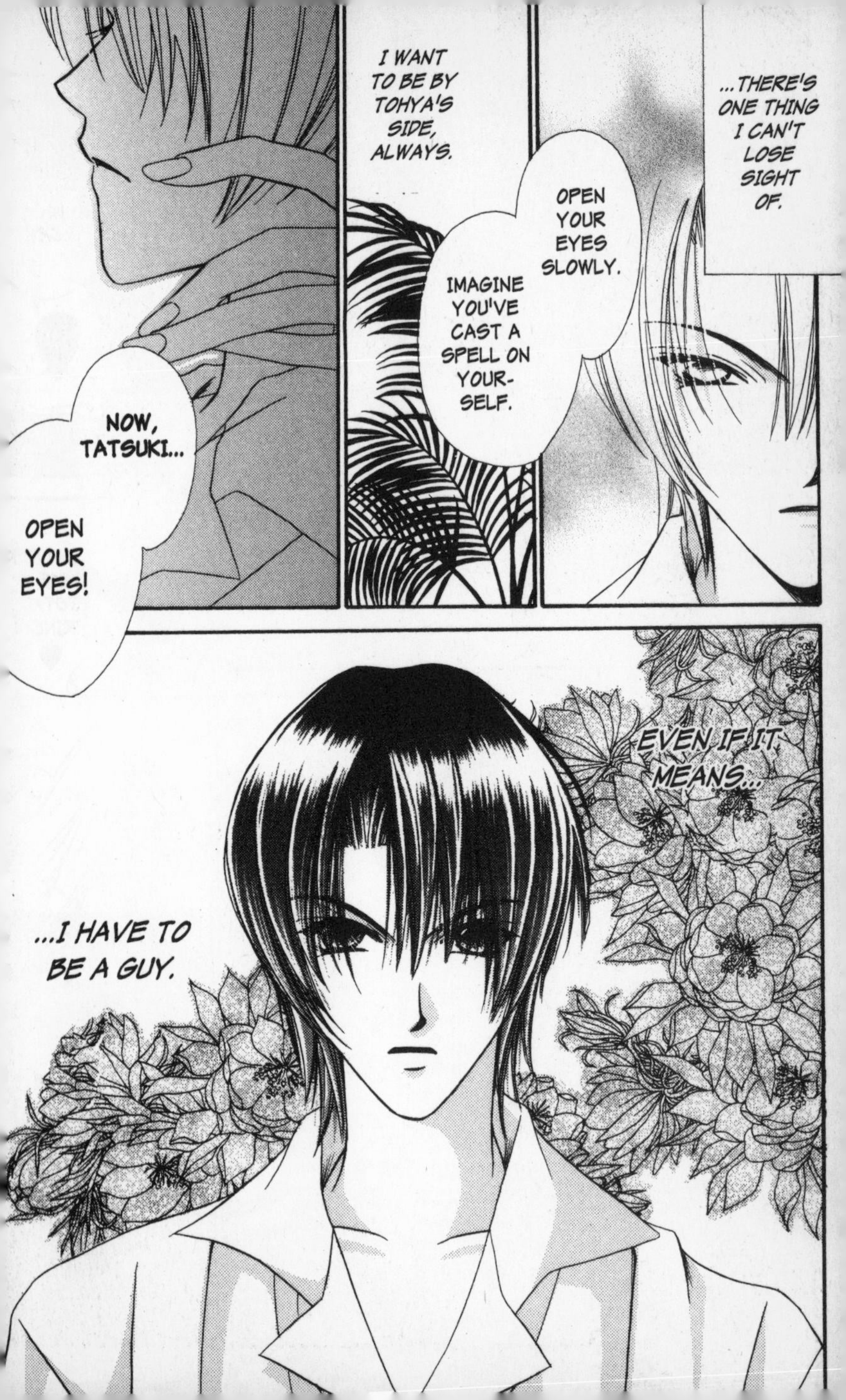
...THERE'S ONE THING I CAN'T LOSE SIGHT OF.
OPEN YOUR EYES SLOWLY.
I WANT TO BE BY TOHYA'S SIDE, ALWAYS.
IMAGINE YOU'VE CAST A SPELL ON YOURSELF.
NOW, TATSUKI...
OPEN YOUR EYES!
EVEN IF IT MEANS...
...I HAVE TO BE A GUY.

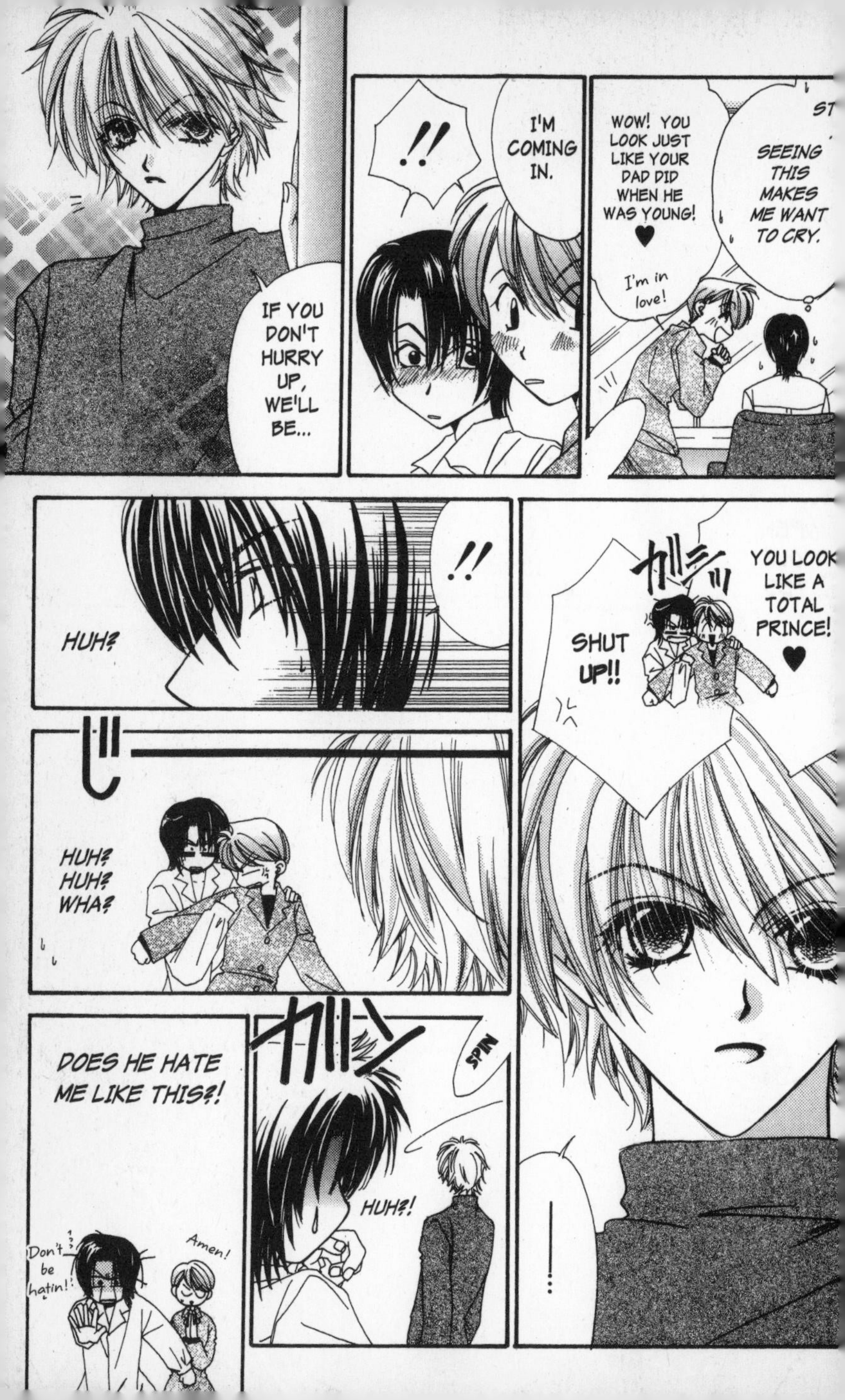

WOW! YOU LOOK JUST LIKE YOUR DAD DID WHEN HE WAS YOUNG! ♥
I'm in love!
SEEING THIS MAKES ME WANT TO CRY.
I'M COMING IN.
!!
IF YOU DON'T HURRY UP, WE'LL BE...
YOU LOOK LIKE A TOTAL PRINCE! ♥
SHUT UP!!
......
!!
HUH?
じー
HUH? HUH? WHA?
カン
SPIN
HUH?!
DOES HE HATE ME LIKE THIS?!
Amen!
Don't be hatin'!

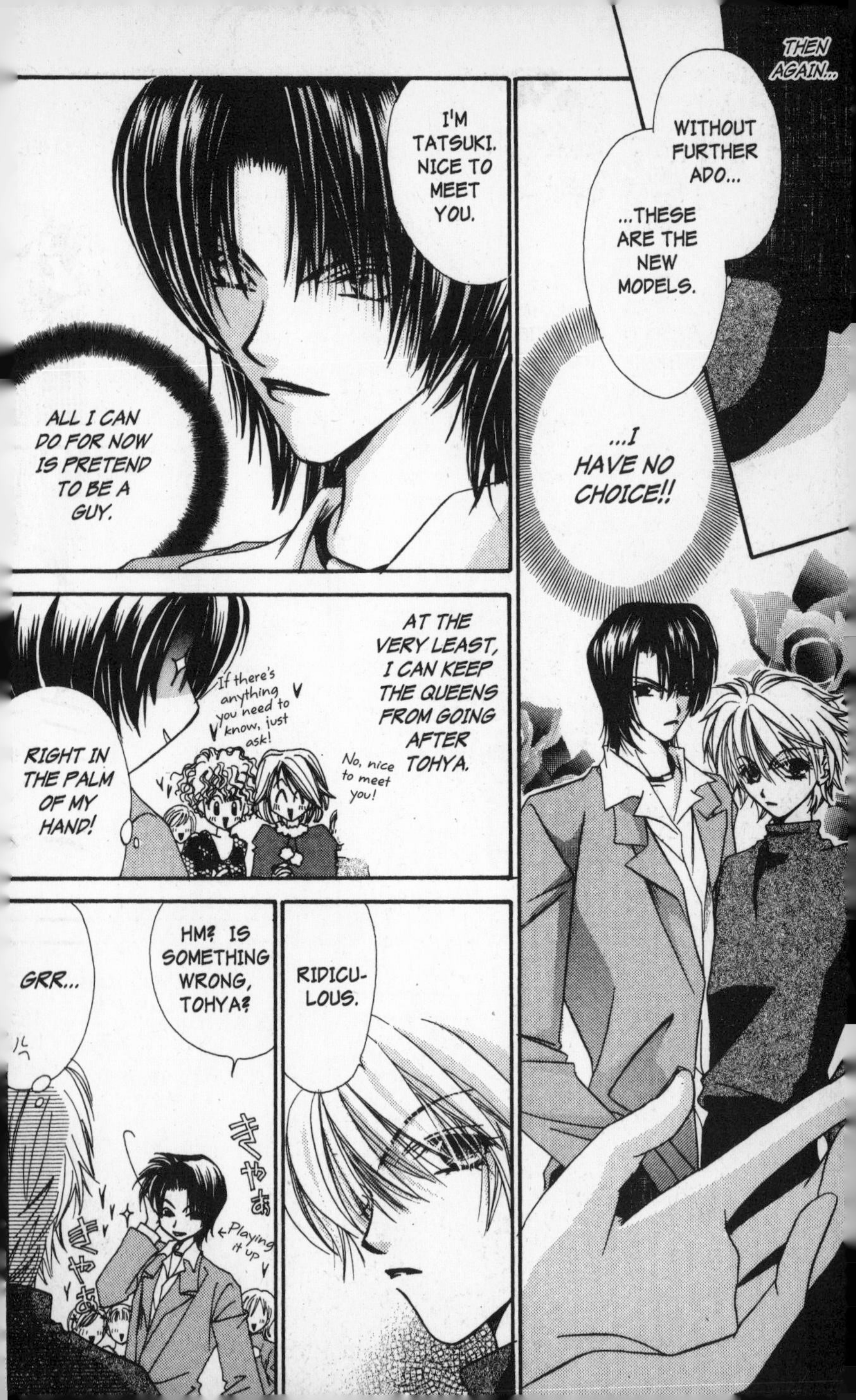

THEN AGAIN...
WITHOUT FURTHER ADO...
...THESE ARE THE NEW MODELS.
...I HAVE NO CHOICE!!
I'M TATSUKI. NICE TO MEET YOU.
ALL I CAN DO FOR NOW IS PRETEND TO BE A GUY.
AT THE VERY LEAST, I CAN KEEP THE QUEENS FROM GOING AFTER TOHYA.
No, nice to meet you!
If there's anything you need to know, just ask!
RIGHT IN THE PALM OF MY HAND!
RIDICU-LOUS.
HM? IS SOMETHING WRONG, TOHYA?
GRR...
きゃあ
きゃあ
←Playing it up

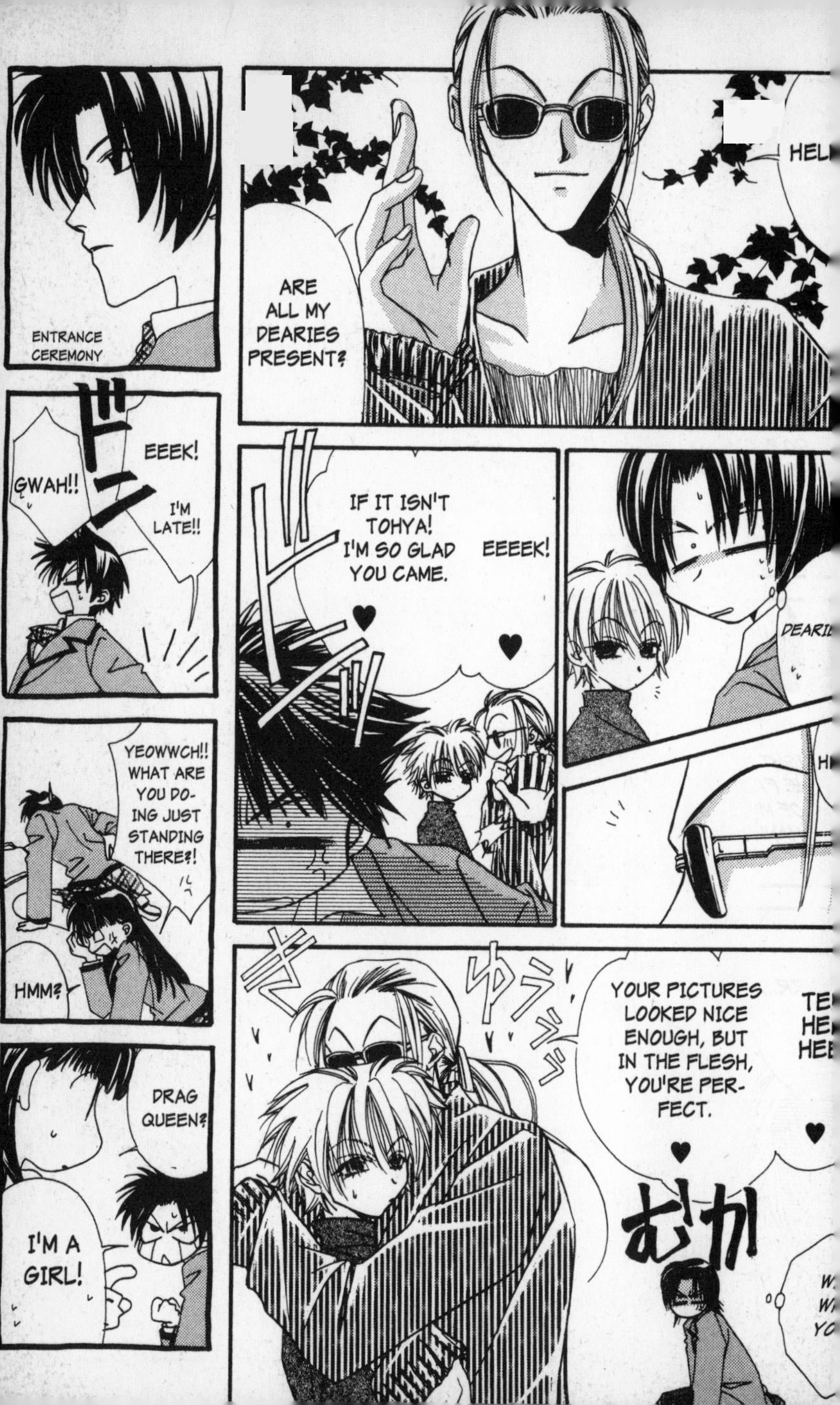
HEL
ARE ALL MY DEARIES PRESENT?
DEARI
HI
EEEEK!
IF IT ISN'T TOHYA! I'M SO GLAD YOU CAME.
ドド
TE
HE
HEE
YOUR PICTURES LOOKED NICE ENOUGH, BUT IN THE FLESH, YOU'RE PER-FECT.
ゆう
き
むか!
ENTRANCE CEREMONY
ドン
EEEK!
I'M LATE!!
GWAH!!
YEOWWCH!! WHAT ARE YOU DO-ING JUST STANDING THERE?!
HMM?
DRAG QUEEN?
I'M A GIRL!

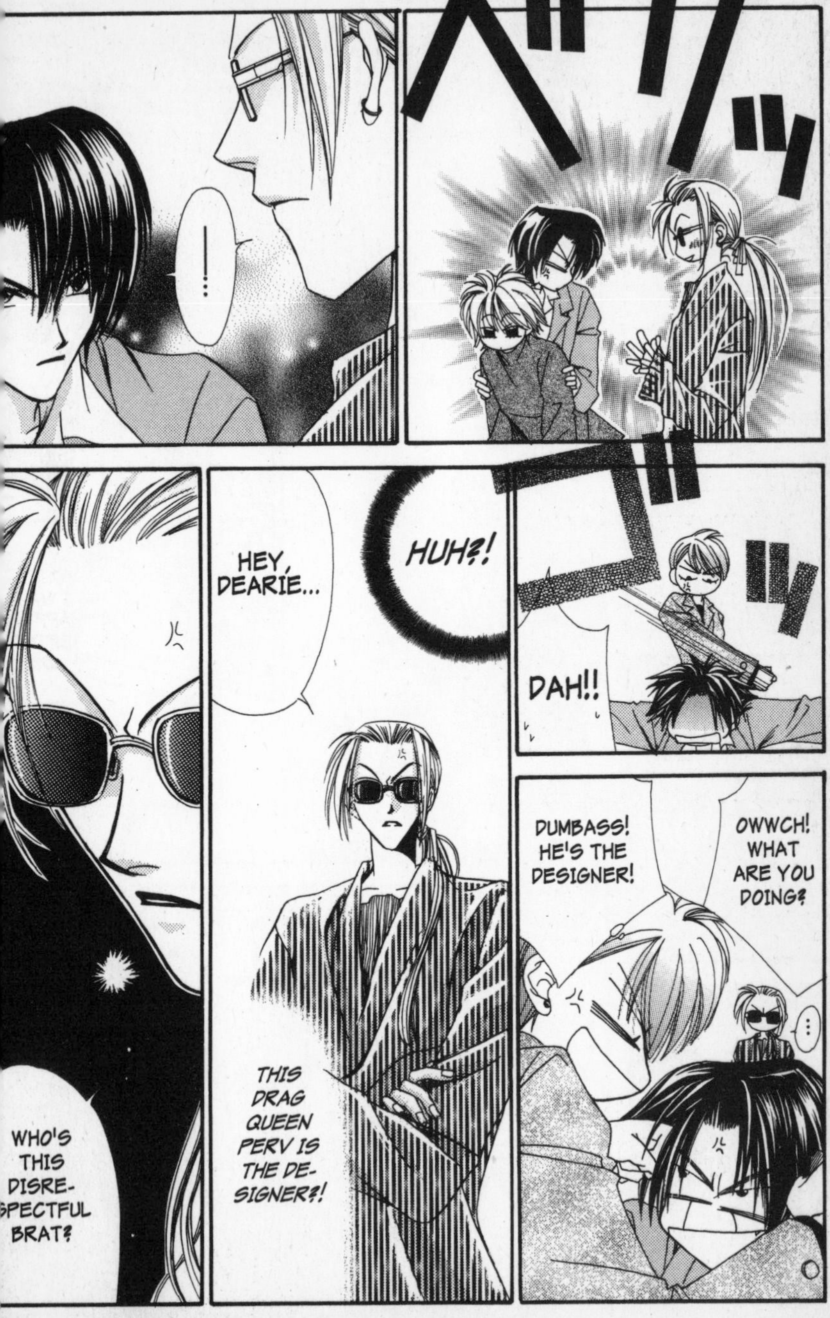
ベリッ
……
ゴッ
DAH!!
OWWCH! WHAT ARE YOU DOING?
DUMBASS! HE'S THE DESIGNER!
…
HUH?!
HEY, DEARIE...
THIS DRAG QUEEN PERV IS THE DE-SIGNER?!
WHO'S THIS DISRE-SPECTFUL BRAT?

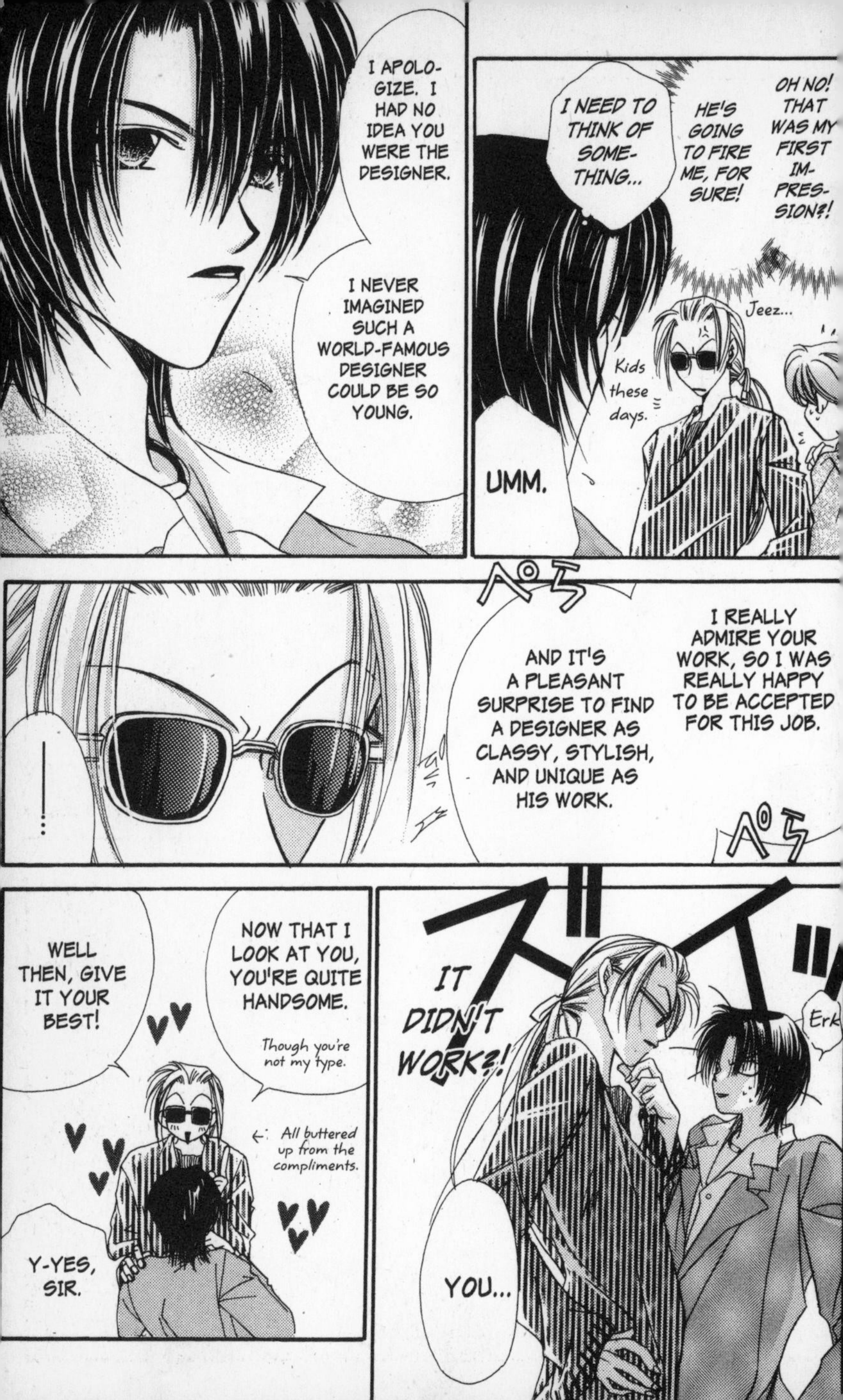
OH NO! THAT WAS MY FIRST IMPRESSION?!
HE'S GOING TO FIRE ME, FOR SURE!
I NEED TO THINK OF SOMETHING...
Jeez...
Kids these days.
UMM.
I APOLOGIZE. I HAD NO IDEA YOU WERE THE DESIGNER.
I NEVER IMAGINED SUCH A WORLD-FAMOUS DESIGNER COULD BE SO YOUNG.
I REALLY ADMIRE YOUR WORK, SO I WAS REALLY HAPPY TO BE ACCEPTED FOR THIS JOB.
AND IT'S A PLEASANT SURPRISE TO FIND A DESIGNER AS CLASSY, STYLISH, AND UNIQUE AS HIS WORK.
Erk
IT DIDN'T WORK?!
YOU...
NOW THAT I LOOK AT YOU, YOU'RE QUITE HANDSOME.
Though you're not my type.
WELL THEN, GIVE IT YOUR BEST!
All buttered up from the compliments.
Y-YES, SIR.

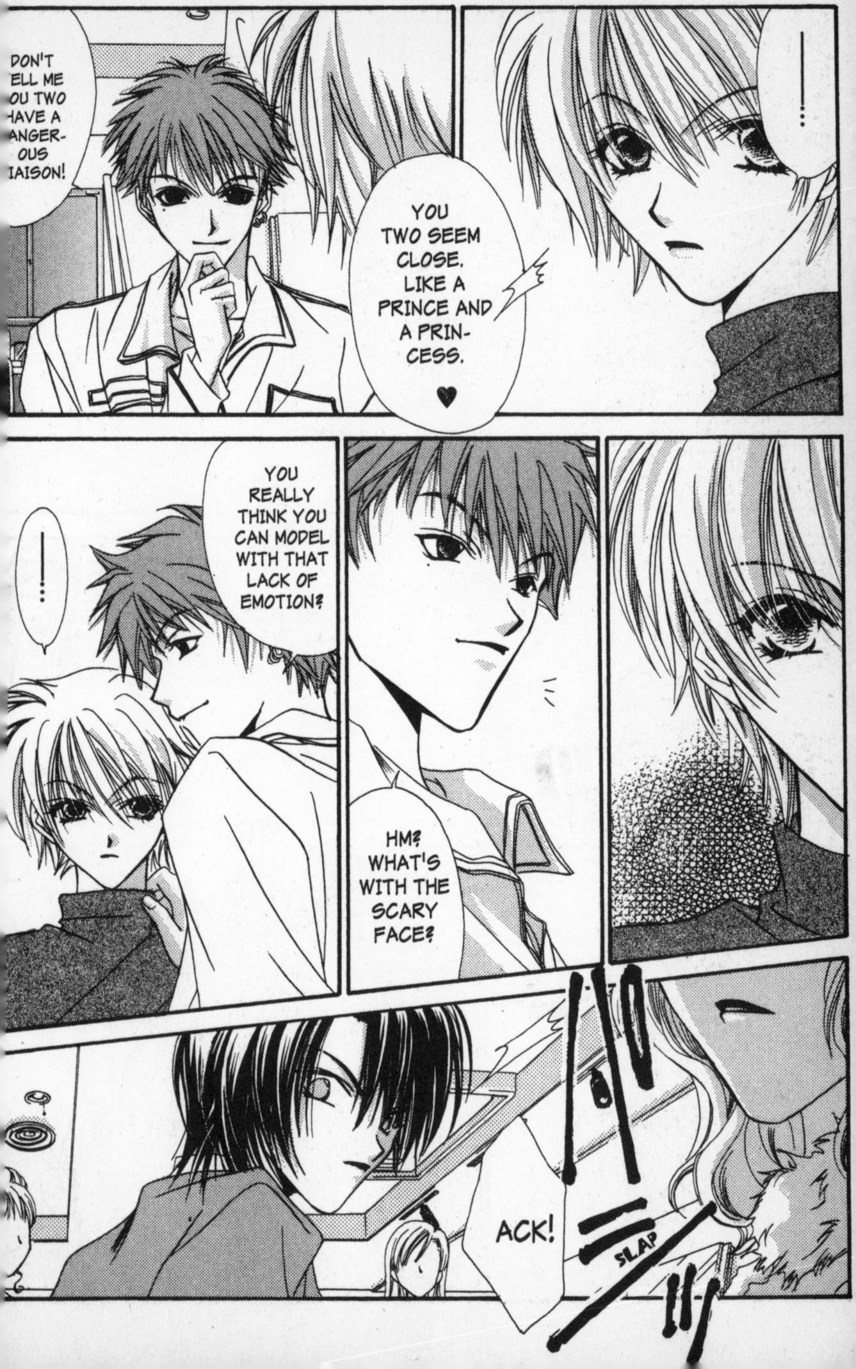

!......
YOU TWO SEEM CLOSE. LIKE A PRINCE AND A PRIN-CESS. ♥
DON'T ELL ME OU TWO HAVE A ANGER-OUS IAISON!
HM? WHAT'S WITH THE SCARY FACE?
YOU REALLY THINK YOU CAN MODEL WITH THAT LACK OF EMOTION?
!......
ACK!
SLAP

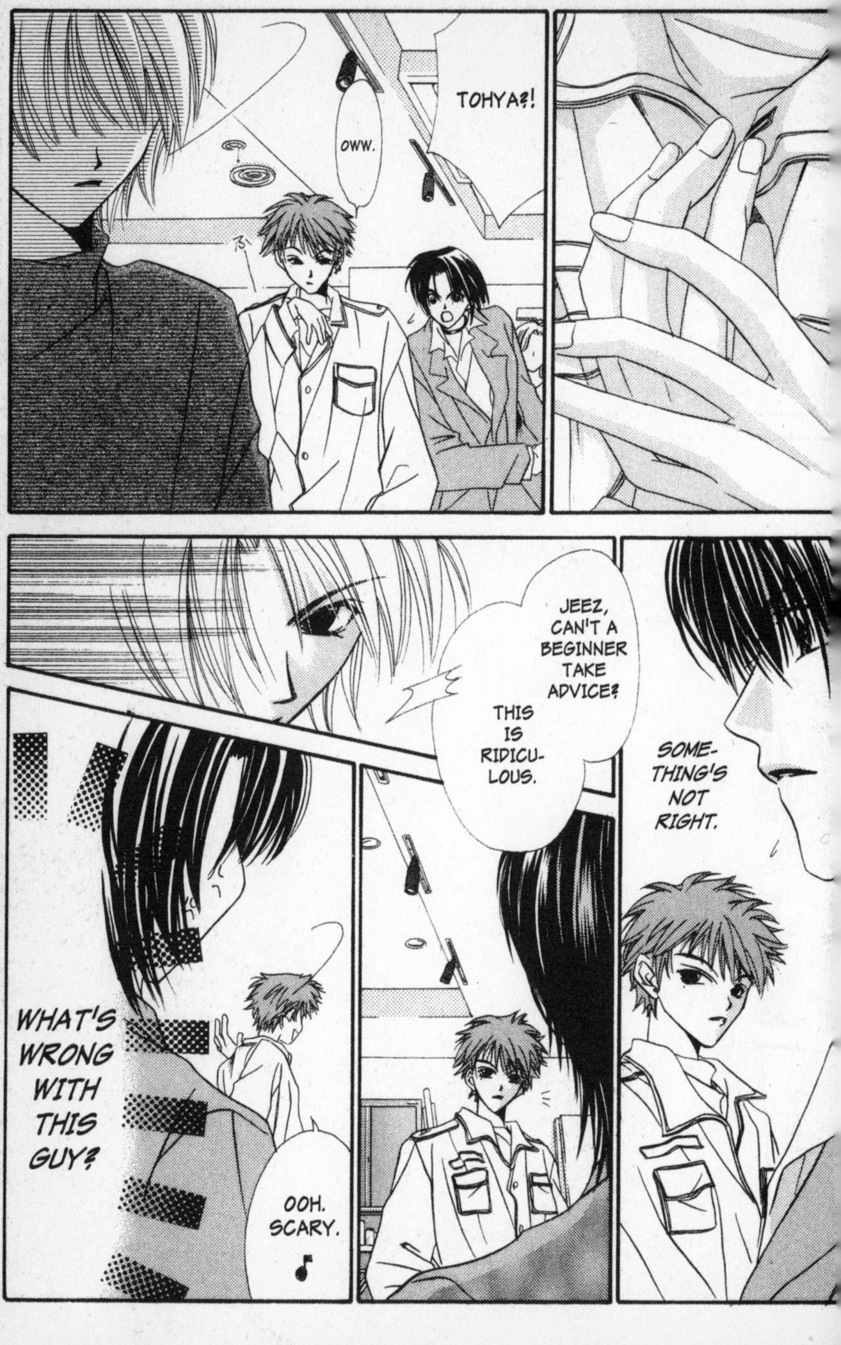
TOHYA?!
OWW.
SOME-THING'S NOT RIGHT.
JEEZ, CAN'T A BEGINNER TAKE ADVICE? THIS IS RIDICU-LOUS.
WHAT'S WRONG WITH THIS GUY?
OOH. SCARY. ♪

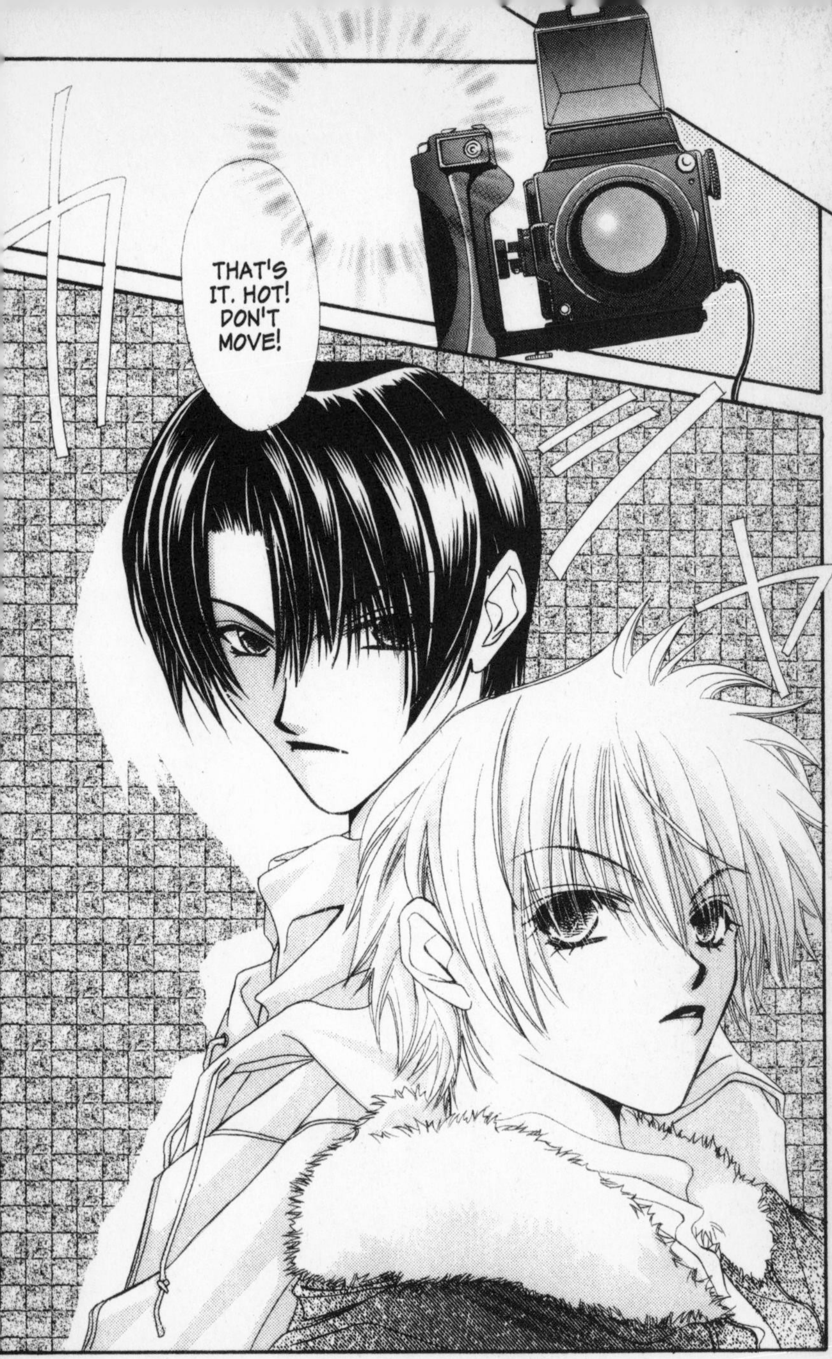
THAT'S IT. HOT! DON'T MOVE!

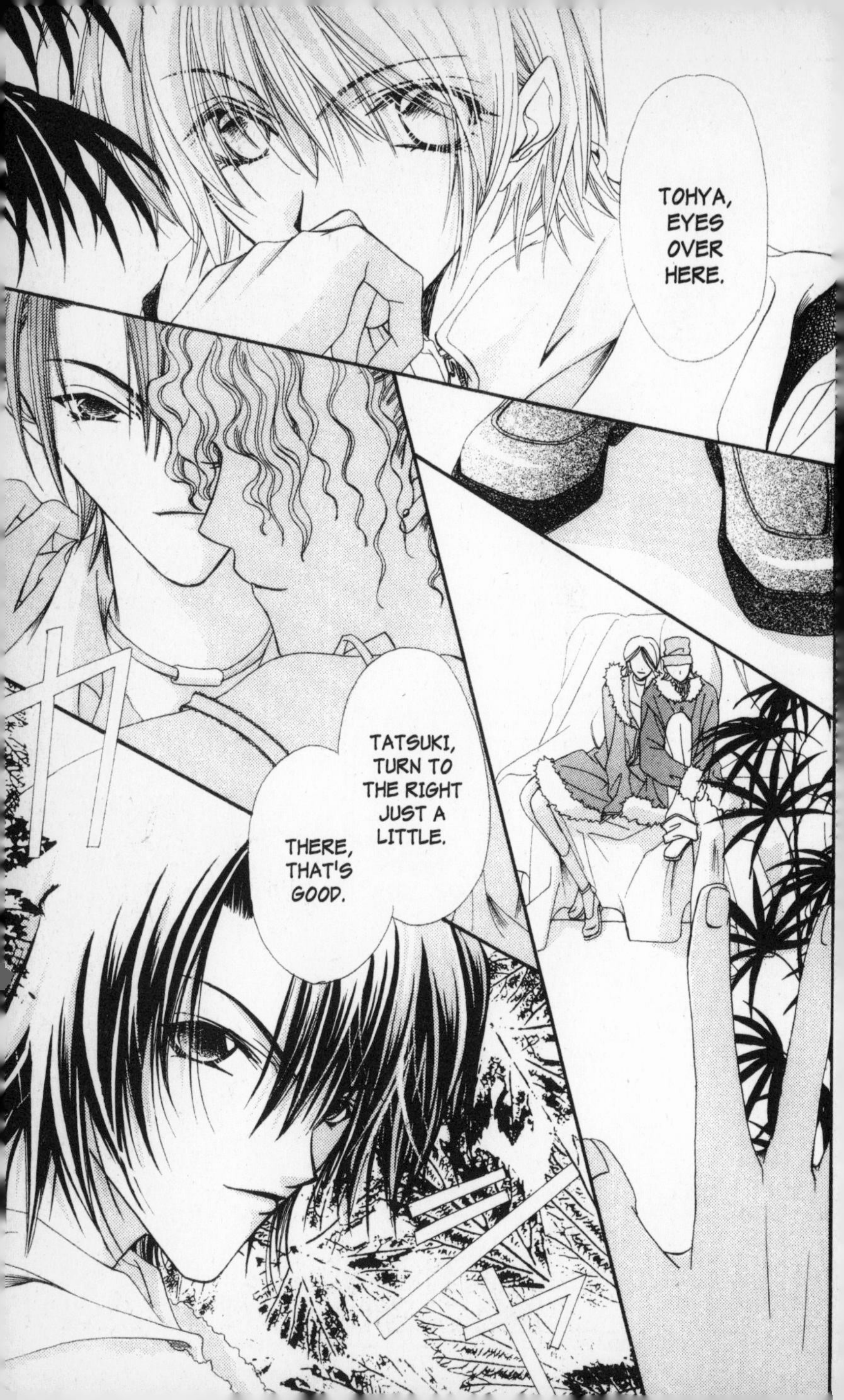
TOHYA, EYES OVER HERE.
TATSUKI, TURN TO THE RIGHT JUST A LITTLE.
THERE, THAT'S GOOD.

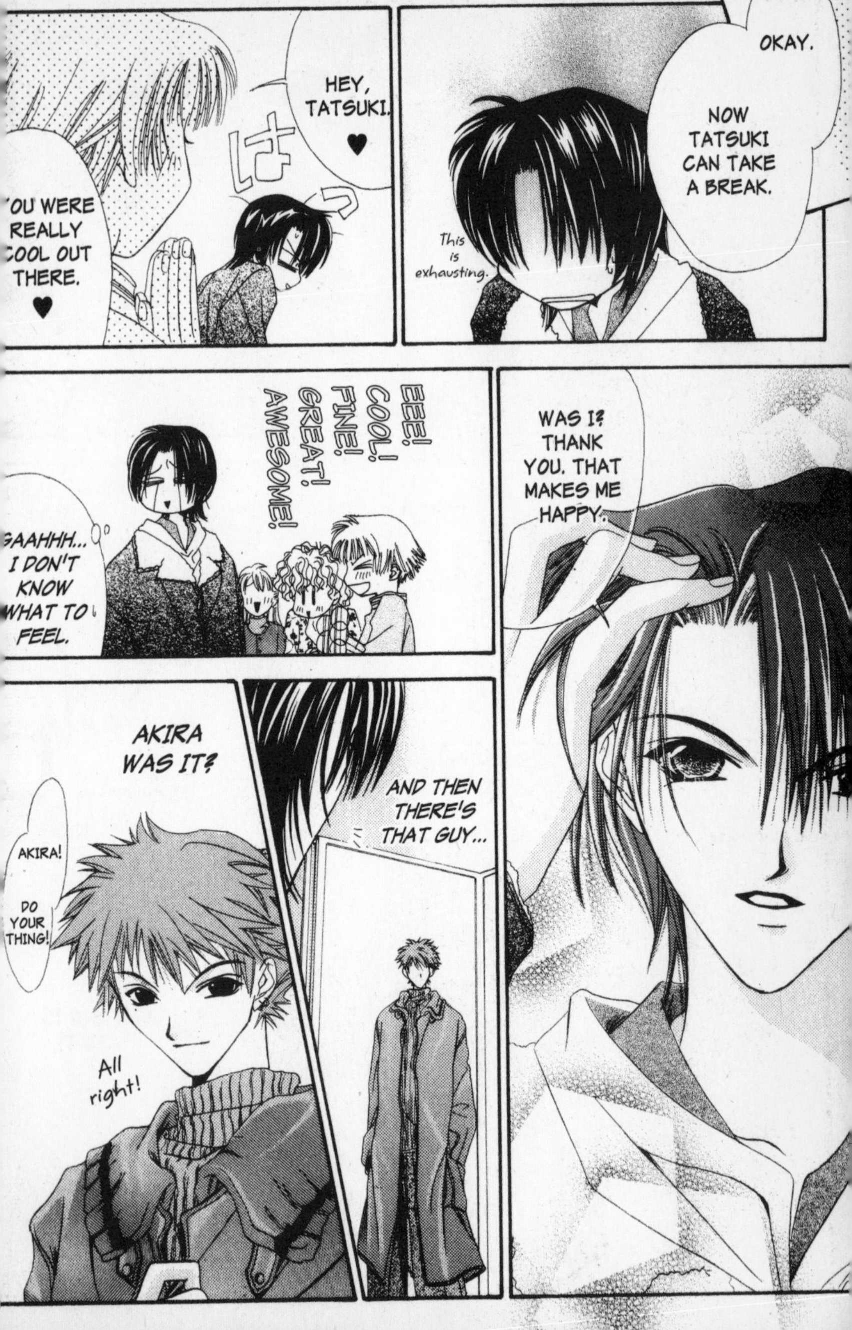
OKAY.
NOW TATSUKI CAN TAKE A BREAK.
This is exhausting.
HEY, TATSUKI. ♥
は
YOU WERE REALLY COOL OUT THERE. ♥
WAS I? THANK YOU. THAT MAKES ME HAPPY.
EEE! COOL! FINE! GREAT! AWESOME!
GAAHHH... I DON'T KNOW WHAT TO FEEL.
AND THEN THERE'S THAT GUY...
AKIRA WAS IT?
AKIRA!
DO YOUR THING!
All right!

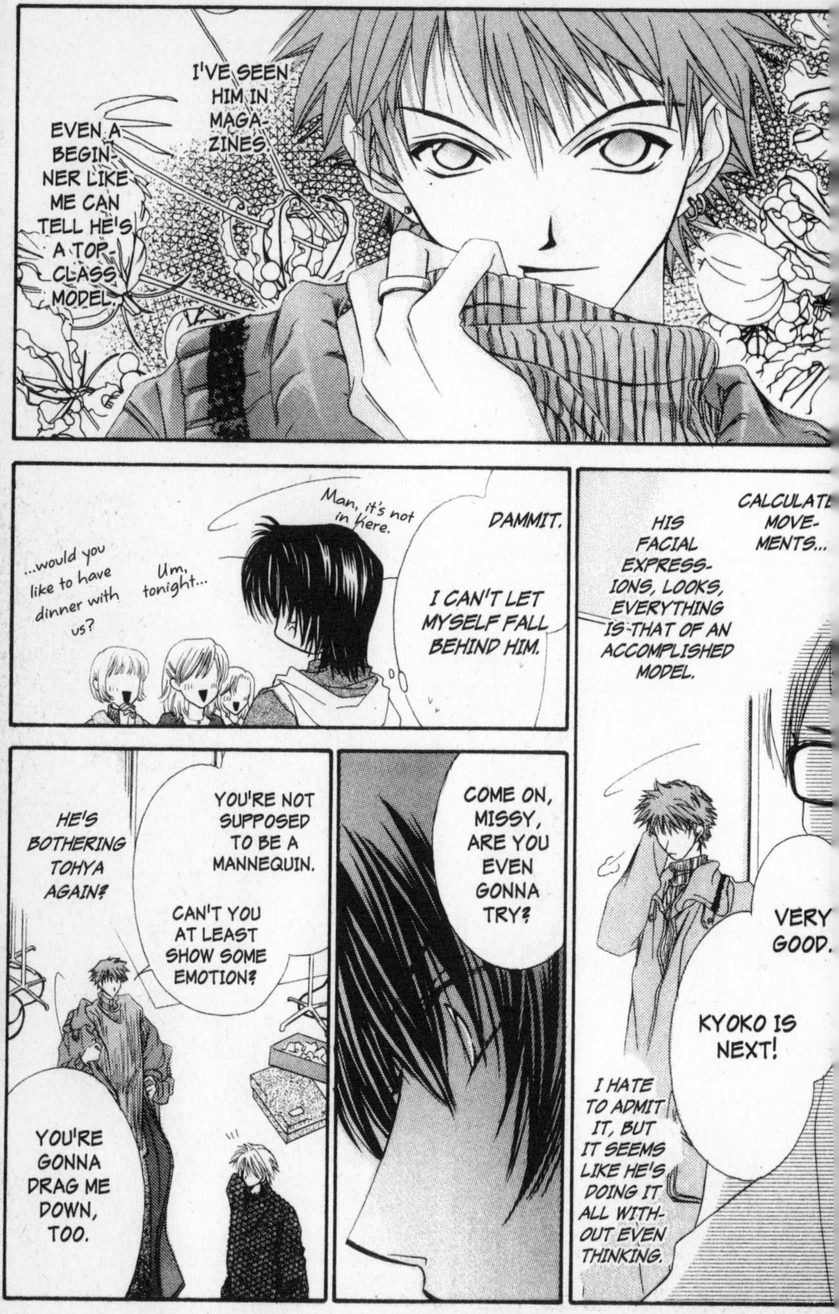
I'VE SEEN HIM IN MAGAZINES.
EVEN A BEGINNER LIKE ME CAN TELL HE'S A TOP-CLASS MODEL.
CALCULATE MOVEMENTS...
HIS FACIAL EXPRESSIONS, LOOKS, EVERYTHING IS THAT OF AN ACCOMPLISHED MODEL.
VERY GOOD.
KYOKO IS NEXT!
I HATE TO ADMIT IT, BUT IT SEEMS LIKE HE'S DOING IT ALL WITHOUT EVEN THINKING.
DAMMIT.
I CAN'T LET MYSELF FALL BEHIND HIM.
Man, it's not in here.
Um, tonight...
...would you like to have dinner with us?
COME ON, MISSY, ARE YOU EVEN GONNA TRY?
YOU'RE NOT SUPPOSED TO BE A MANNEQUIN.
CAN'T YOU AT LEAST SHOW SOME EMOTION?
HE'S BOTHERING TOHYA AGAIN?
YOU'RE GONNA DRAG ME DOWN, TOO.

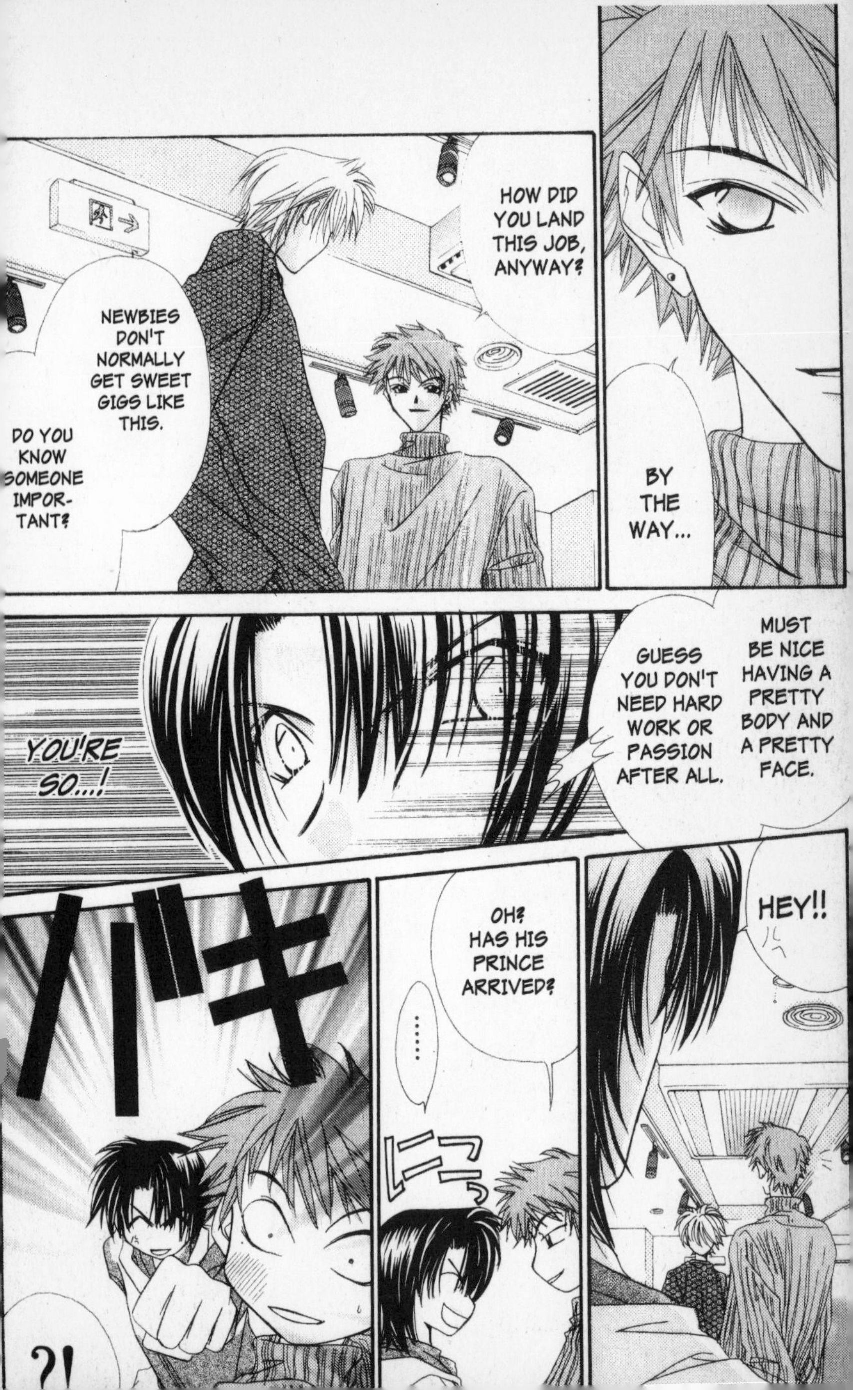
BY THE WAY...
HOW DID YOU LAND THIS JOB, ANYWAY?
NEWBIES DON'T NORMALLY GET SWEET GIGS LIKE THIS.
DO YOU KNOW SOMEONE IMPOR-TANT?
MUST BE NICE HAVING A PRETTY BODY AND A PRETTY FACE.
GUESS YOU DON'T NEED HARD WORK OR PASSION AFTER ALL.
YOU'RE SO...!
HEY!!
OH? HAS HIS PRINCE ARRIVED?
......
にこっ
バキ
?!

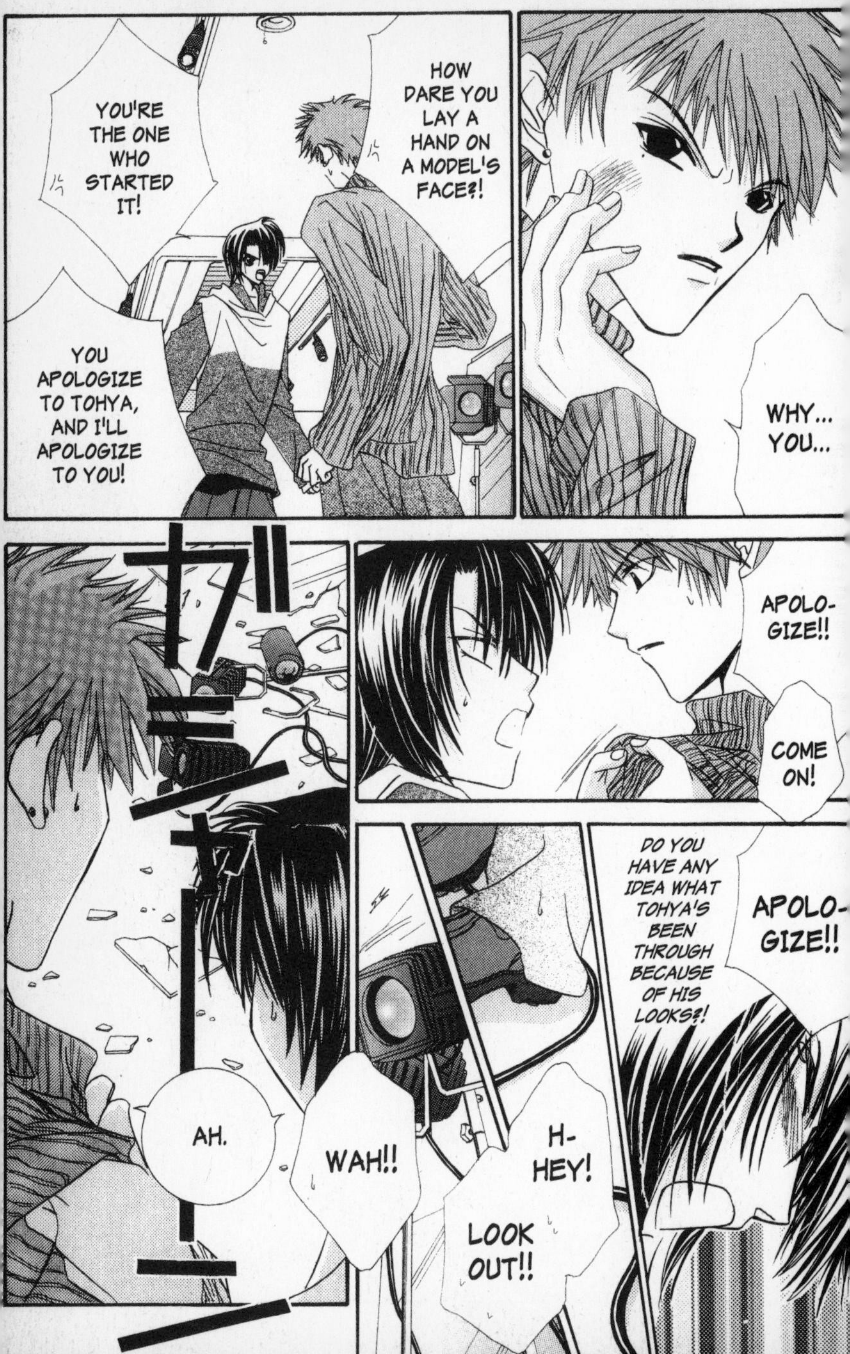

WHY... YOU...
HOW DARE YOU LAY A HAND ON A MODEL'S FACE?!
YOU'RE THE ONE WHO STARTED IT!
YOU APOLOGIZE TO TOHYA, AND I'LL APOLOGIZE TO YOU!
APOLO-GIZE!!
COME ON!
APOLO-GIZE!!
DO YOU HAVE ANY IDEA WHAT TOHYA'S BEEN THROUGH BECAUSE OF HIS LOOKS?!
H-HEY!
LOOK OUT!!
WAH!!
AH.

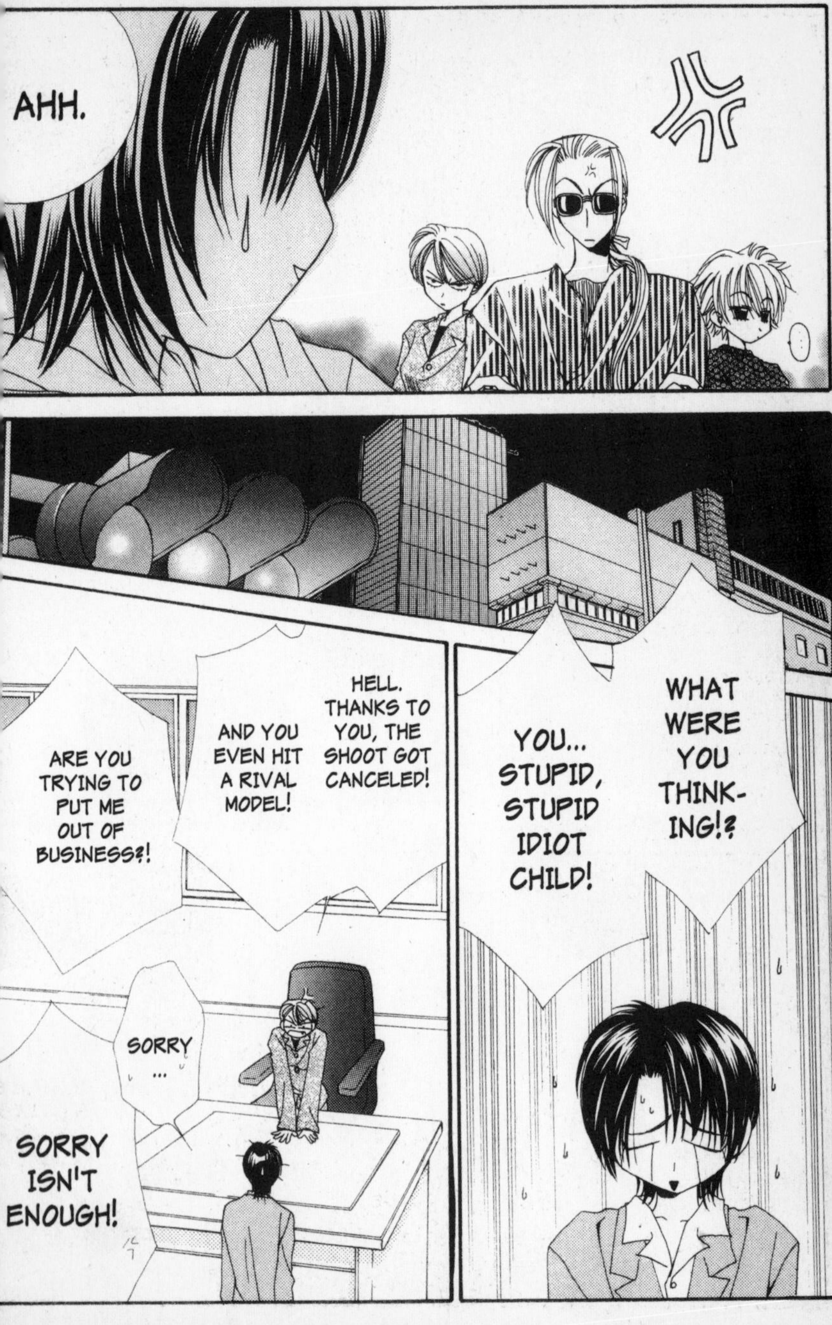
AHH.
...
WHAT WERE YOU THINKING!?
YOU... STUPID, STUPID IDIOT CHILD!
HELL. THANKS TO YOU, THE SHOOT GOT CANCELED!
AND YOU EVEN HIT A RIVAL MODEL!
ARE YOU TRYING TO PUT ME OUT OF BUSINESS?!
SORRY ...
SORRY ISN'T ENOUGH!

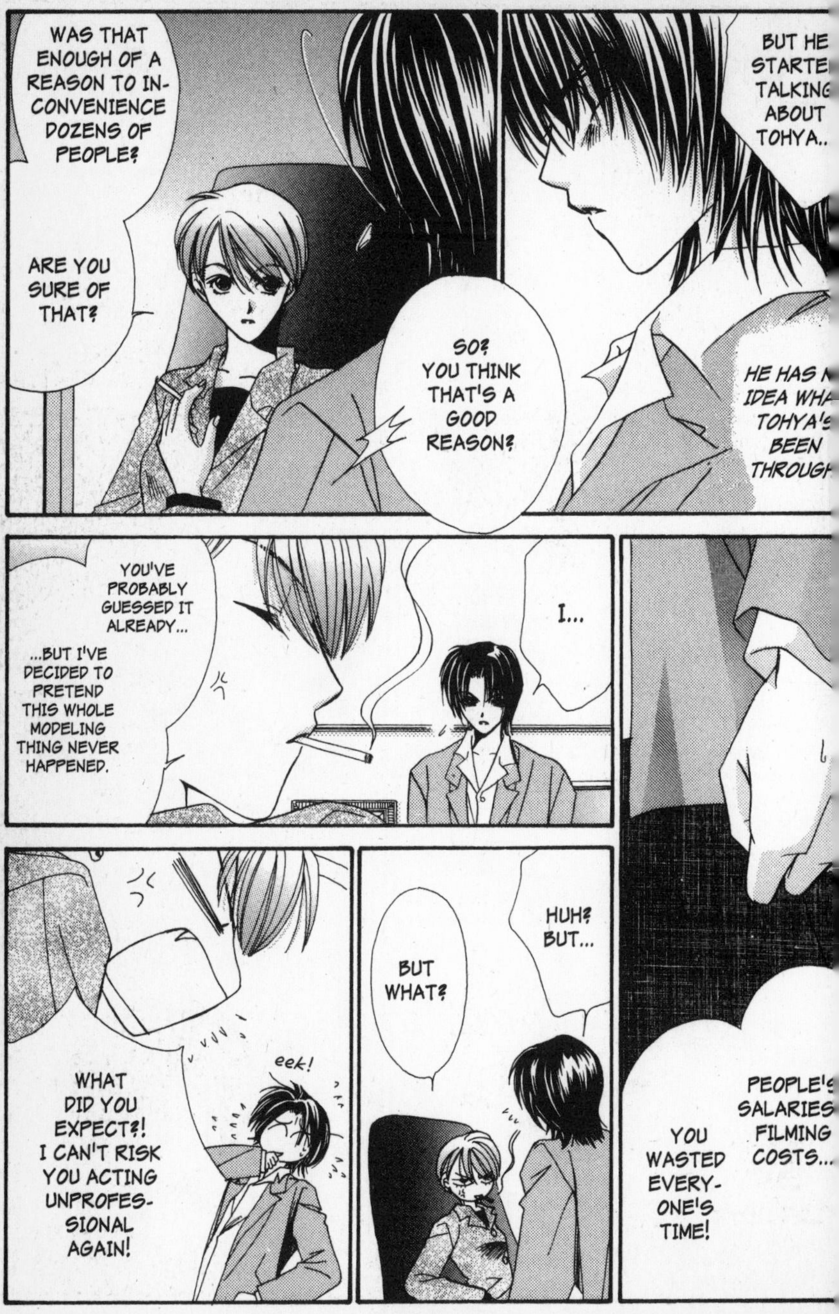
BUT HE STARTE TALKING ABOUT TOHYA..
HE HAS N IDEA WHA TOHYA'S BEEN THROUGH
SO? YOU THINK THAT'S A GOOD REASON?
WAS THAT ENOUGH OF A REASON TO IN-CONVENIENCE DOZENS OF PEOPLE?
ARE YOU SURE OF THAT?
PEOPLE'S SALARIES FILMING COSTS...
YOU WASTED EVERY-ONE'S TIME!
I...
YOU'VE PROBABLY GUESSED IT ALREADY...
...BUT I'VE DECIDED TO PRETEND THIS WHOLE MODELING THING NEVER HAPPENED.
HUH? BUT...
BUT WHAT?
eek!
WHAT DID YOU EXPECT?! I CAN'T RISK YOU ACTING UNPROFES-SIONAL AGAIN!

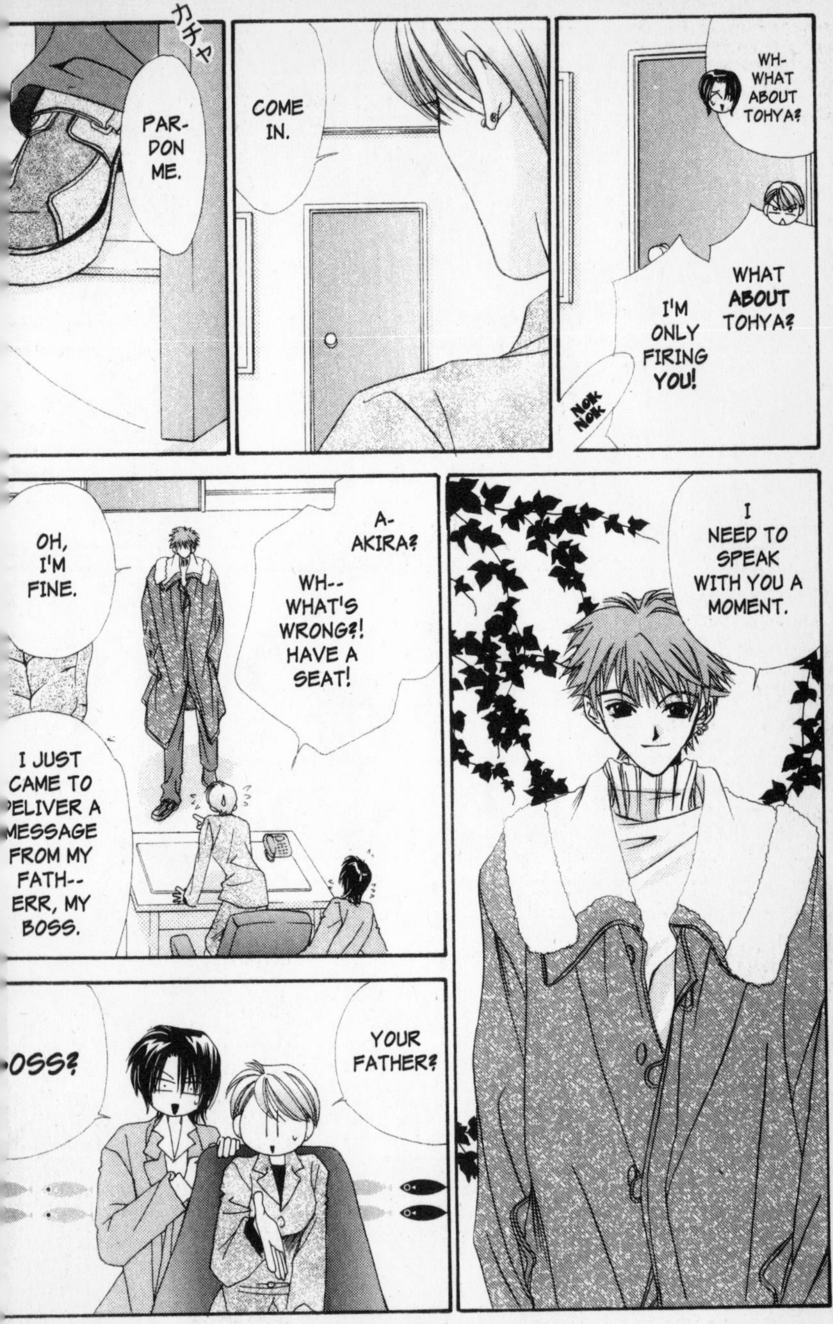
WH- WHAT ABOUT TOHYA?
WHAT ABOUT TOHYA?
I'M ONLY FIRING YOU!
NOK NOK
COME IN.
カチャ
PAR-DON ME.
I NEED TO SPEAK WITH YOU A MOMENT.
A- AKIRA?
WH-- WHAT'S WRONG?! HAVE A SEAT!
OH, I'M FINE.
I JUST CAME TO ELIVER A ESSAGE FROM MY FATH-- ERR, MY BOSS.
YOUR FATHER?
OSS?

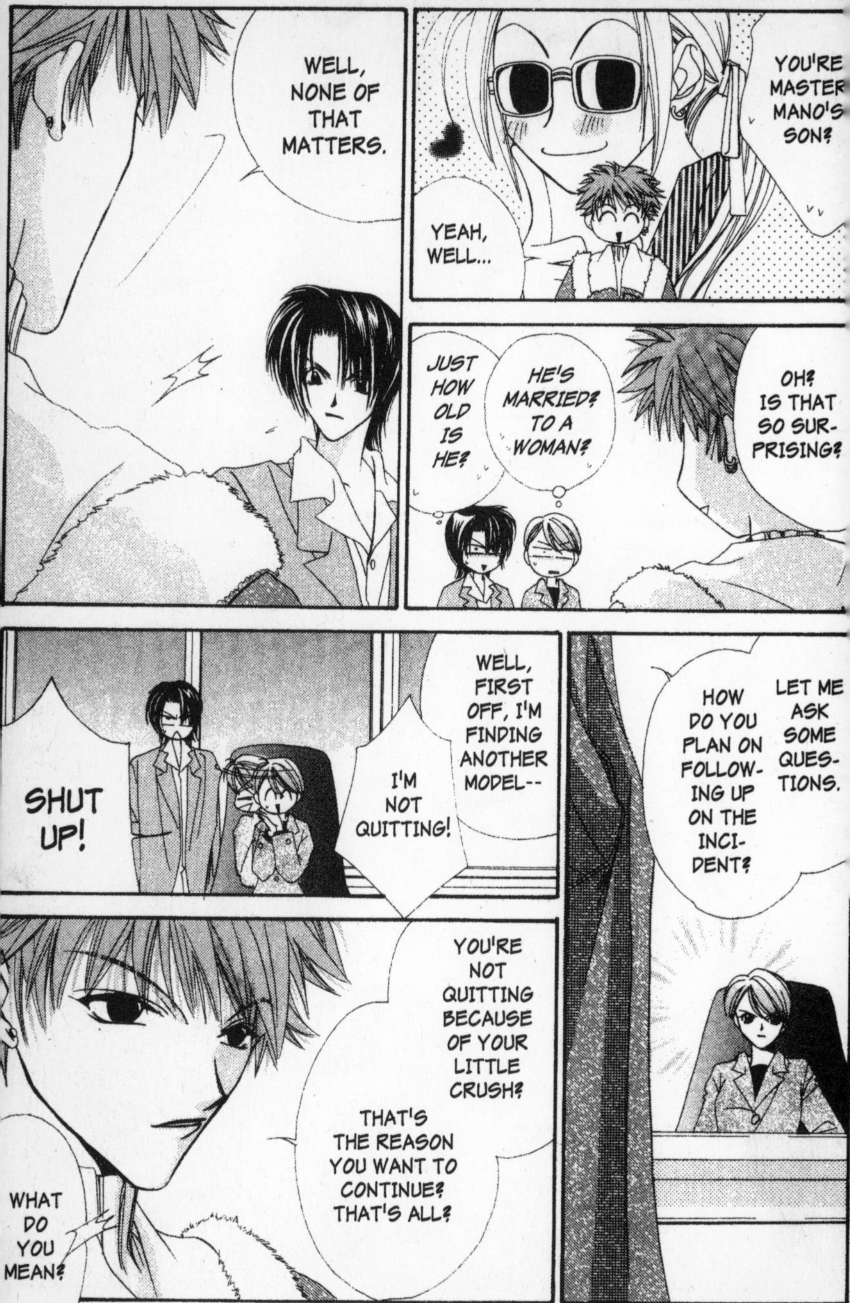

YOU'RE MASTER MANO'S SON?
YEAH, WELL...
OH? IS THAT SO SURPRISING?
HE'S MARRIED? TO A WOMAN?
JUST HOW OLD IS HE?
WELL, NONE OF THAT MATTERS.
LET ME ASK SOME QUESTIONS.
HOW DO YOU PLAN ON FOLLOWING UP ON THE INCIDENT?
WELL, FIRST OFF, I'M FINDING ANOTHER MODEL--
I'M NOT QUITTING!
SHUT UP!
YOU'RE NOT QUITTING BECAUSE OF YOUR LITTLE CRUSH?
THAT'S THE REASON YOU WANT TO CONTINUE? THAT'S ALL?
WHAT DO YOU MEAN?

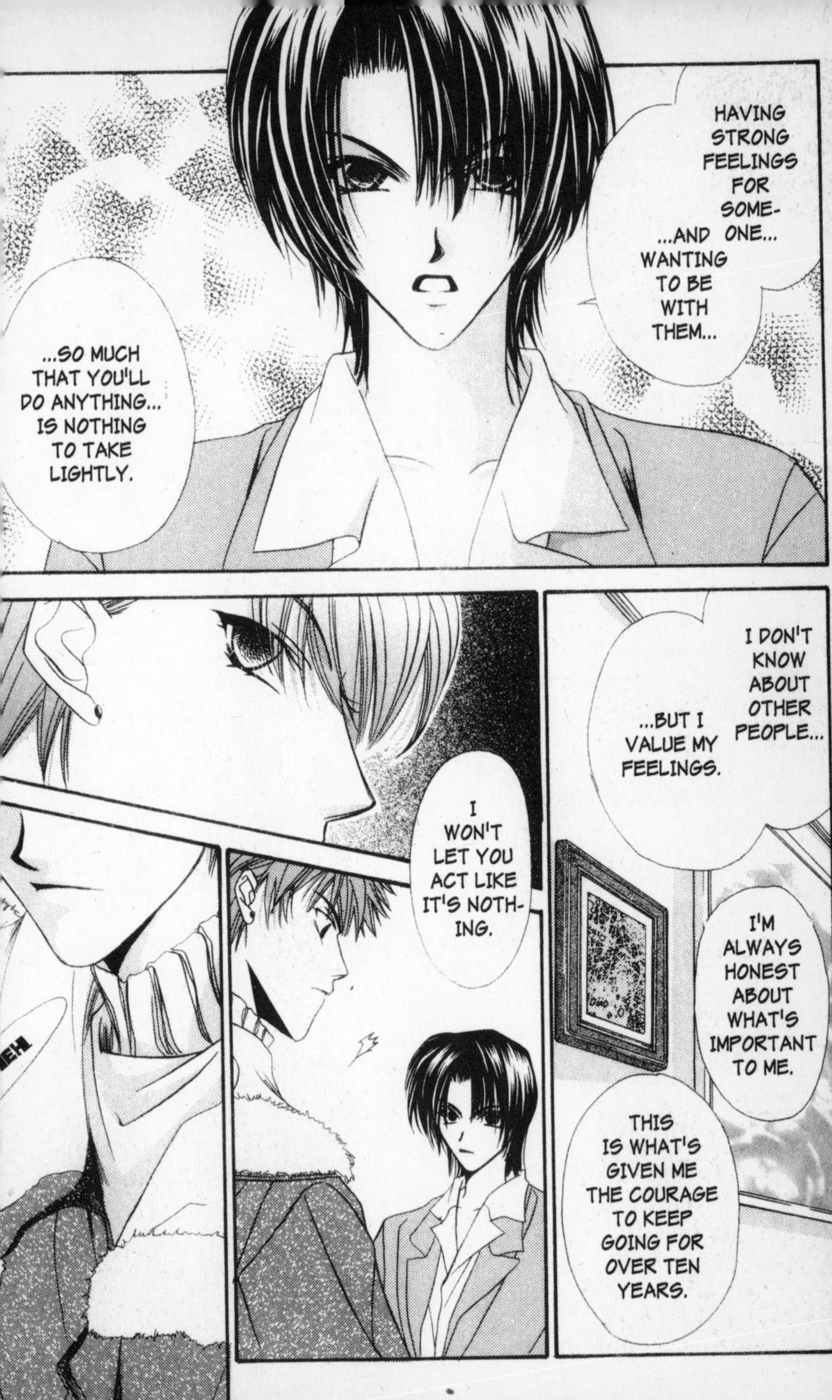
HAVING STRONG FEELINGS FOR SOME-ONE...
...AND WANTING TO BE WITH THEM...
...SO MUCH THAT YOU'LL DO ANYTHING... IS NOTHING TO TAKE LIGHTLY.
I DON'T KNOW ABOUT OTHER PEOPLE...
...BUT I VALUE MY FEELINGS.
I'M ALWAYS HONEST ABOUT WHAT'S IMPORTANT TO ME.
THIS IS WHAT'S GIVEN ME THE COURAGE TO KEEP GOING FOR OVER TEN YEARS.
I WON'T LET YOU ACT LIKE IT'S NOTH-ING.
HEH

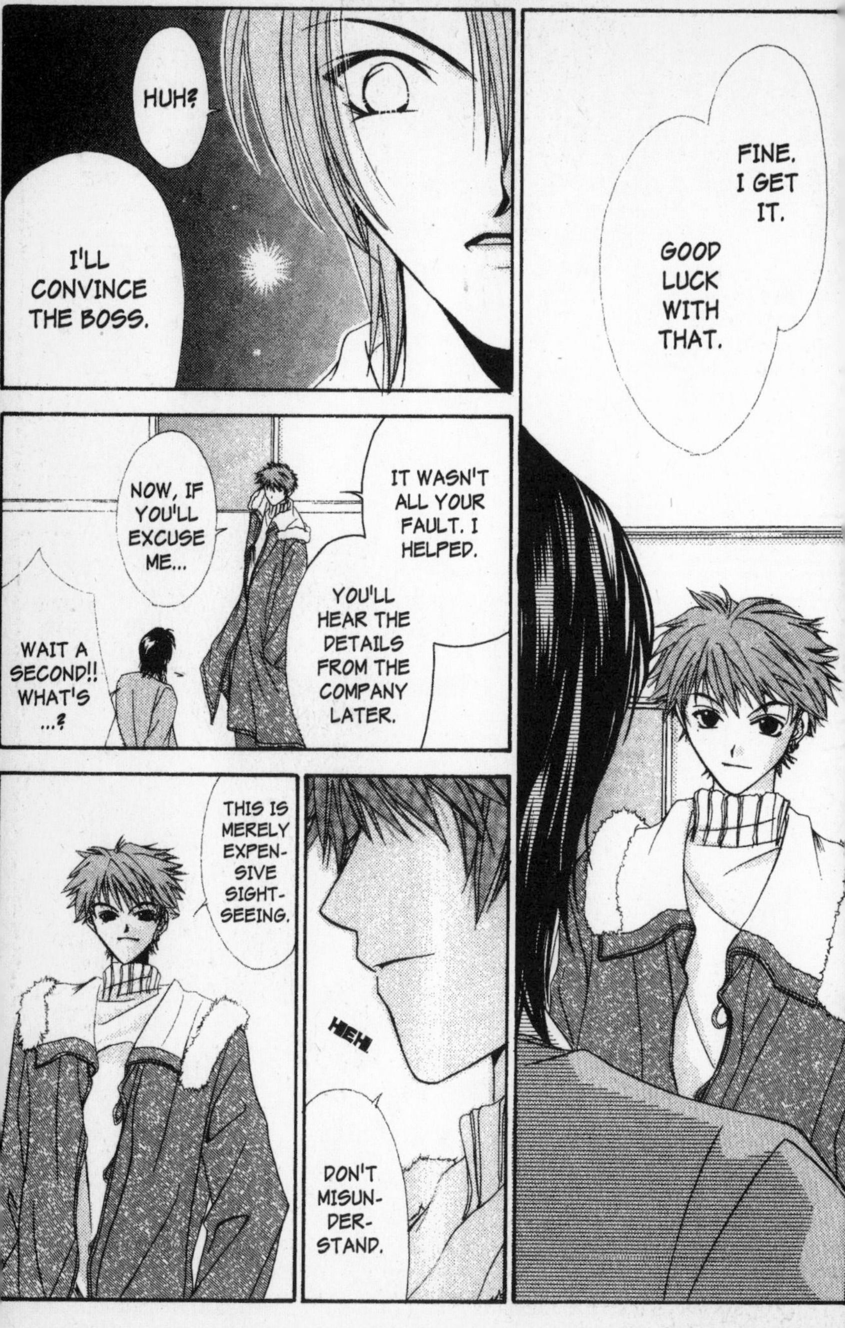
FINE. I GET IT.
GOOD LUCK WITH THAT.
HUH?
I'LL CONVINCE THE BOSS.
IT WASN'T ALL YOUR FAULT. I HELPED.
YOU'LL HEAR THE DETAILS FROM THE COMPANY LATER.
NOW, IF YOU'LL EXCUSE ME...
WAIT A SECOND!! WHAT'S ...?
HEH
DON'T MISUNDERSTAND.
THIS IS MERELY EXPENSIVE SIGHTSEEING.

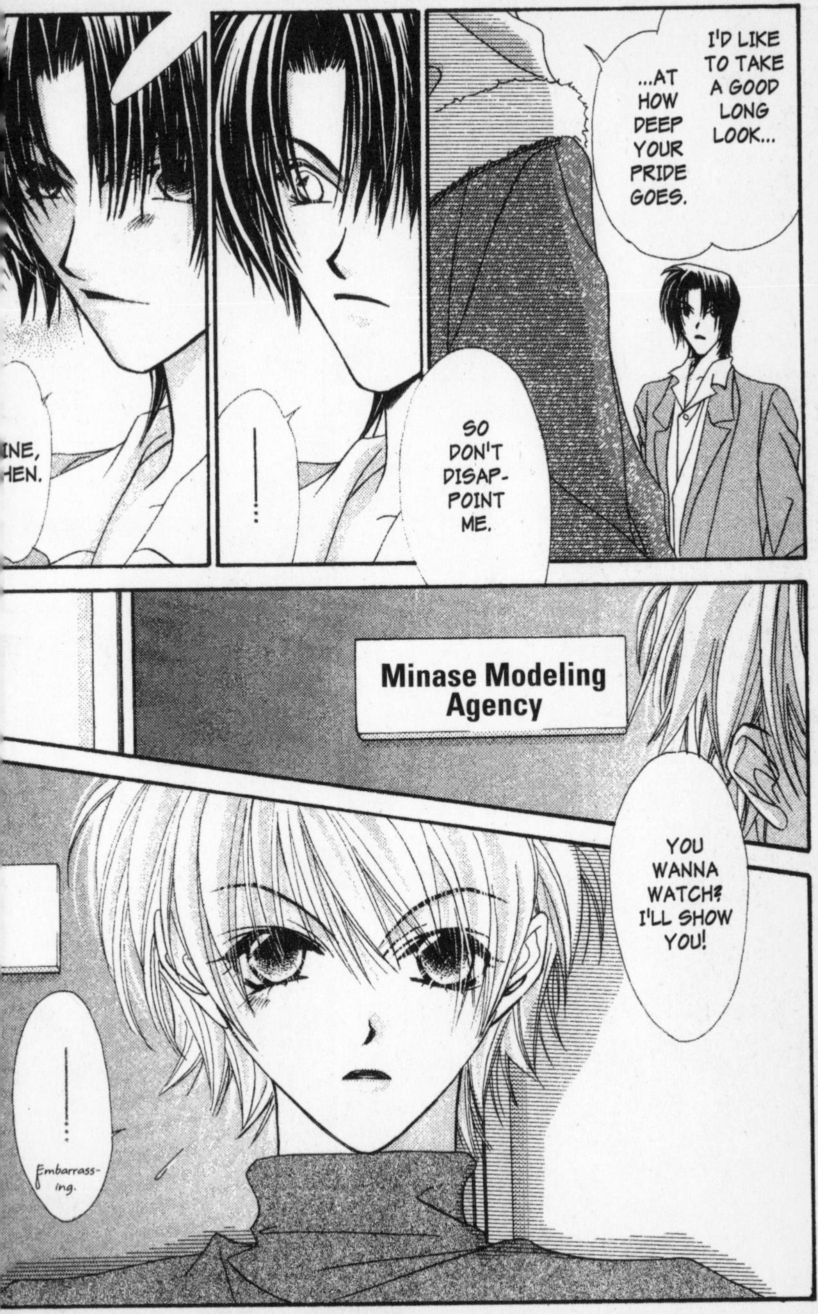
I'D LIKE TO TAKE A GOOD LONG LOOK...
...AT HOW DEEP YOUR PRIDE GOES.
SO DON'T DISAP- POINT ME.
......
INE, HEN.
Minase Modeling Agency
YOU WANNA WATCH? I'LL SHOW YOU!
......
Embarrass- ing.

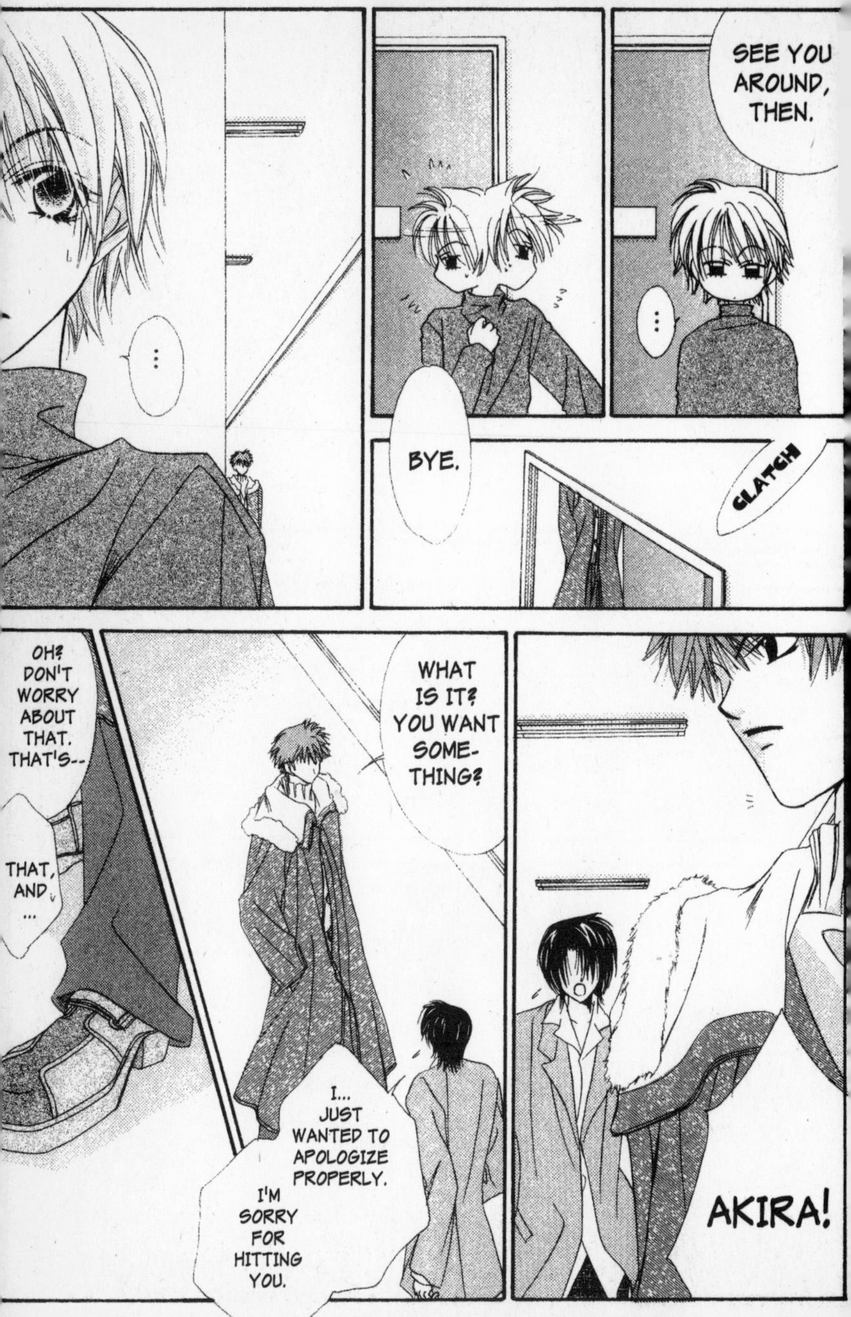
SEE YOU AROUND, THEN.
...
BYE.
CLATCH
...
AKIRA!
WHAT IS IT? YOU WANT SOME-THING?
I... JUST WANTED TO APOLOGIZE PROPERLY.
I'M SORRY FOR HITTING YOU.
OH? DON'T WORRY ABOUT THAT. THAT'S--
THAT, AND ...

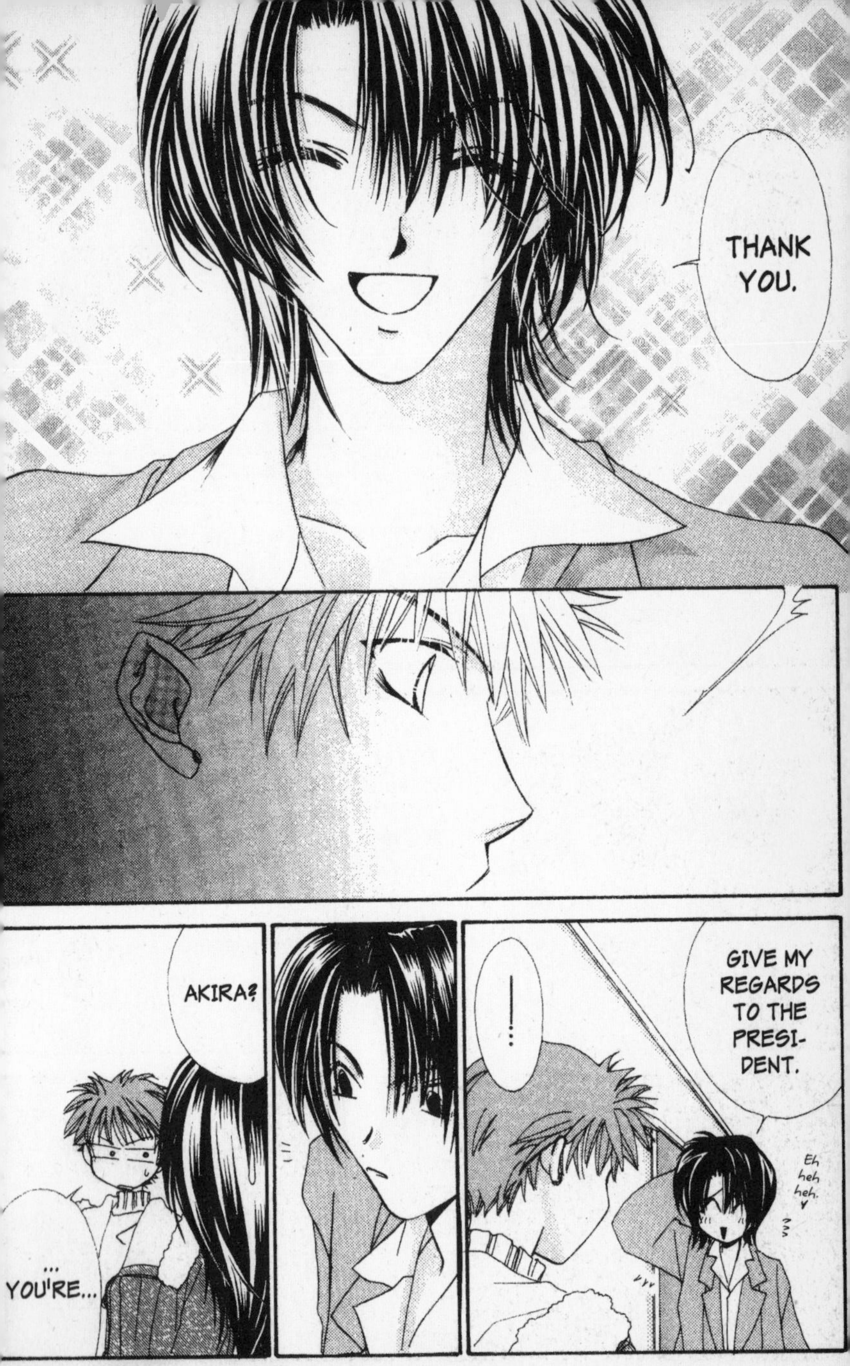
THANK YOU.
GIVE MY REGARDS TO THE PRESIDENT.
!...
Eh heh heh.
AKIRA?
... YOU'RE...

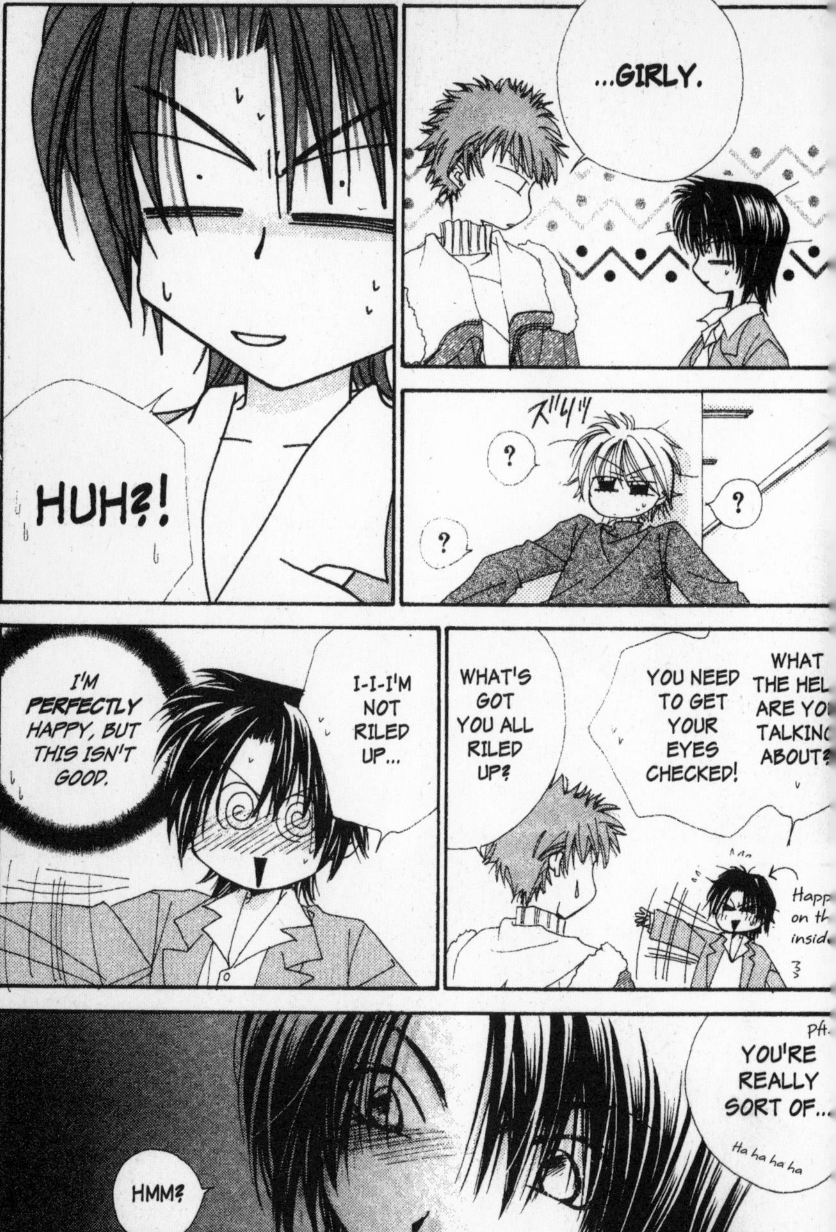
...GIRLY.
ズリッ
?
?
?
HUH?!
WHAT THE HEL ARE YO TALKIN ABOUT?
YOU NEED TO GET YOUR EYES CHECKED!
WHAT'S GOT YOU ALL RILED UP?
Happ on th insid
I-I-I'M NOT RILED UP...
I'M PERFECTLY HAPPY, BUT THIS ISN'T GOOD.
Pft.
YOU'RE REALLY SORT OF...
Ha ha ha ha
HMM?

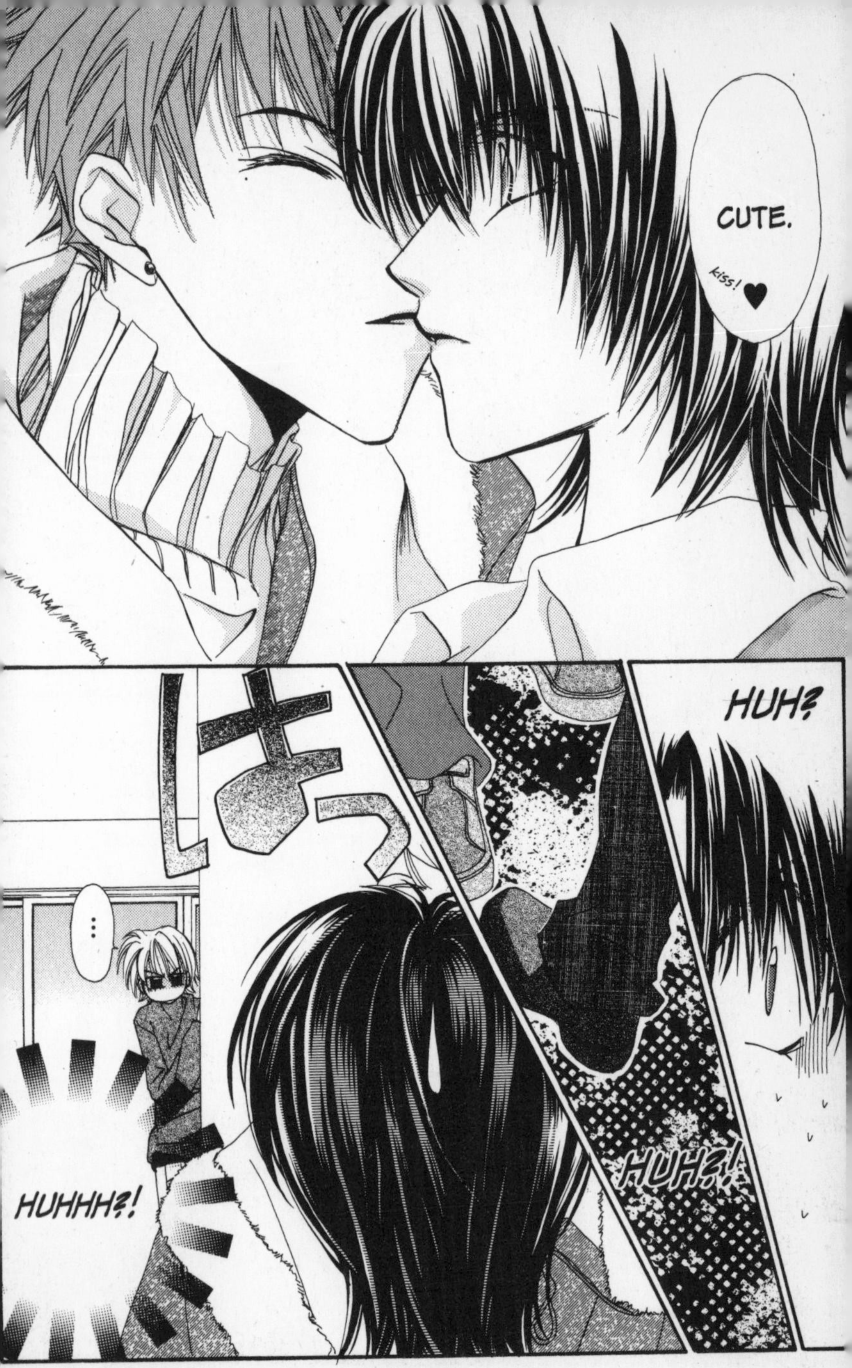
CUTE.
kiss! ♥
HUH?
HUH?!
はっ
...
HUHHH?!

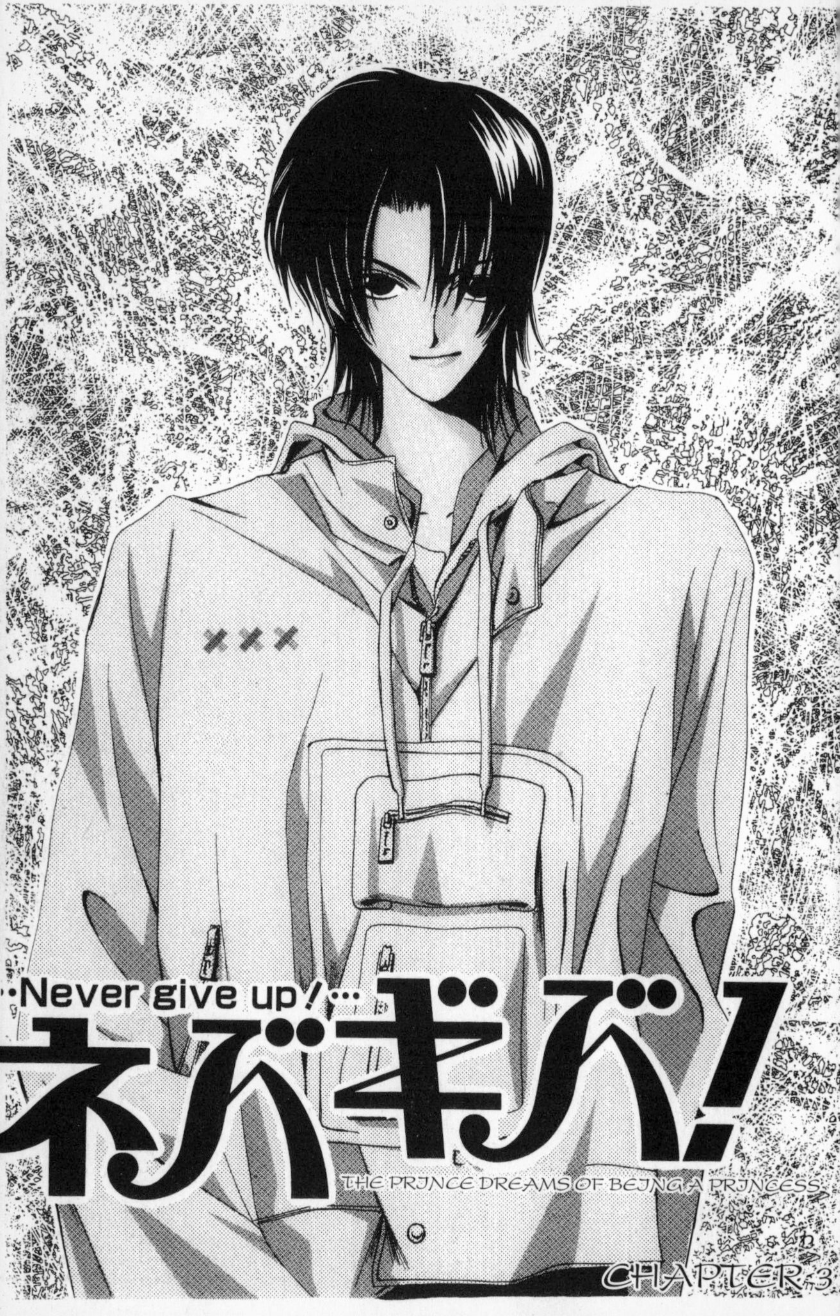
··Never give up!···
ネバギバ!
THE PRINCE DREAMS OF BEING A PRINCESS
CHAPTER 3

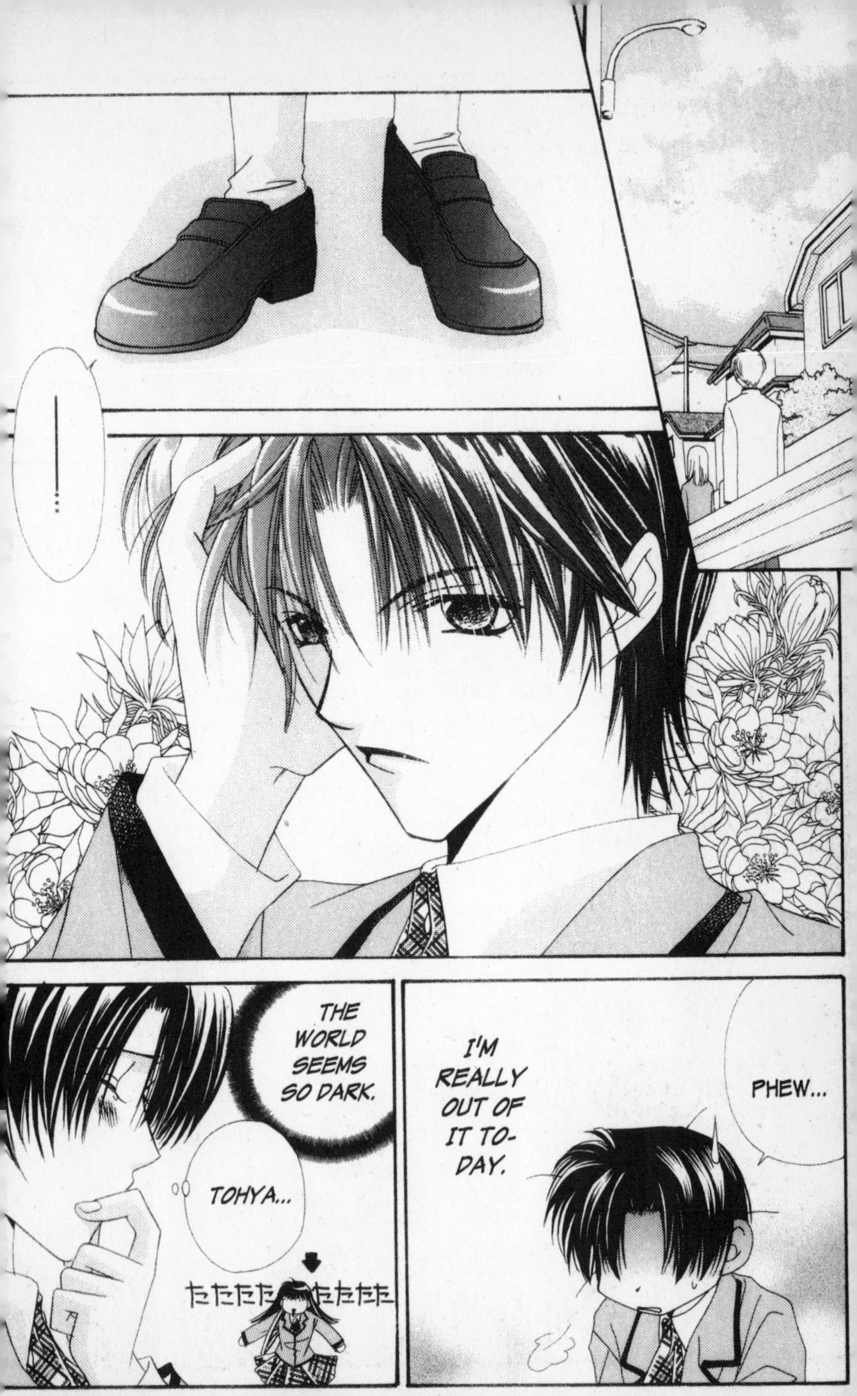
——……
PHEW...
I'M REALLY OUT OF IT TO-DAY.
THE WORLD SEEMS SO DARK.
TOHYA...
たたたた
たたたた

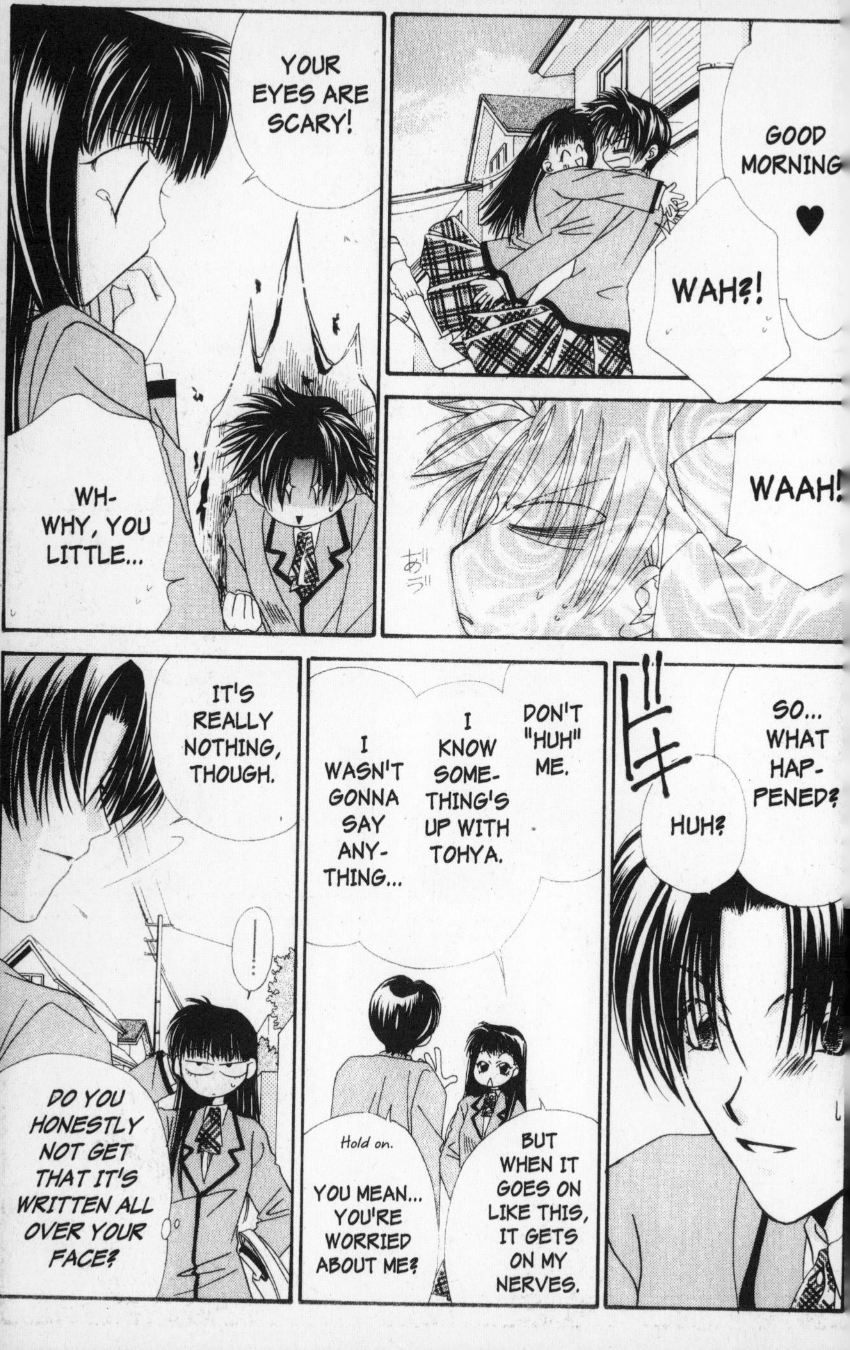
GOOD MORNING ♥
WAH?!
WAAH!
YOUR EYES ARE SCARY!
WH- WHY, YOU LITTLE...
ドキ
SO... WHAT HAPPENED?
HUH?
DON'T "HUH" ME.
I KNOW SOMETHING'S UP WITH TOHYA.
I WASN'T GONNA SAY ANYTHING...
BUT WHEN IT GOES ON LIKE THIS, IT GETS ON MY NERVES.
Hold on.
YOU MEAN... YOU'RE WORRIED ABOUT ME?
IT'S REALLY NOTHING, THOUGH.
!...
DO YOU HONESTLY NOT GET THAT IT'S WRITTEN ALL OVER YOUR FACE?

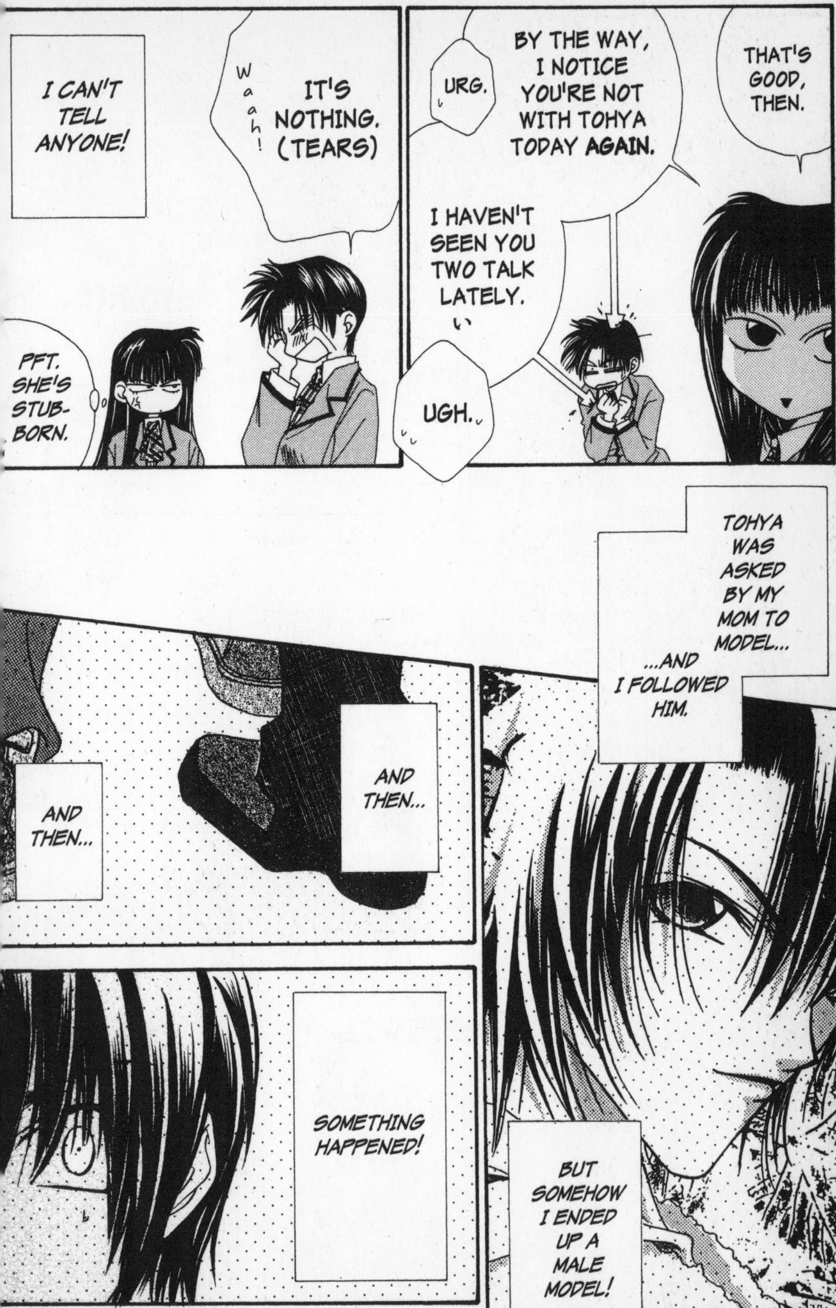
THAT'S GOOD, THEN.
BY THE WAY, I NOTICE YOU'RE NOT WITH TOHYA TODAY AGAIN.
URG.
I HAVEN'T SEEN YOU TWO TALK LATELY.
UGH.
IT'S NOTHING. (TEARS)
Waah!
I CAN'T TELL ANYONE!
PFT. SHE'S STUB-BORN.
TOHYA WAS ASKED BY MY MOM TO MODEL...
...AND I FOLLOWED HIM.
BUT SOMEHOW I ENDED UP A MALE MODEL!
AND THEN...
AND THEN...
SOMETHING HAPPENED!

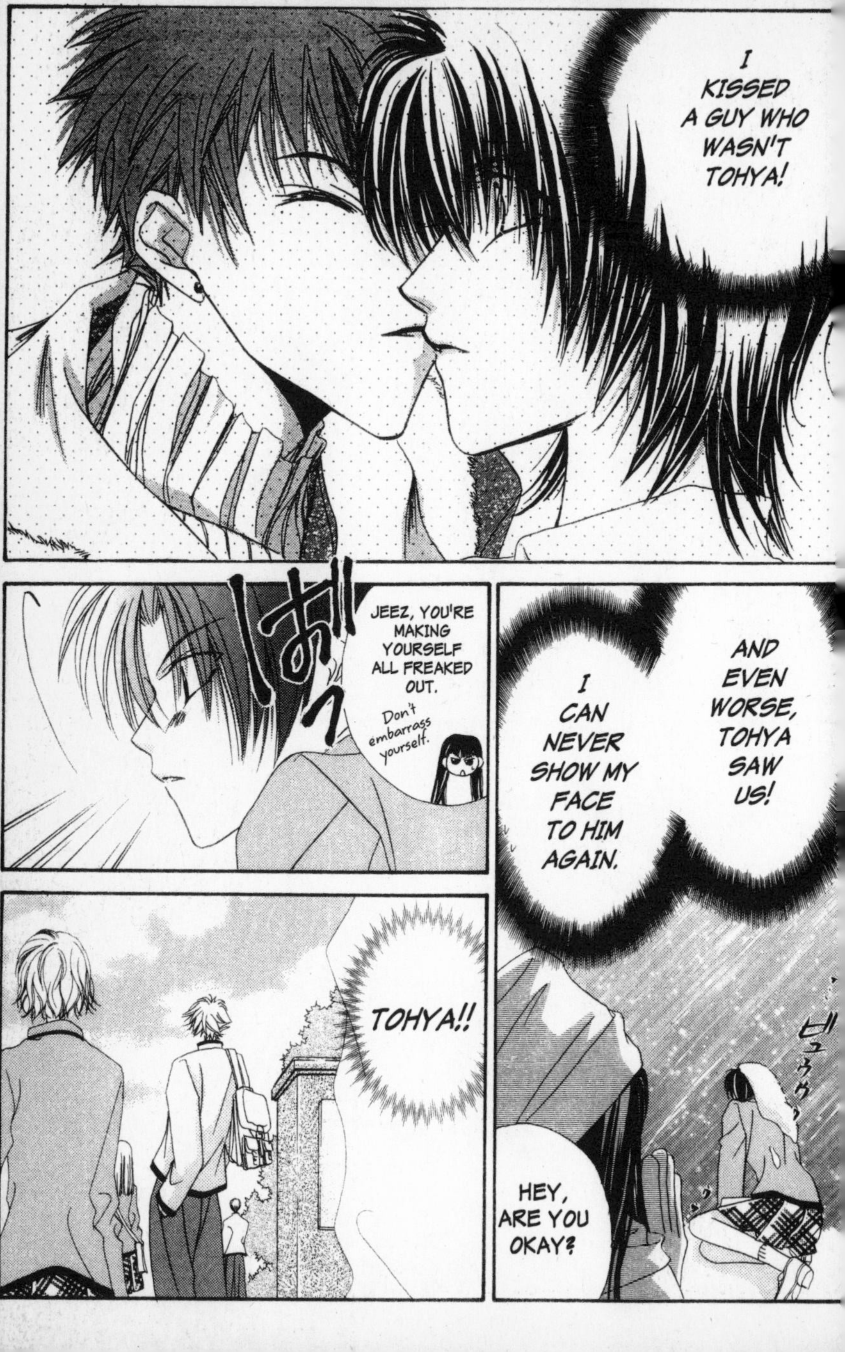
I KISSED A GUY WHO WASN'T TOHYA!
AND EVEN WORSE, TOHYA SAW US!
I CAN NEVER SHOW MY FACE TO HIM AGAIN.
JEEZ, YOU'RE MAKING YOURSELF ALL FREAKED OUT.
Don't embarrass yourself.
HEY, ARE YOU OKAY?
TOHYA!!

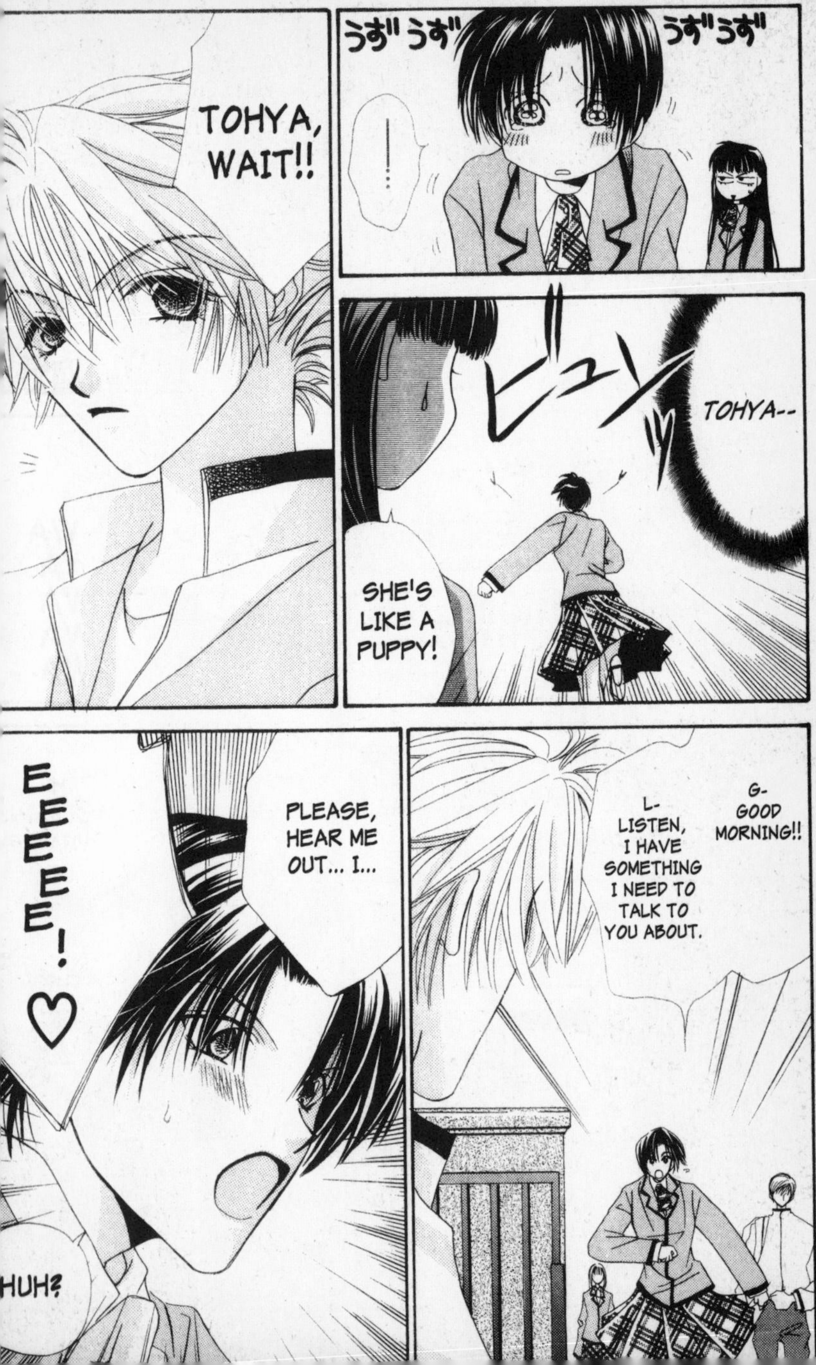
うずうず
うずうず
TOHYA--
ビュンッ
SHE'S LIKE A PUPPY!
TOHYA, WAIT!!
G- GOOD MORNING!!
L- LISTEN, I HAVE SOMETHING I NEED TO TALK TO YOU ABOUT.
PLEASE, HEAR ME OUT... I...
EEEEE! ♥
HUH?

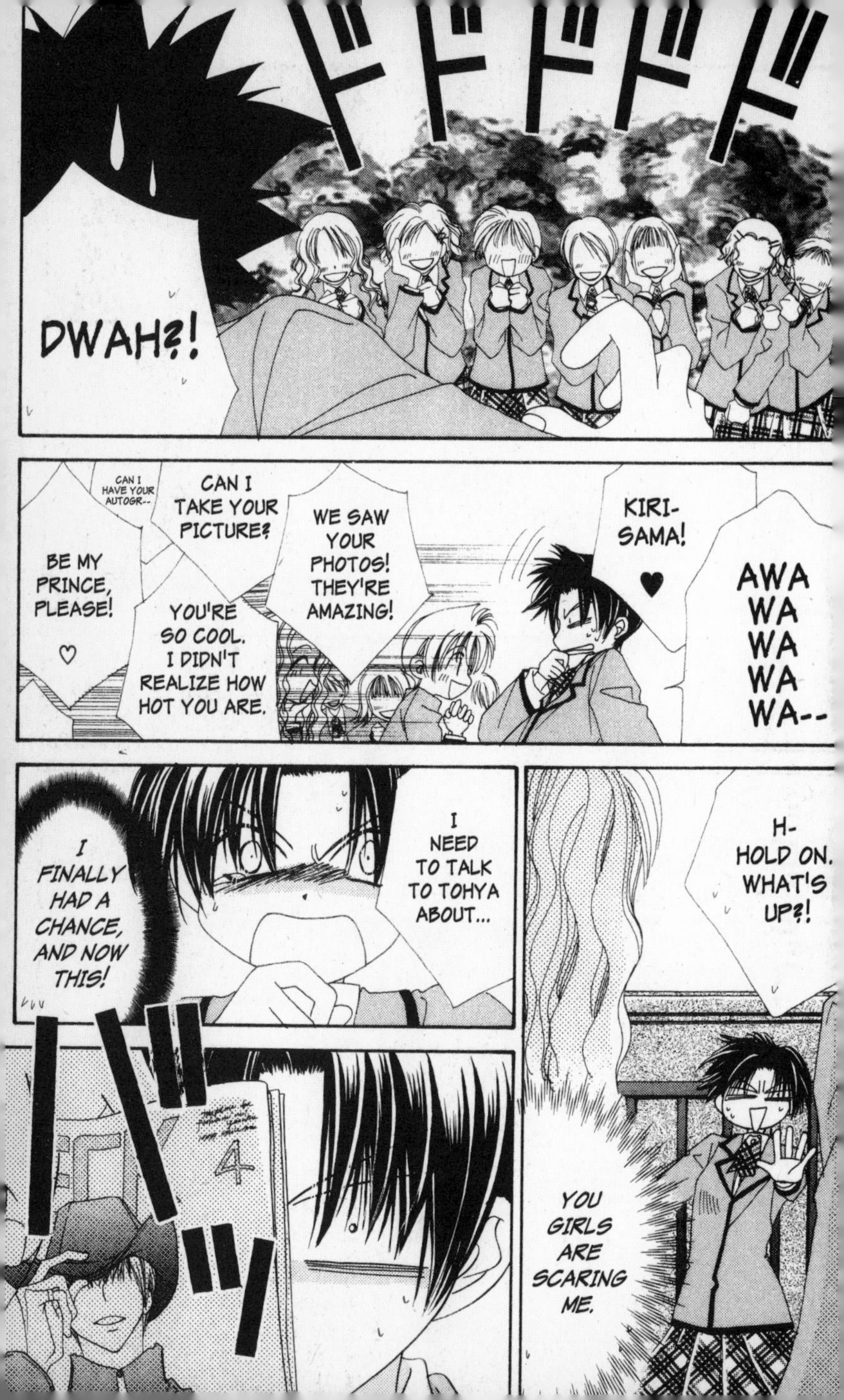
ドドドドド
DWAH?!
AWA WA WA WA WA--
KIRI-SAMA! ♥
WE SAW YOUR PHOTOS! THEY'RE AMAZING!
CAN I TAKE YOUR PICTURE?
CAN I HAVE YOUR AUTOGR--
YOU'RE SO COOL. I DIDN'T REALIZE HOW HOT YOU ARE.
BE MY PRINCE, PLEASE! ♡
H- HOLD ON. WHAT'S UP?!
I NEED TO TALK TO TOHYA ABOUT...
I FINALLY HAD A CHANCE, AND NOW THIS!
YOU GIRLS ARE SCARING ME.

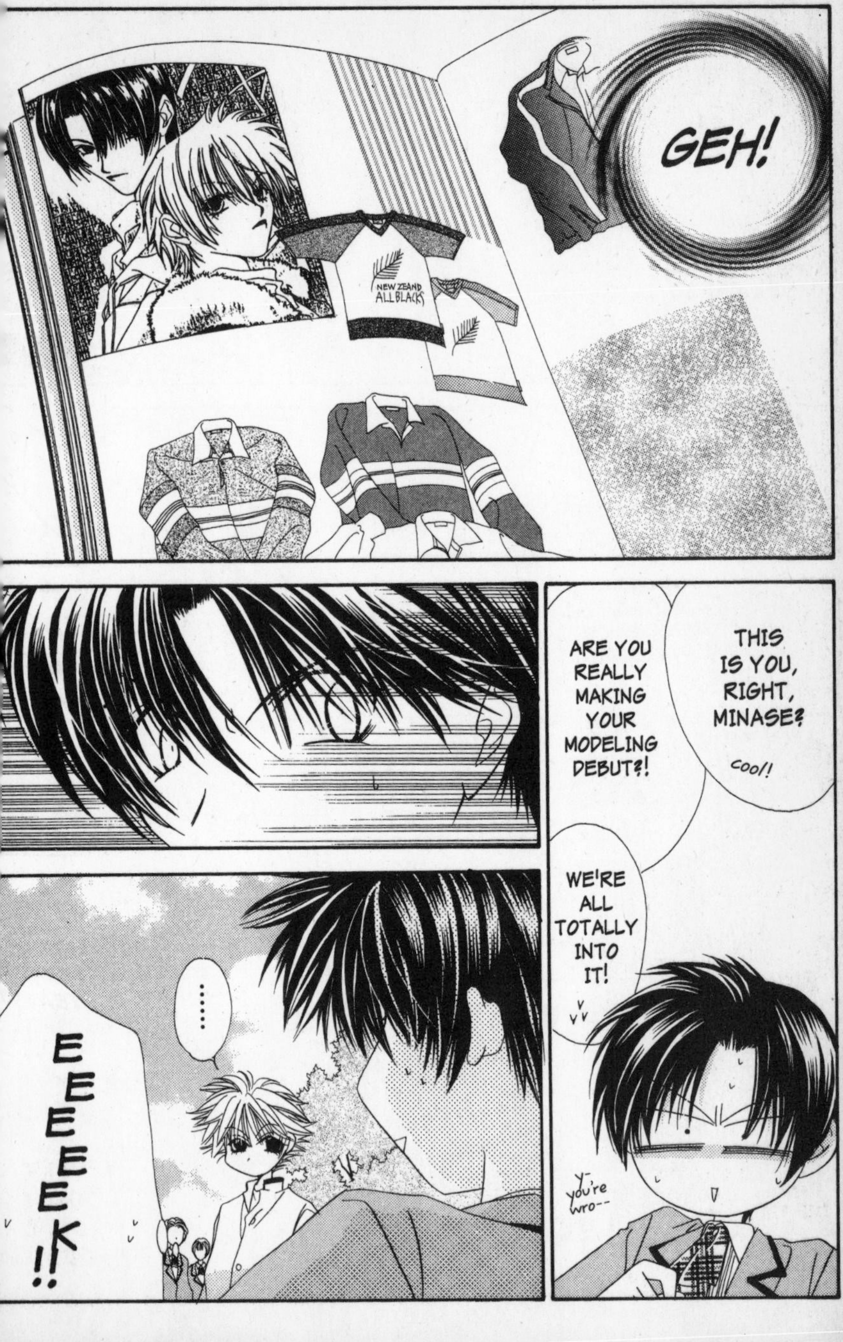
GEH!
NEW ZEAND ALLBLACKS
THIS IS YOU, RIGHT, MINASE?
cool!
ARE YOU REALLY MAKING YOUR MODELING DEBUT?!
WE'RE ALL TOTALLY INTO IT!
y-you're wro--
......
EEEEEK!!

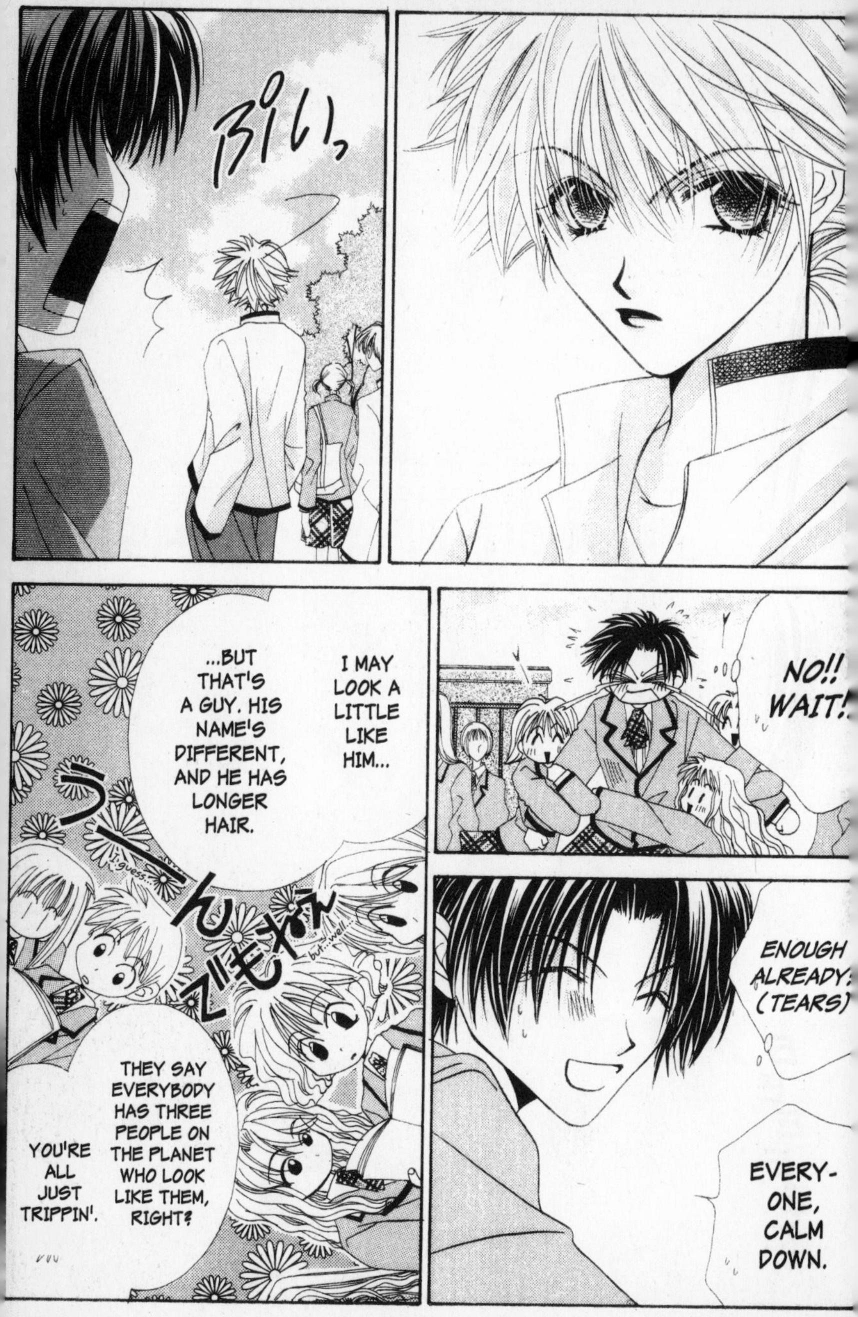
ぷいっ
NO!! WAIT!!
ENOUGH ALREADY! (TEARS)
EVERY-ONE, CALM DOWN.
I MAY LOOK A LITTLE LIKE HIM...
...BUT THAT'S A GUY. HIS NAME'S DIFFERENT, AND HE HAS LONGER HAIR.
I guess...
but...well...
THEY SAY EVERYBODY HAS THREE PEOPLE ON THE PLANET WHO LOOK LIKE THEM, RIGHT?
YOU'RE ALL JUST TRIPPIN'.

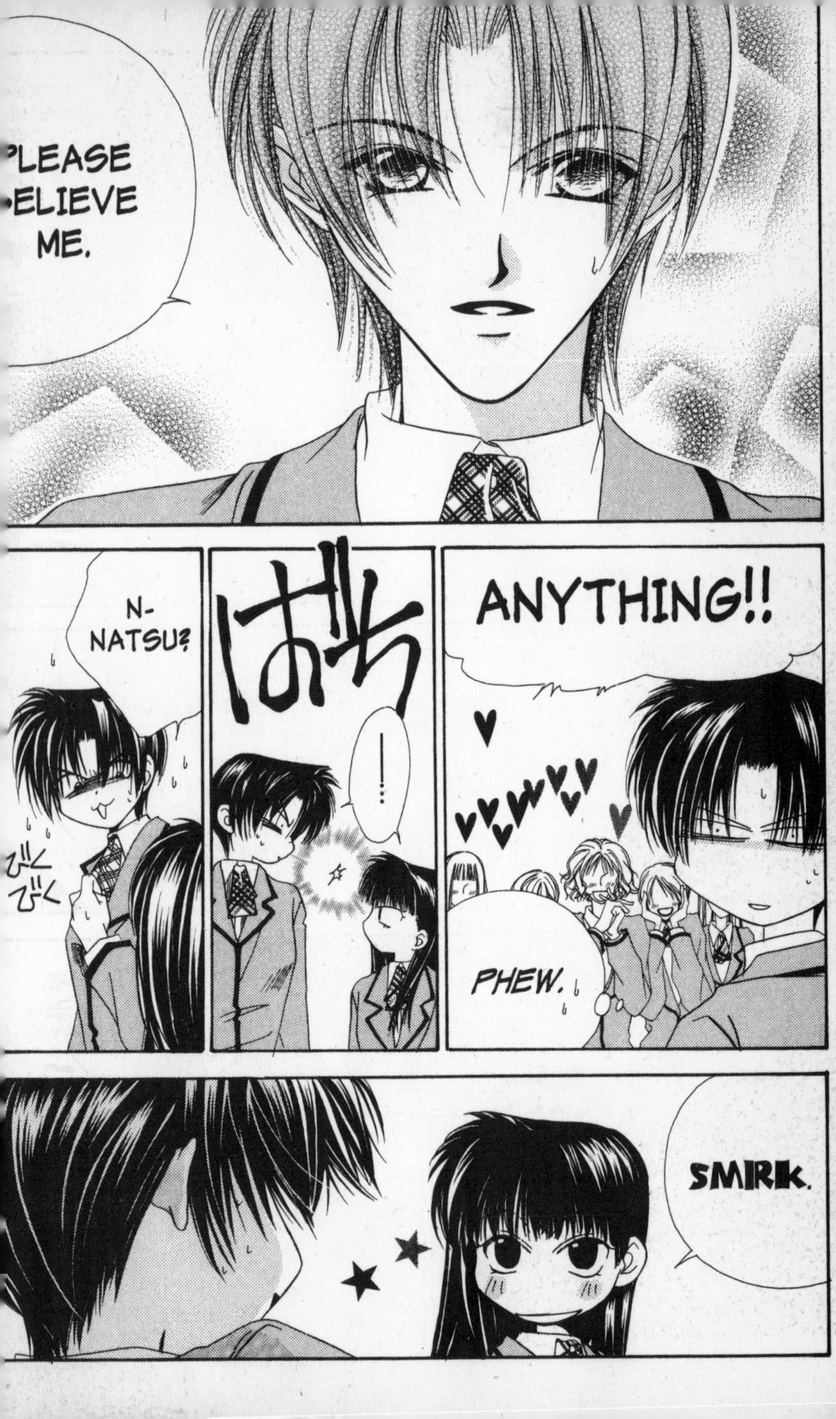

PLEASE BELIEVE ME.
ANYTHING!!
PHEW.
ばち
!...
N-NATSU?
びくびく
SMIRK.

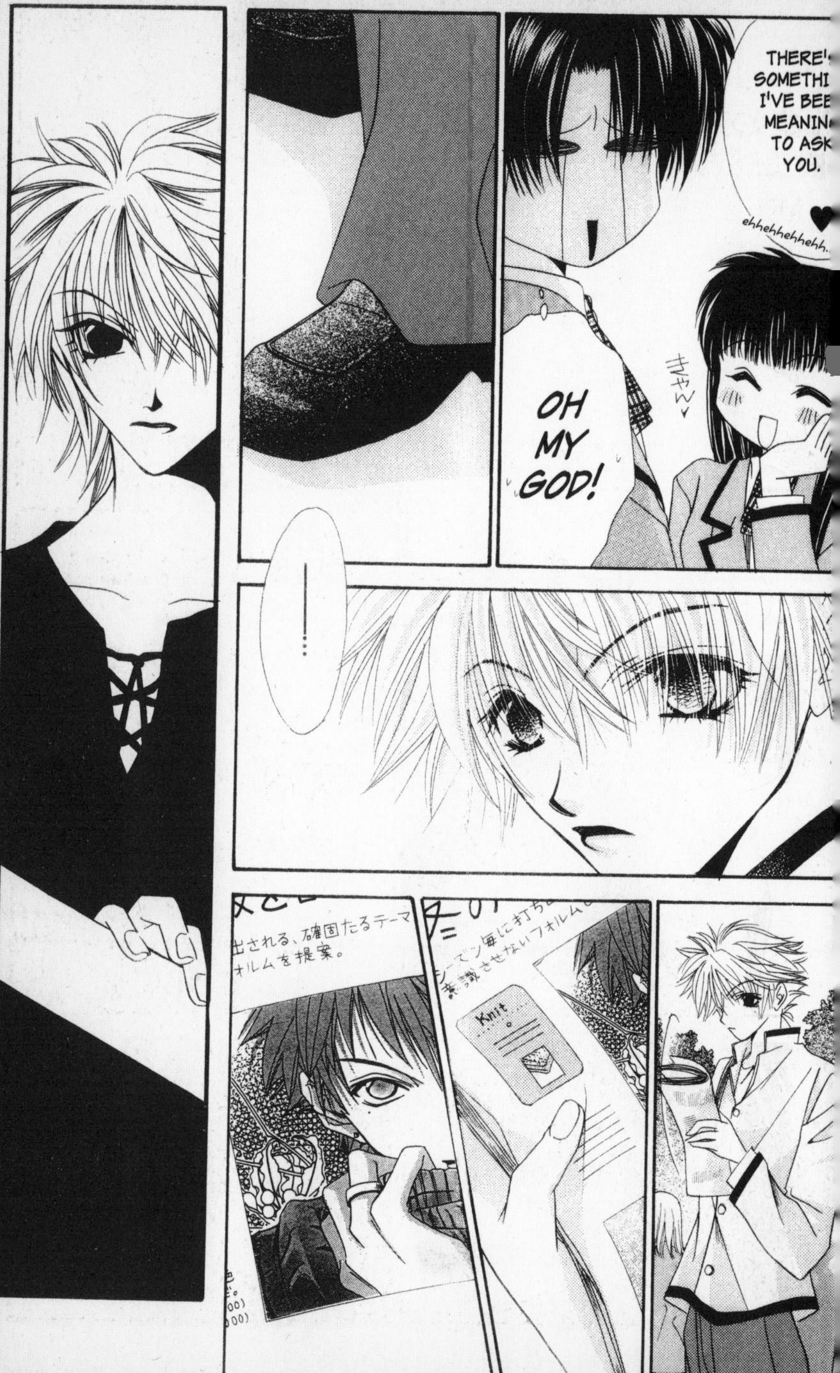
THERE'S SOMETHI I'VE BEE MEANIN TO ASK YOU.
ehhehhehhehh..
きゃん
OH MY GOD!
……!
出される、確固たるテーマ
ォルムを提案。
シーズン毎に打ち
意識させないフォルム
Knit

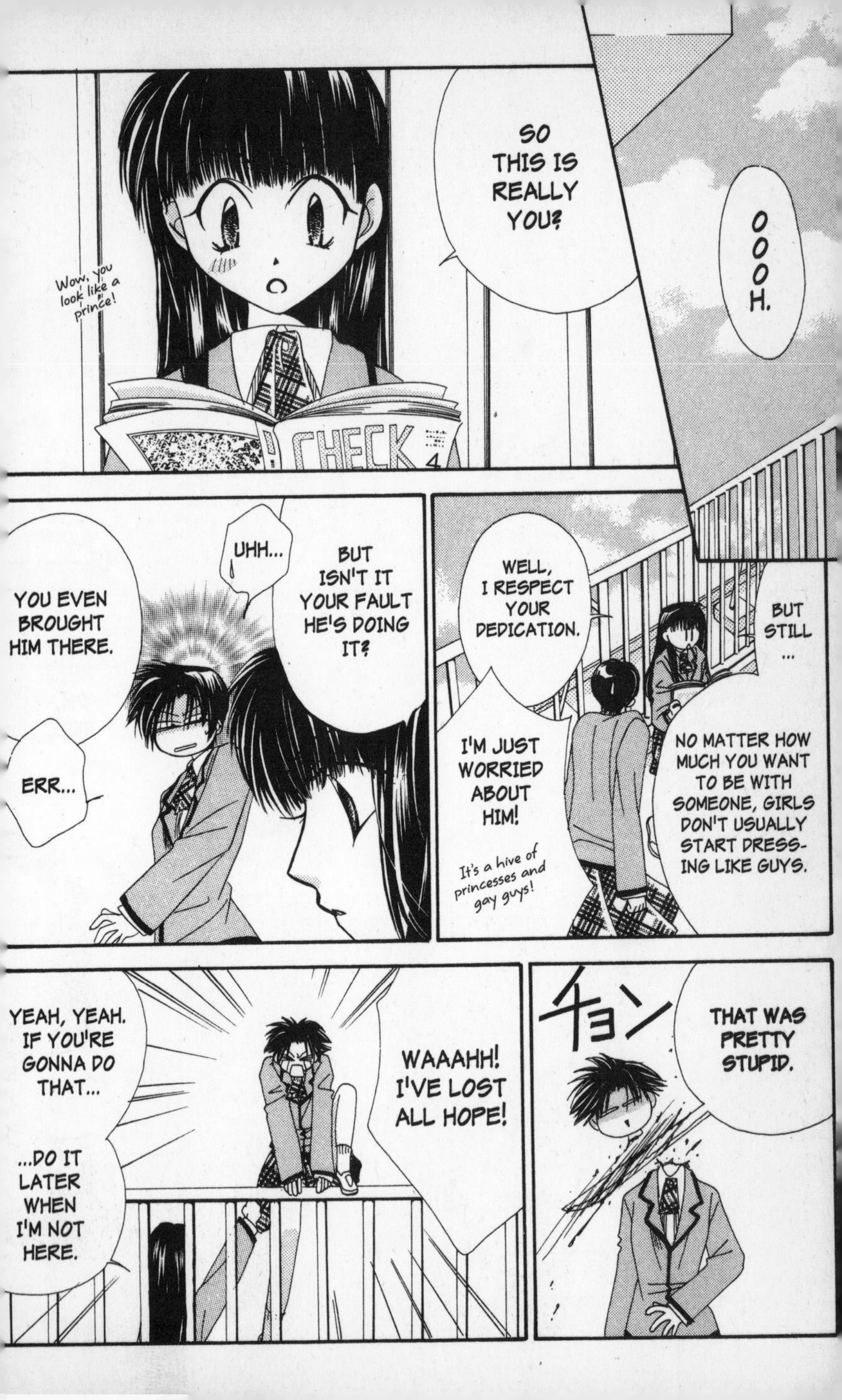

OOOH.
SO THIS IS REALLY YOU?
Wow, you look like a prince!
BUT STILL ...
NO MATTER HOW MUCH YOU WANT TO BE WITH SOMEONE, GIRLS DON'T USUALLY START DRESSING LIKE GUYS.
WELL, I RESPECT YOUR DEDICATION.
I'M JUST WORRIED ABOUT HIM!
It's a hive of princesses and gay guys!
BUT ISN'T IT YOUR FAULT HE'S DOING IT?
UHH...
YOU EVEN BROUGHT HIM THERE.
ERR...
チョン
THAT WAS PRETTY STUPID.
WAAAHH! I'VE LOST ALL HOPE!
YEAH, YEAH. IF YOU'RE GONNA DO THAT...
...DO IT LATER WHEN I'M NOT HERE.

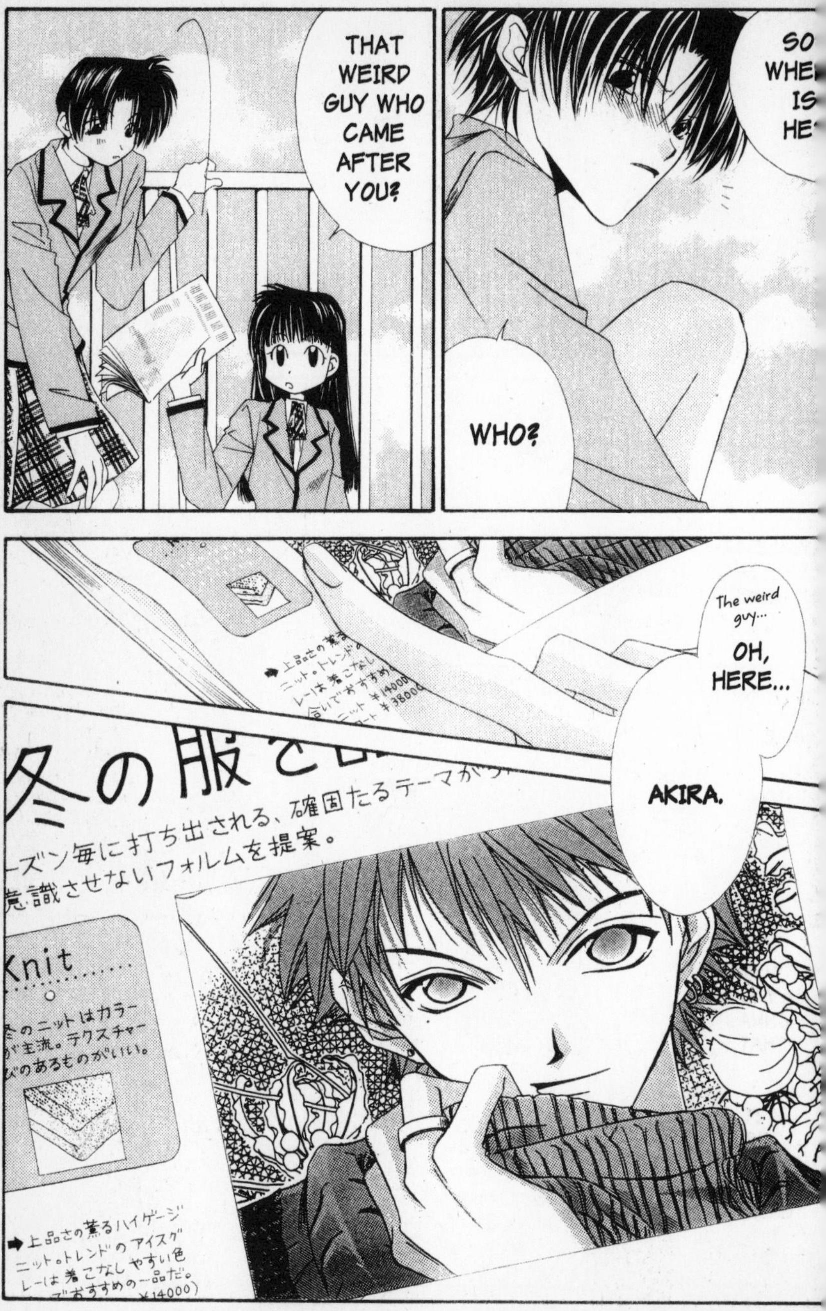

SO WHE IS HE
WHO?
THAT WEIRD GUY WHO CAME AFTER YOU?
The weird guy... OH, HERE...
AKIRA.
冬の服を
ーズン毎に打ち出される、確固たるテーマが
意識させないフォルムを提案。
Knit
冬のニットはカラー
が主流。テクスチャー
びのあるものがいい。
上品さの薫るハイゲージ
ニット。トレンドのアイスグ
レーは着こなしやすい色
でおすすめの一品だ。
¥14000)

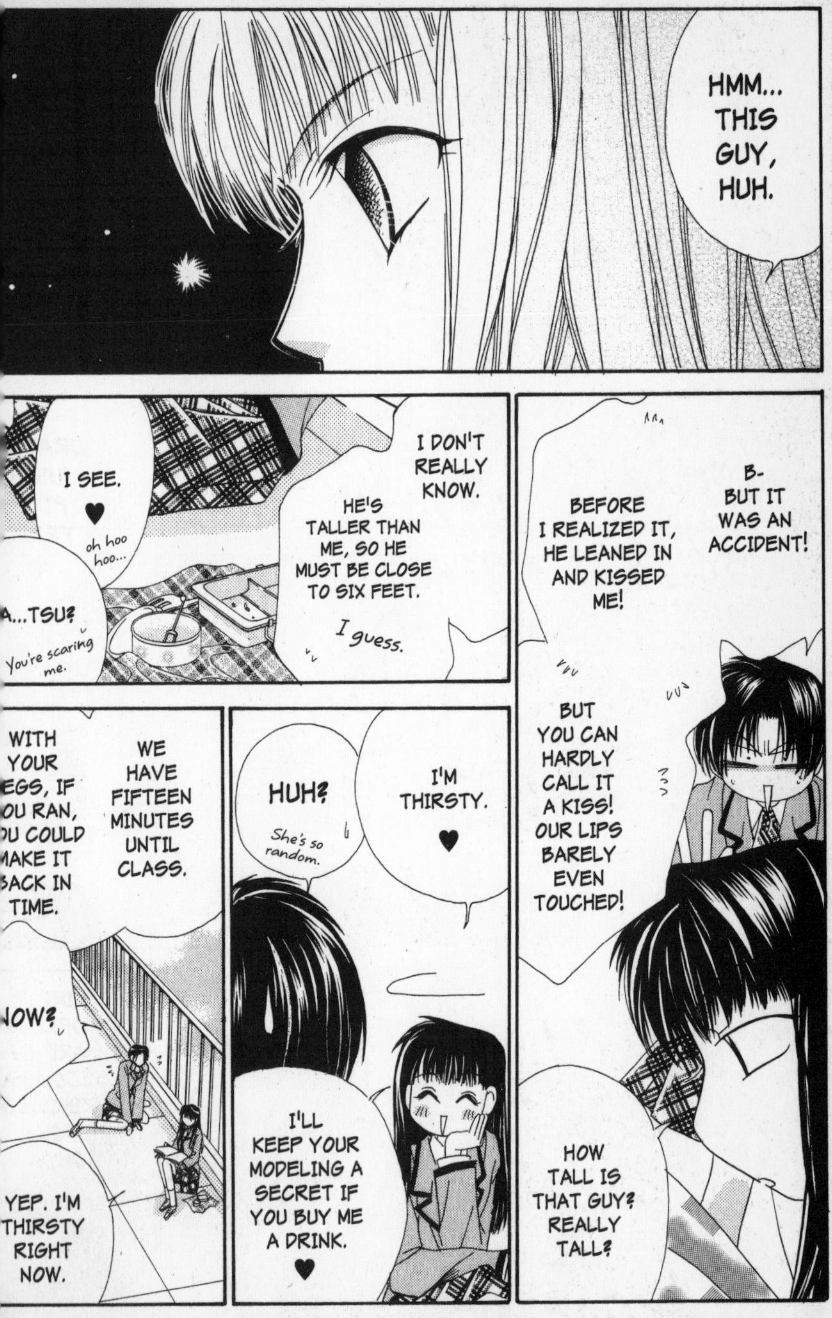
HMM... THIS GUY, HUH.
B- BUT IT WAS AN ACCIDENT!
BEFORE I REALIZED IT, HE LEANED IN AND KISSED ME!
BUT YOU CAN HARDLY CALL IT A KISS! OUR LIPS BARELY EVEN TOUCHED!
HOW TALL IS THAT GUY? REALLY TALL?
I DON'T REALLY KNOW.
HE'S TALLER THAN ME, SO HE MUST BE CLOSE TO SIX FEET.
I guess.
I SEE. ♥
oh hoo hoo...
A...TSU?
You're scaring me.
I'M THIRSTY. ♥
HUH?
She's so random.
I'LL KEEP YOUR MODELING A SECRET IF YOU BUY ME A DRINK. ♥
WE HAVE FIFTEEN MINUTES UNTIL CLASS.
WITH YOUR EGS, IF OU RAN, U COULD AKE IT ACK IN TIME.
NOW?
YEP. I'M THIRSTY RIGHT NOW.

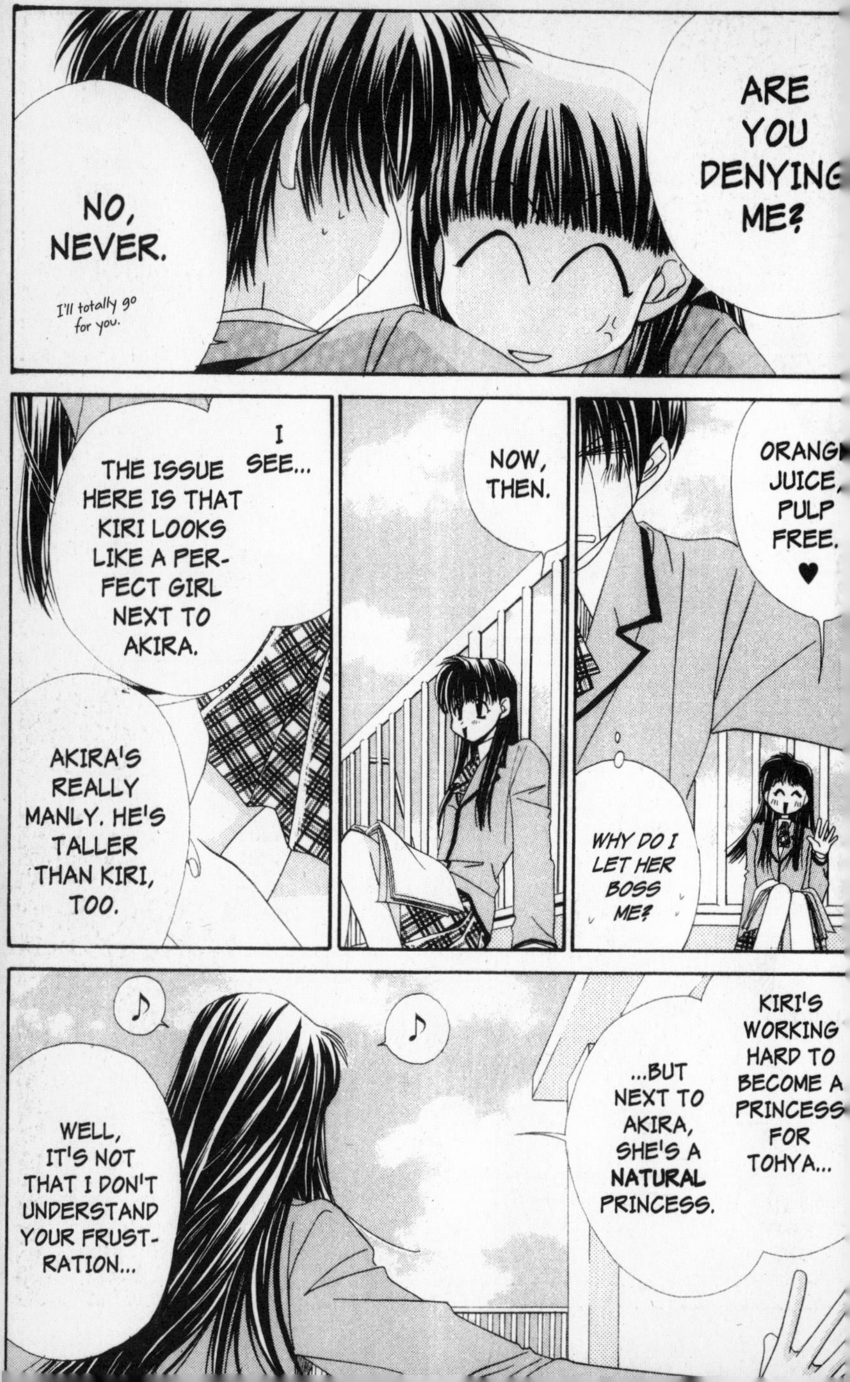
ARE YOU DENYING ME?
NO, NEVER.
I'll totally go for you.
ORANG JUICE, PULP FREE. ♥
WHY DO I LET HER BOSS ME?
NOW, THEN.
I SEE...
THE ISSUE HERE IS THAT KIRI LOOKS LIKE A PER-FECT GIRL NEXT TO AKIRA.
AKIRA'S REALLY MANLY. HE'S TALLER THAN KIRI, TOO.
KIRI'S WORKING HARD TO BECOME A PRINCESS FOR TOHYA...
...BUT NEXT TO AKIRA, SHE'S A NATURAL PRINCESS.
♪
♪
WELL, IT'S NOT THAT I DON'T UNDERSTAND YOUR FRUST-RATION...

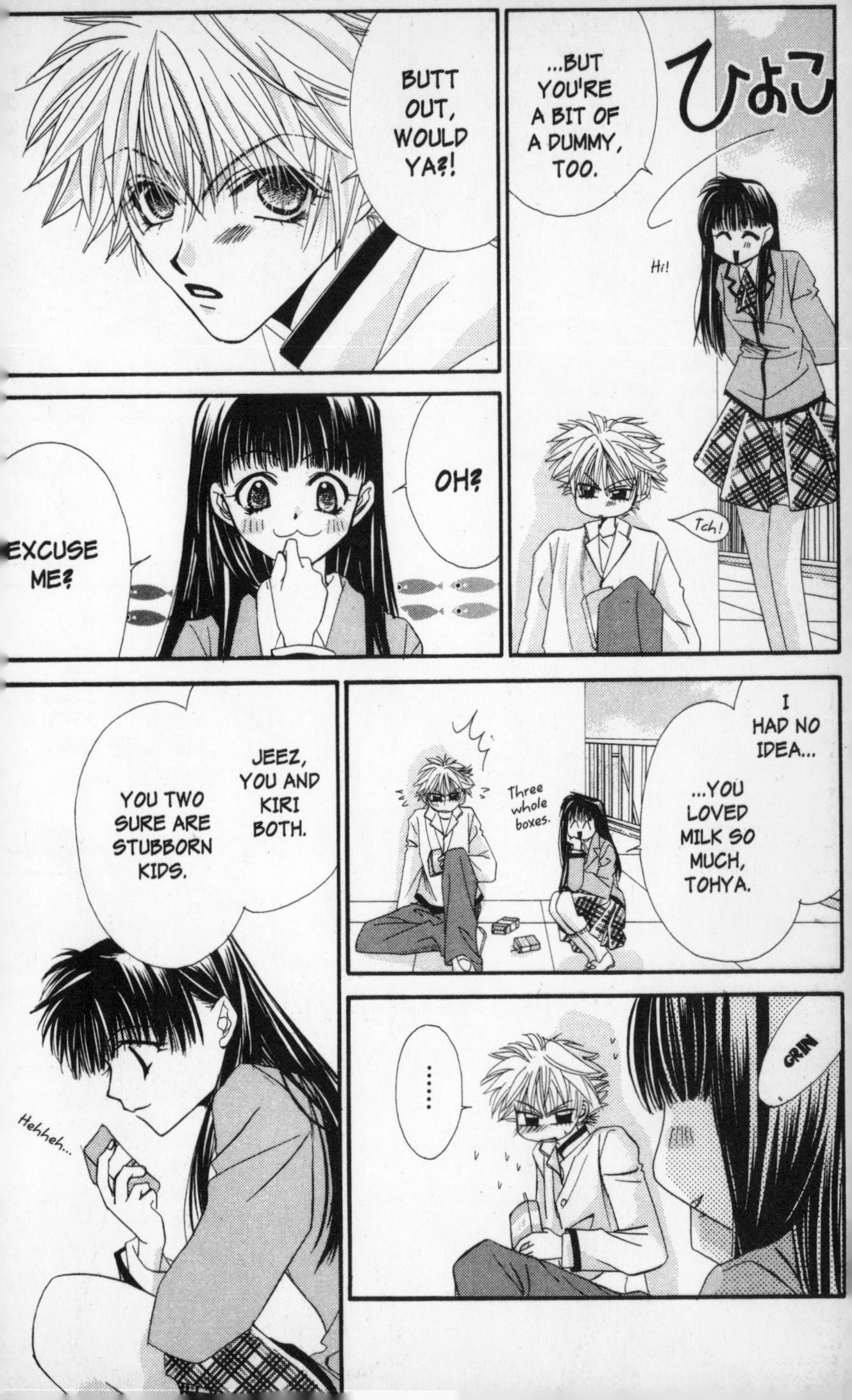
ひよこ
...BUT YOU'RE A BIT OF A DUMMY, TOO.
Hi!
Tch!
BUTT OUT, WOULD YA?!
OH?
EXCUSE ME?
I HAD NO IDEA...
...YOU LOVED MILK SO MUCH, TOHYA.
Three whole boxes.
GRIN
......
JEEZ, YOU AND KIRI BOTH.
YOU TWO SURE ARE STUBBORN KIDS.
Hehheh...

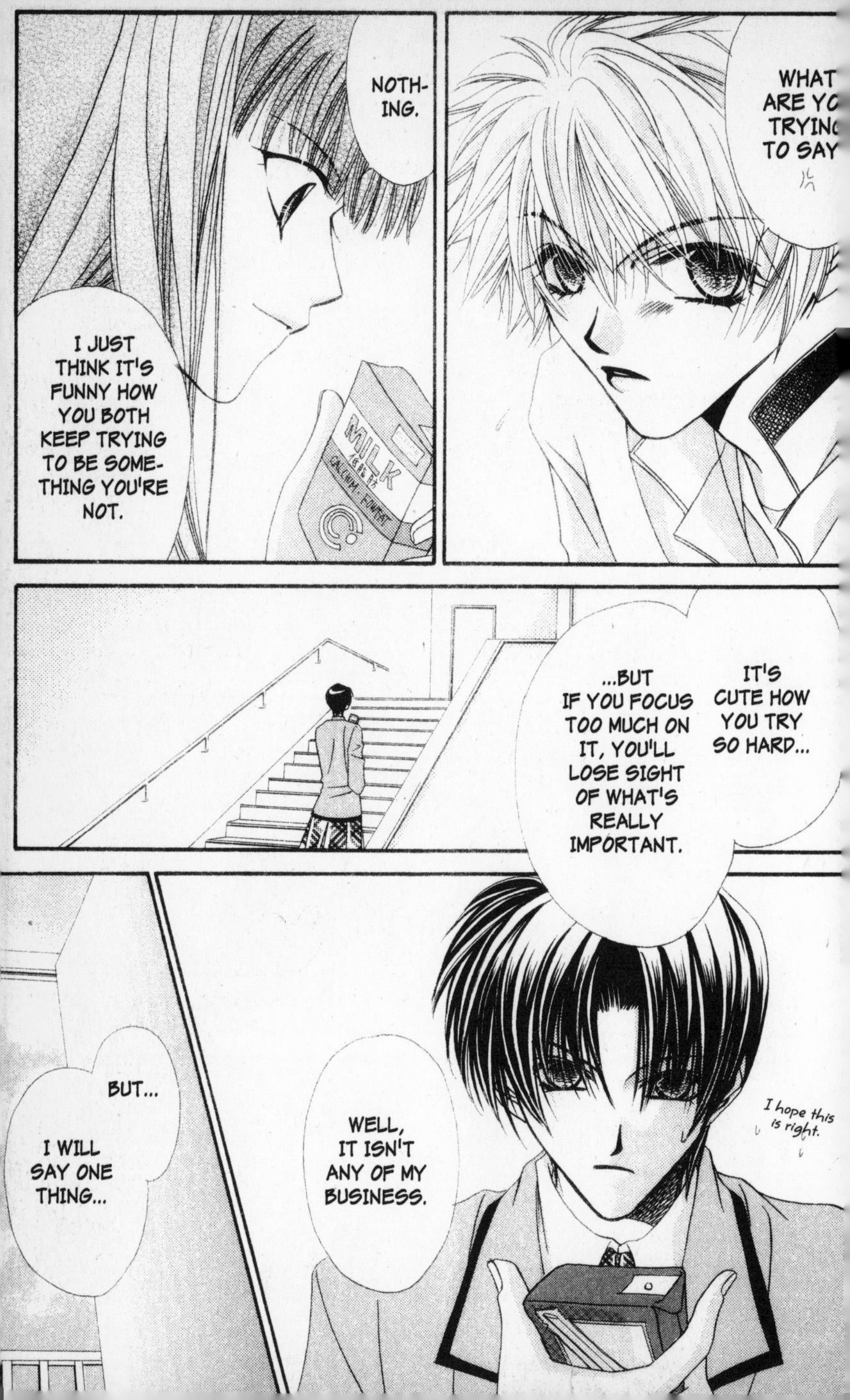
WHAT ARE YO TRYING TO SAY
NOTH-ING.
I JUST THINK IT'S FUNNY HOW YOU BOTH KEEP TRYING TO BE SOME-THING YOU'RE NOT.
MILK
IT'S CUTE HOW YOU TRY SO HARD...
...BUT IF YOU FOCUS TOO MUCH ON IT, YOU'LL LOSE SIGHT OF WHAT'S REALLY IMPORTANT.
I hope this is right.
WELL, IT ISN'T ANY OF MY BUSINESS.
BUT...
I WILL SAY ONE THING...

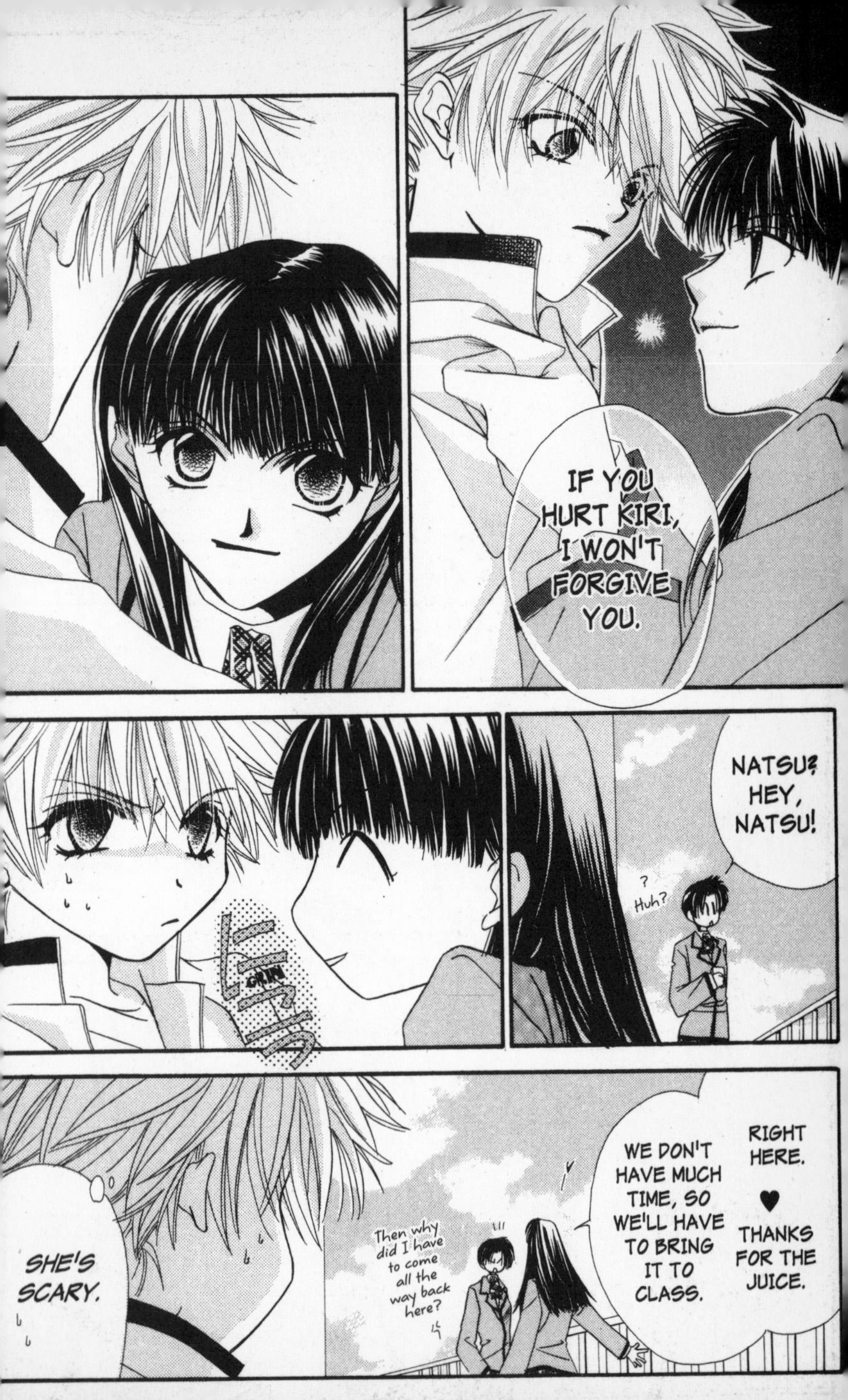
IF YOU HURT KIRI, I WON'T FORGIVE YOU.
NATSU? HEY, NATSU!
? Huh?
GRIN
RIGHT HERE. ♥ THANKS FOR THE JUICE.
WE DON'T HAVE MUCH TIME, SO WE'LL HAVE TO BRING IT TO CLASS.
Then why did I have to come all the way back here?
SHE'S SCARY.

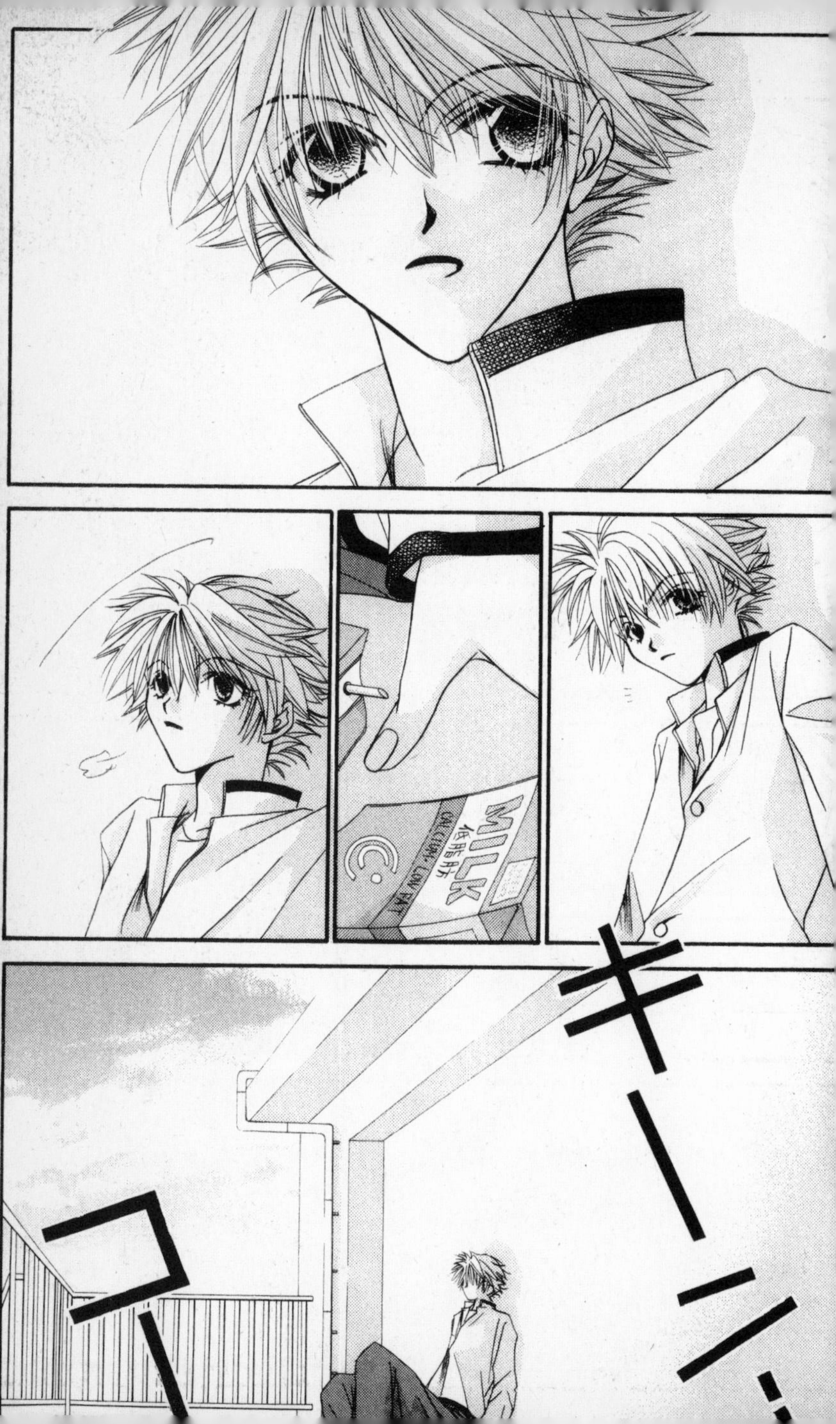
MILK
低脂肪
CALCIUM · LOW FAT
キーン!
コ

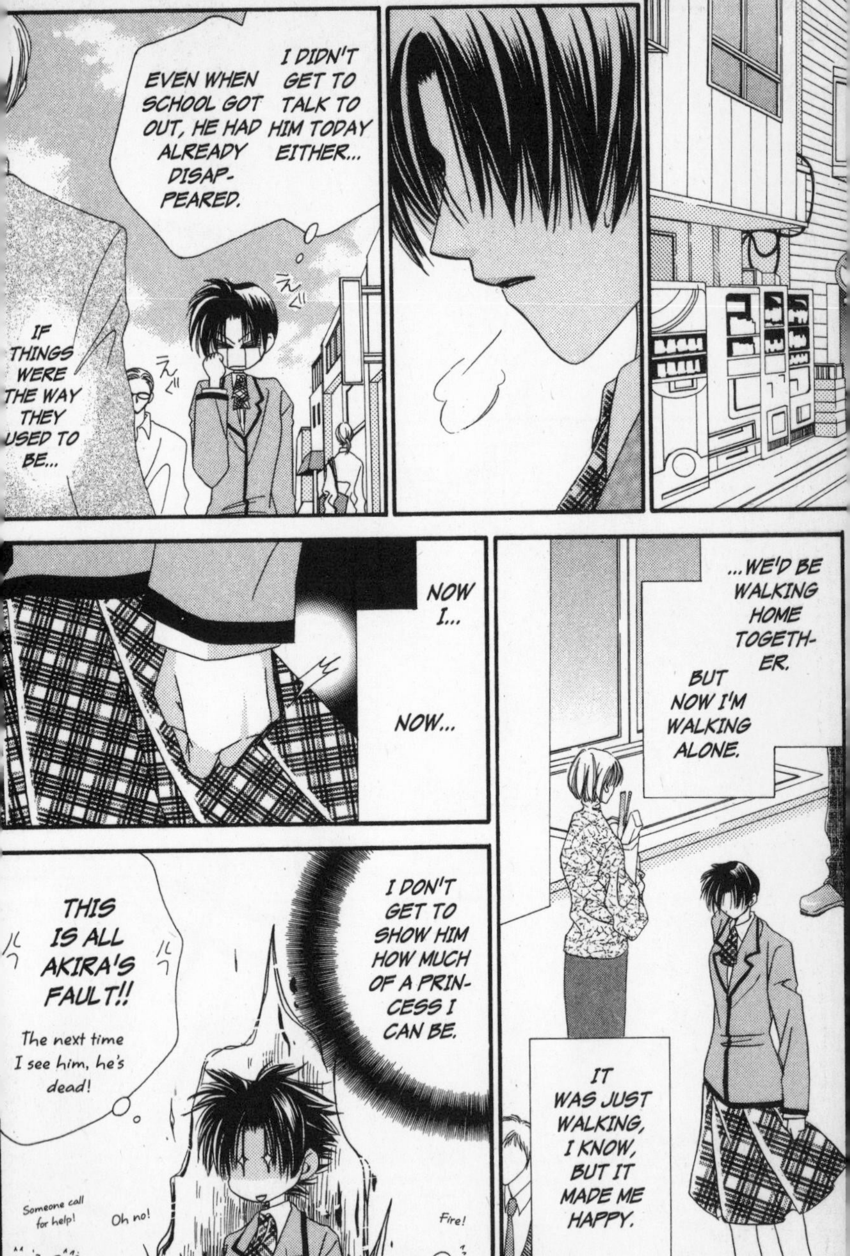
I DIDN'T GET TO TALK TO HIM TODAY EITHER...
EVEN WHEN SCHOOL GOT OUT, HE HAD ALREADY DISAP-PEARED.
IF THINGS WERE THE WAY THEY USED TO BE...
...WE'D BE WALKING HOME TOGETH-ER.
BUT NOW I'M WALKING ALONE.
IT WAS JUST WALKING, I KNOW, BUT IT MADE ME HAPPY.
NOW I...
NOW...
I DON'T GET TO SHOW HIM HOW MUCH OF A PRIN-CESS I CAN BE.
THIS IS ALL AKIRA'S FAULT!!
The next time I see him, he's dead!
Fire!
Oh no!
Someone call for help!

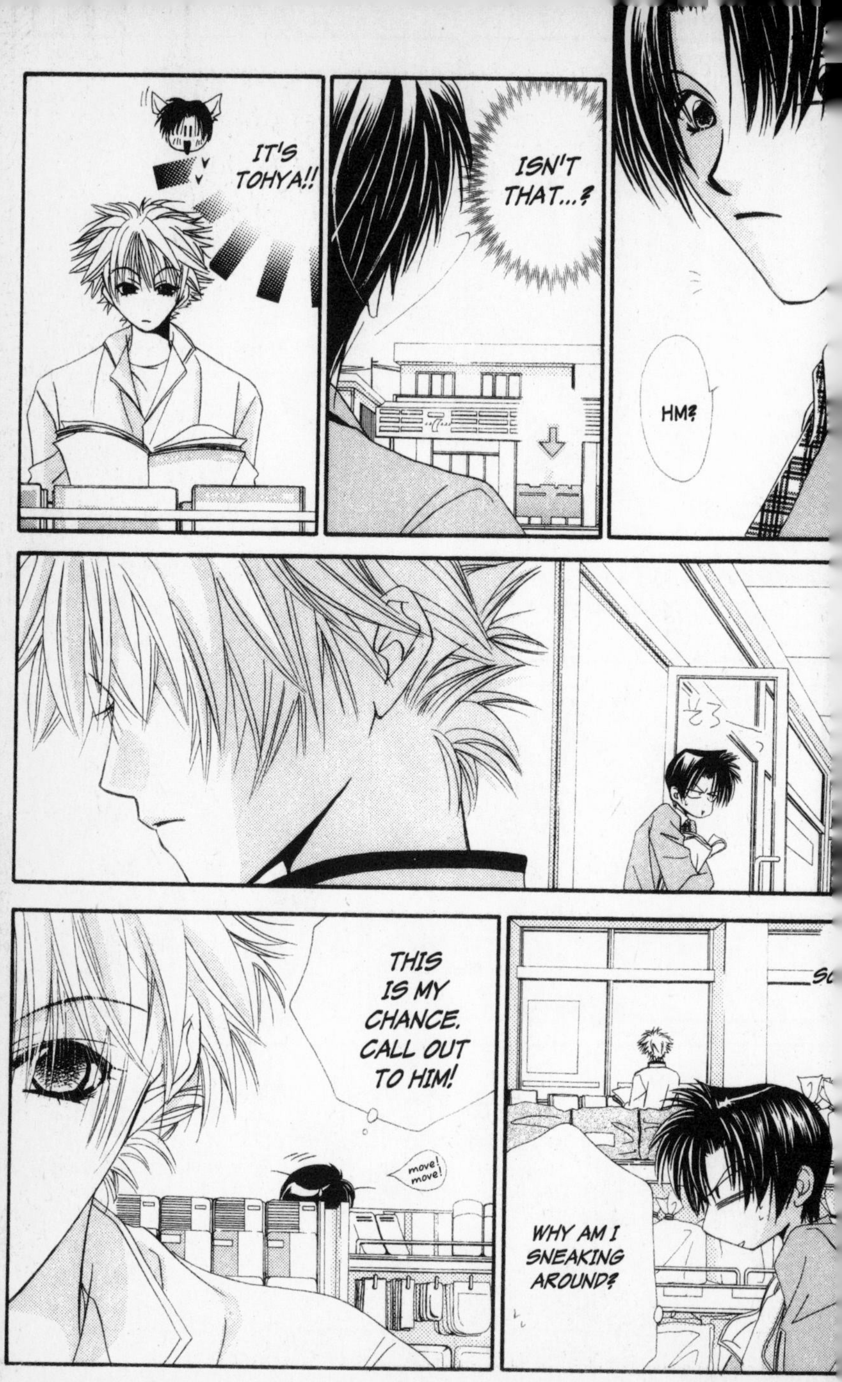
HM?
ISN'T THAT...?
IT'S TOHYA!!
WHY AM I SNEAKING AROUND?
THIS IS MY CHANCE. CALL OUT TO HIM!
move! move!

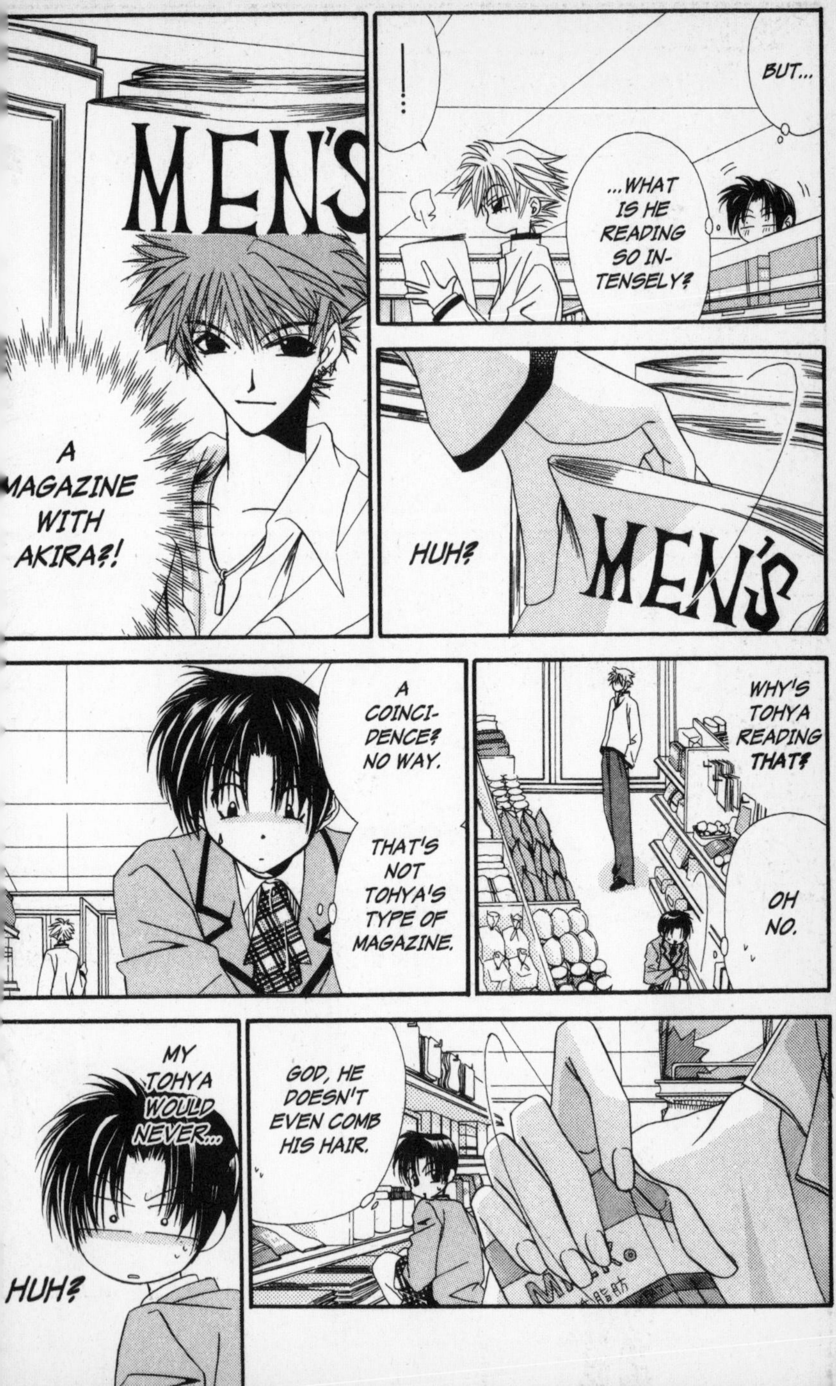
BUT...
!...
...WHAT IS HE READING SO INTENSELY?
MEN'S
HUH?
MEN'S
A MAGAZINE WITH AKIRA?!
WHY'S TOHYA READING THAT?
OH NO.
A COINCIDENCE? NO WAY.
THAT'S NOT TOHYA'S TYPE OF MAGAZINE.
GOD, HE DOESN'T EVEN COMB HIS HAIR.
MY TOHYA WOULD NEVER...
HUH?

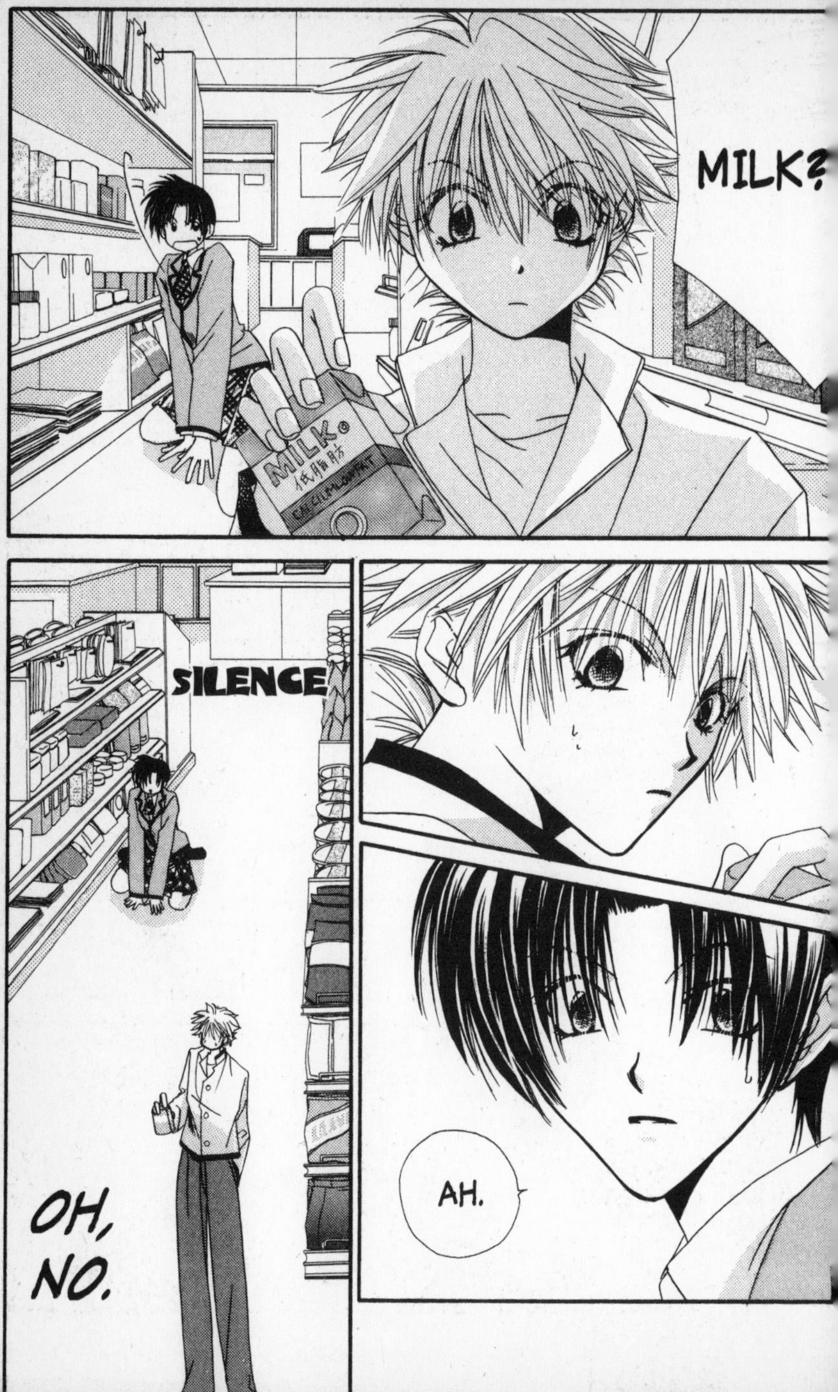

MILK?
MILK
低脂肪
AH.
SILENCE
OH, NO.

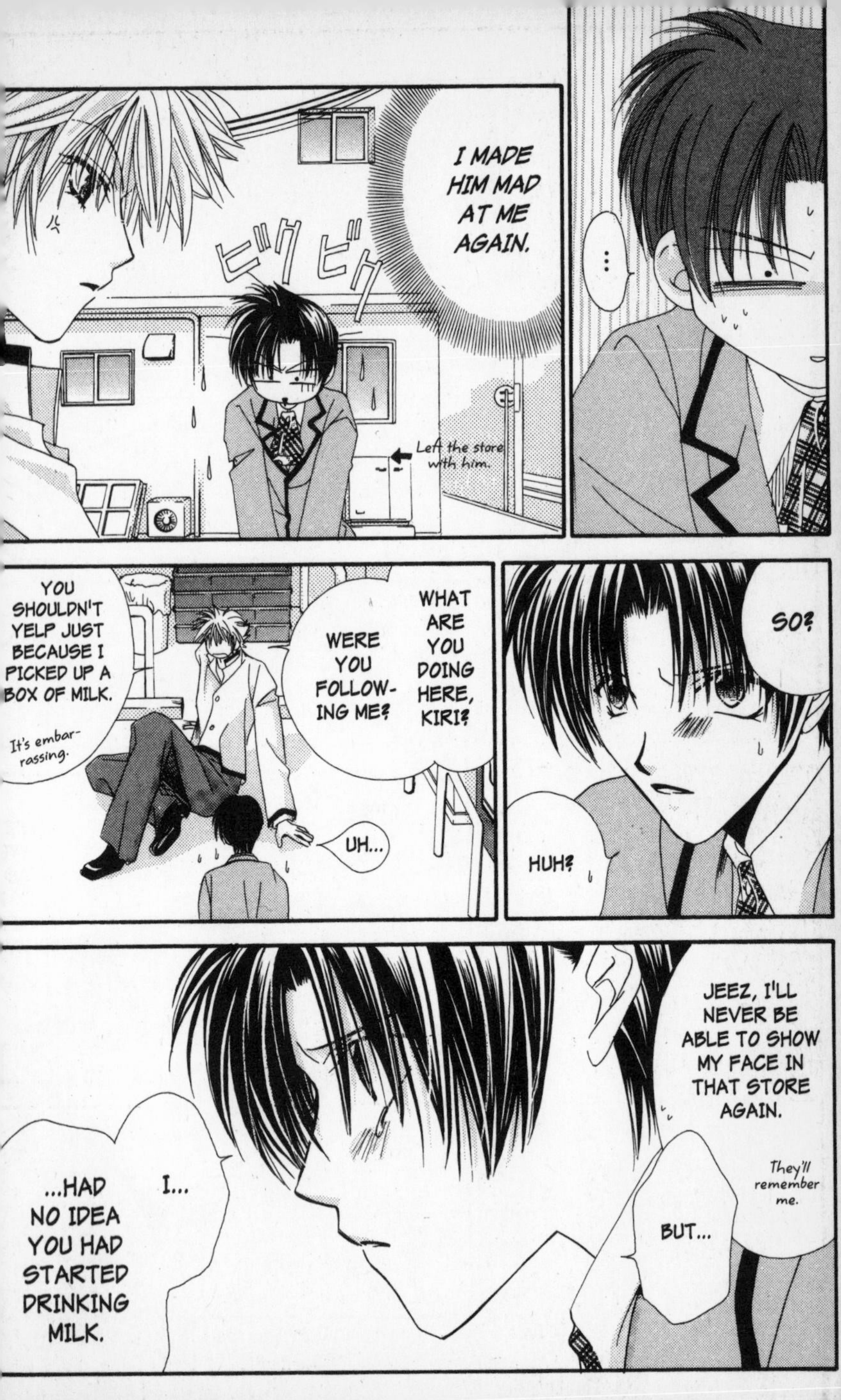
...
I MADE HIM MAD AT ME AGAIN.
ビクビク
Left the store with him.
SO?
HUH?
WHAT ARE YOU DOING HERE, KIRI?
WERE YOU FOLLOW-ING ME?
UH...
YOU SHOULDN'T YELP JUST BECAUSE I PICKED UP A BOX OF MILK.
It's embar-rassing.
JEEZ, I'LL NEVER BE ABLE TO SHOW MY FACE IN THAT STORE AGAIN.
They'll remember me.
BUT...
I...
...HAD NO IDEA YOU HAD STARTED DRINKING MILK.

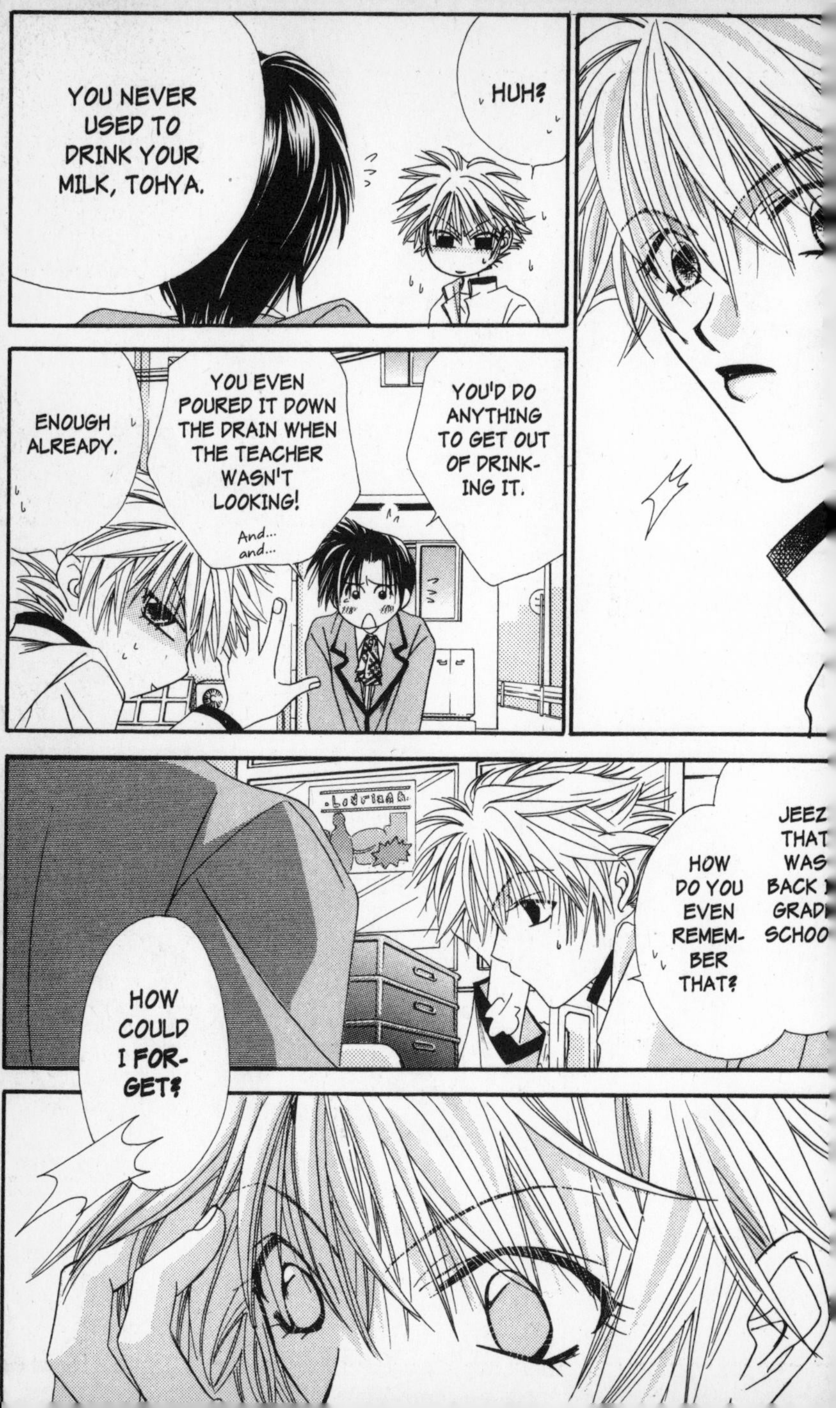
HUH?
YOU NEVER USED TO DRINK YOUR MILK, TOHYA.
YOU'D DO ANYTHING TO GET OUT OF DRINK-ING IT.
YOU EVEN POURED IT DOWN THE DRAIN WHEN THE TEACHER WASN'T LOOKING!
And... and...
ENOUGH ALREADY.
JEEZ THAT WAS BACK GRAD SCHOO
HOW DO YOU EVEN REMEM-BER THAT?
HOW COULD I FOR-GET?

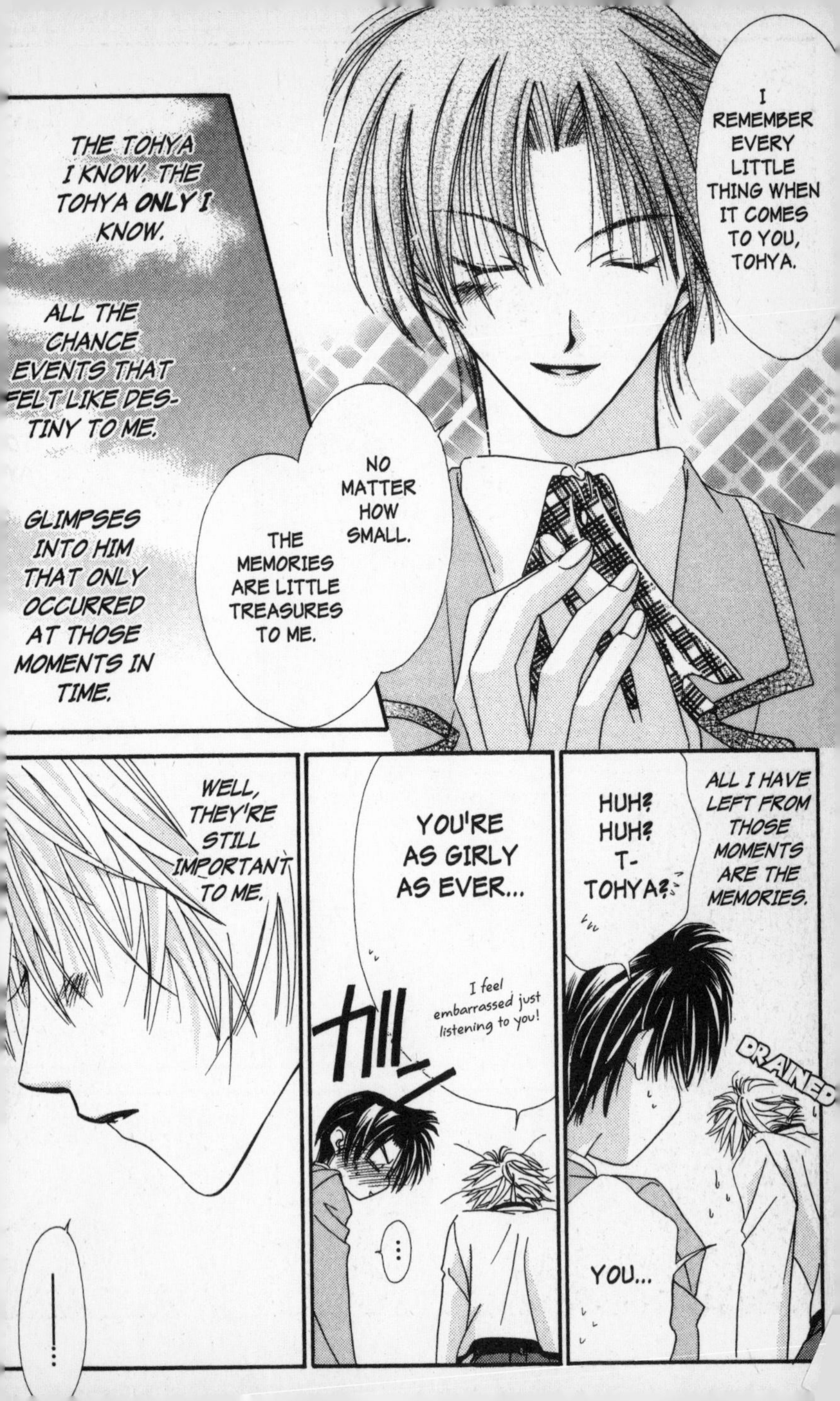

I REMEMBER EVERY LITTLE THING WHEN IT COMES TO YOU, TOHYA.
NO MATTER HOW SMALL.
THE MEMORIES ARE LITTLE TREASURES TO ME.
THE TOHYA I KNOW. THE TOHYA ONLY I KNOW.
ALL THE CHANCE EVENTS THAT FELT LIKE DESTINY TO ME.
GLIMPSES INTO HIM THAT ONLY OCCURRED AT THOSE MOMENTS IN TIME.
ALL I HAVE LEFT FROM THOSE MOMENTS ARE THE MEMORIES.
HUH? HUH? T-TOHYA?
DRAINED
YOU...
YOU'RE AS GIRLY AS EVER...
I feel embarrassed just listening to you!
...
WELL, THEY'RE STILL IMPORTANT TO ME.
......

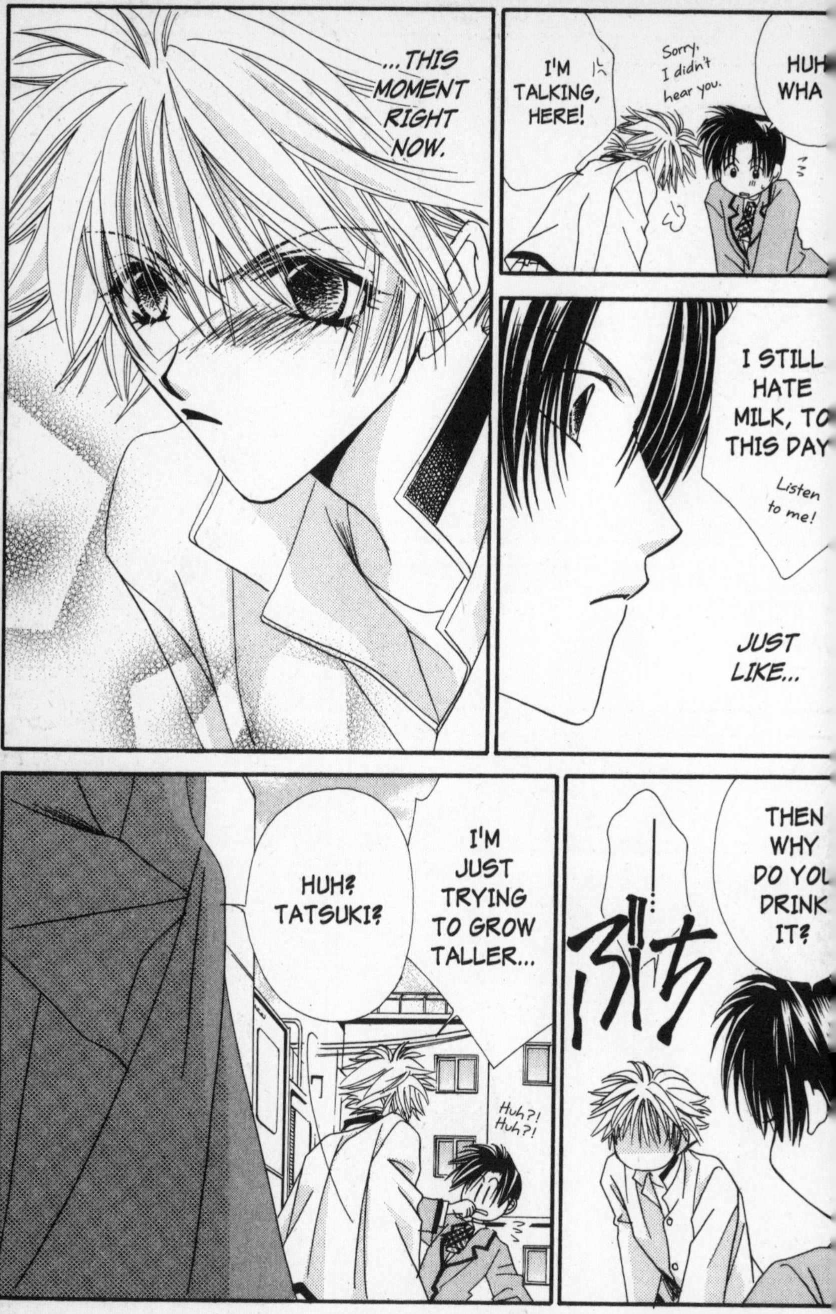
HUH WHA
Sorry, I didn't hear you.
I'M TALKING, HERE!
I STILL HATE MILK, TO THIS DAY
Listen to me!
JUST LIKE...
...THIS MOMENT RIGHT NOW.
THEN WHY DO YOU DRINK IT?
ぶち
...!
I'M JUST TRYING TO GROW TALLER...
HUH? TATSUKI?
Huh?! Huh?!

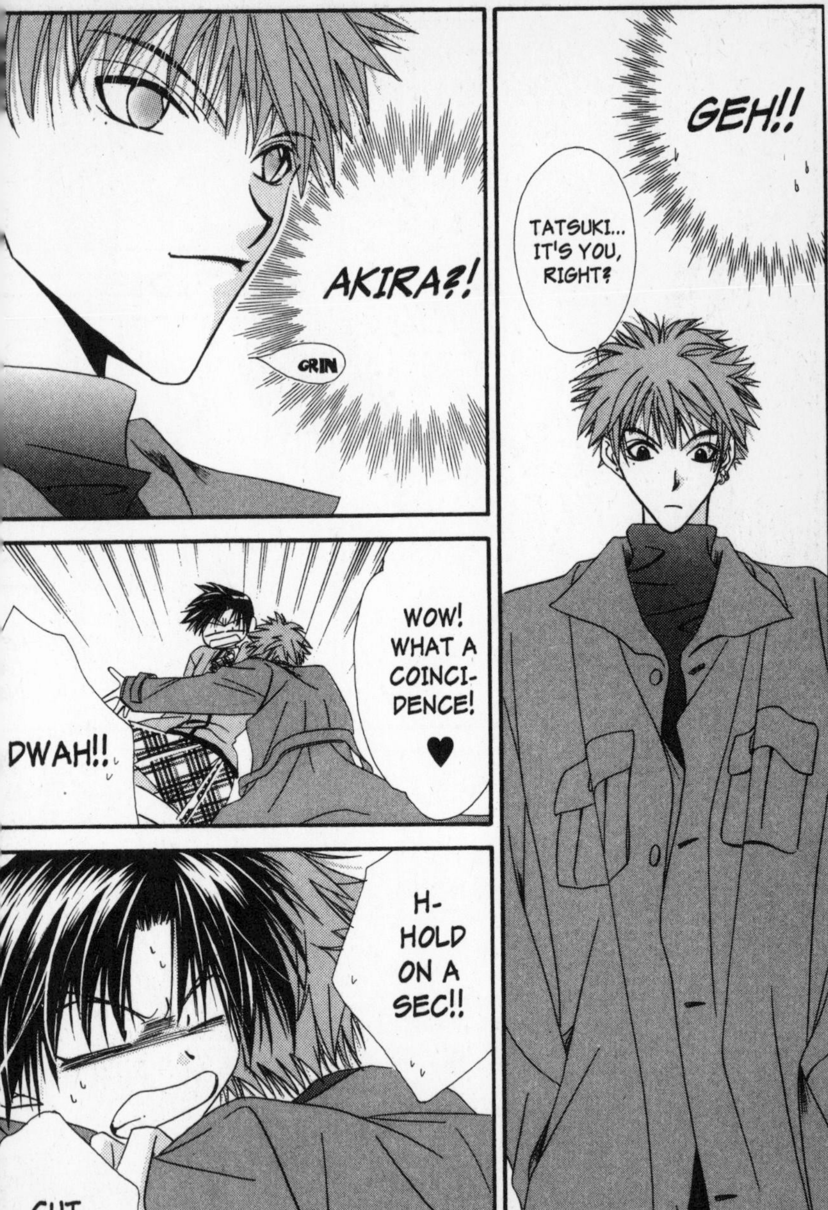
GEH!!
TATSUKI... IT'S YOU, RIGHT?
AKIRA?!
GRIN
WOW! WHAT A COINCI-DENCE! ♥
DWAH!!
H-HOLD ON A SEC!!
CUT IT...

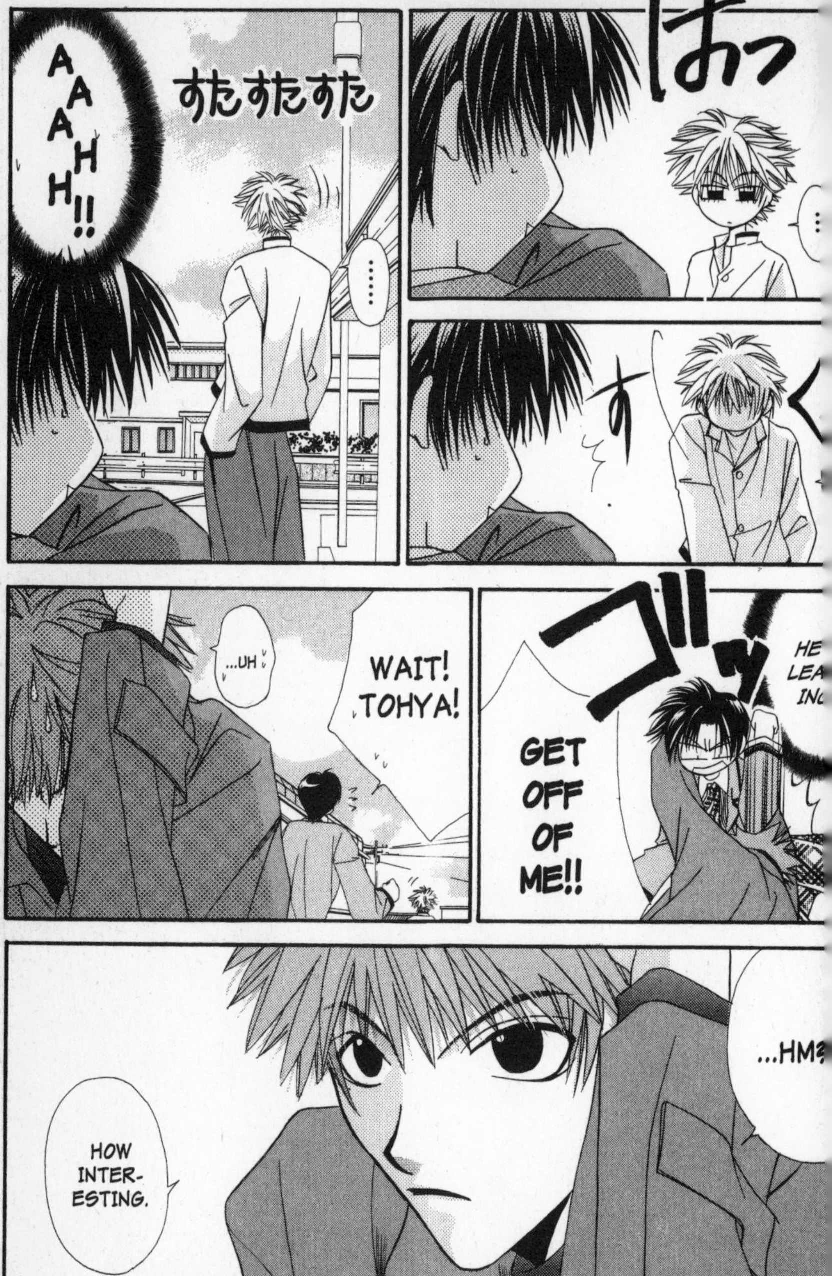

はっ
...
すく
AAAHH!!
すたすたすた
......
ゴッ
GET OFF OF ME!!
WAIT! TOHYA!
...UH
...HM?
HOW INTER-ESTING.

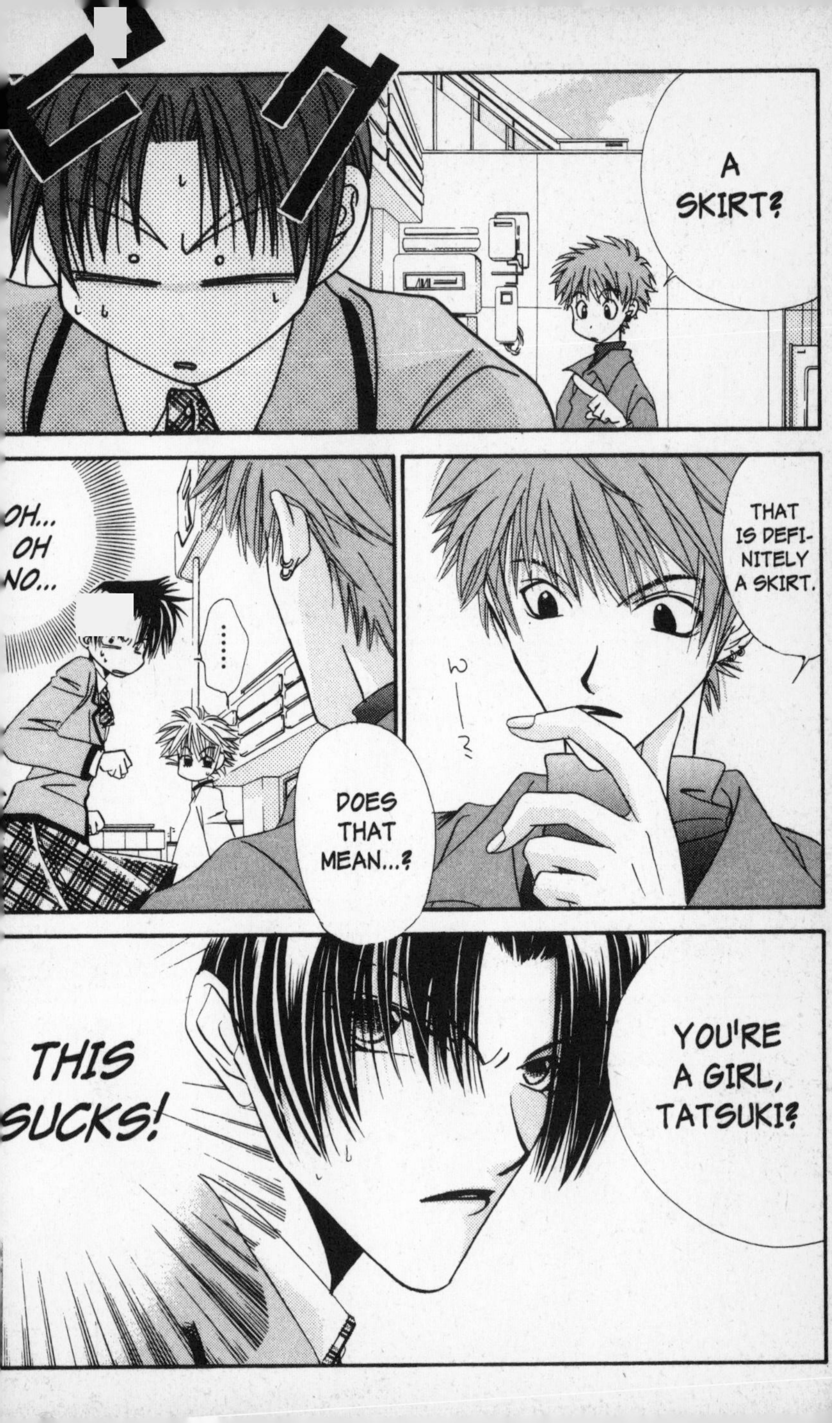
A SKIRT?
THAT IS DEFINITELY A SKIRT.
DOES THAT MEAN...?
......
OH... OH NO...
YOU'RE A GIRL, TATSUKI?
THIS SUCKS!

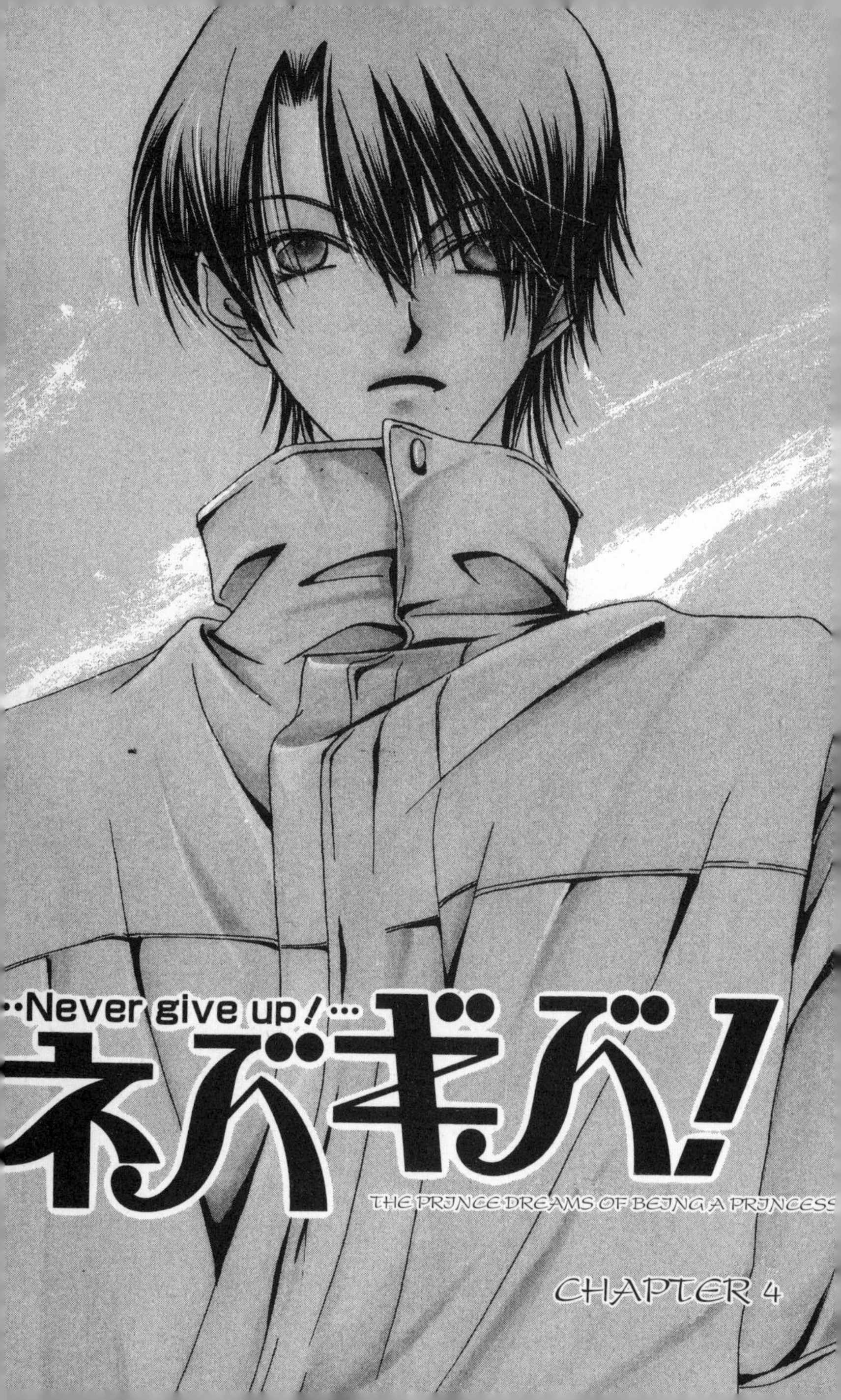

…Never give up!…
ネバギバ!
THE PRINCE DREAMS OF BEING A PRINCESS
CHAPTER 4

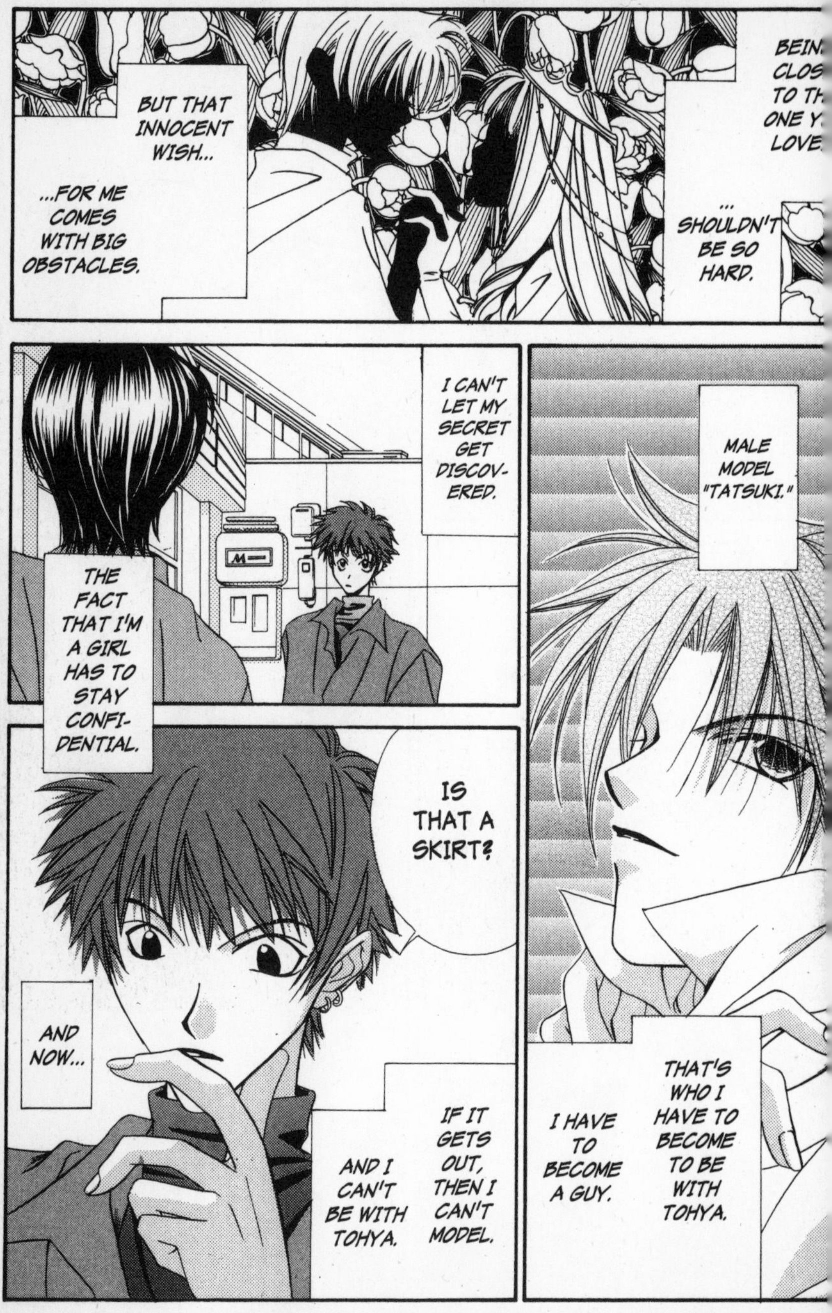
BEIN CLOS TO TH ONE Y LOVE
...SHOULDN'T BE SO HARD.
BUT THAT INNOCENT WISH...
...FOR ME COMES WITH BIG OBSTACLES.
MALE MODEL "TATSUKI."
THAT'S WHO I HAVE TO BECOME TO BE WITH TOHYA.
I HAVE TO BECOME A GUY.
I CAN'T LET MY SECRET GET DISCOVERED.
THE FACT THAT I'M A GIRL HAS TO STAY CONFIDENTIAL.
IS THAT A SKIRT?
IF IT GETS OUT, THEN I CAN'T MODEL.
AND I CAN'T BE WITH TOHYA.
AND NOW...

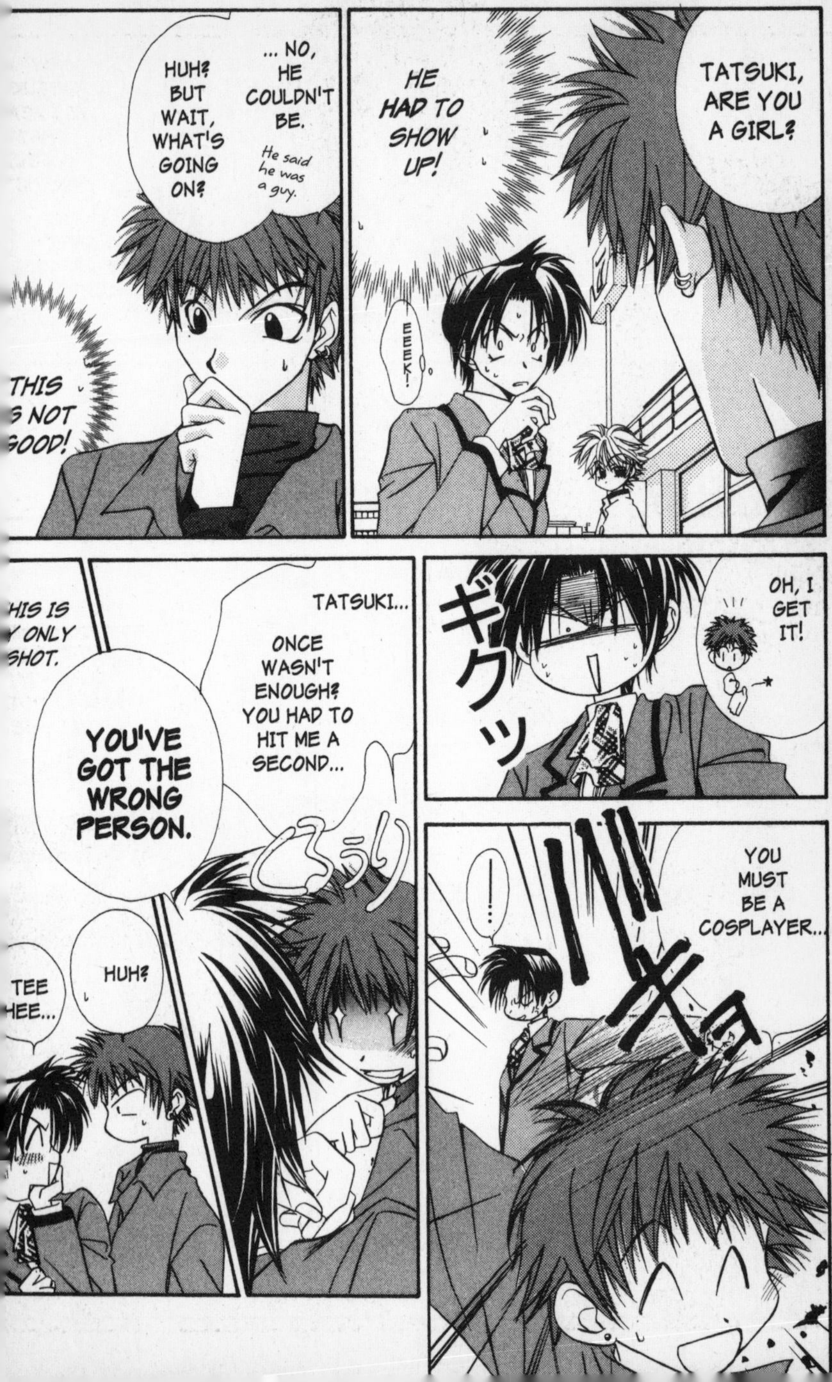
TATSUKI, ARE YOU A GIRL?
HE HAD TO SHOW UP!
EEEK!
... NO, HE COULDN'T BE.
He said he was a guy.
HUH? BUT WAIT, WHAT'S GOING ON?
THIS
S NOT
GOOD!
OH, I GET IT!
ギクッ
YOU MUST BE A COSPLAYER...
!...
TATSUKI...
ONCE WASN'T ENOUGH? YOU HAD TO HIT ME A SECOND...
YOU'VE GOT THE WRONG PERSON.
HIS IS
Y ONLY
SHOT.
HUH?
TEE
HEE...

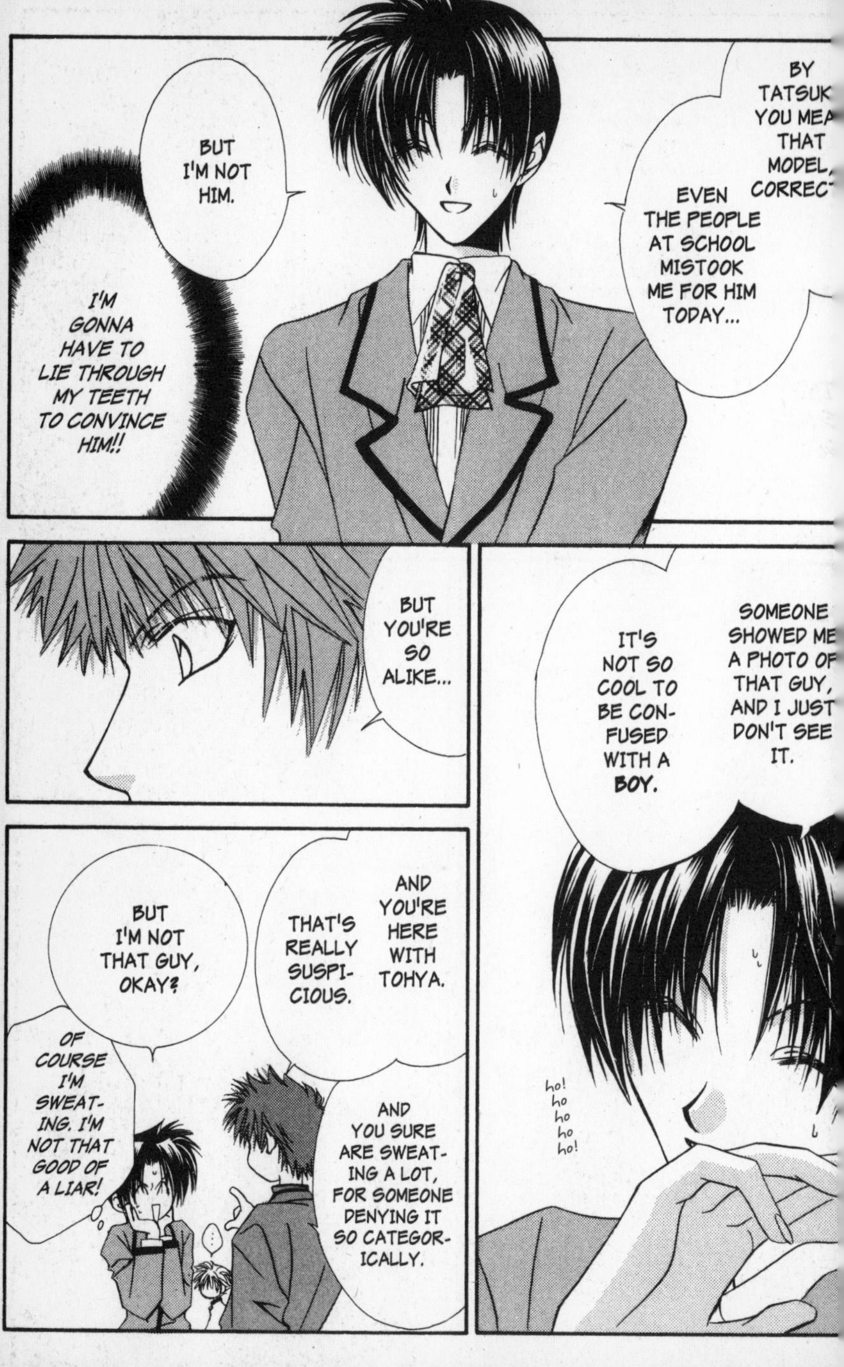
BY TATSUK YOU MEA THAT MODEL, CORREC
EVEN THE PEOPLE AT SCHOOL MISTOOK ME FOR HIM TODAY...
BUT I'M NOT HIM.
I'M GONNA HAVE TO LIE THROUGH MY TEETH TO CONVINCE HIM!!
SOMEONE SHOWED ME A PHOTO OF THAT GUY, AND I JUST DON'T SEE IT.
IT'S NOT SO COOL TO BE CON-FUSED WITH A **BOY.**
ho! ho ho ho ho!
BUT YOU'RE SO ALIKE...
AND YOU'RE HERE WITH TOHYA.
THAT'S REALLY SUSPICIOUS.
BUT I'M NOT THAT GUY, OKAY?
AND YOU SURE ARE SWEAT-ING A LOT, FOR SOMEONE DENYING IT SO CATEGOR-ICALLY.
OF COURSE I'M SWEAT-ING. I'M NOT THAT GOOD OF A LIAR!
...

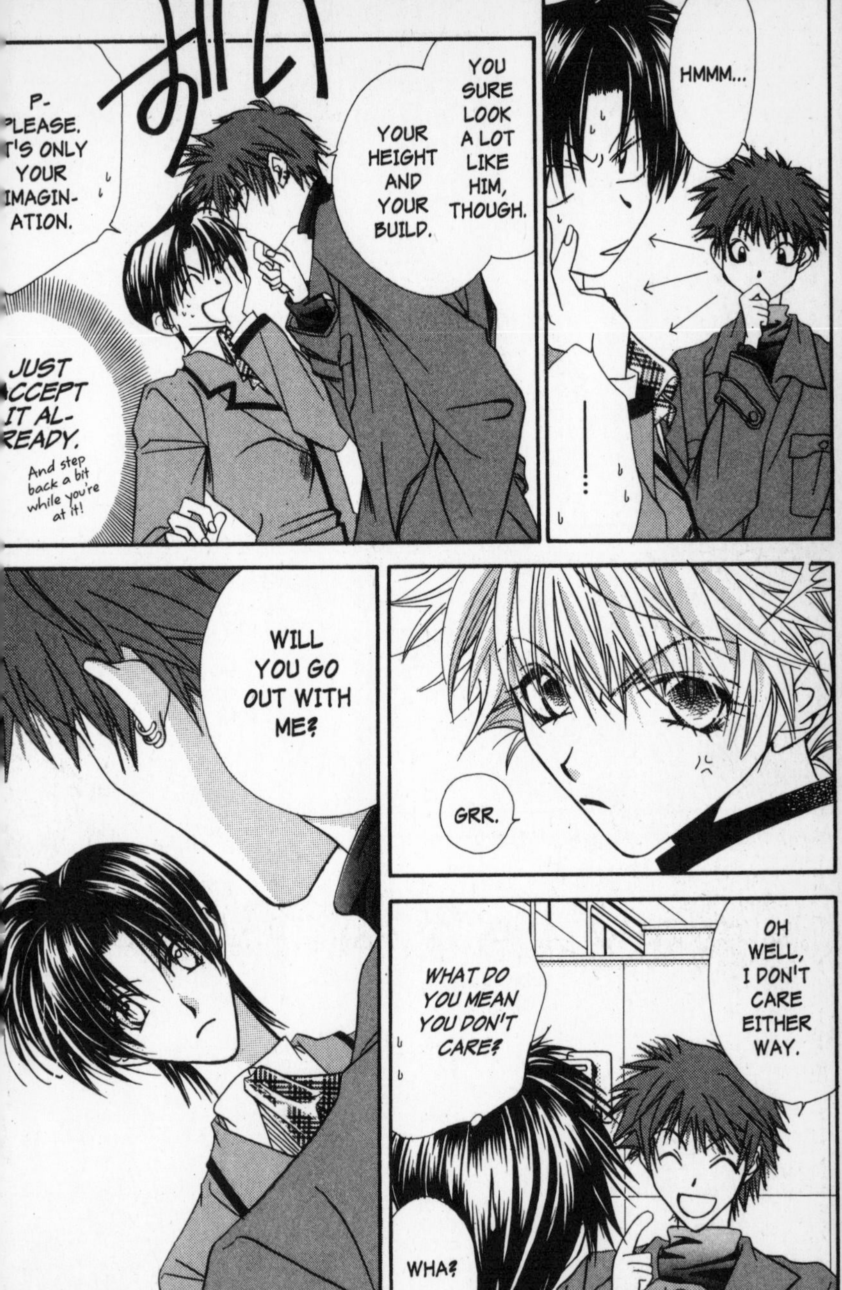
HMMM...
YOU SURE LOOK A LOT LIKE HIM, THOUGH.
YOUR HEIGHT AND YOUR BUILD.
おい
P-PLEASE. IT'S ONLY YOUR IMAGINATION.
JUST ACCEPT IT ALREADY.
And step back a bit while you're at it!
GRR.
OH WELL, I DON'T CARE EITHER WAY.
WHAT DO YOU MEAN YOU DON'T CARE?
WHA?
WILL YOU GO OUT WITH ME?

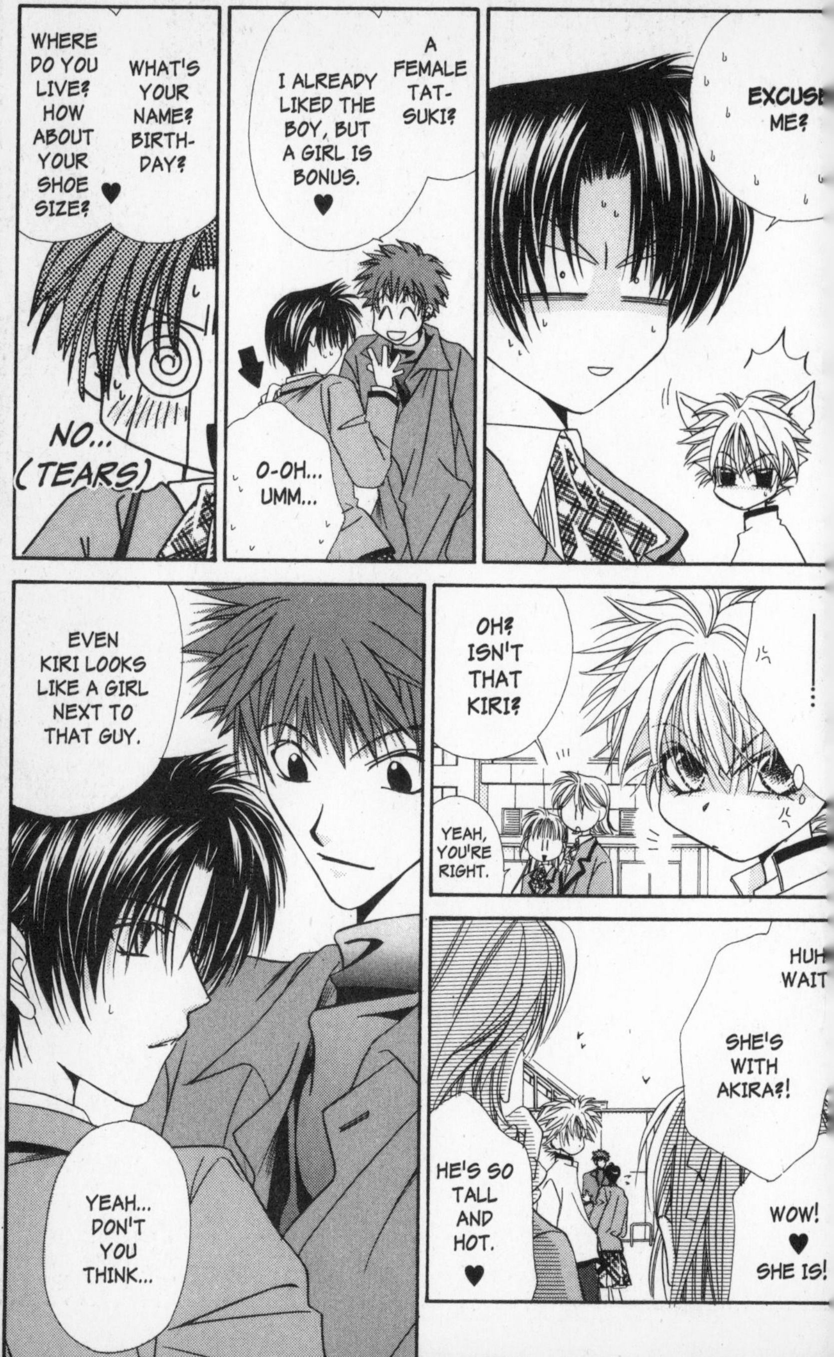
EXCUSE ME?
A FEMALE TAT-SUKI?
I ALREADY LIKED THE BOY, BUT A GIRL IS BONUS. ♥
O-OH... UMM...
WHAT'S YOUR NAME? BIRTH-DAY?
WHERE DO YOU LIVE? HOW ABOUT YOUR SHOE SIZE? ♥
NO... (TEARS)
OH? ISN'T THAT KIRI?
YEAH, YOU'RE RIGHT.
HUH WAIT
SHE'S WITH AKIRA?!
WOW! ♥ SHE IS!
HE'S SO TALL AND HOT. ♥
EVEN KIRI LOOKS LIKE A GIRL NEXT TO THAT GUY.
YEAH... DON'T YOU THINK...

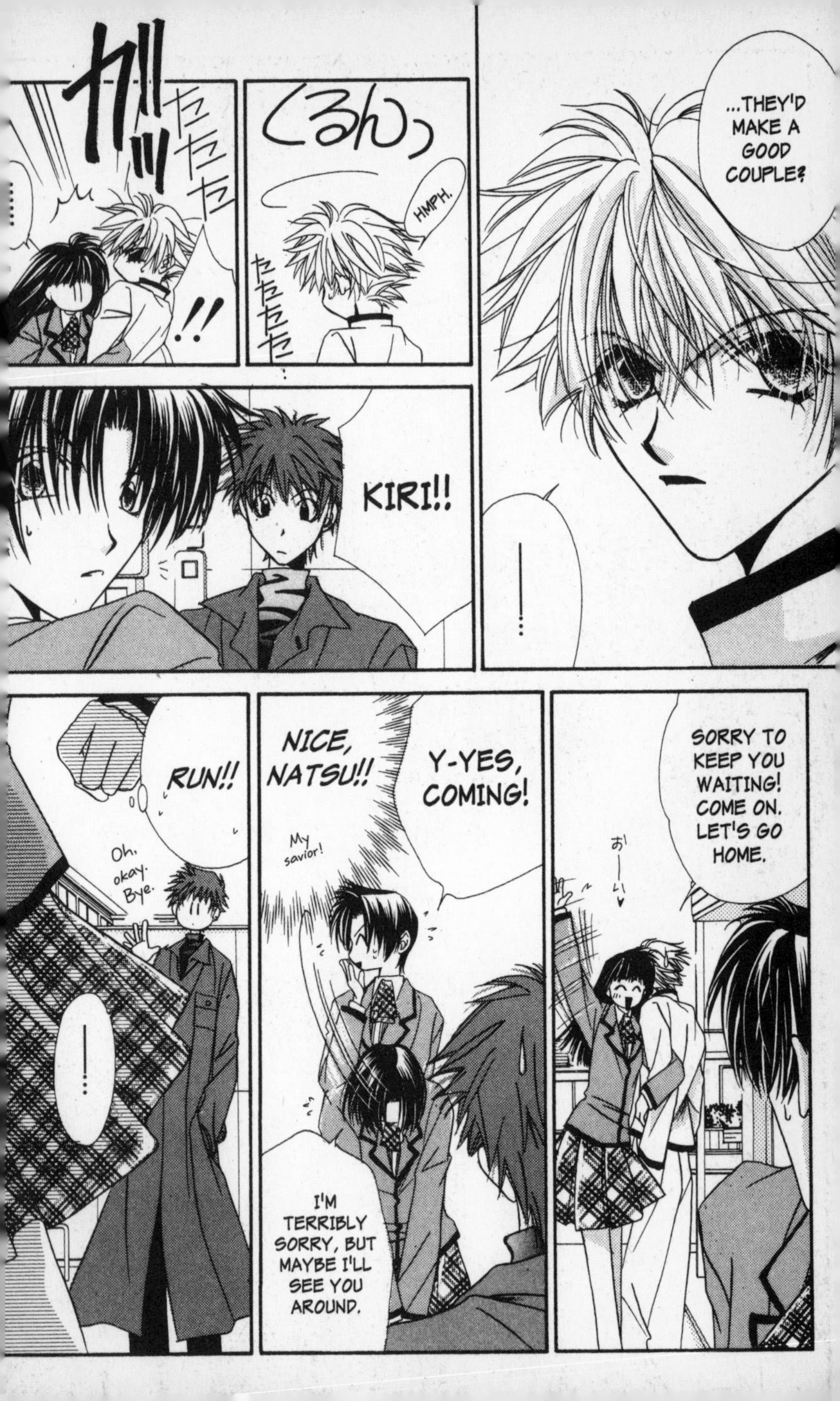
...THEY'D MAKE A GOOD COUPLE?
......
くるんっ
HMPH.
たたたた
カッ
たたた
!!
KIRI!!
SORRY TO KEEP YOU WAITING! COME ON. LET'S GO HOME.
おーい
Y-YES, COMING!
NICE, NATSU!!
My savior!
I'M TERRIBLY SORRY, BUT MAYBE I'LL SEE YOU AROUND.
RUN!!
Oh, okay. Bye.
......

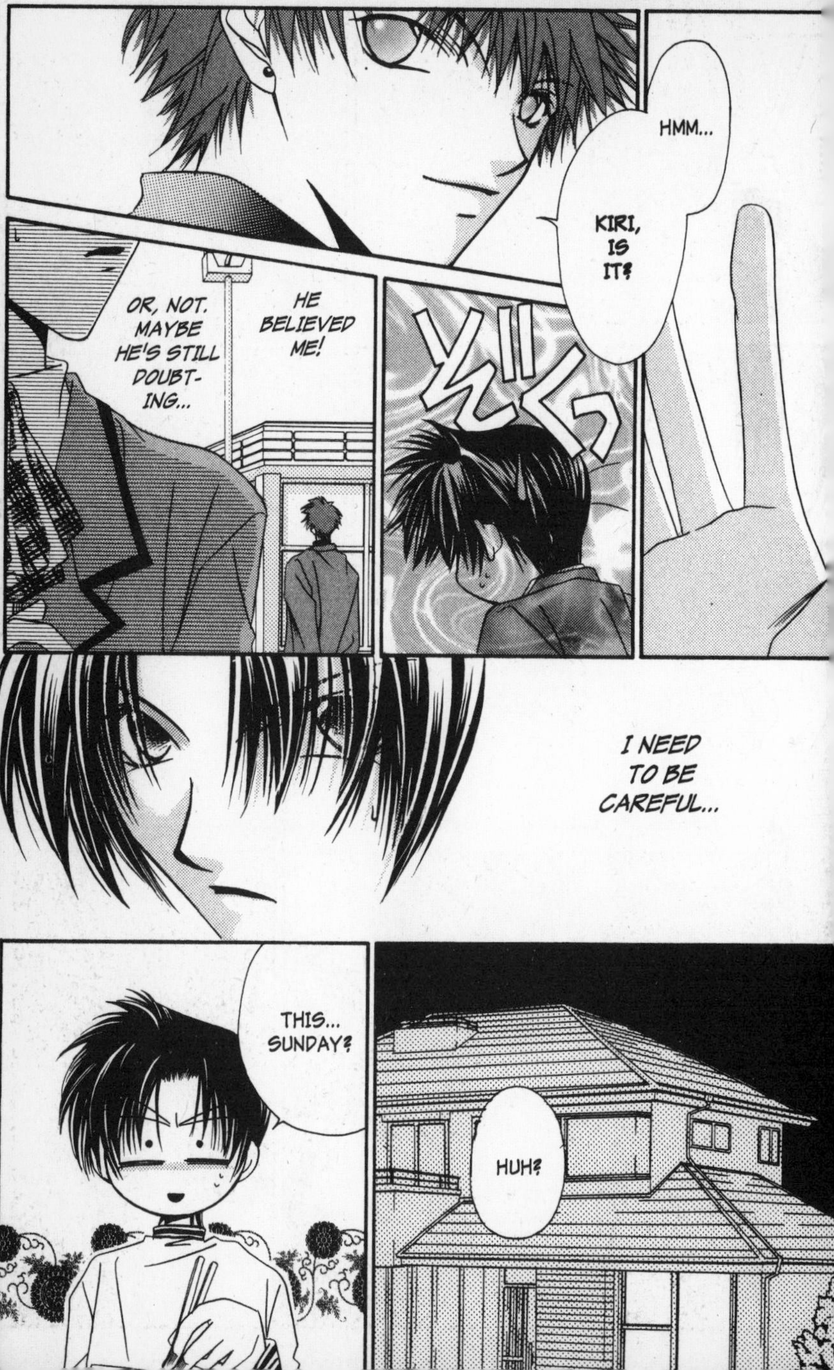
HMM...
KIRI, IS IT?
ぞくっ
HE BELIEVED ME!
OR, NOT. MAYBE HE'S STILL DOUBTING...
I NEED TO BE CAREFUL...
HUH?
THIS... SUNDAY?

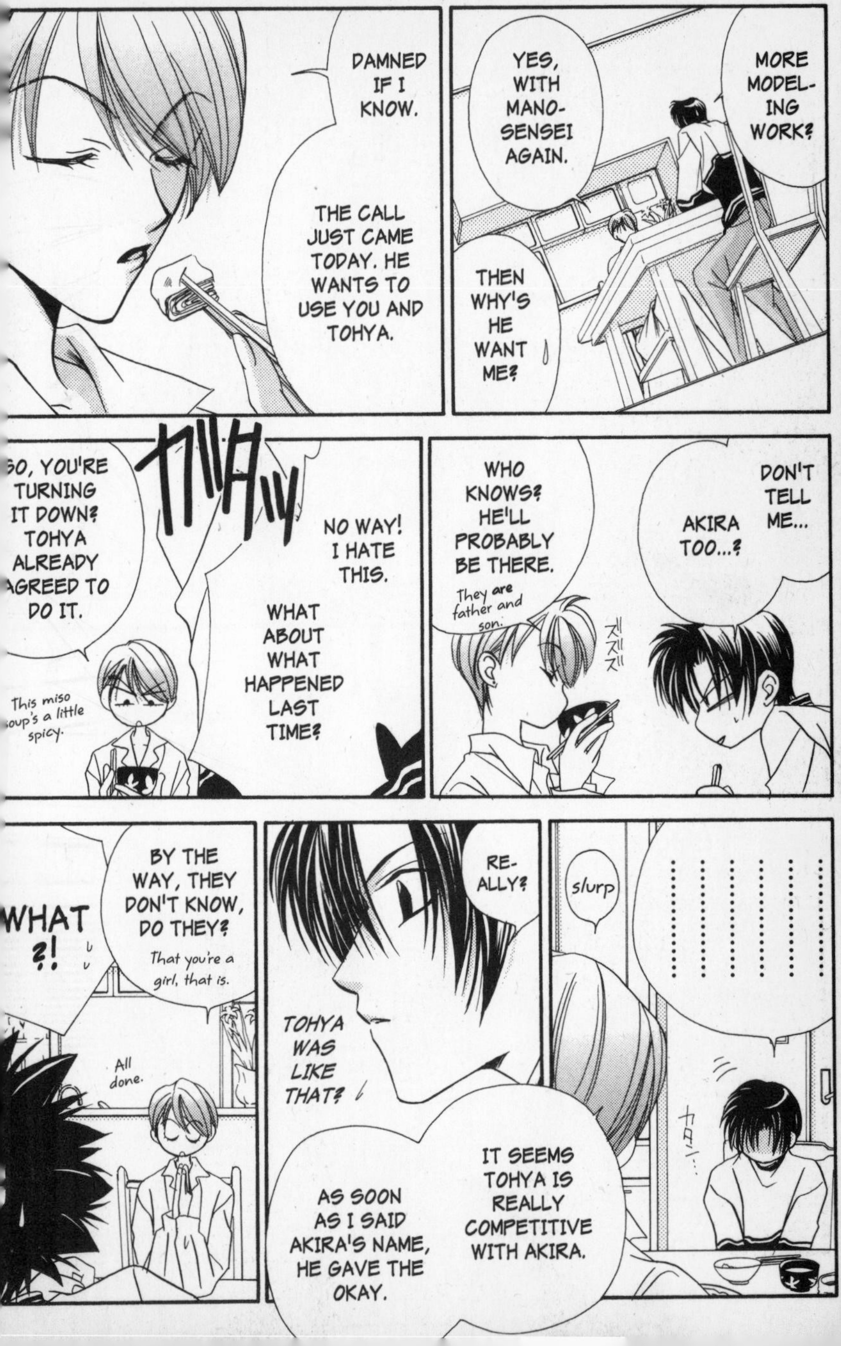
MORE MODELING WORK?
YES, WITH MANO-SENSEI AGAIN.
THEN WHY'S HE WANT ME?
DAMNED IF I KNOW.
THE CALL JUST CAME TODAY. HE WANTS TO USE YOU AND TOHYA.
DON'T TELL ME...
AKIRA TOO...?
WHO KNOWS? HE'LL PROBABLY BE THERE.
They are father and son.
ズズズ
NO WAY! I HATE THIS.
WHAT ABOUT WHAT HAPPENED LAST TIME?
SO, YOU'RE TURNING IT DOWN? TOHYA ALREADY AGREED TO DO IT.
This miso soup's a little spicy.
....
slurp
RE-ALLY?
TOHYA WAS LIKE THAT?
IT SEEMS TOHYA IS REALLY COMPETITIVE WITH AKIRA.
AS SOON AS I SAID AKIRA'S NAME, HE GAVE THE OKAY.
BY THE WAY, THEY DON'T KNOW, DO THEY?
That you're a girl, that is.
WHAT?!
All done.

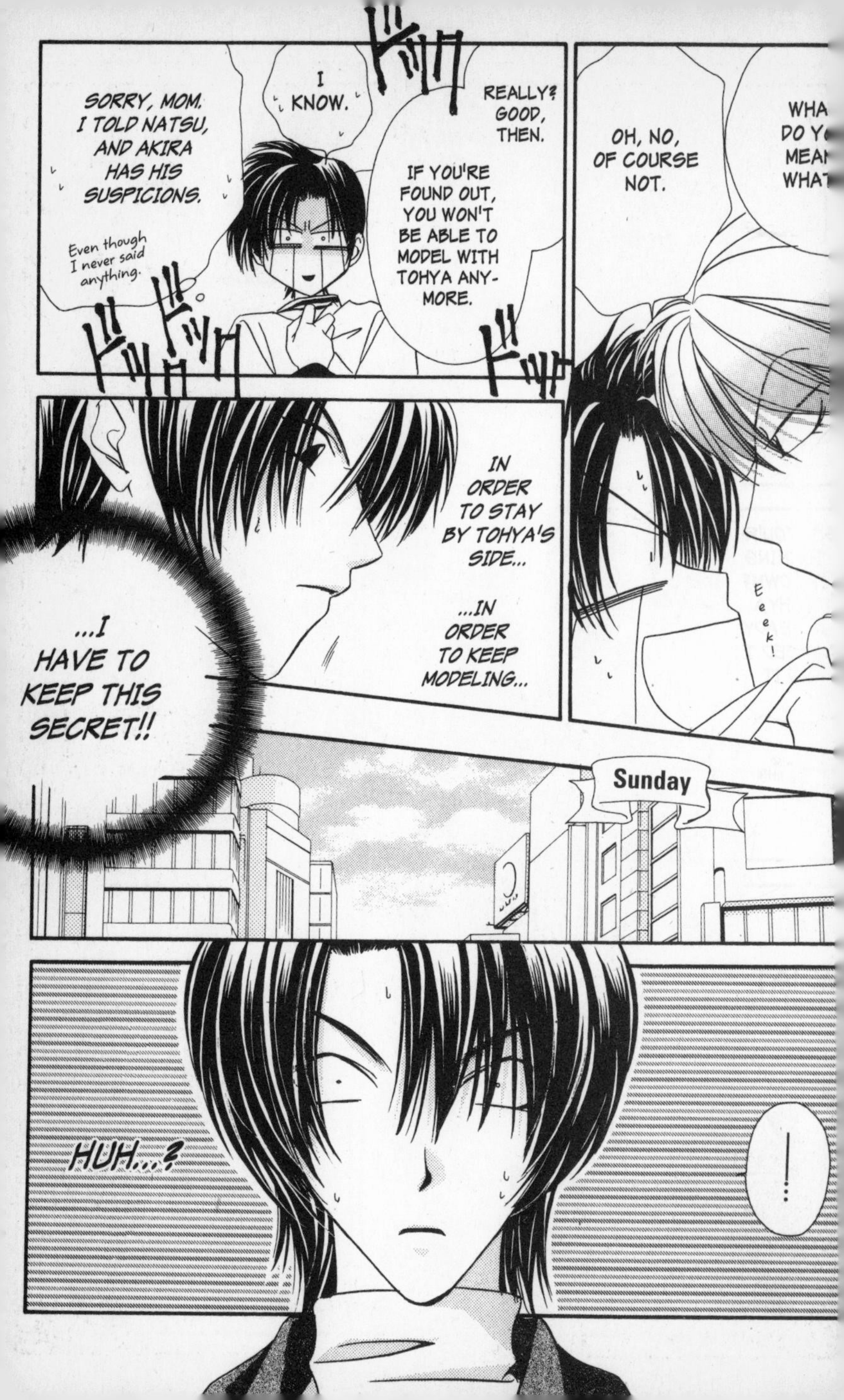
WHA DO YO MEAN WHAT
OH, NO, OF COURSE NOT.
REALLY? GOOD, THEN.
IF YOU'RE FOUND OUT, YOU WON'T BE ABLE TO MODEL WITH TOHYA ANY-MORE.
I KNOW.
SORRY, MOM. I TOLD NATSU, AND AKIRA HAS HIS SUSPICIONS.
Even though I never said anything.
Eeek!
IN ORDER TO STAY BY TOHYA'S SIDE...
...IN ORDER TO KEEP MODELING...
...I HAVE TO KEEP THIS SECRET!!
Sunday
!...
HUH...?

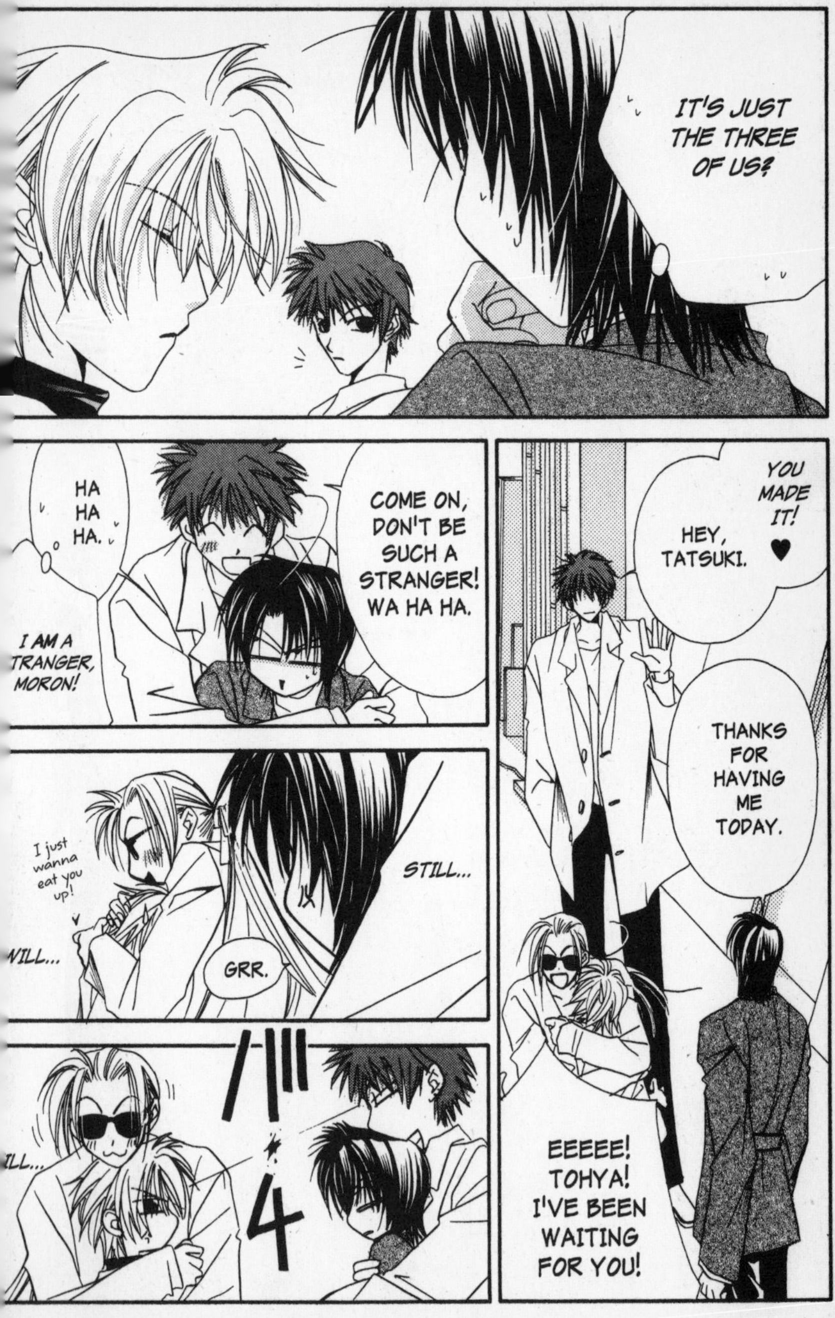
IT'S JUST THE THREE OF US?
YOU MADE IT! ♥
HEY, TATSUKI.
THANKS FOR HAVING ME TODAY.
EEEEE! TOHYA! I'VE BEEN WAITING FOR YOU!
COME ON, DON'T BE SUCH A STRANGER! WA HA HA.
HA HA HA.
I AM A TRANGER, MORON!
STILL...
GRR.
I just wanna eat you up! ♥
ILL...
ILL...

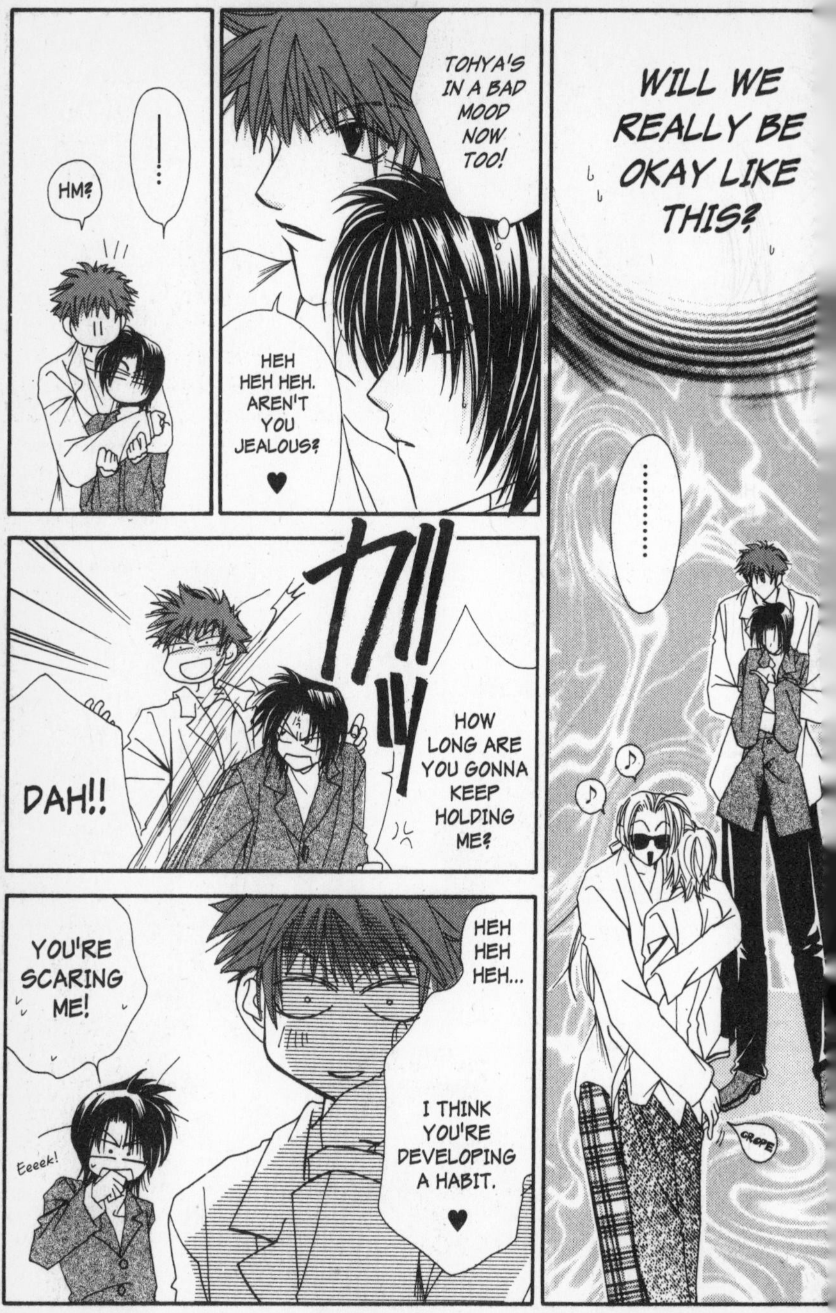
WILL WE REALLY BE OKAY LIKE THIS?
......
GROPE
TOHYA'S IN A BAD MOOD NOW TOO!
HEH HEH HEH. AREN'T YOU JEALOUS? ♥
!......
HM?
HOW LONG ARE YOU GONNA KEEP HOLDING ME?
DAH!!
HEH HEH HEH...
I THINK YOU'RE DEVELOPING A HABIT. ♥
YOU'RE SCARING ME!
Eeeek!

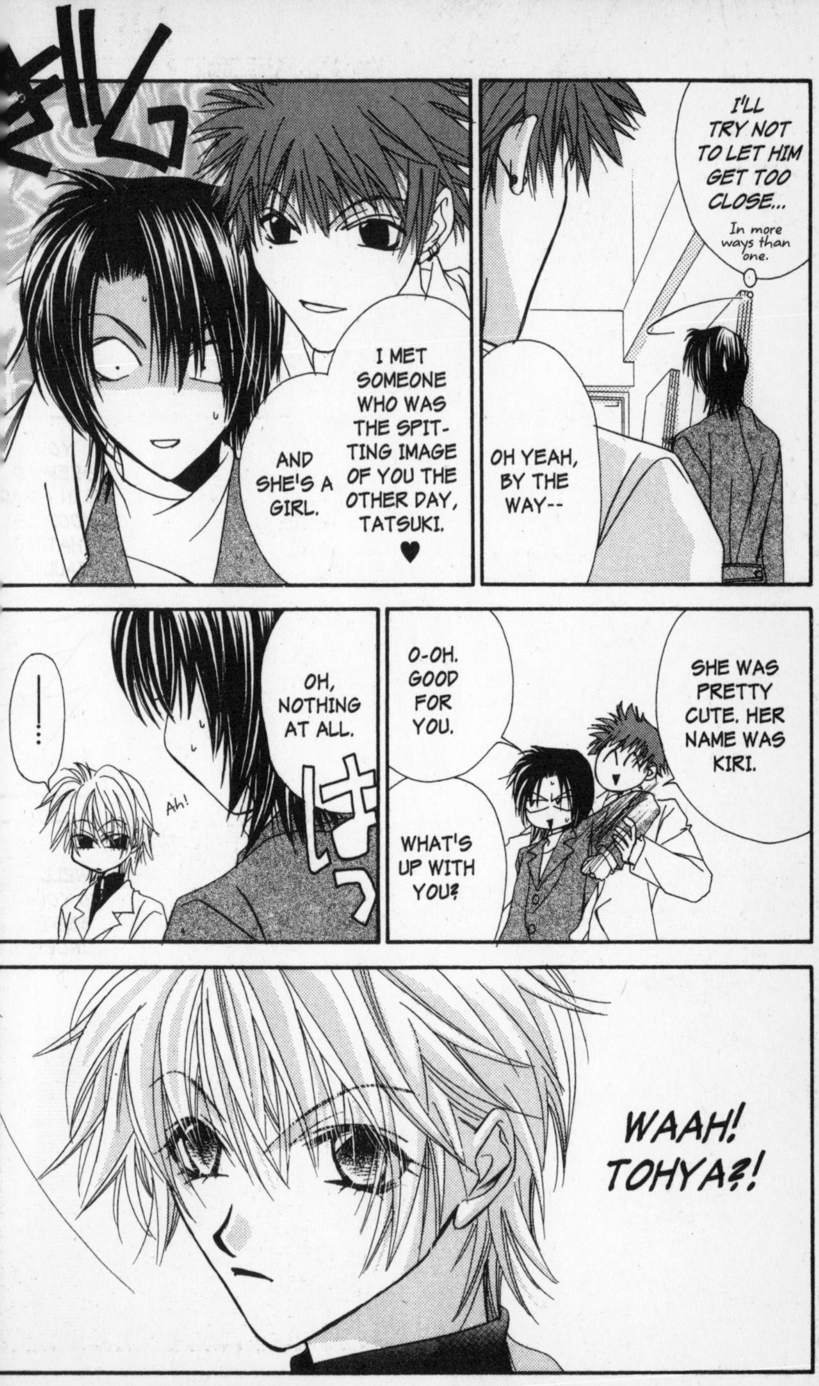
I'LL TRY NOT TO LET HIM GET TOO CLOSE...
In more ways than one.
OH YEAH, BY THE WAY--
I MET SOMEONE WHO WAS THE SPITTING IMAGE OF YOU THE OTHER DAY, TATSUKI. ♥
AND SHE'S A GIRL.
SHE WAS PRETTY CUTE. HER NAME WAS KIRI.
O-OH. GOOD FOR YOU.
WHAT'S UP WITH YOU?
OH, NOTHING AT ALL.
はっ
Ah!
—!...
WAAH! TOHYA?!

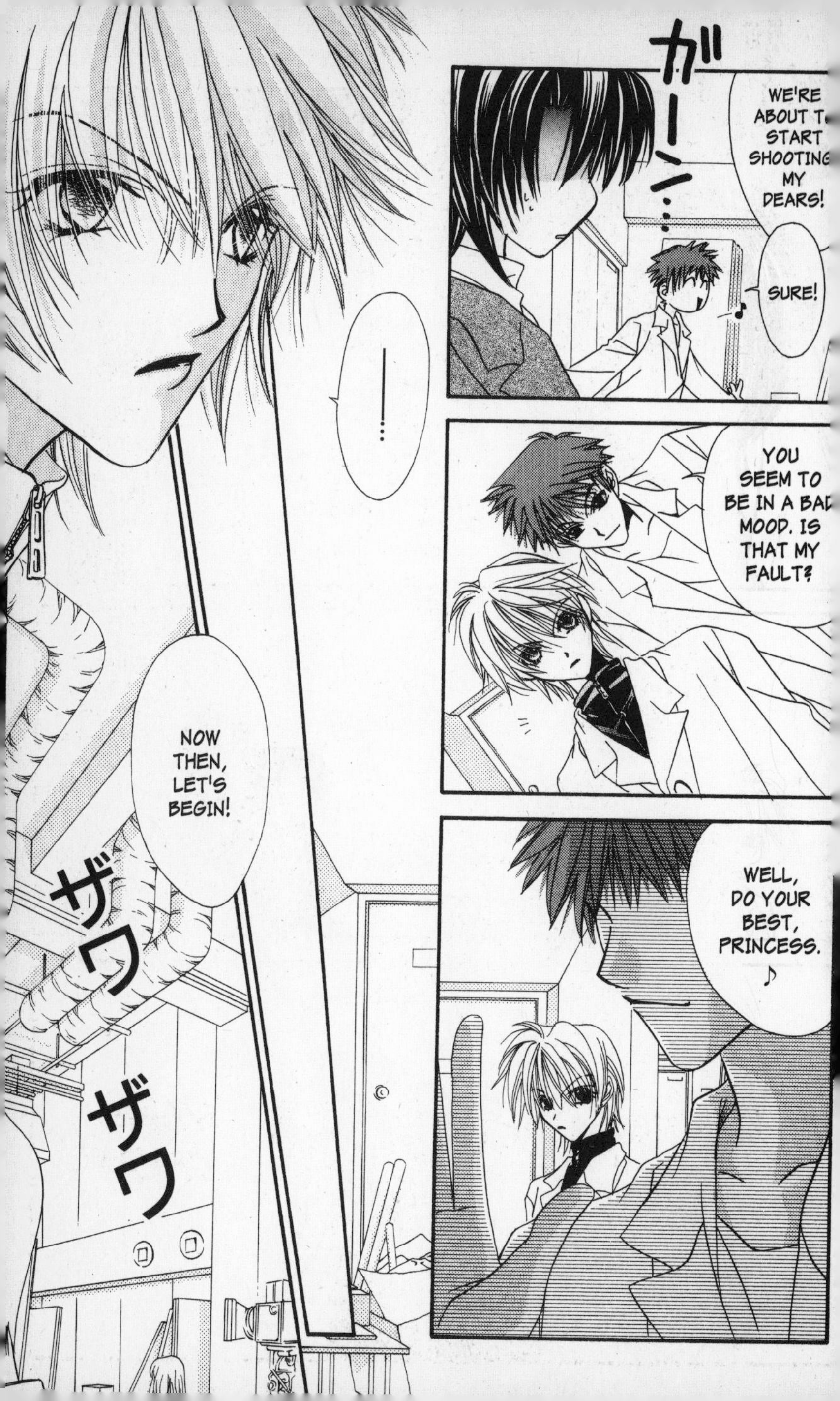
WE'RE ABOUT T START SHOOTING MY DEARS!
ガーン…
SURE!
YOU SEEM TO BE IN A BAD MOOD. IS THAT MY FAULT?
WELL, DO YOUR BEST, PRINCESS. ♪
—…
NOW THEN, LET'S BEGIN!
ザワ ザワ

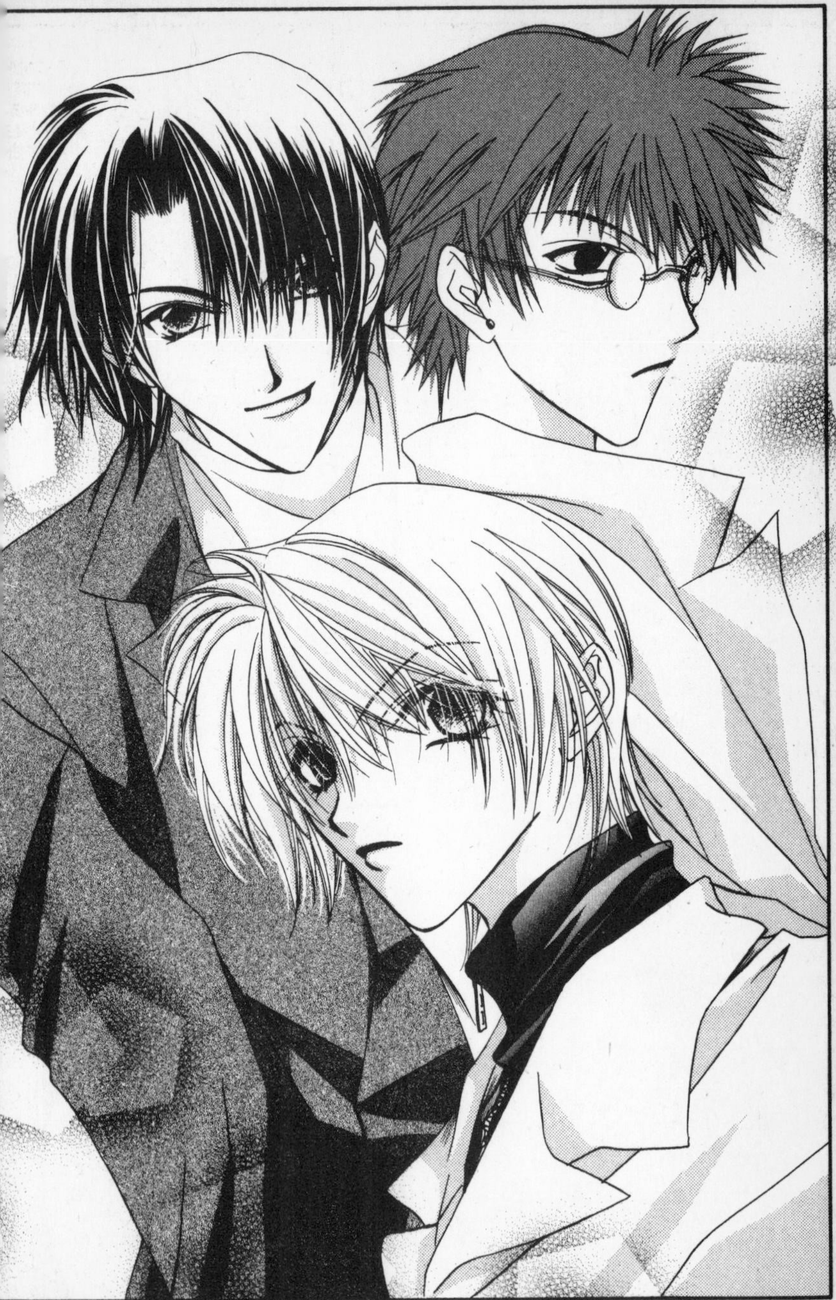

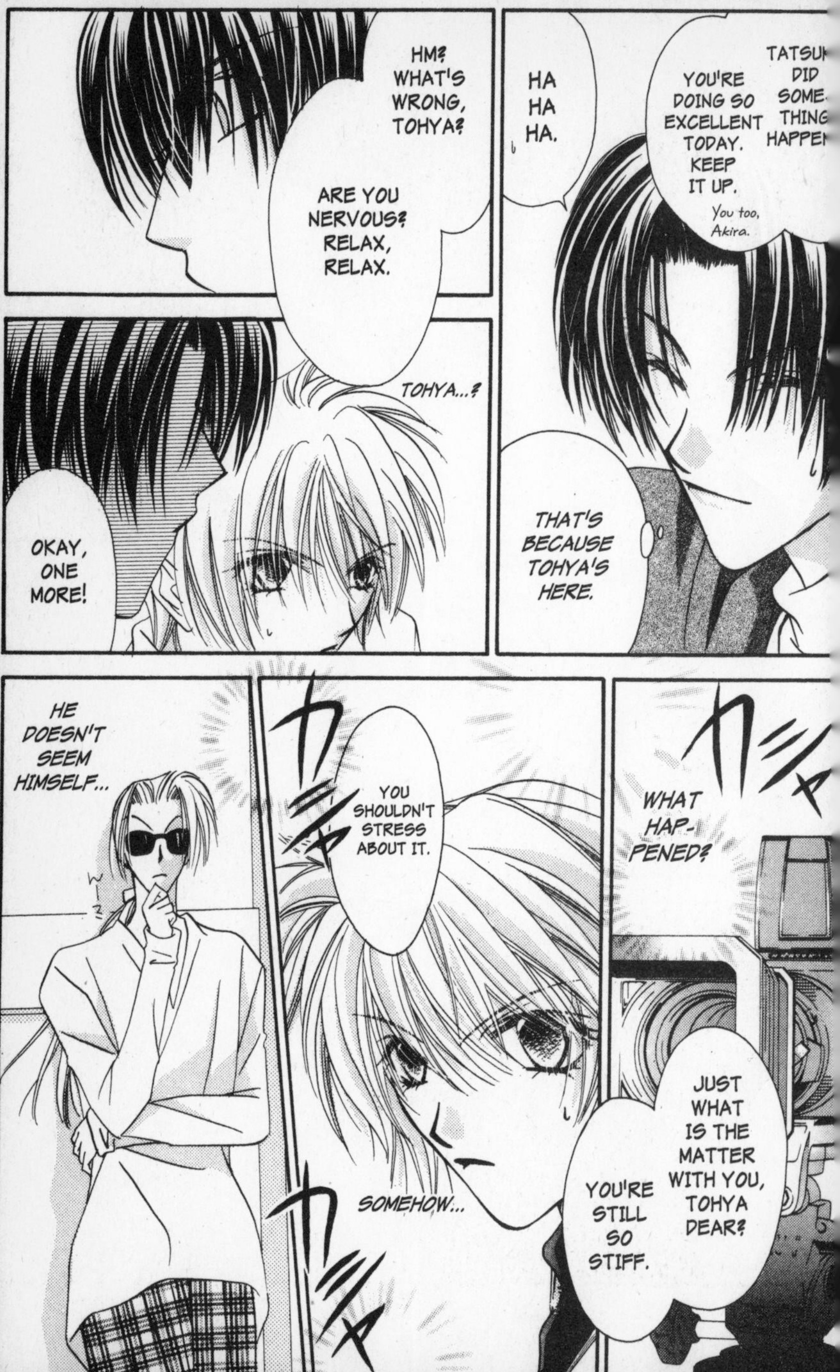

TATSU DID SOME- THING HAPPE
YOU'RE DOING SO EXCELLENT TODAY. KEEP IT UP.
You too, Akira.
HA HA HA.
THAT'S BECAUSE TOHYA'S HERE.
HM? WHAT'S WRONG, TOHYA?
ARE YOU NERVOUS? RELAX, RELAX.
TOHYA...?
OKAY, ONE MORE!
WHAT HAP-PENED?
JUST WHAT IS THE MATTER WITH YOU, TOHYA DEAR?
YOU'RE STILL SO STIFF.
YOU SHOULDN'T STRESS ABOUT IT.
SOMEHOW...
HE DOESN'T SEEM HIMSELF...

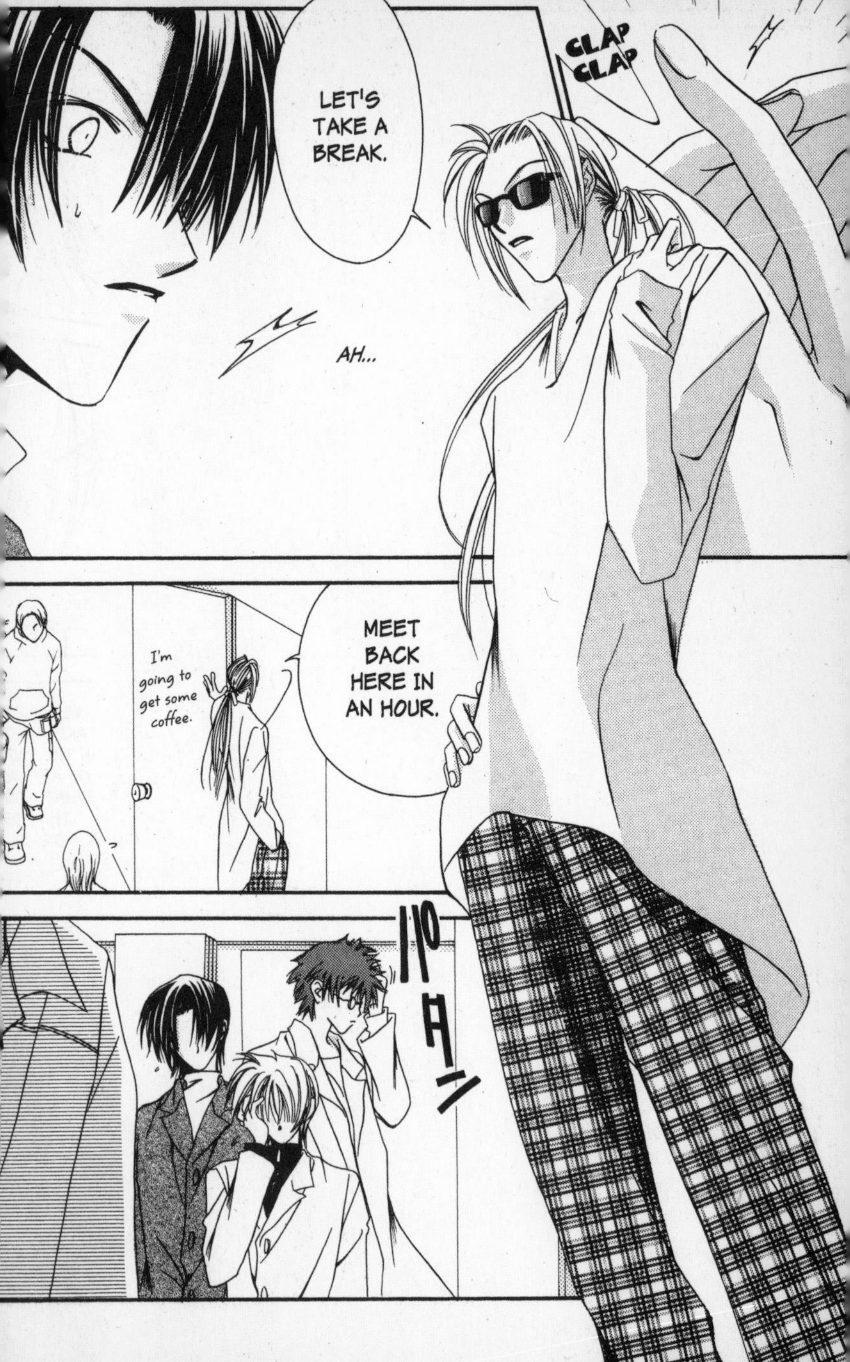
CLAP
CLAP
LET'S TAKE A BREAK.
AH...
MEET BACK HERE IN AN HOUR.
I'm going to get some coffee.
パタン

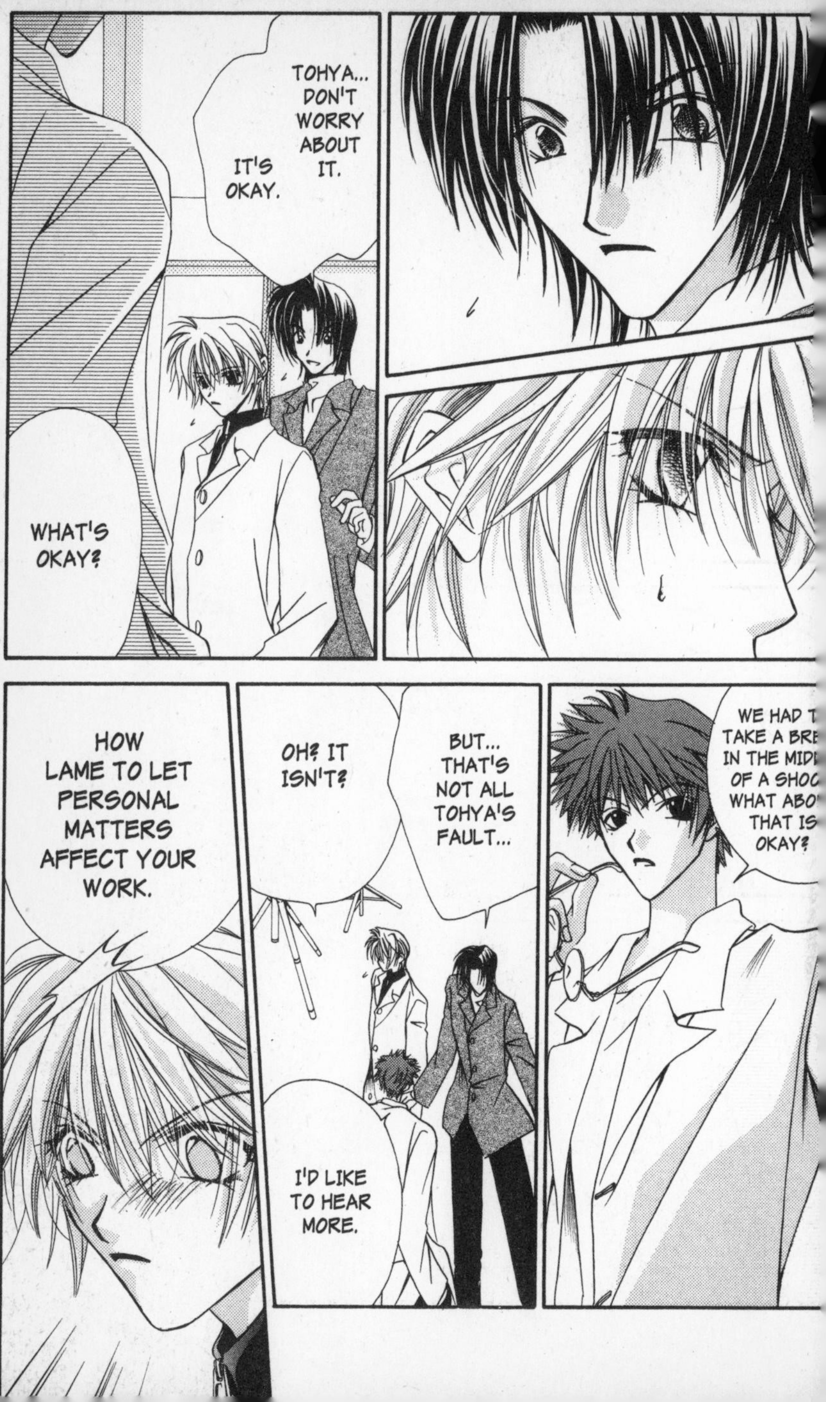
TOHYA... DON'T WORRY ABOUT IT.
IT'S OKAY.
WHAT'S OKAY?
WE HAD T TAKE A BRE IN THE MIDI OF A SHOC WHAT ABO THAT IS OKAY?
BUT... THAT'S NOT ALL TOHYA'S FAULT...
OH? IT ISN'T?
I'D LIKE TO HEAR MORE.
HOW LAME TO LET PERSONAL MATTERS AFFECT YOUR WORK.

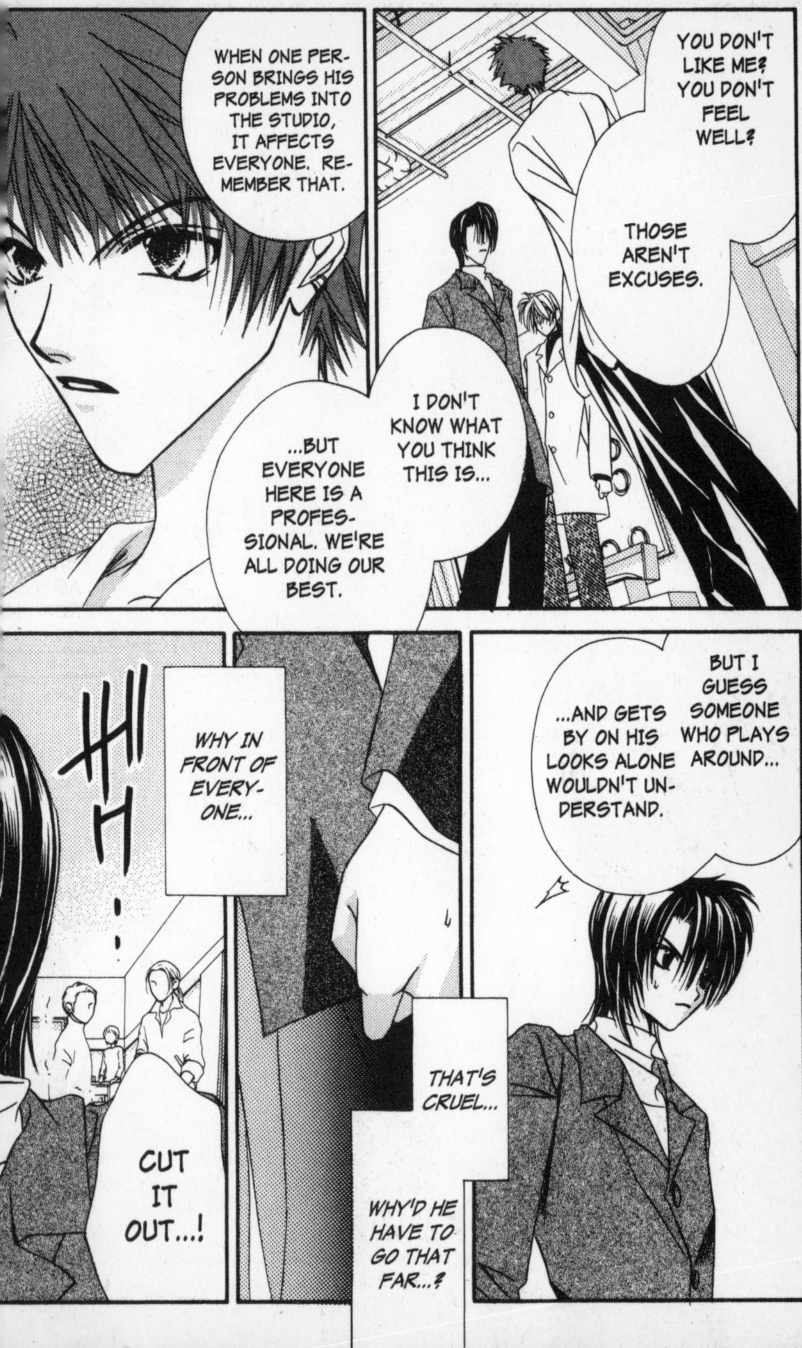
YOU DON'T LIKE ME? YOU DON'T FEEL WELL?
THOSE AREN'T EXCUSES.
I DON'T KNOW WHAT YOU THINK THIS IS...
...BUT EVERYONE HERE IS A PROFES-SIONAL. WE'RE ALL DOING OUR BEST.
WHEN ONE PER-SON BRINGS HIS PROBLEMS INTO THE STUDIO, IT AFFECTS EVERYONE. RE-MEMBER THAT.
BUT I GUESS SOMEONE WHO PLAYS AROUND...
...AND GETS BY ON HIS LOOKS ALONE WOULDN'T UN-DERSTAND.
WHY IN FRONT OF EVERY-ONE...
THAT'S CRUEL...
WHY'D HE HAVE TO GO THAT FAR...?
CUT IT OUT...!

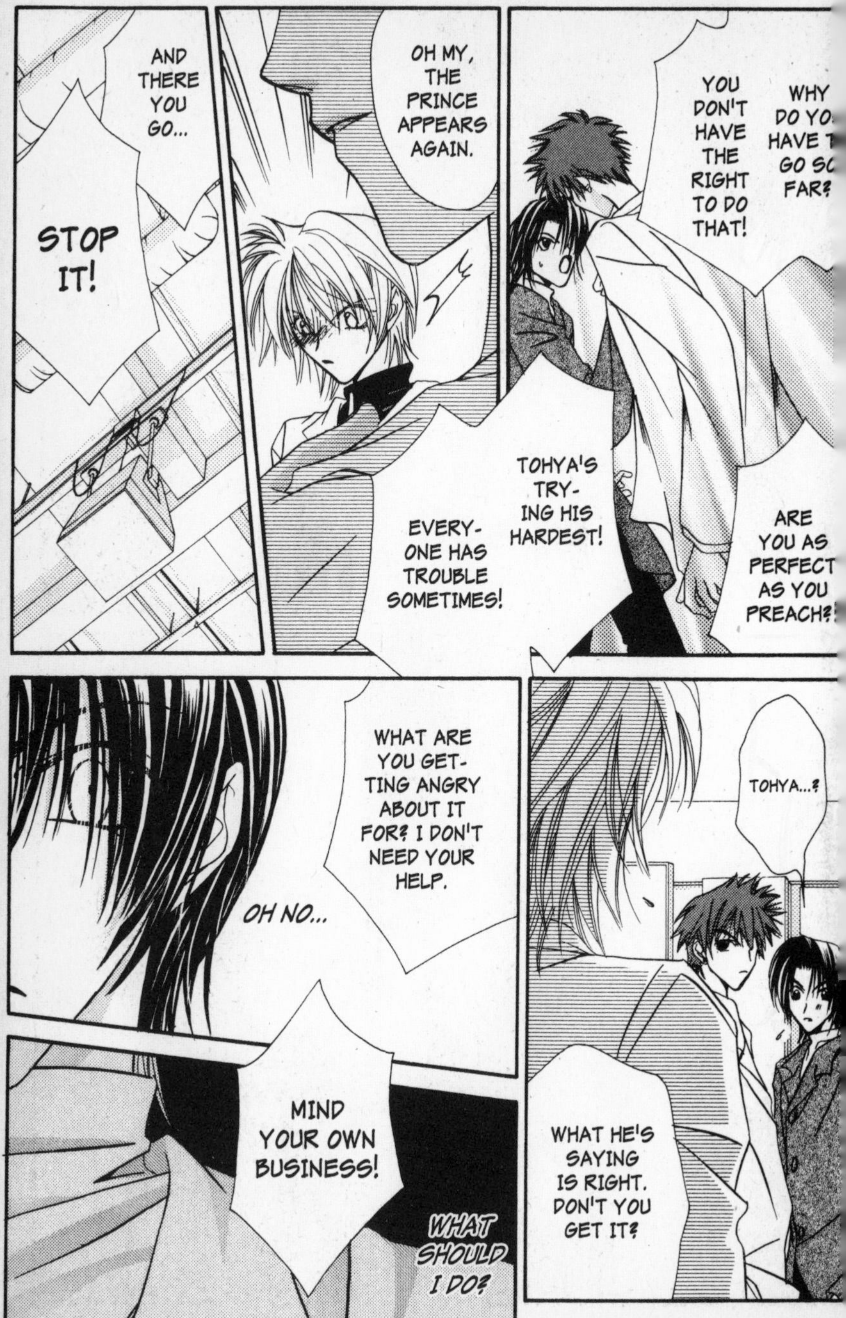
WHY DO YO HAVE T GO SC FAR?
YOU DON'T HAVE THE RIGHT TO DO THAT!
ARE YOU AS PERFECT AS YOU PREACH?!
TOHYA'S TRYING HIS HARDEST!
OH MY, THE PRINCE APPEARS AGAIN.
EVERYONE HAS TROUBLE SOMETIMES!
AND THERE YOU GO...
STOP IT!
TOHYA...?
WHAT HE'S SAYING IS RIGHT. DON'T YOU GET IT?
WHAT ARE YOU GETTING ANGRY ABOUT IT FOR? I DON'T NEED YOUR HELP.
OH NO...
MIND YOUR OWN BUSINESS!
WHAT SHOULD I DO?

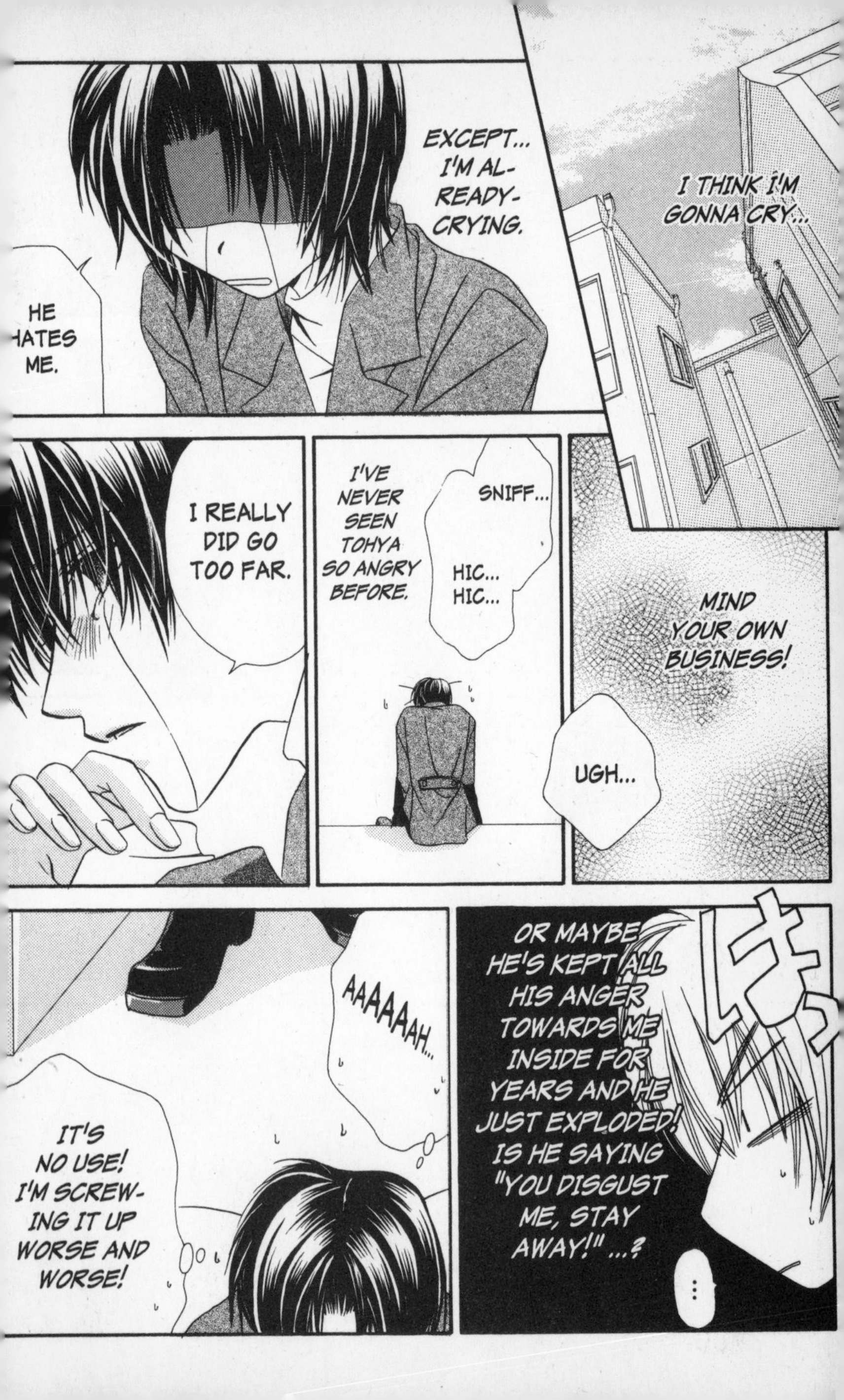
I THINK I'M GONNA CRY...
EXCEPT... I'M AL-READY-CRYING.
HE HATES ME.
MIND YOUR OWN BUSINESS!
UGH...
SNIFF...
HIC... HIC...
I'VE NEVER SEEN TOHYA SO ANGRY BEFORE.
I REALLY DID GO TOO FAR.
はっ
OR MAYBE HE'S KEPT ALL HIS ANGER TOWARDS ME INSIDE FOR YEARS AND HE JUST EXPLODED! IS HE SAYING "YOU DISGUST ME, STAY AWAY!" ...?
...
AAAAAAH...
IT'S NO USE! I'M SCREW-ING IT UP WORSE AND WORSE!

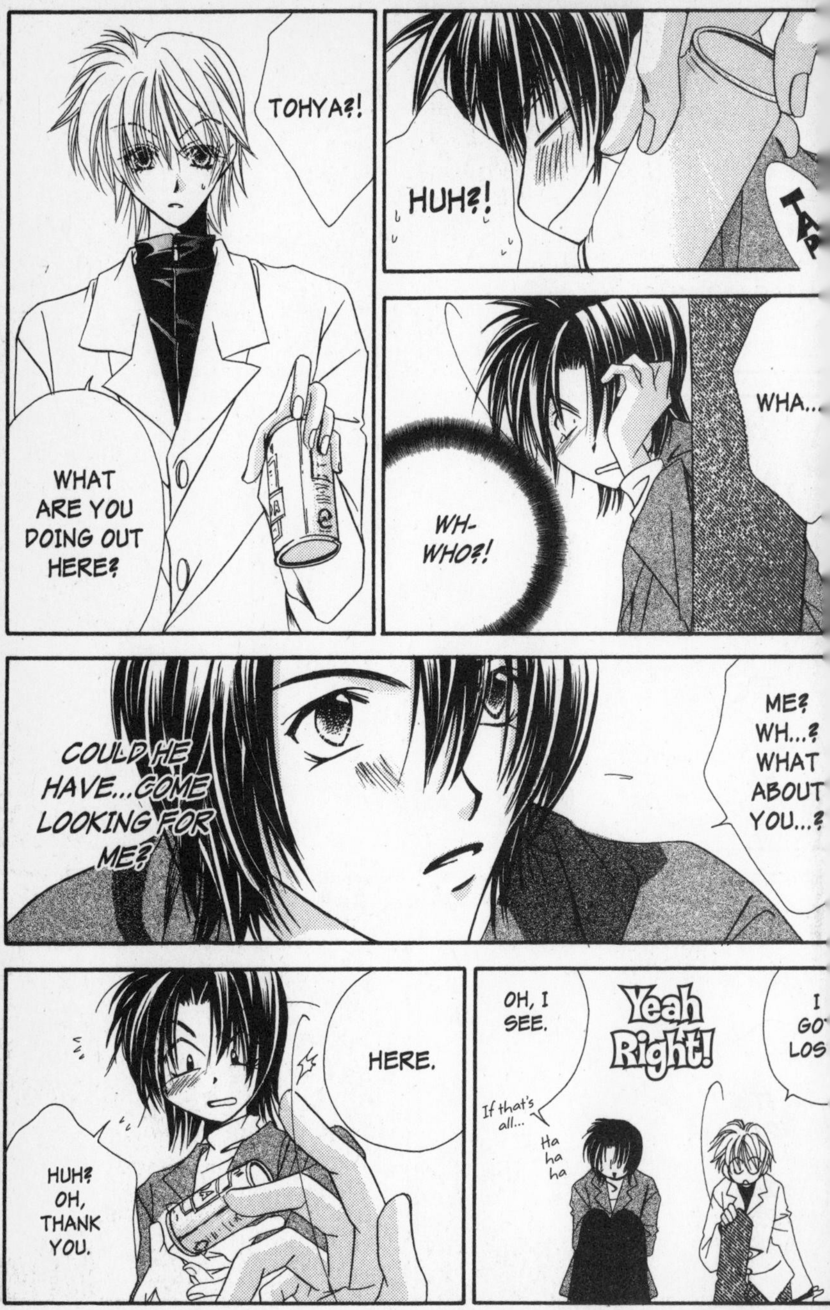
TAP
HUH?!
WHA...
WH-WHO?!
TOHYA?!
WHAT ARE YOU DOING OUT HERE?
ME? WH...? WHAT ABOUT YOU...?
COULD HE HAVE...COME LOOKING FOR ME?
I GO LOS
Yeah Right!
OH, I SEE.
If that's all...
Ha ha ha
HERE.
HUH? OH, THANK YOU.

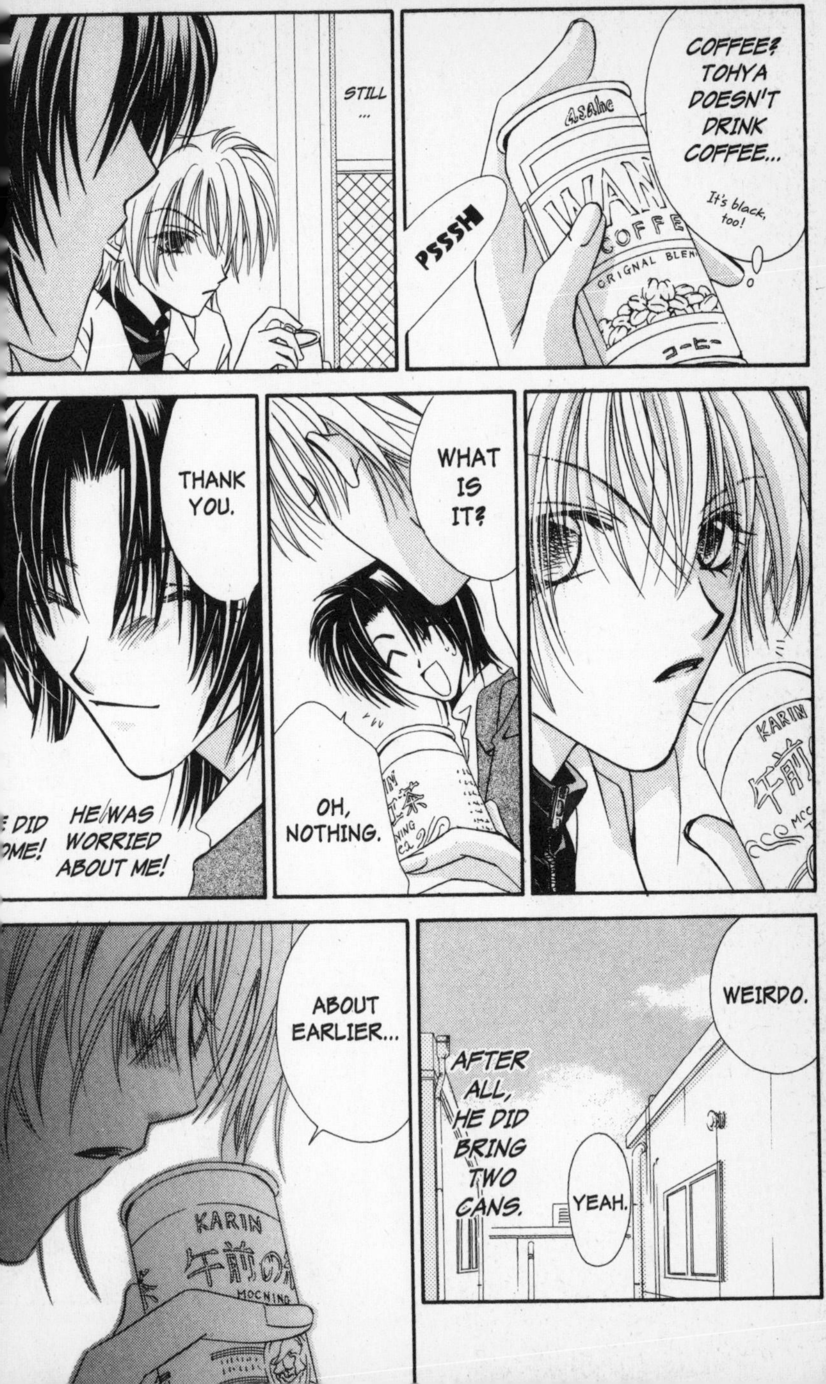
COFFEE? TOHYA DOESN'T DRINK COFFEE...
It's black, too!
PSSSH
STILL ...
WHAT IS IT?
OH, NOTHING.
THANK YOU.
HE WAS WORRIED ABOUT ME!
WEIRDO.
AFTER ALL, HE DID BRING TWO CANS.
YEAH.
ABOUT EARLIER...

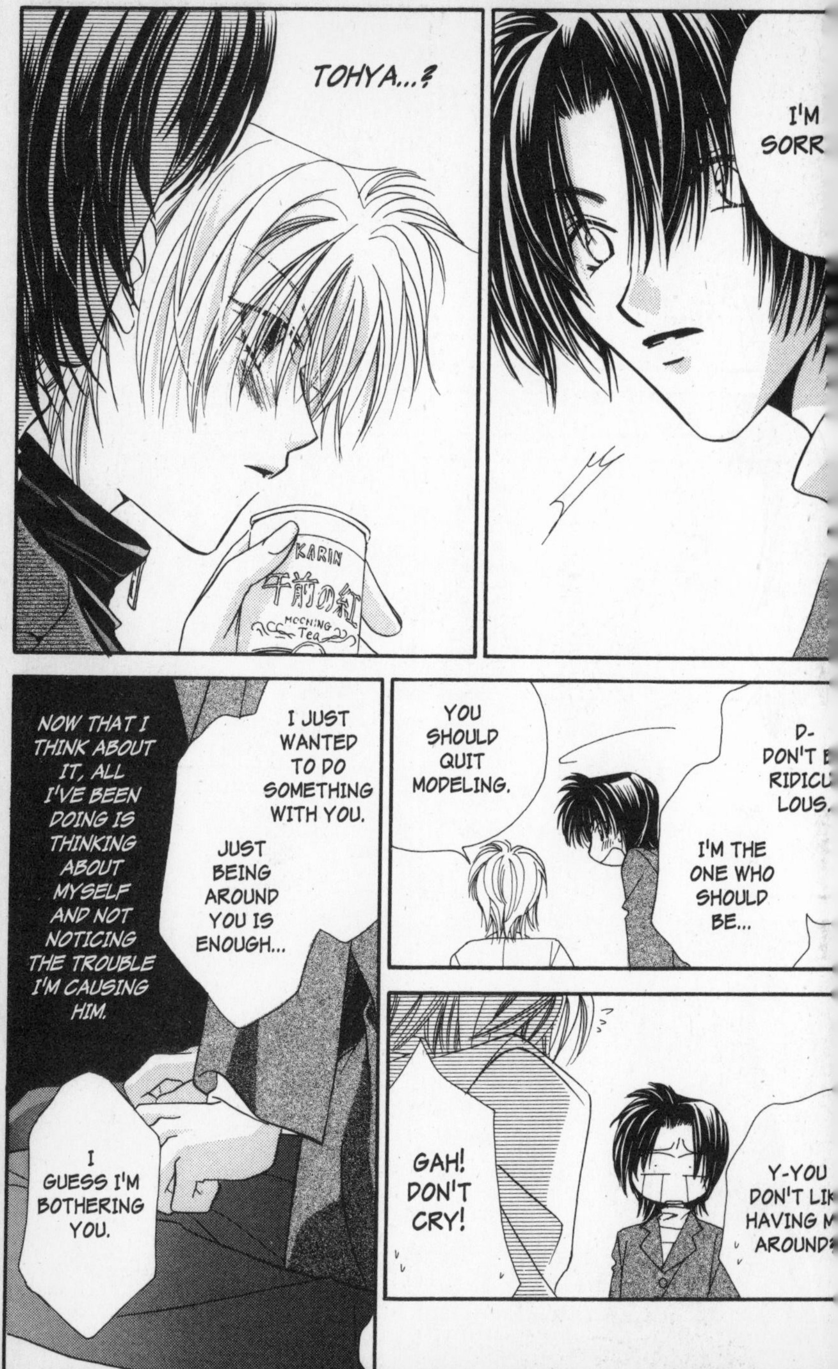
I'M SORR
TOHYA...?
KARIN
D-DON'T B RIDICU LOUS.
I'M THE ONE WHO SHOULD BE...
YOU SHOULD QUIT MODELING.
Y-YOU DON'T LIK HAVING M AROUND?
GAH! DON'T CRY!
I JUST WANTED TO DO SOMETHING WITH YOU.
JUST BEING AROUND YOU IS ENOUGH...
NOW THAT I THINK ABOUT IT, ALL I'VE BEEN DOING IS THINKING ABOUT MYSELF AND NOT NOTICING THE TROUBLE I'M CAUSING HIM.
I GUESS I'M BOTHERING YOU.

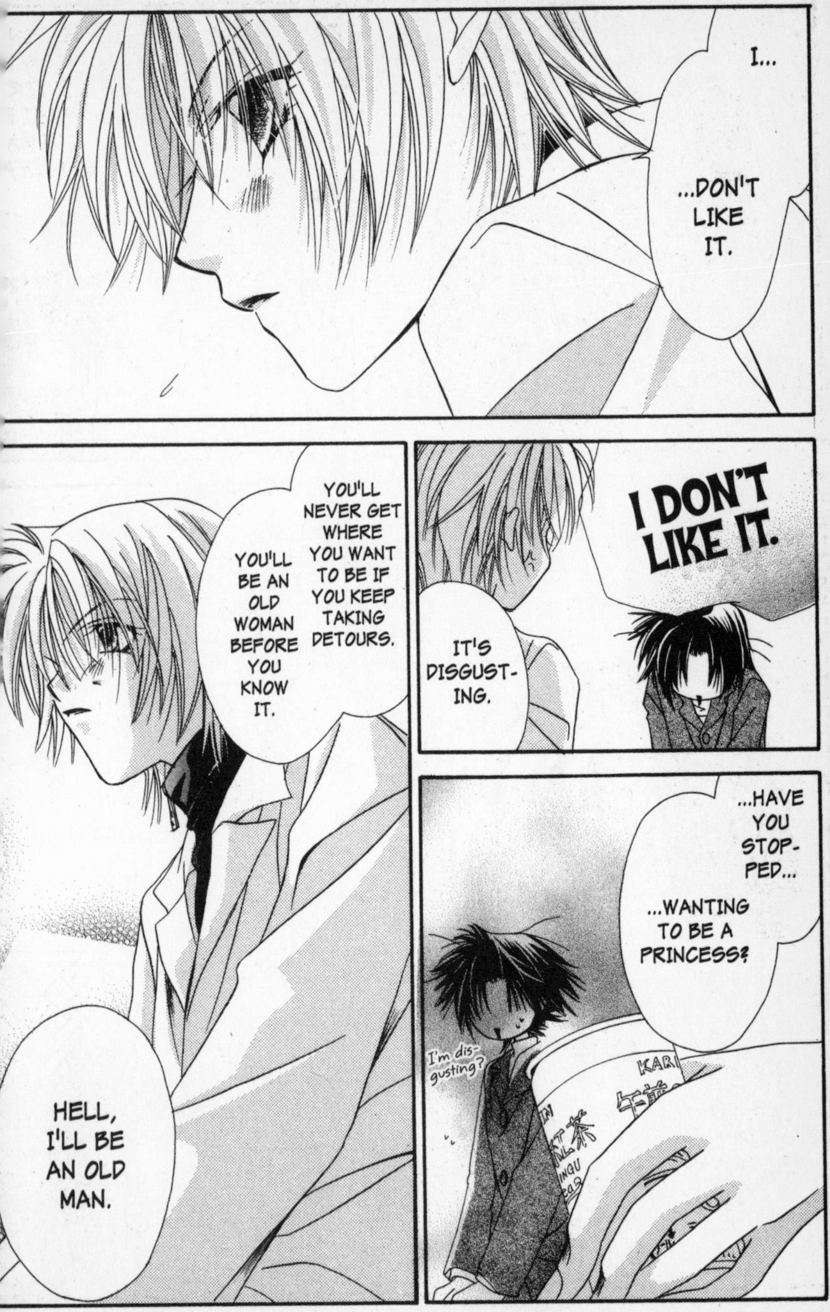
I...
...DON'T LIKE IT.
I DON'T LIKE IT.
IT'S DISGUST-ING.
...HAVE YOU STOP-PED...
...WANTING TO BE A PRINCESS?
I'm dis-gusting?
YOU'LL NEVER GET WHERE YOU WANT TO BE IF YOU KEEP TAKING DETOURS.
YOU'LL BE AN OLD WOMAN BEFORE YOU KNOW IT.
HELL, I'LL BE AN OLD MAN.

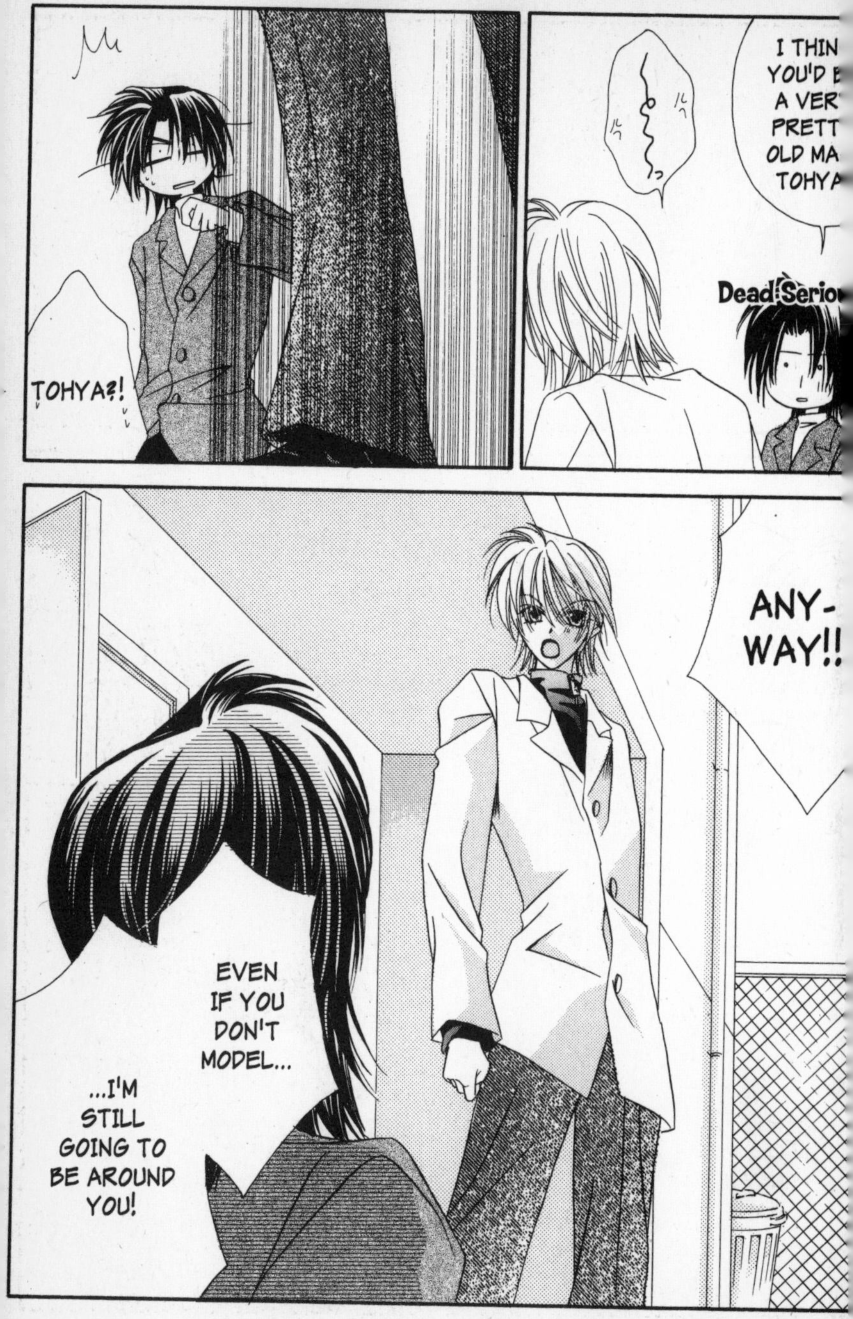
I THIN YOU'D B A VER PRETT OLD MA TOHYA
Dead Serio
TOHYA?!
ANY-WAY!!
EVEN IF YOU DON'T MODEL...
...I'M STILL GOING TO BE AROUND YOU!

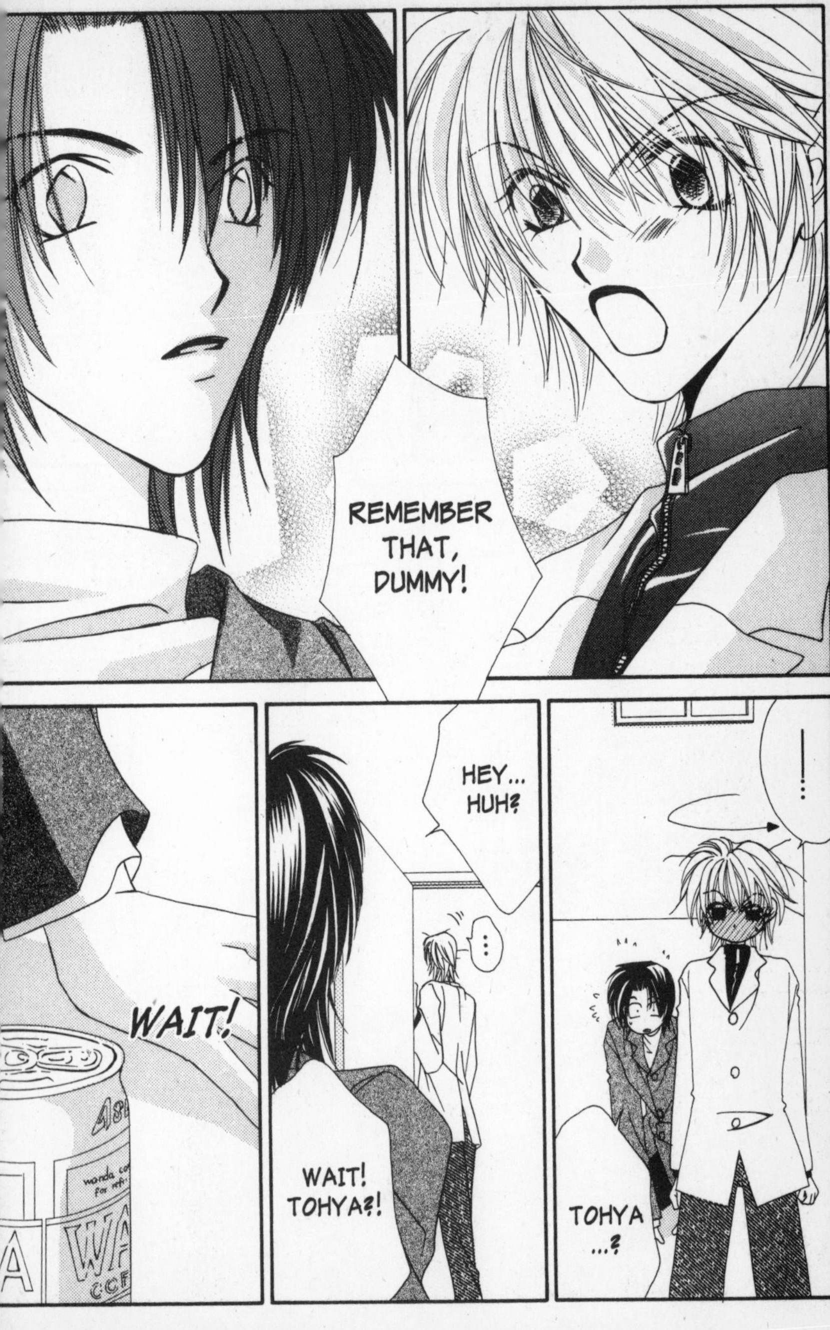
REMEMBER THAT, DUMMY!
...!
TOHYA ...?
HEY... HUH?
...
WAIT! TOHYA?!
WAIT!

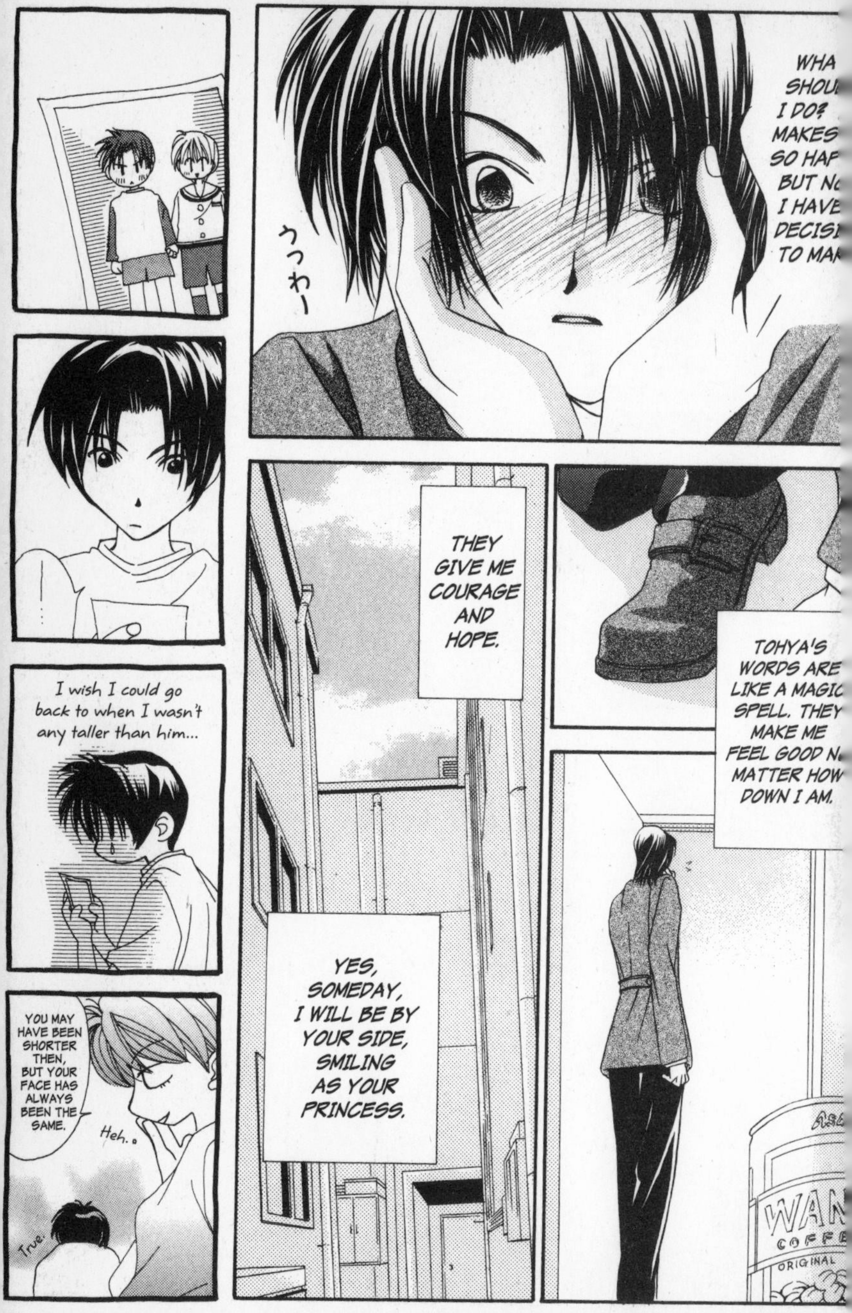
WHA
SHOU
I DO?
MAKES
SO HAP
BUT N
I HAVE
DECISI
TO MA
うっわー
TOHYA'S WORDS ARE LIKE A MAGIC SPELL. THEY MAKE ME FEEL GOOD N MATTER HOW DOWN I AM.
WAN
COFFE
ORIGINAL
THEY GIVE ME COURAGE AND HOPE.
YES, SOMEDAY, I WILL BE BY YOUR SIDE, SMILING AS YOUR PRINCESS.
I wish I could go back to when I wasn't any taller than him...
YOU MAY HAVE BEEN SHORTER THEN, BUT YOUR FACE HAS ALWAYS BEEN THE SAME.
Heh.
True.

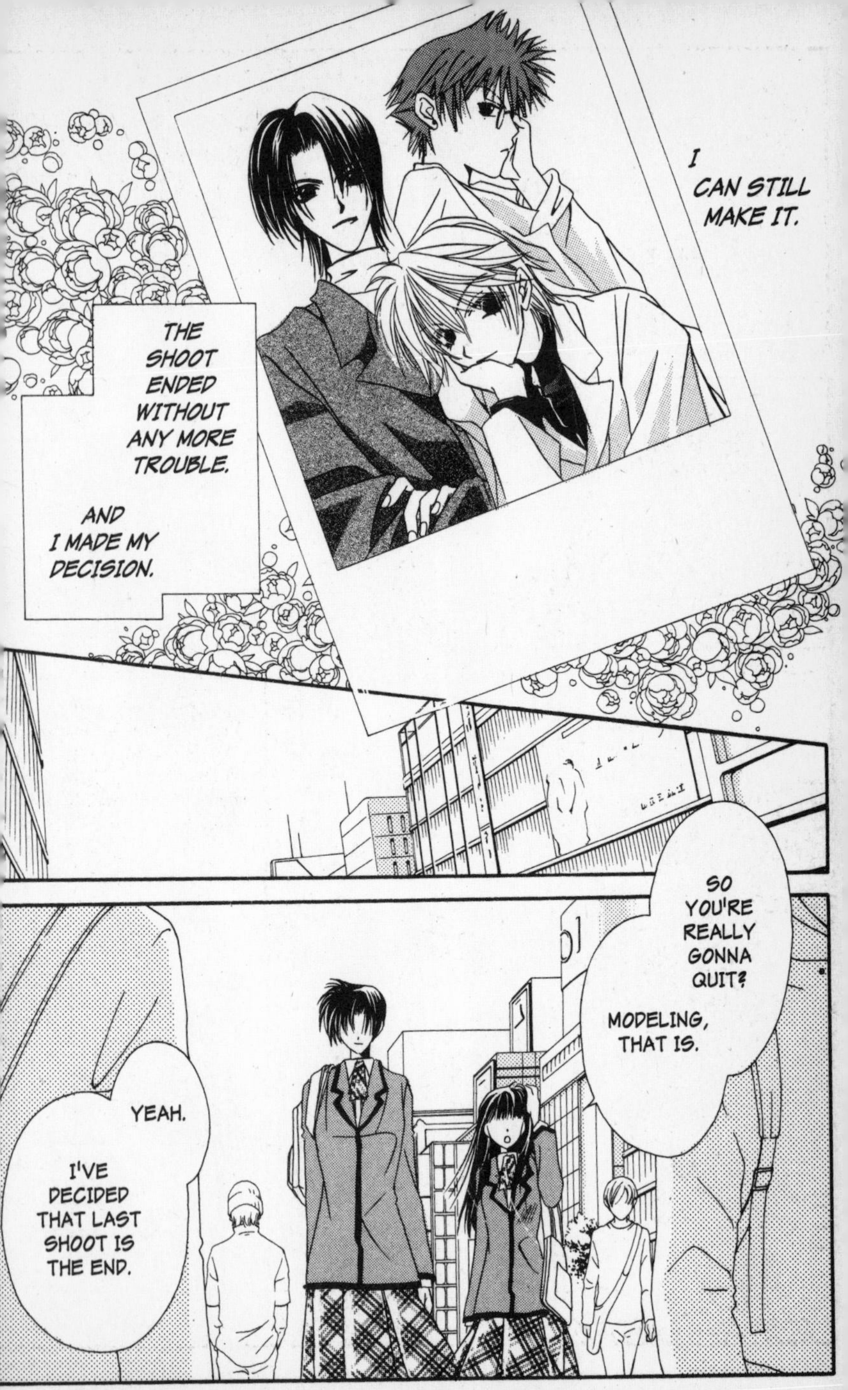

I CAN STILL MAKE IT.
THE SHOOT ENDED WITHOUT ANY MORE TROUBLE.
AND I MADE MY DECISION.
SO YOU'RE REALLY GONNA QUIT?
MODELING, THAT IS.
YEAH.
I'VE DECIDED THAT LAST SHOOT IS THE END.

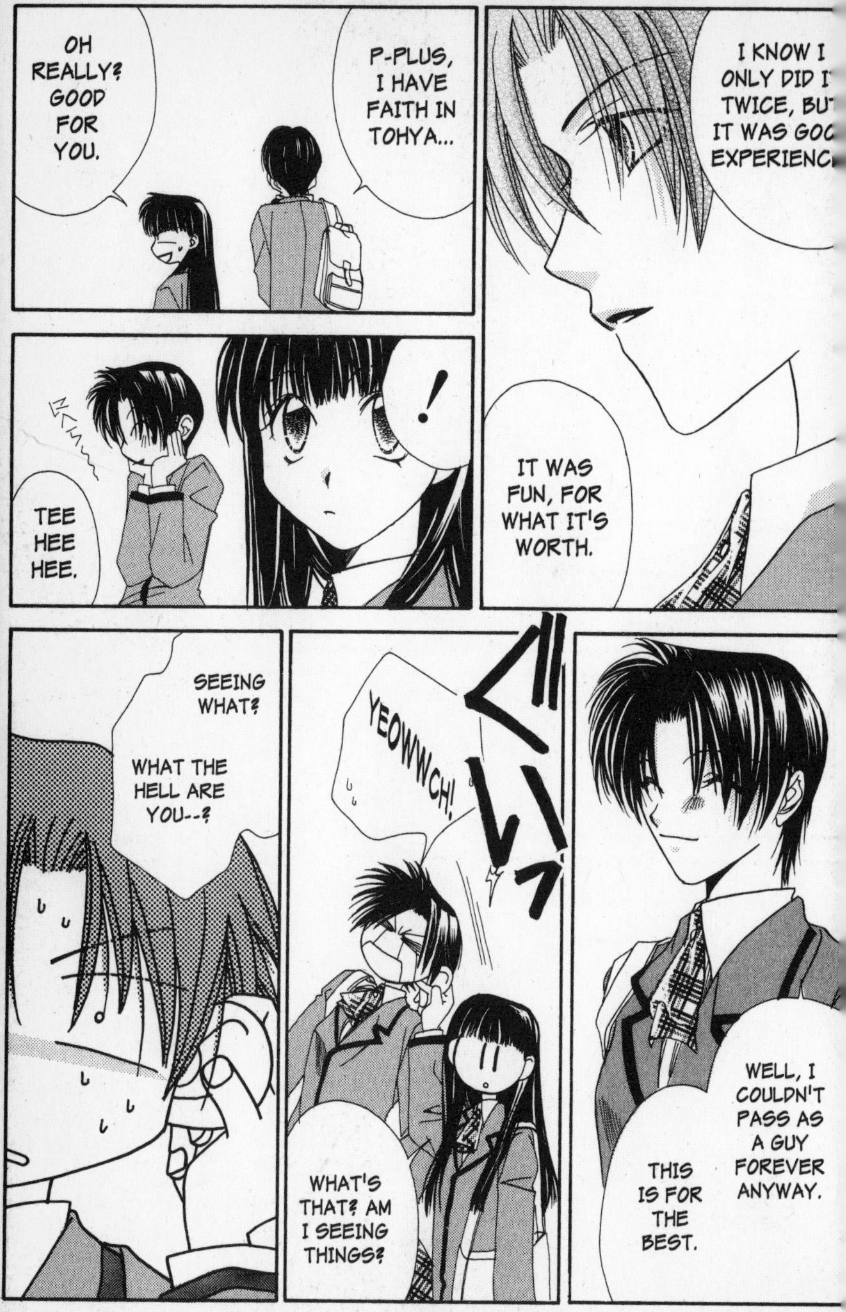

I KNOW I ONLY DID IT TWICE, BUT IT WAS GOO EXPERIENC
IT WAS FUN, FOR WHAT IT'S WORTH.
P-PLUS, I HAVE FAITH IN TOHYA...
OH REALLY? GOOD FOR YOU.
!
TEE HEE HEE.
WELL, I COULDN'T PASS AS A GUY FOREVER ANYWAY.
THIS IS FOR THE BEST.
YEOWWCH!
WHAT'S THAT? AM I SEEING THINGS?
SEEING WHAT?
WHAT THE HELL ARE YOU--?

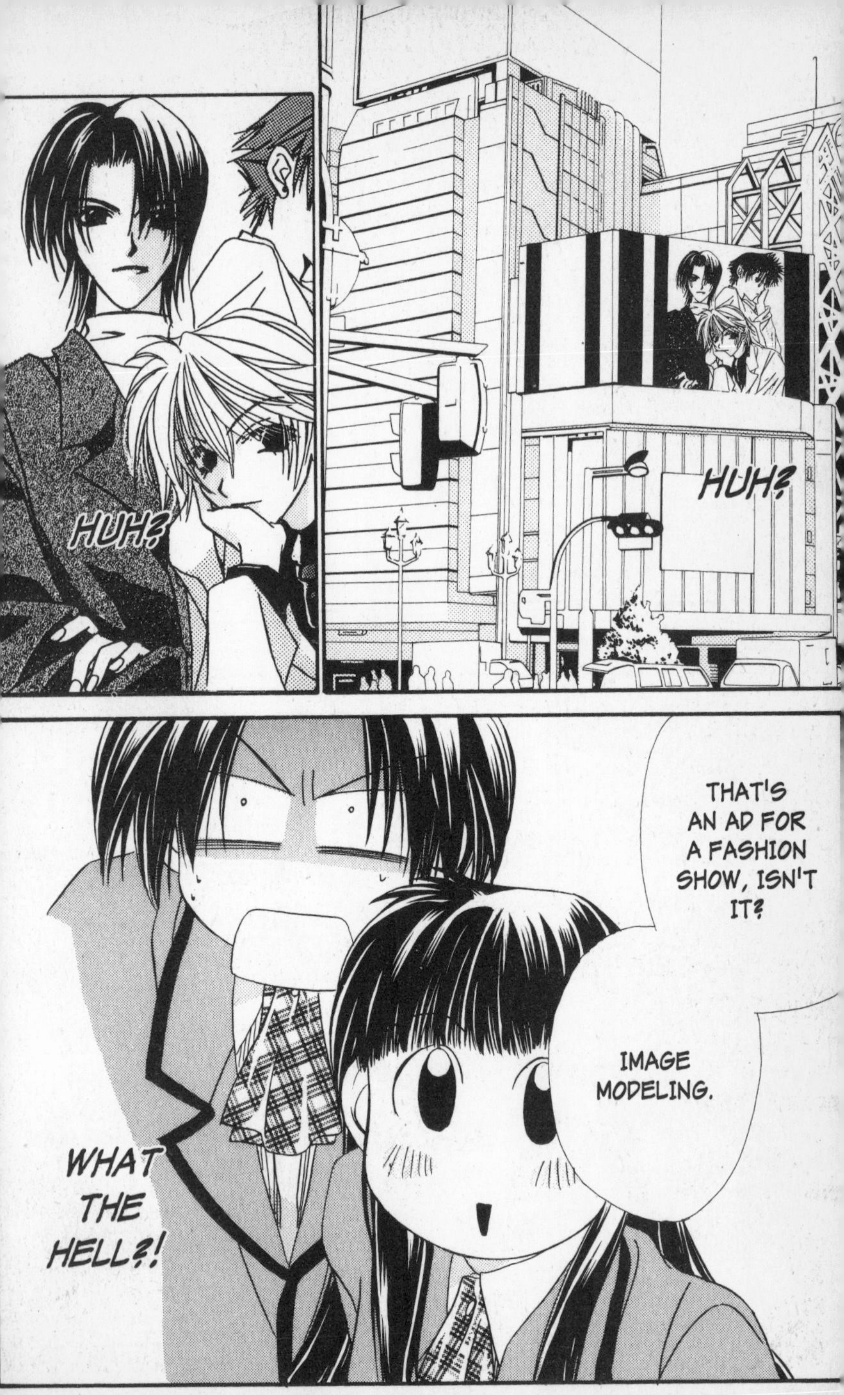
HUH?
HUH?
THAT'S AN AD FOR A FASHION SHOW, ISN'T IT?
IMAGE MODELING.
WHAT THE HELL?!

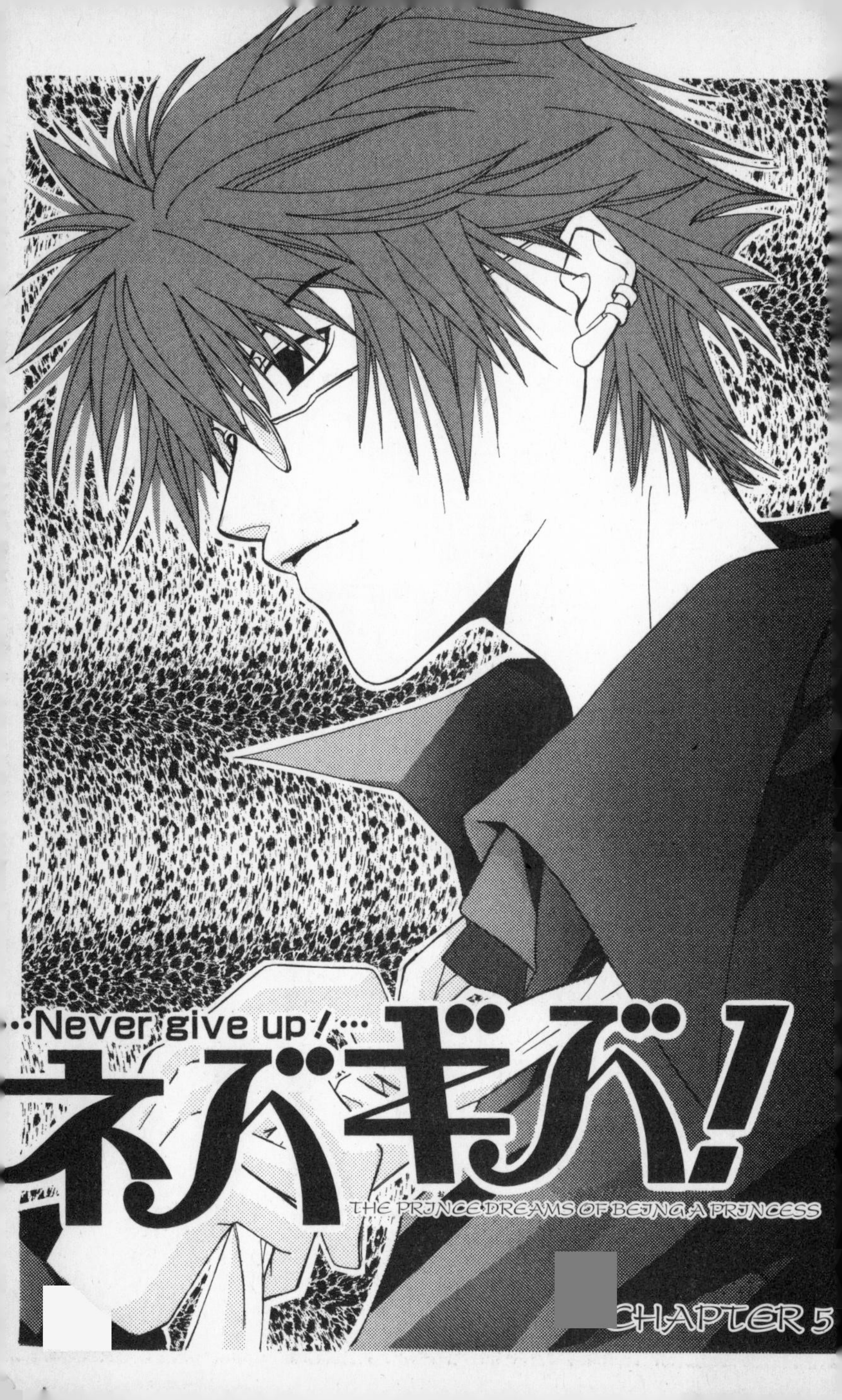

···Never give up!···
ネバギバ!
THE PRINCE DREAMS OF BEING A PRINCESS
CHAPTER 5

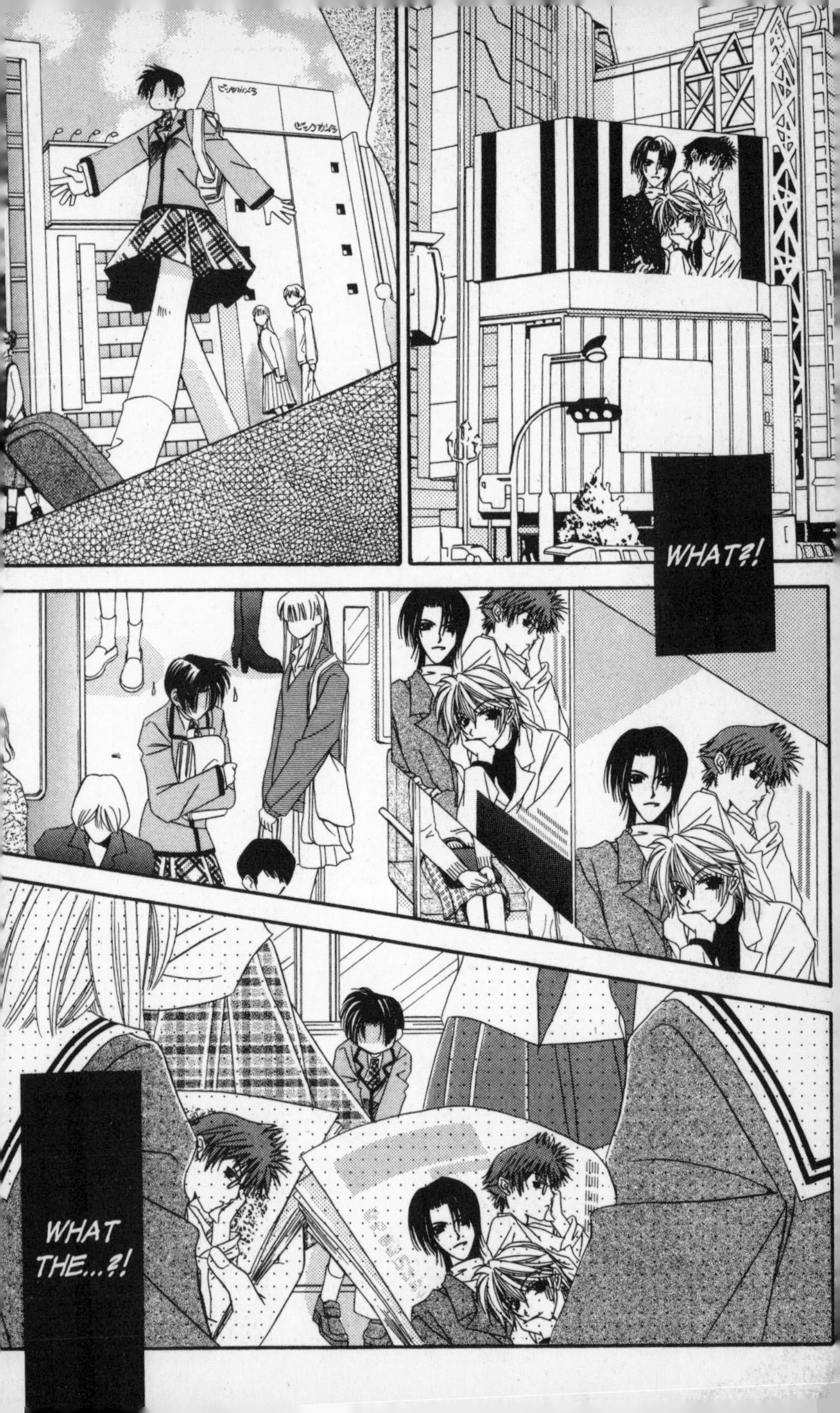
WHAT?!
WHAT THE...?!

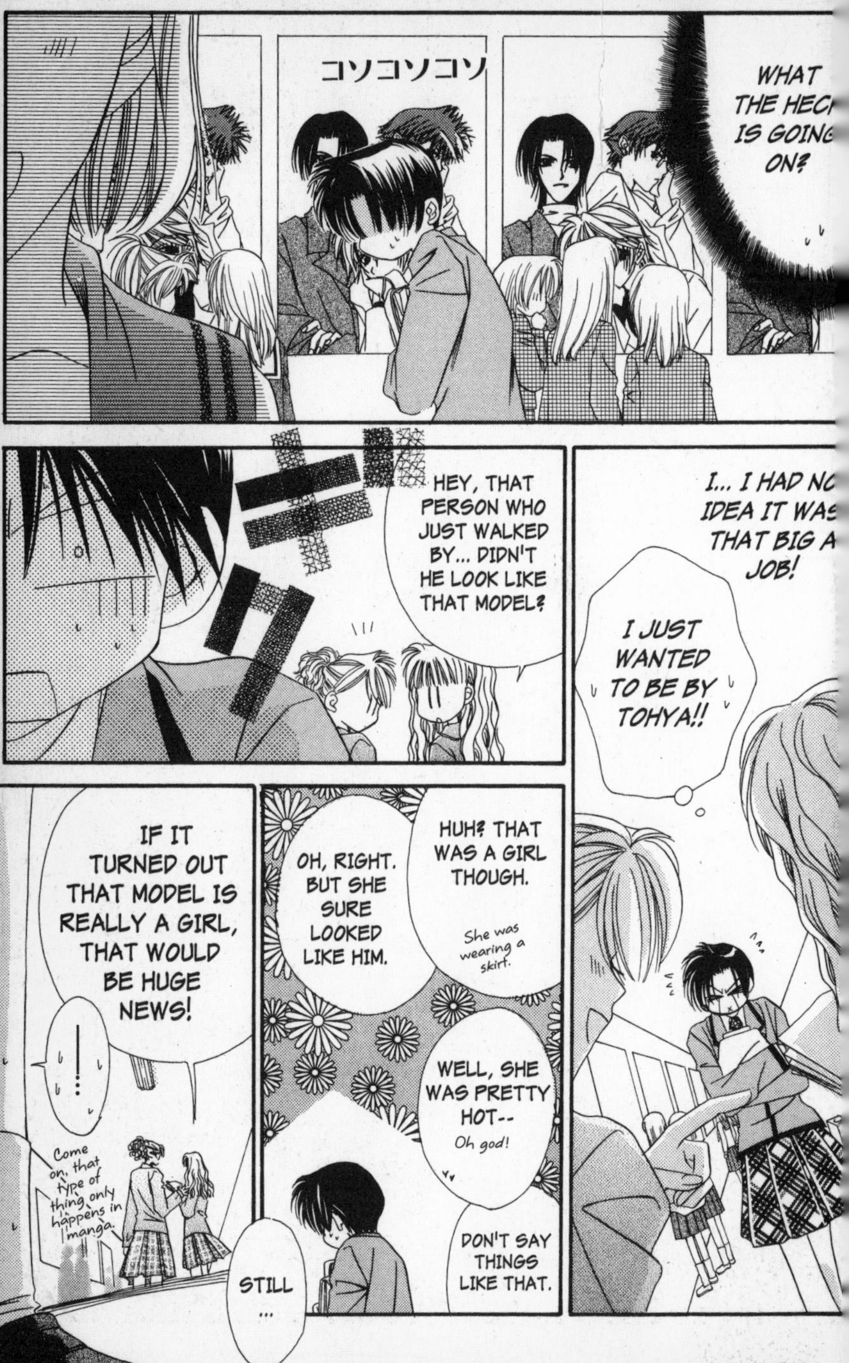
WHAT THE HEC IS GOING ON?
コソコソコソ
I... I HAD NO IDEA IT WAS THAT BIG A JOB!
I JUST WANTED TO BE BY TOHYA!!
HEY, THAT PERSON WHO JUST WALKED BY... DIDN'T HE LOOK LIKE THAT MODEL?
HUH? THAT WAS A GIRL THOUGH.
She was wearing a skirt.
OH, RIGHT. BUT SHE SURE LOOKED LIKE HIM.
WELL, SHE WAS PRETTY HOT--
Oh god!
DON'T SAY THINGS LIKE THAT.
STILL ...
IF IT TURNED OUT THAT MODEL IS REALLY A GIRL, THAT WOULD BE HUGE NEWS!
...!
Come on, that type of thing only happens in manga.

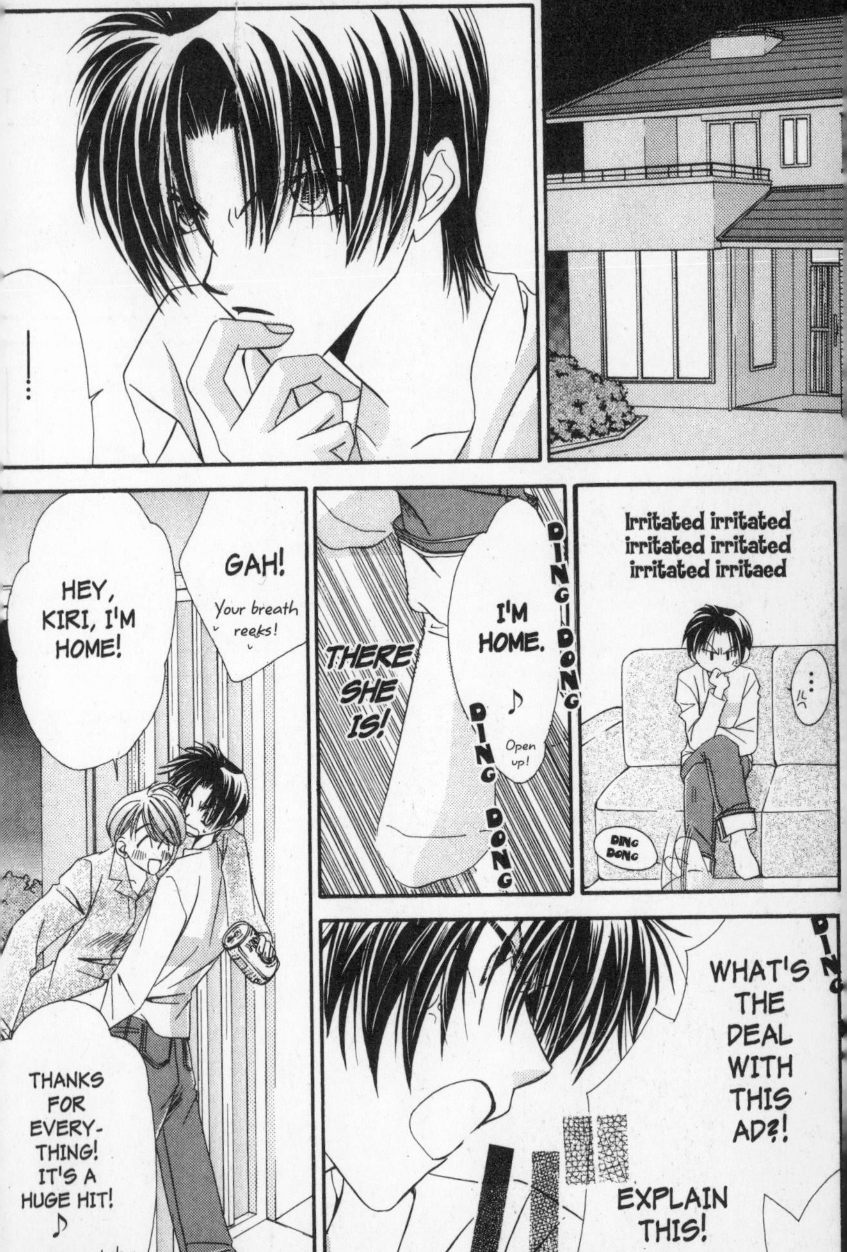

…
Irritated irritated irritated irritated irritated irritaed
…ん
DING DONG
DING DONG
I'M HOME. ♪
Open up!
DING DONG
THERE SHE IS!
DING
WHAT'S THE DEAL WITH THIS AD?!
EXPLAIN THIS!
HEY, KIRI, I'M HOME!
GAH!
Your breath reeks!
THANKS FOR EVERYTHING! IT'S A HUGE HIT! ♪
Heh heh heh...

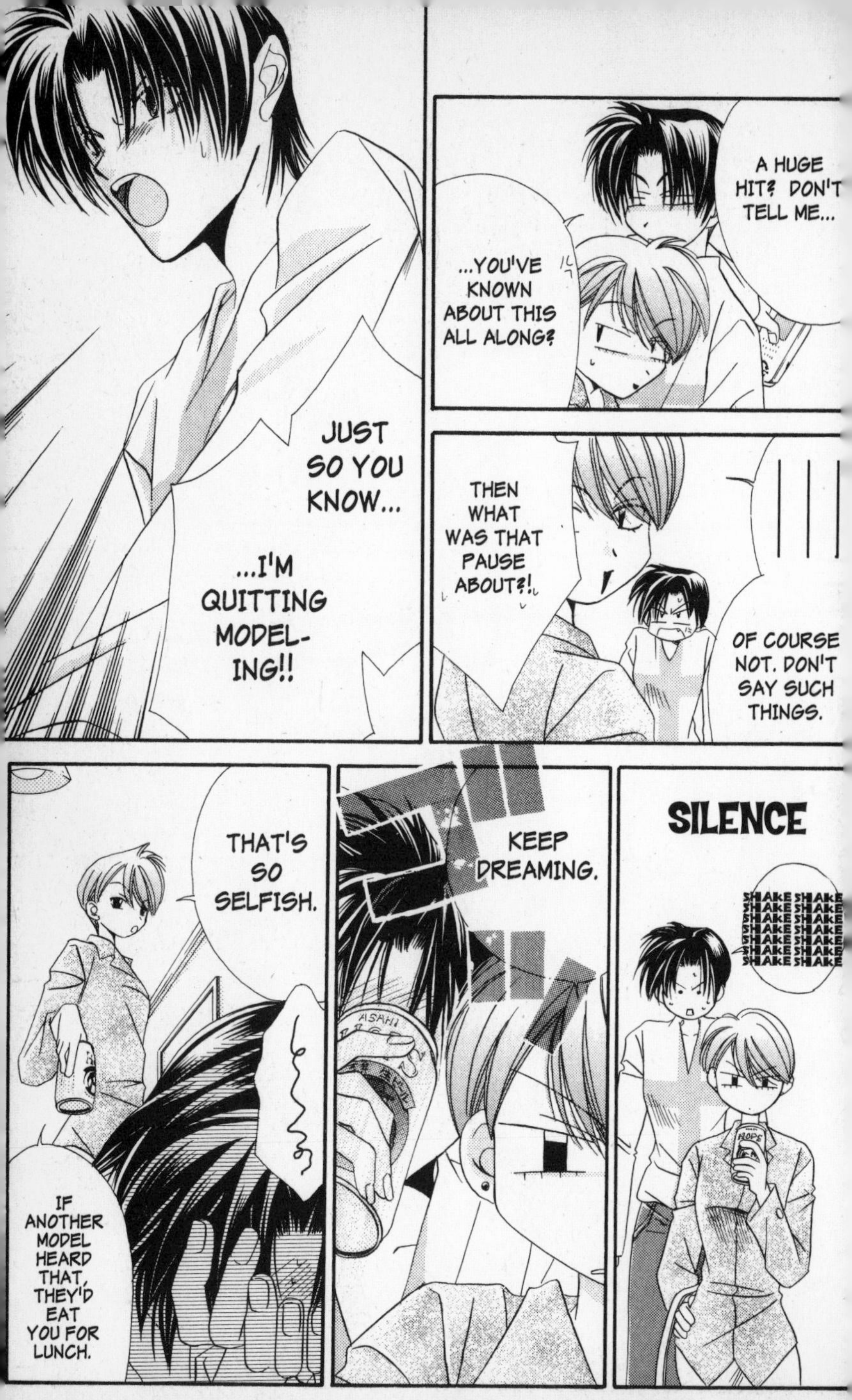
A HUGE HIT? DON'T TELL ME...
...YOU'VE KNOWN ABOUT THIS ALL ALONG?
OF COURSE NOT. DON'T SAY SUCH THINGS.
THEN WHAT WAS THAT PAUSE ABOUT?!
JUST SO YOU KNOW...
...I'M QUITTING MODEL-ING!!
SILENCE
SHAKE SHAKE SHAKE SHAKE SHAKE SHAKE SHAKE SHAKE SHAKE SHAKE SHAKE SHAKE SHAKE SHAKE
KEEP DREAMING.
THAT'S SO SELFISH.
IF ANOTHER MODEL HEARD THAT, THEY'D EAT YOU FOR LUNCH.

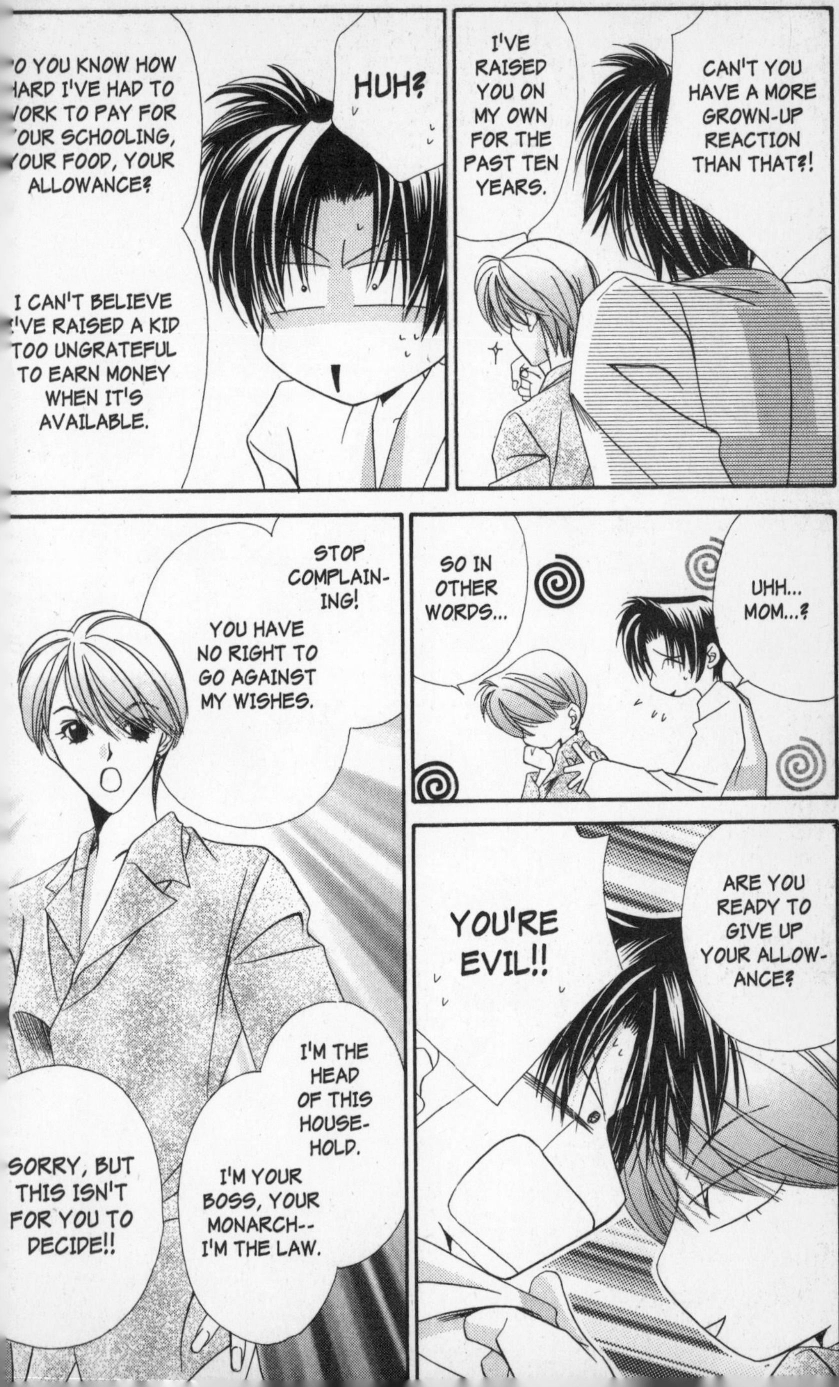

CAN'T YOU HAVE A MORE GROWN-UP REACTION THAN THAT?!
I'VE RAISED YOU ON MY OWN FOR THE PAST TEN YEARS.
HUH?
DO YOU KNOW HOW HARD I'VE HAD TO WORK TO PAY FOR YOUR SCHOOLING, YOUR FOOD, YOUR ALLOWANCE?
I CAN'T BELIEVE I'VE RAISED A KID TOO UNGRATEFUL TO EARN MONEY WHEN IT'S AVAILABLE.
UHH... MOM...?
SO IN OTHER WORDS...
ARE YOU READY TO GIVE UP YOUR ALLOW-ANCE?
YOU'RE EVIL!!
STOP COMPLAIN-ING!
YOU HAVE NO RIGHT TO GO AGAINST MY WISHES.
I'M THE HEAD OF THIS HOUSE-HOLD.
I'M YOUR BOSS, YOUR MONARCH-- I'M THE LAW.
SORRY, BUT THIS ISN'T FOR YOU TO DECIDE!!

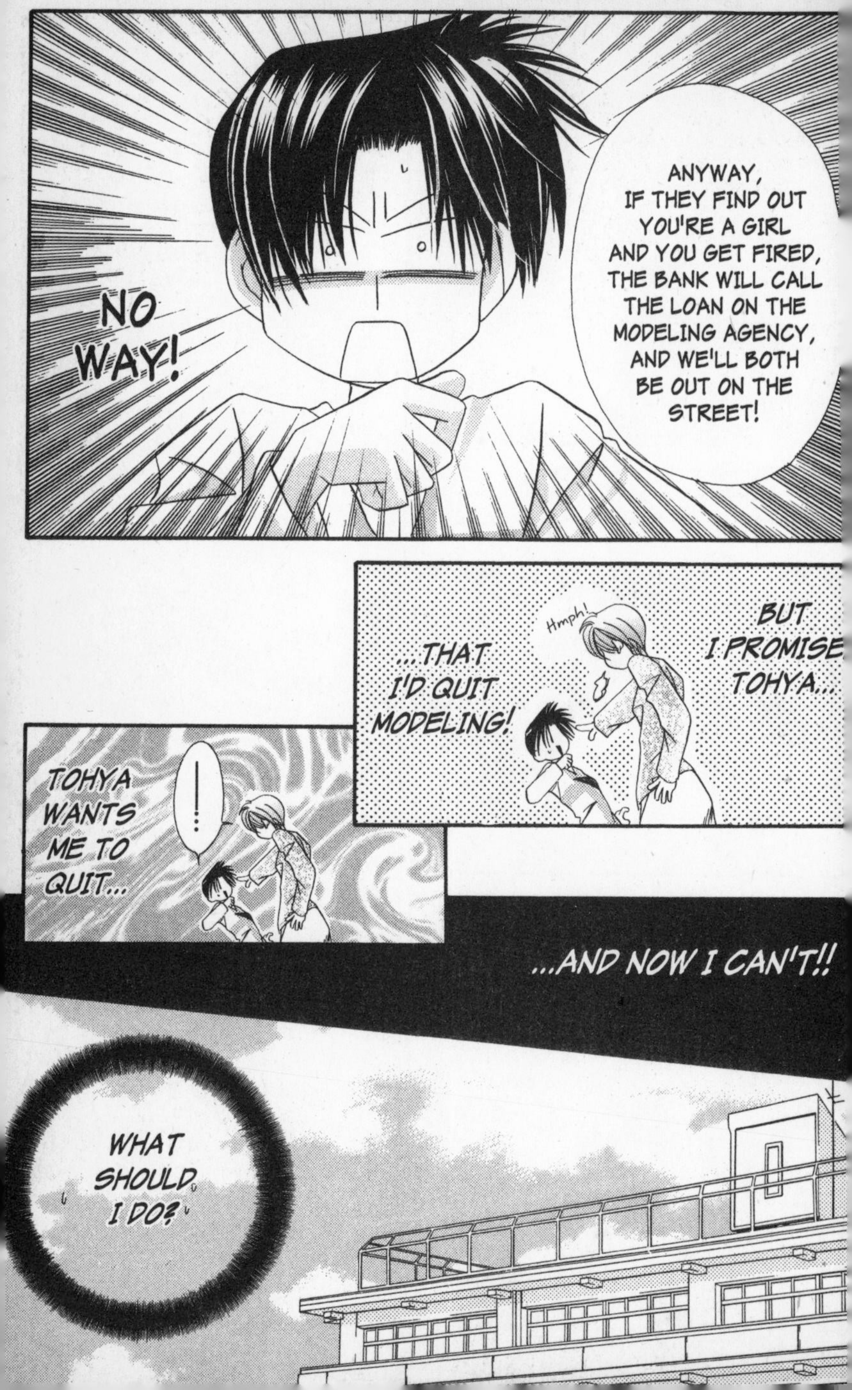

ANYWAY, IF THEY FIND OUT YOU'RE A GIRL AND YOU GET FIRED, THE BANK WILL CALL THE LOAN ON THE MODELING AGENCY, AND WE'LL BOTH BE OUT ON THE STREET!
NO WAY!
BUT I PROMISE TOHYA...
Hmph!
...THAT I'D QUIT MODELING!
TOHYA WANTS ME TO QUIT...
!
...AND NOW I CAN'T!!
WHAT SHOULD I DO?

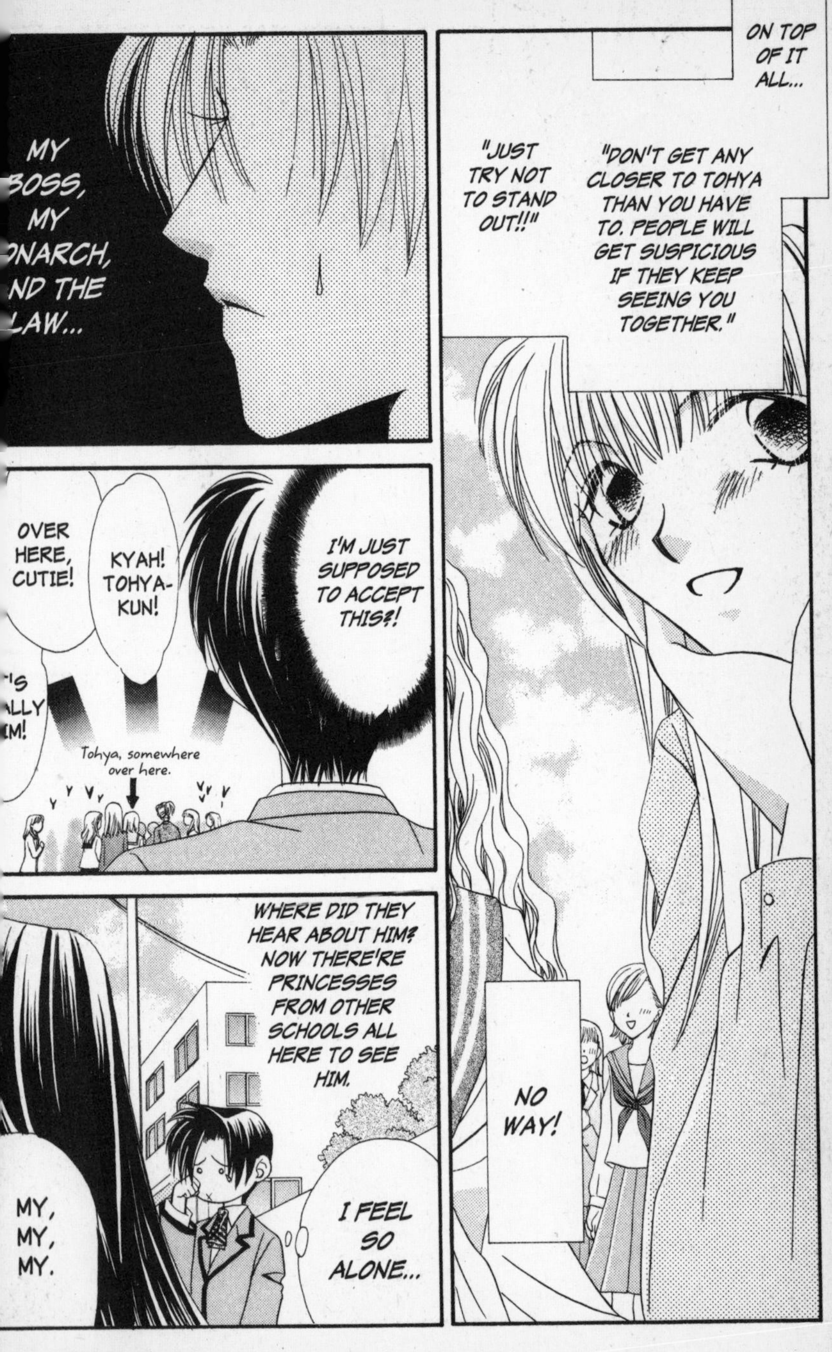
ON TOP OF IT ALL...
"DON'T GET ANY CLOSER TO TOHYA THAN YOU HAVE TO. PEOPLE WILL GET SUSPICIOUS IF THEY KEEP SEEING YOU TOGETHER."
"JUST TRY NOT TO STAND OUT!!"
NO WAY!
MY BOSS, MY ONARCH, ND THE LAW...
I'M JUST SUPPOSED TO ACCEPT THIS?!
KYAH! TOHYA-KUN!
OVER HERE, CUTIE!
Tohya, somewhere over here.
WHERE DID THEY HEAR ABOUT HIM? NOW THERE'RE PRINCESSES FROM OTHER SCHOOLS ALL HERE TO SEE HIM.
I FEEL SO ALONE...
MY, MY, MY.

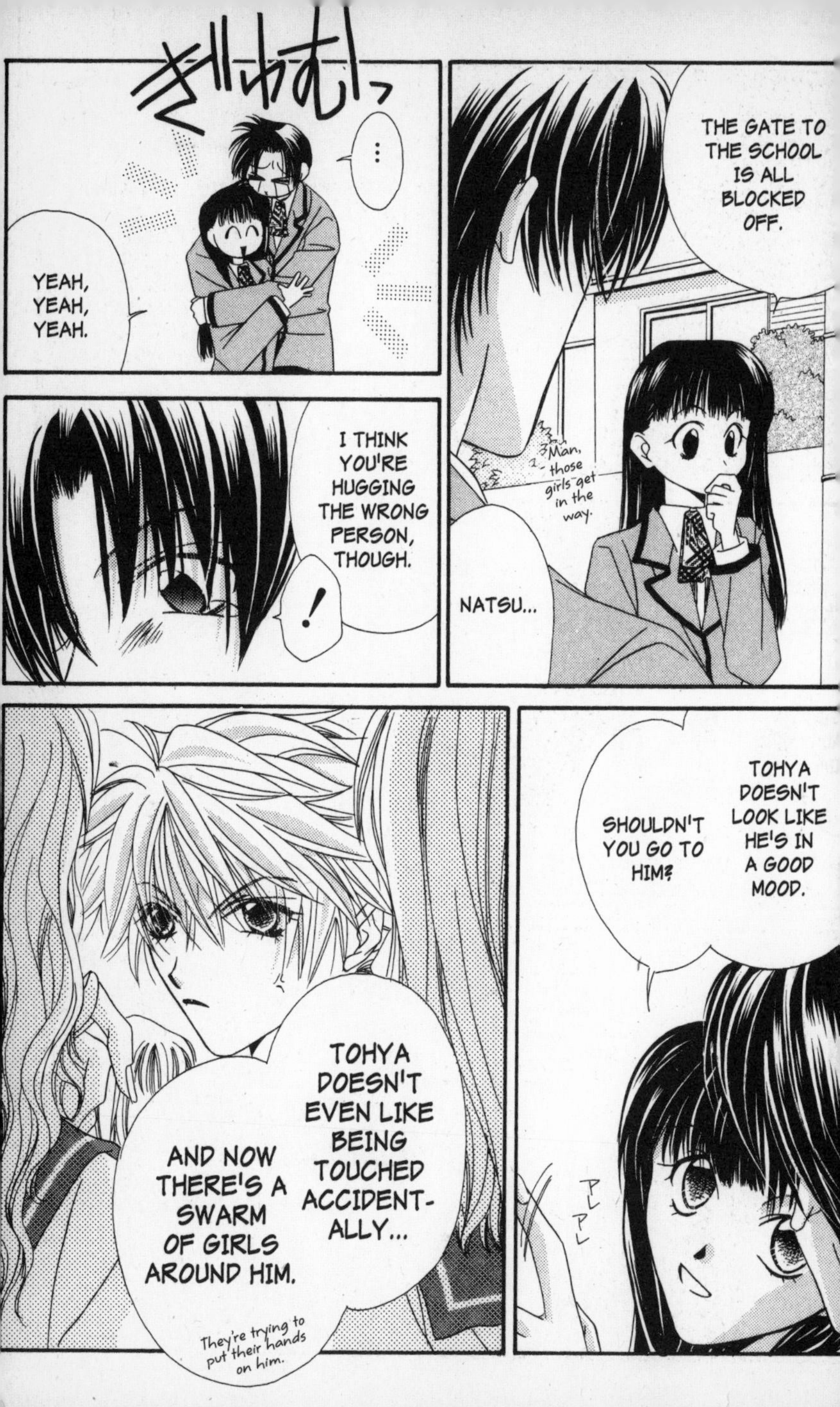
THE GATE TO THE SCHOOL IS ALL BLOCKED OFF.
Man, those girls get in the way.
NATSU...
きゅむっ
...
YEAH, YEAH, YEAH.
I THINK YOU'RE HUGGING THE WRONG PERSON, THOUGH.
!
TOHYA DOESN'T LOOK LIKE HE'S IN A GOOD MOOD.
SHOULDN'T YOU GO TO HIM?
TOHYA DOESN'T EVEN LIKE BEING TOUCHED ACCIDENT-ALLY...
AND NOW THERE'S A SWARM OF GIRLS AROUND HIM.
They're trying to put their hands on him.

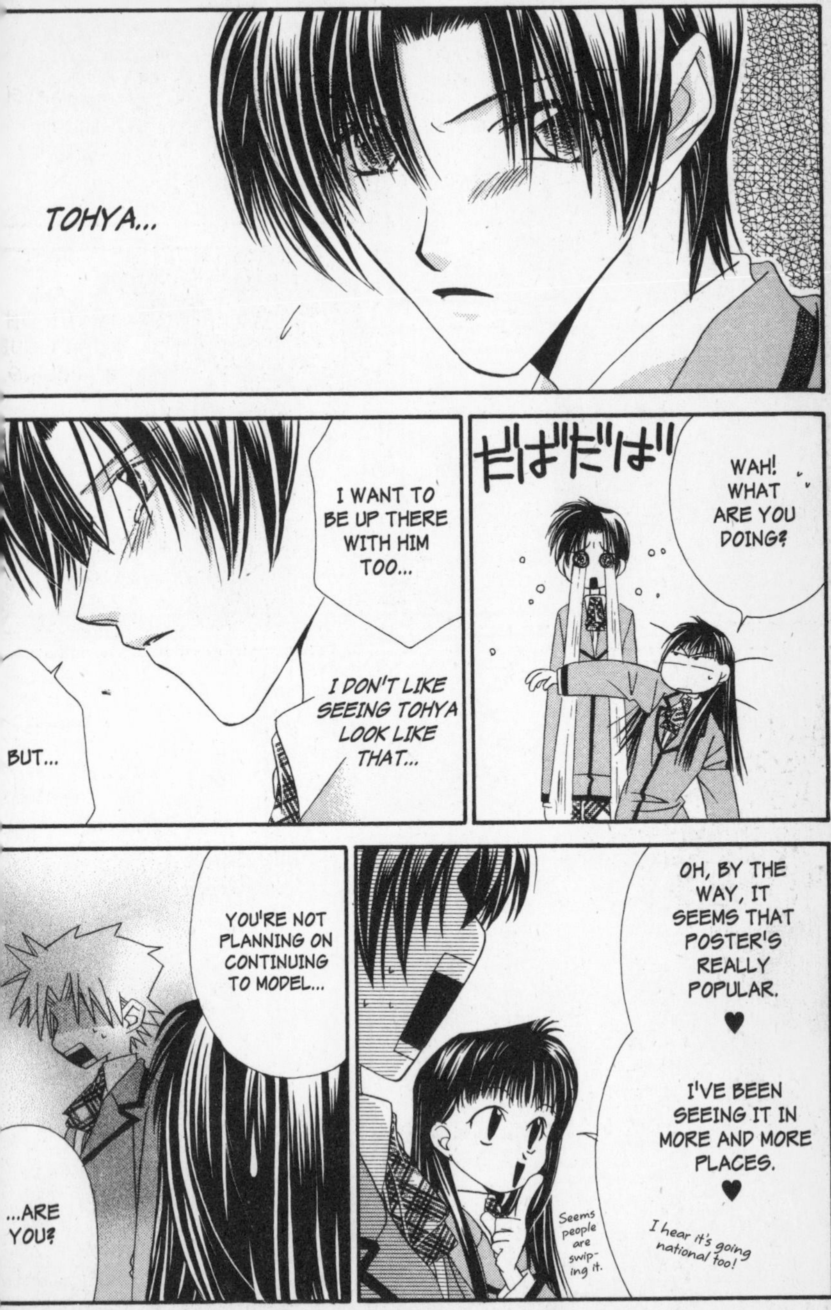
TOHYA...
だばだば
WAH! WHAT ARE YOU DOING?
I WANT TO BE UP THERE WITH HIM TOO...
I DON'T LIKE SEEING TOHYA LOOK LIKE THAT...
BUT...
OH, BY THE WAY, IT SEEMS THAT POSTER'S REALLY POPULAR. ♥
I'VE BEEN SEEING IT IN MORE AND MORE PLACES. ♥
I hear it's going national too!
Seems people are swip-ing it.
YOU'RE NOT PLANNING ON CONTINUING TO MODEL...
...ARE YOU?

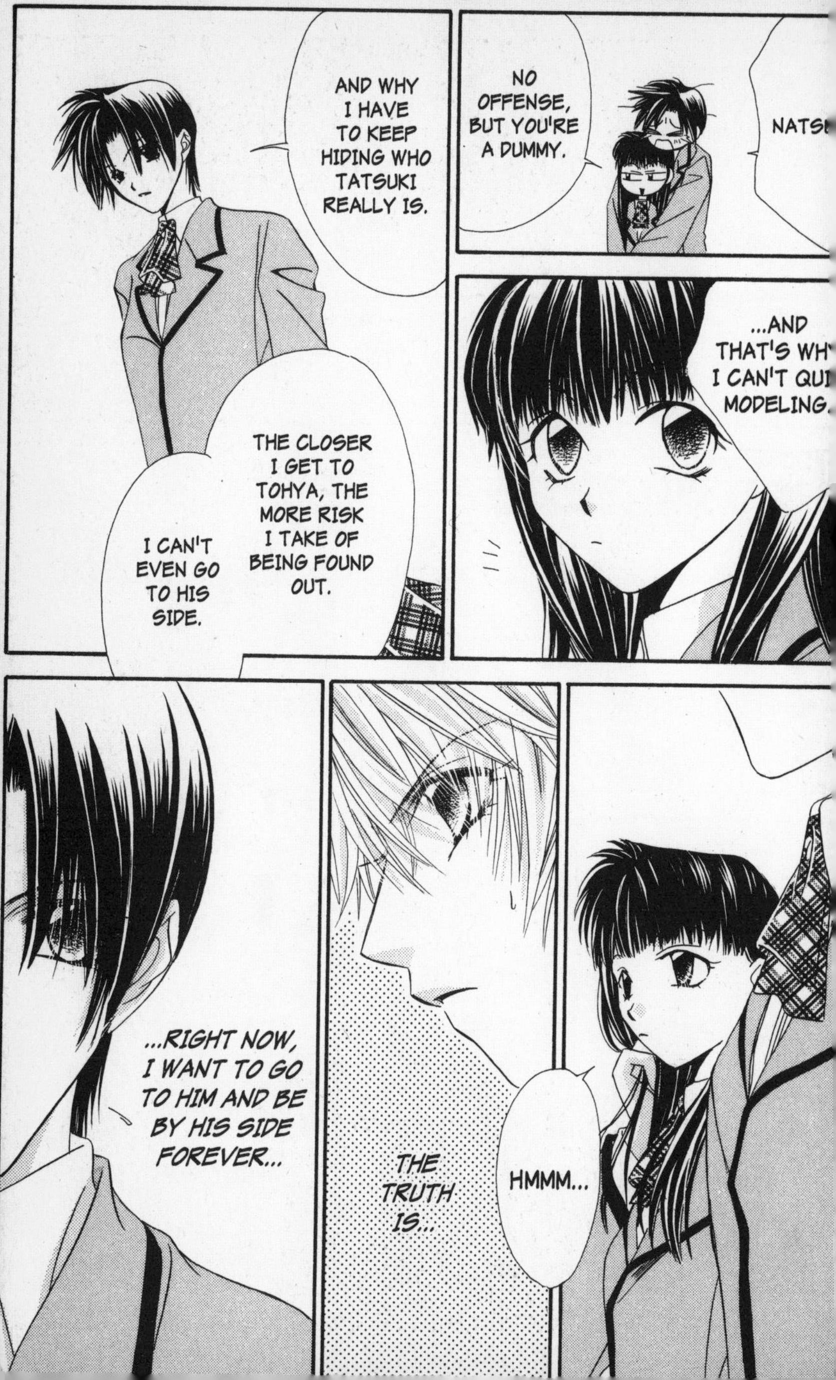
NATS
NO OFFENSE, BUT YOU'RE A DUMMY.
...AND THAT'S WH I CAN'T QUI MODELING.
AND WHY I HAVE TO KEEP HIDING WHO TATSUKI REALLY IS.
THE CLOSER I GET TO TOHYA, THE MORE RISK I TAKE OF BEING FOUND OUT.
I CAN'T EVEN GO TO HIS SIDE.
HMMM...
THE TRUTH IS...
...RIGHT NOW, I WANT TO GO TO HIM AND BE BY HIS SIDE FOREVER...

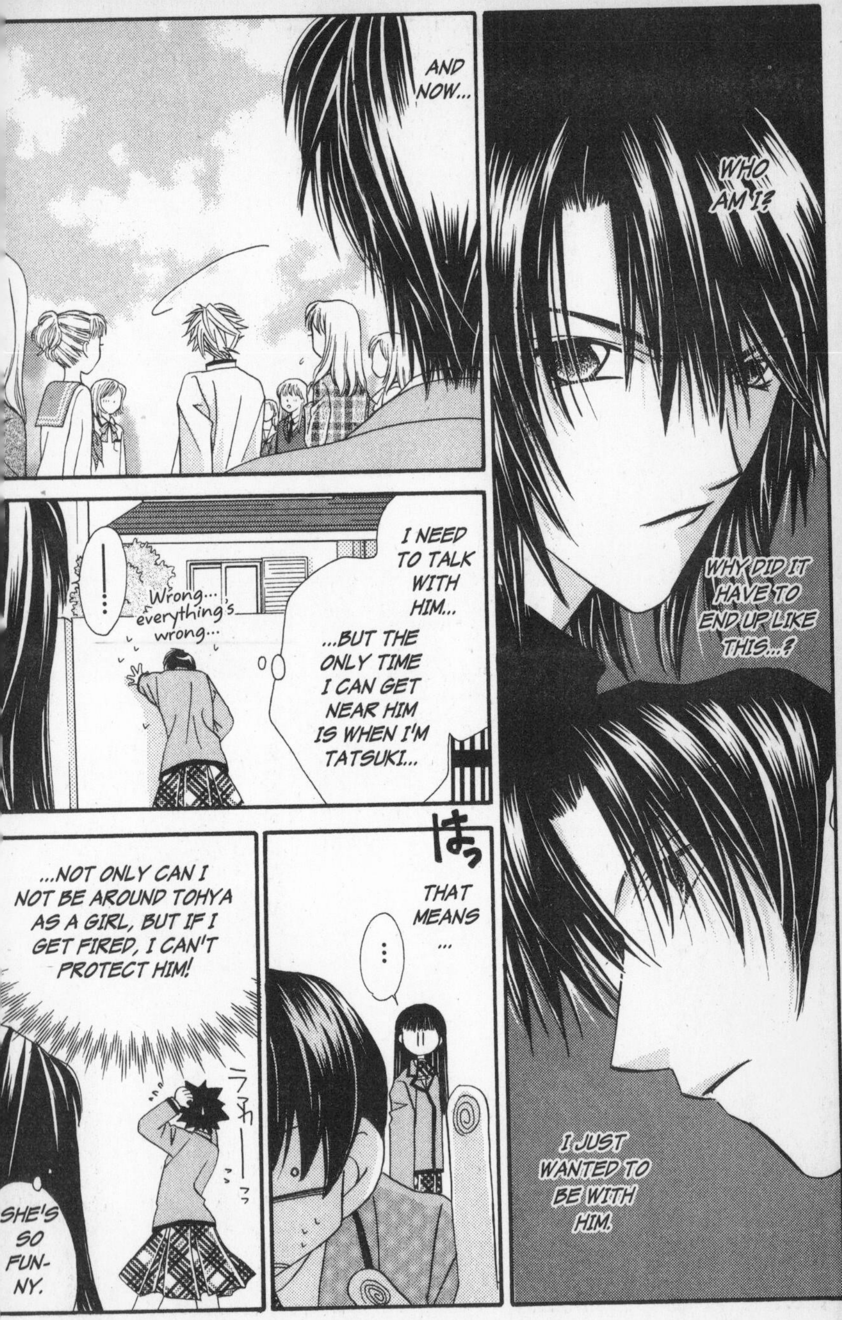
WHO AM I?
WHY DID IT HAVE TO END UP LIKE THIS...?
I JUST WANTED TO BE WITH HIM.
AND NOW...
I NEED TO TALK WITH HIM...
...BUT THE ONLY TIME I CAN GET NEAR HIM IS WHEN I'M TATSUKI...
!...
Wrong... everything's wrong...
はっ
THAT MEANS...
...
...NOT ONLY CAN I NOT BE AROUND TOHYA AS A GIRL, BUT IF I GET FIRED, I CAN'T PROTECT HIM!
SHE'S SO FUN-NY.

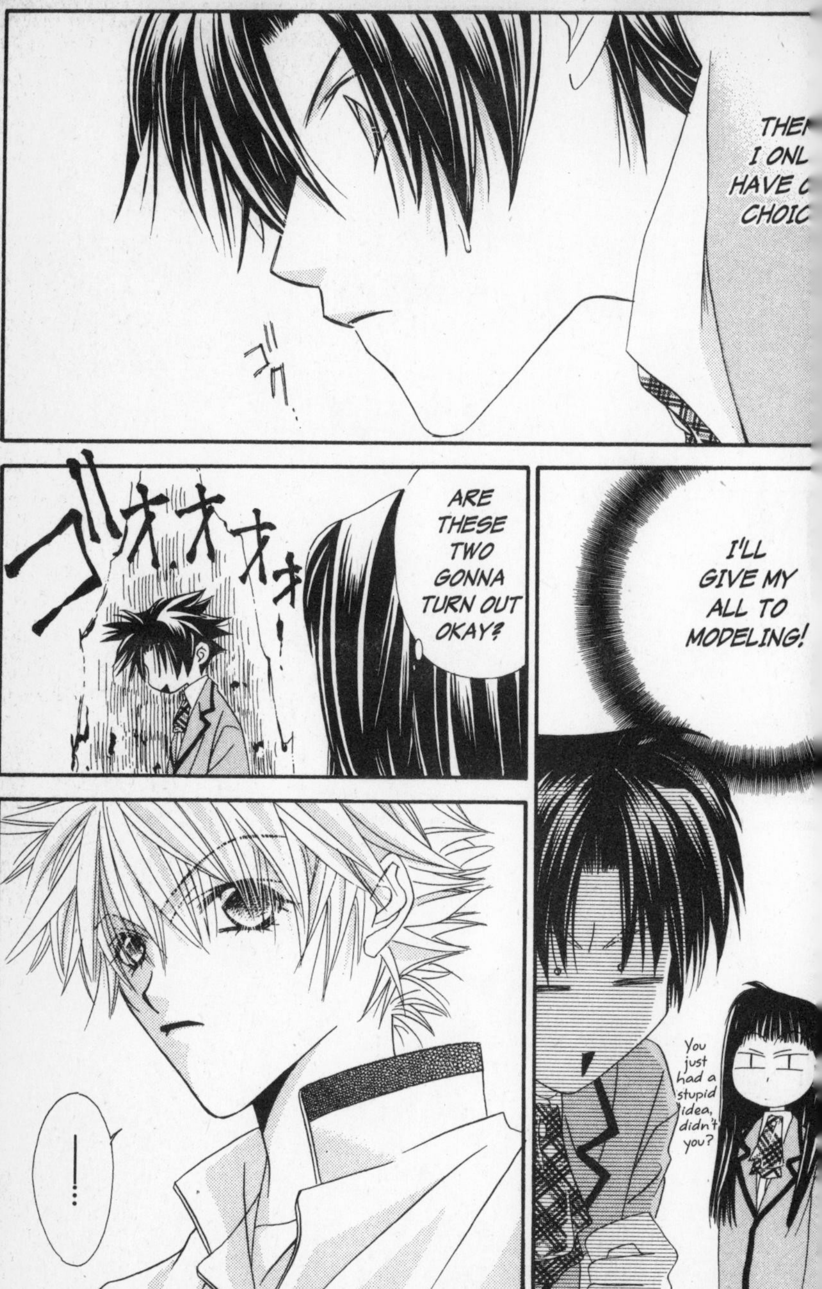
THE
I ONL
HAVE
CHOIC
ゴク…
I'LL GIVE MY ALL TO MODELING!
You just had a stupid idea, didn't you?
ARE THESE TWO GONNA TURN OUT OKAY?
—……

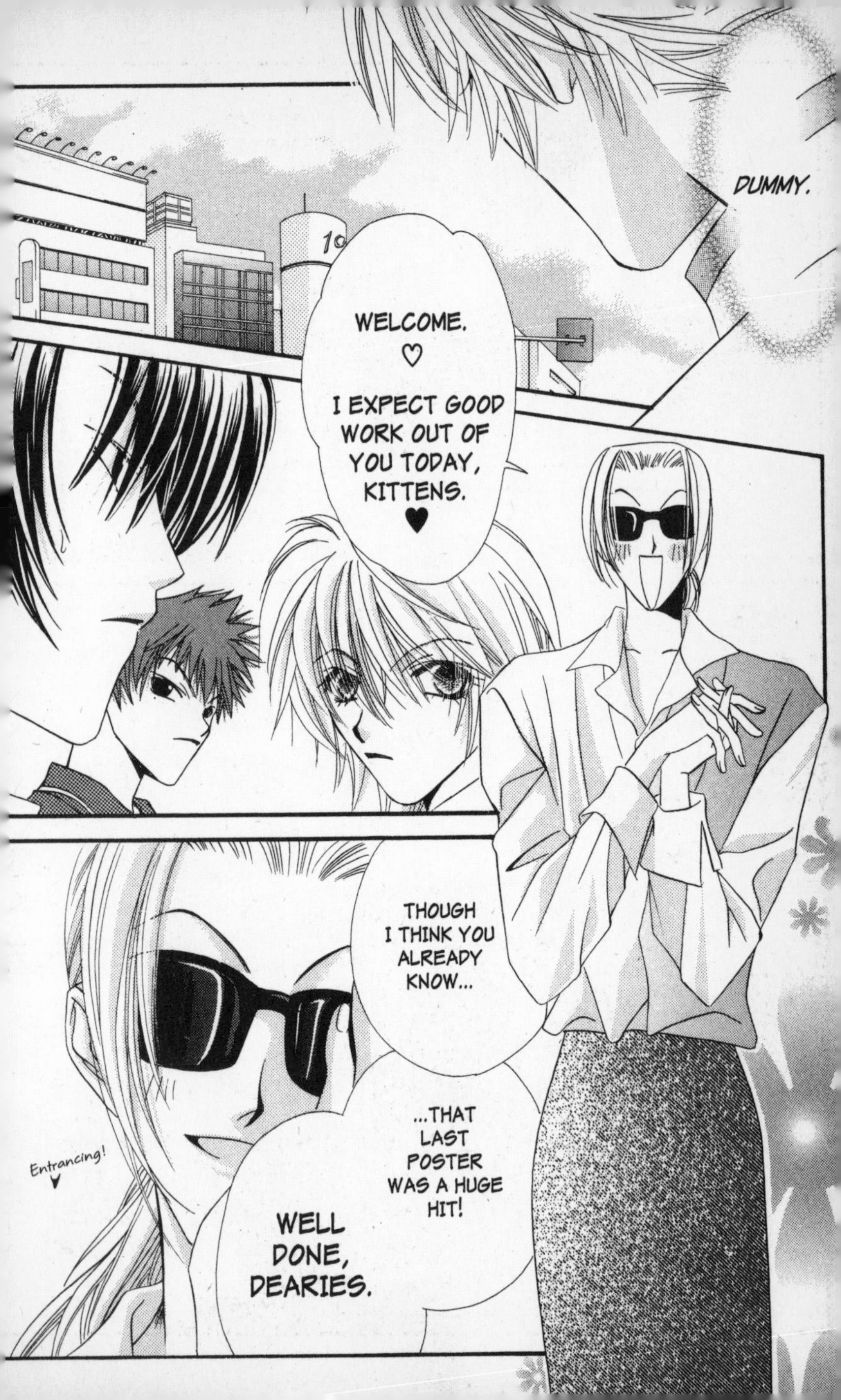
DUMMY.
WELCOME. ♡ I EXPECT GOOD WORK OUT OF YOU TODAY, KITTENS. ♥
THOUGH I THINK YOU ALREADY KNOW...
...THAT LAST POSTER WAS A HUGE HIT!
WELL DONE, DEARIES.
Entrancing!

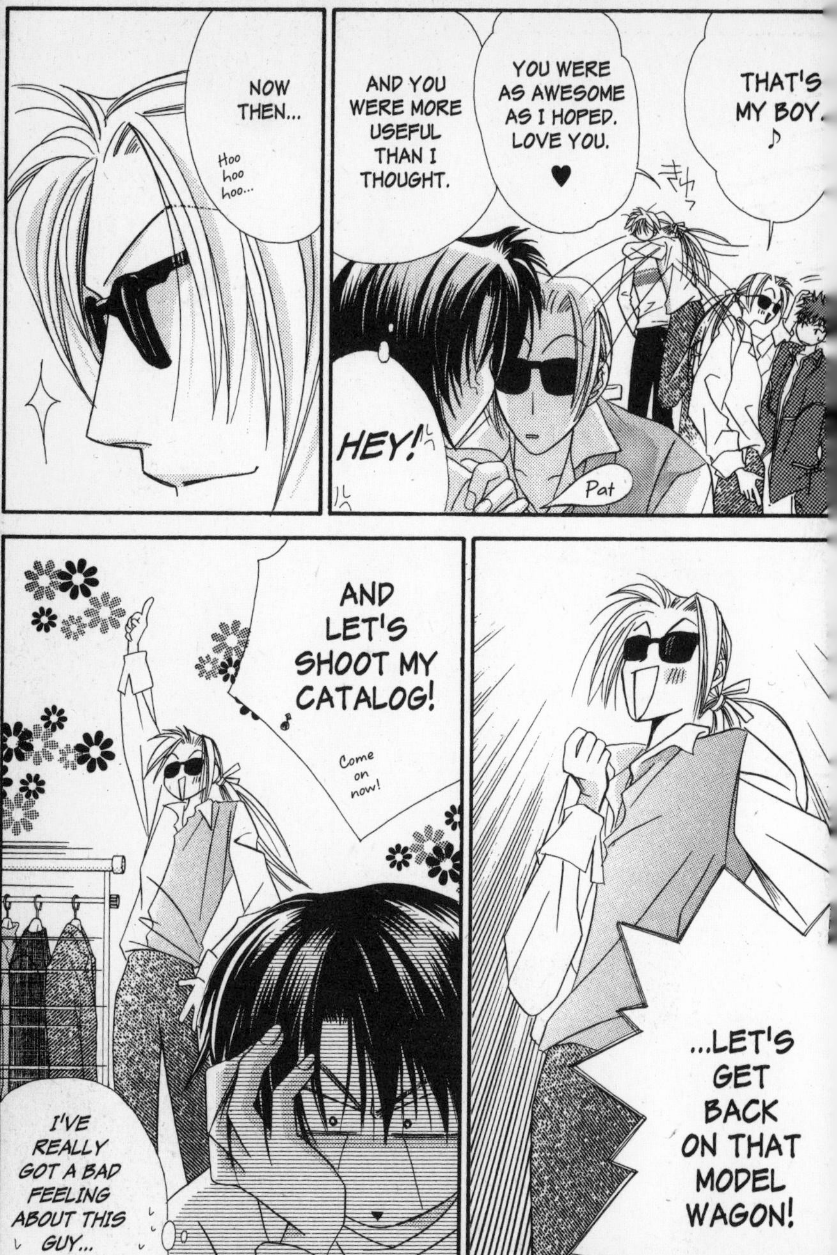
THAT'S MY BOY. ♪
YOU WERE AS AWESOME AS I HOPED. LOVE YOU. ♥
AND YOU WERE MORE USEFUL THAN I THOUGHT.
HEY!
Pat
NOW THEN...
Hoo hoo hoo...
...LET'S GET BACK ON THAT MODEL WAGON!
AND LET'S SHOOT MY CATALOG!
Come on now!
I'VE REALLY GOT A BAD FEELING ABOUT THIS GUY...

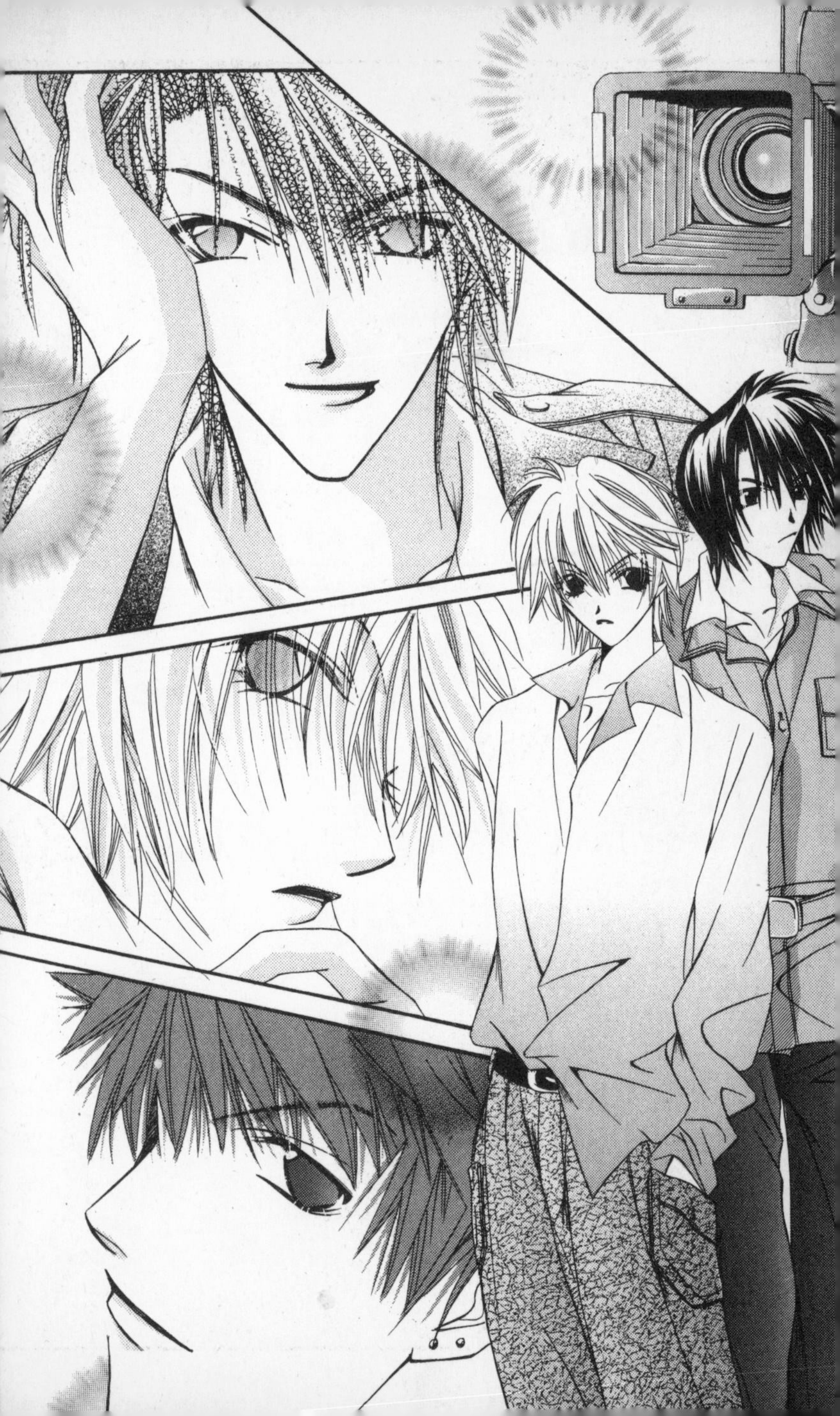

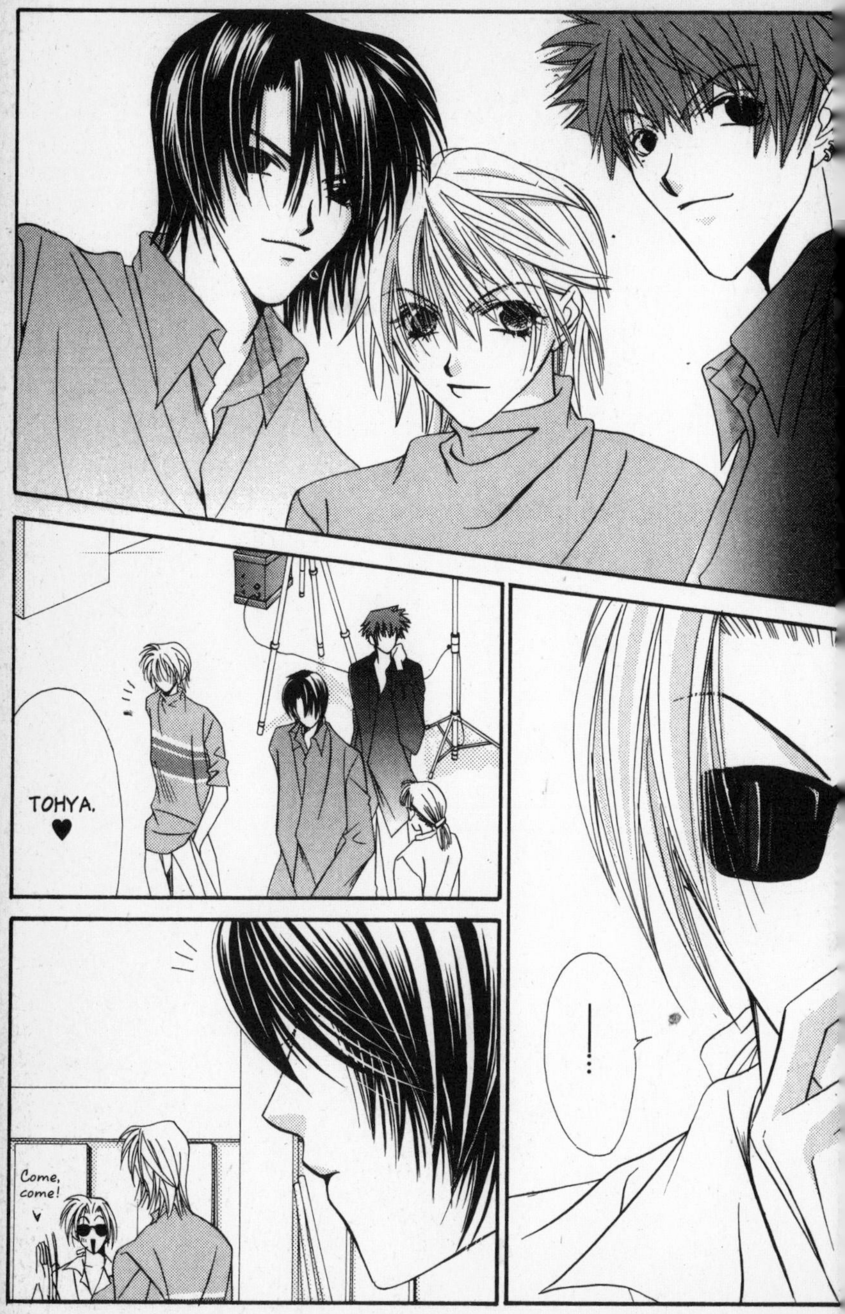
TOHYA. ♥
…!
Come, come!

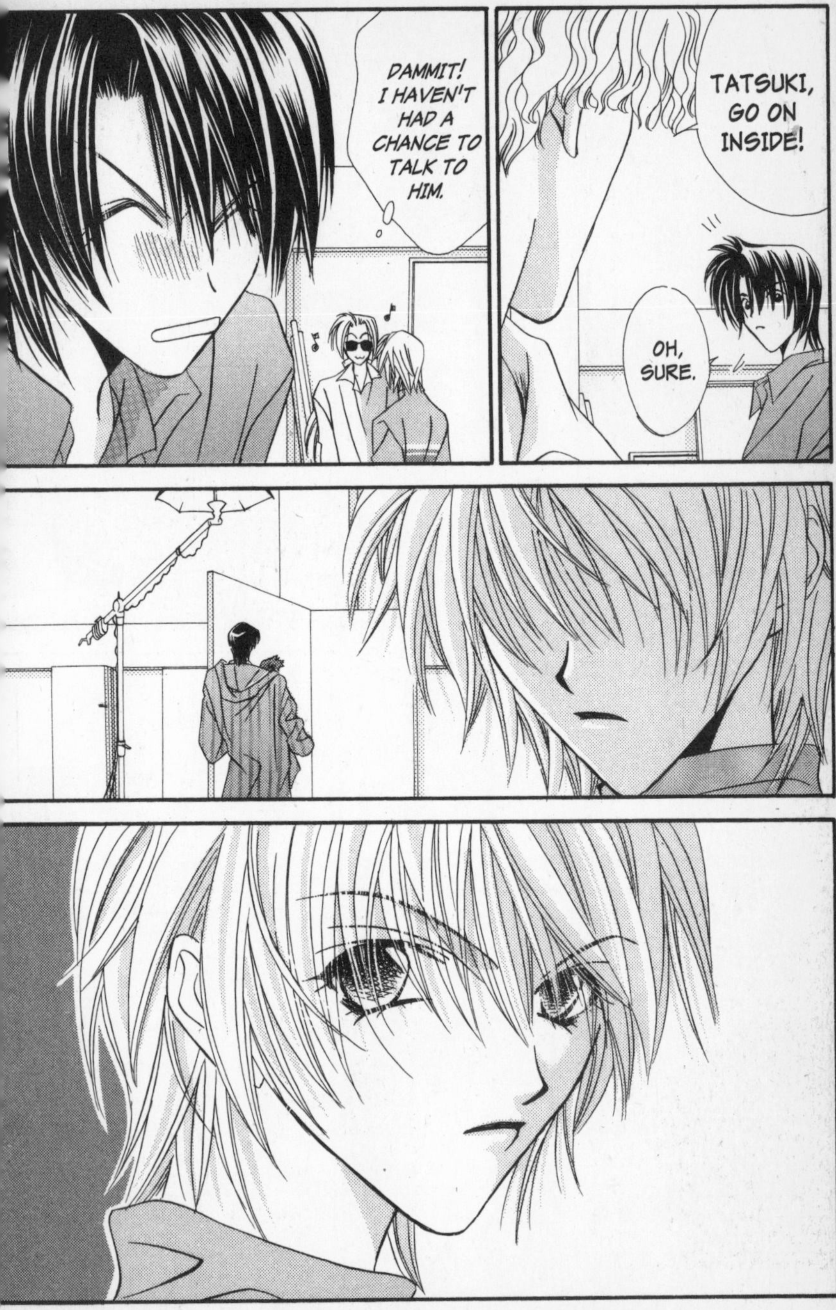
TATSUKI, GO ON INSIDE!
OH, SURE.
DAMMIT! I HAVEN'T HAD A CHANCE TO TALK TO HIM.

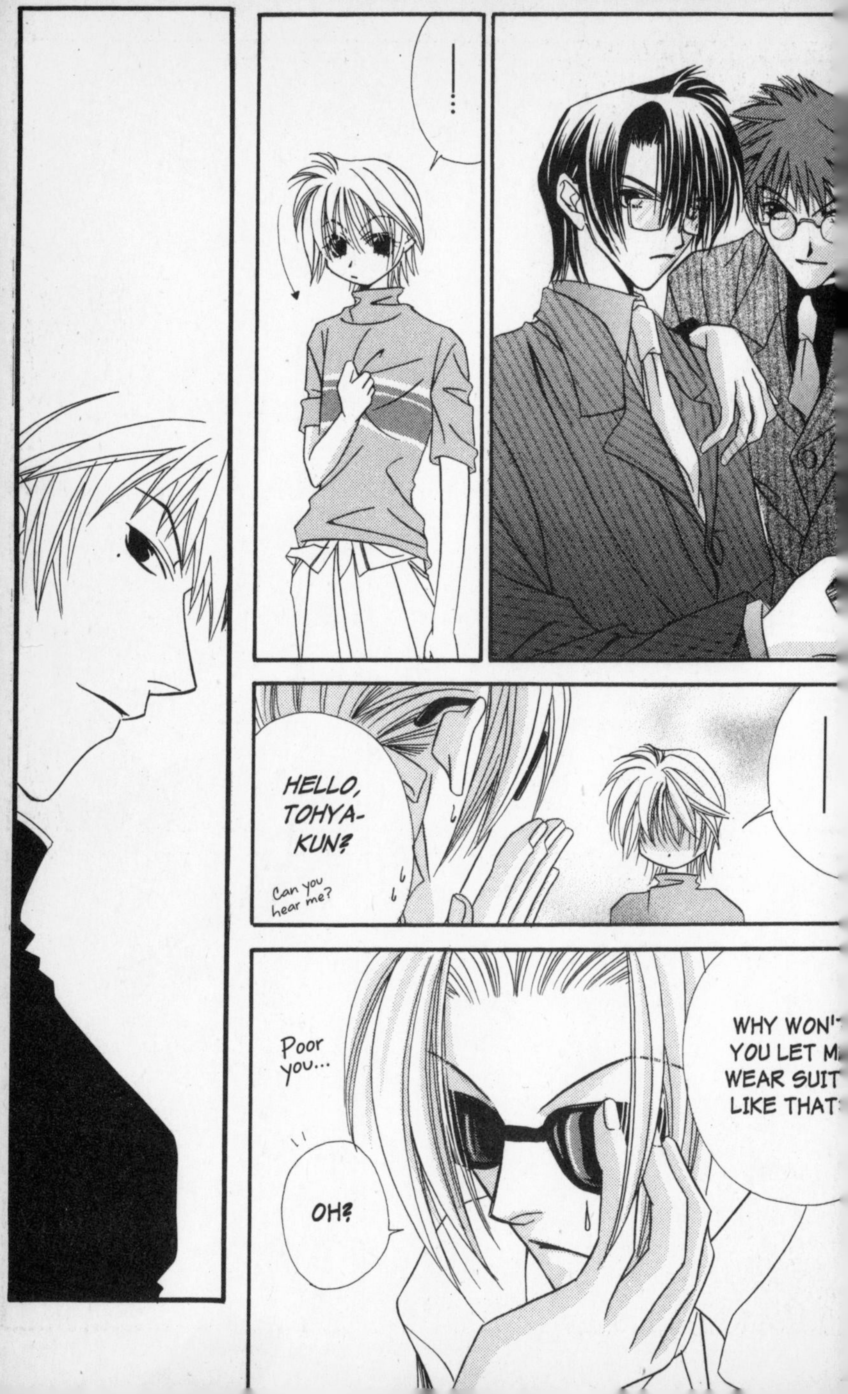

!......
HELLO, TOHYA-KUN?
Can you hear me?
WHY WON'T YOU LET M WEAR SUIT LIKE THAT
Poor you...
OH?

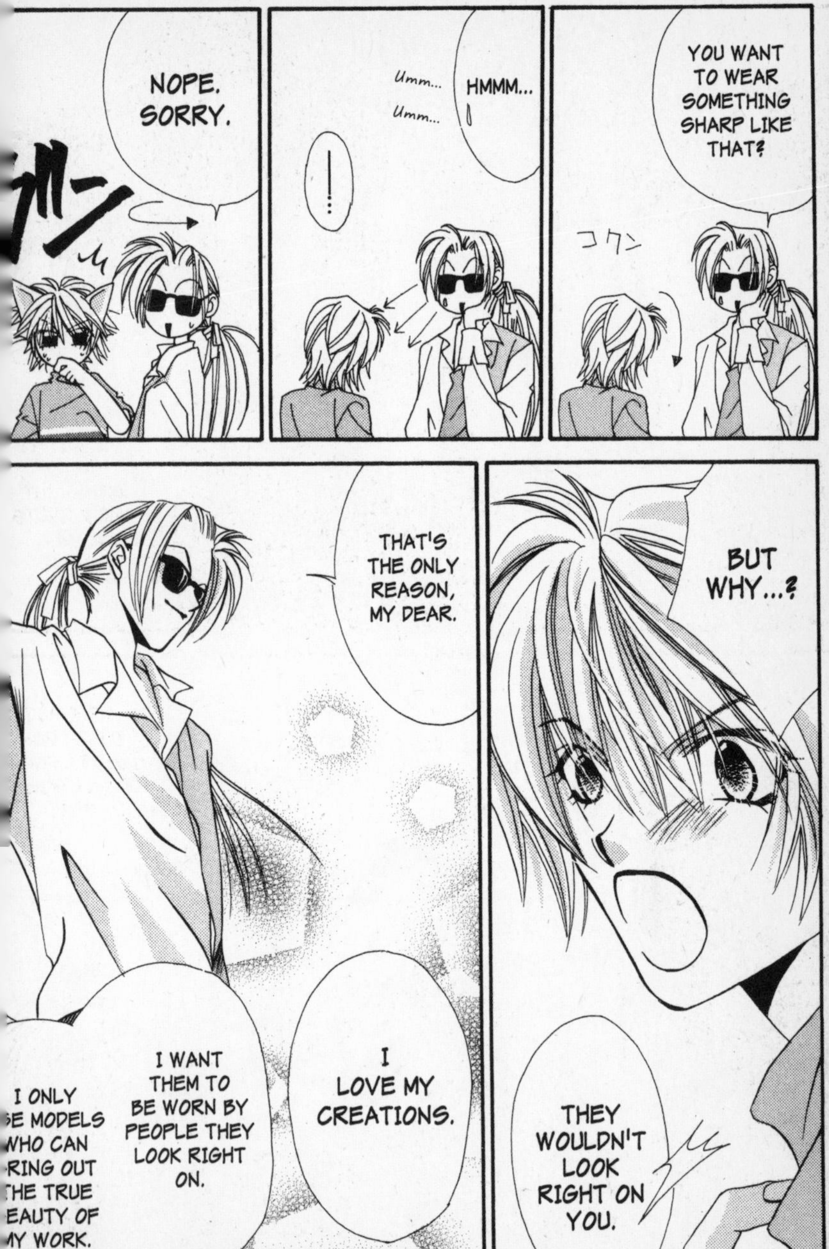
YOU WANT TO WEAR SOMETHING SHARP LIKE THAT?
コクン
HMMM...
Umm...
Umm...
!......
NOPE. SORRY.
BUT WHY...?
THEY WOULDN'T LOOK RIGHT ON YOU.
THAT'S THE ONLY REASON, MY DEAR.
I LOVE MY CREATIONS.
I WANT THEM TO BE WORN BY PEOPLE THEY LOOK RIGHT ON.
I ONLY SE MODELS WHO CAN RING OUT THE TRUE EAUTY OF MY WORK.

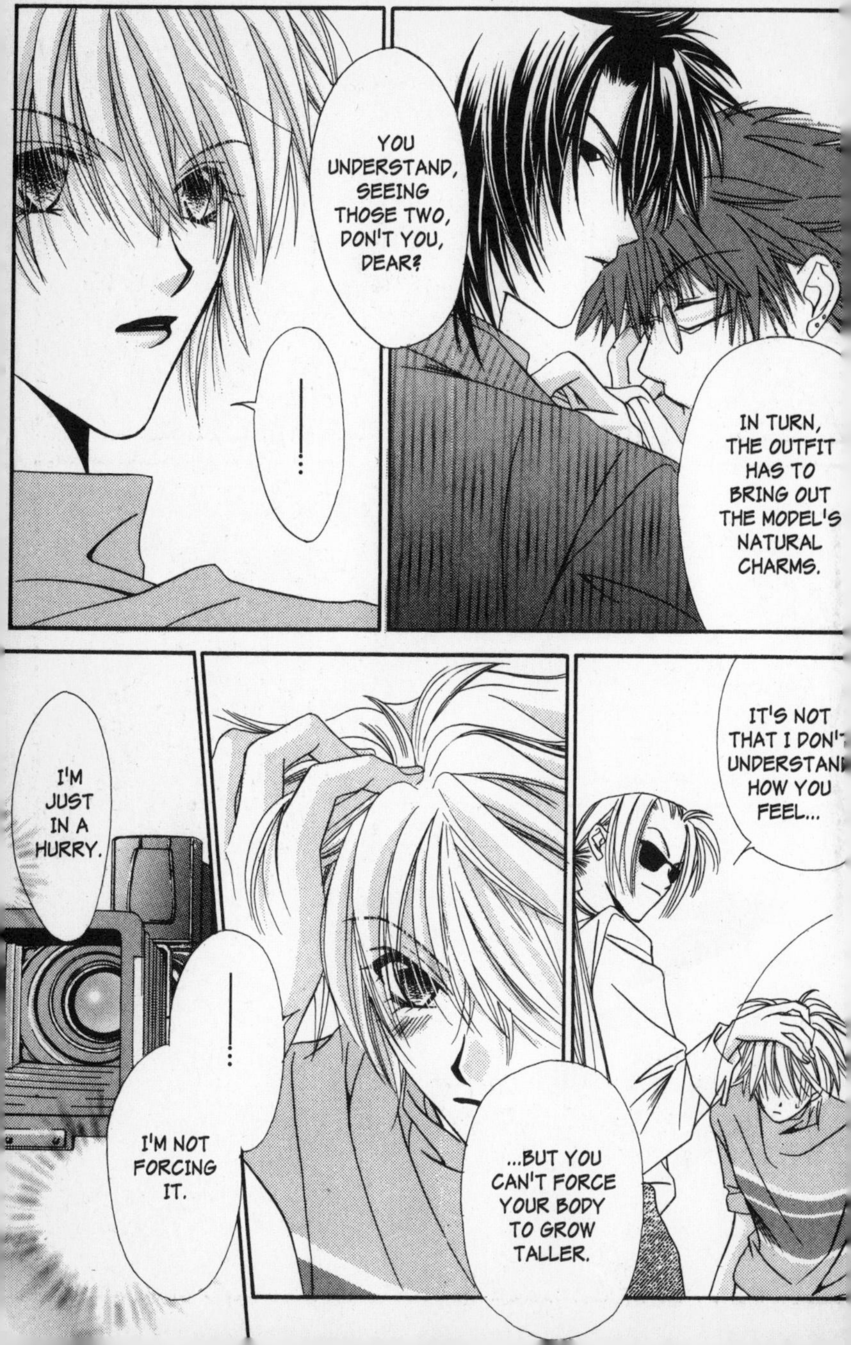
IN TURN, THE OUTFIT HAS TO BRING OUT THE MODEL'S NATURAL CHARMS.
YOU UNDERSTAND, SEEING THOSE TWO, DON'T YOU, DEAR?
......
IT'S NOT THAT I DON' UNDERSTAN HOW YOU FEEL...
...BUT YOU CAN'T FORCE YOUR BODY TO GROW TALLER.
......
I'M NOT FORCING IT.
I'M JUST IN A HURRY.

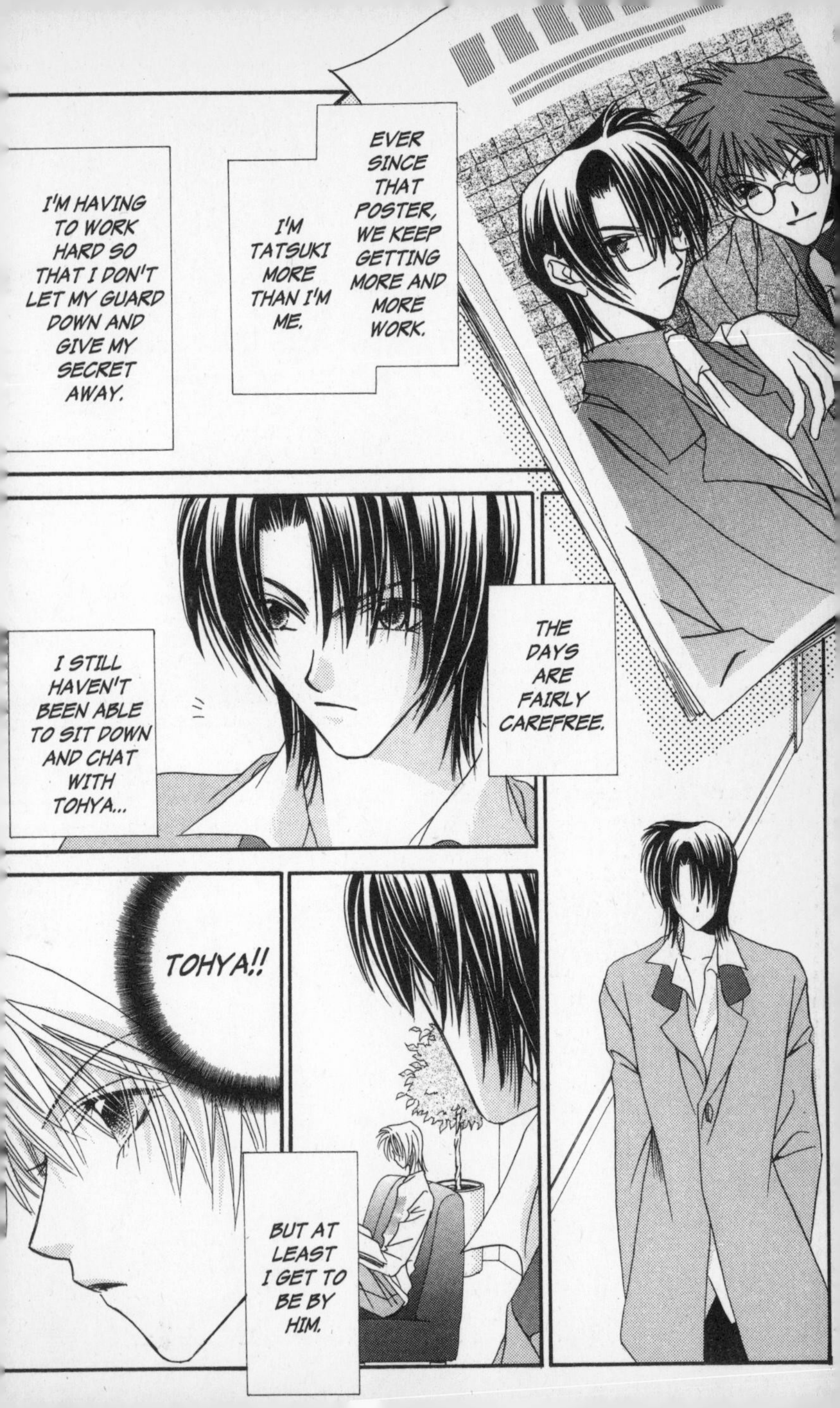
EVER SINCE THAT POSTER, WE KEEP GETTING MORE AND MORE WORK.
I'M TATSUKI MORE THAN I'M ME.
I'M HAVING TO WORK HARD SO THAT I DON'T LET MY GUARD DOWN AND GIVE MY SECRET AWAY.
THE DAYS ARE FAIRLY CAREFREE.
I STILL HAVEN'T BEEN ABLE TO SIT DOWN AND CHAT WITH TOHYA...
BUT AT LEAST I GET TO BE BY HIM.
TOHYA!!

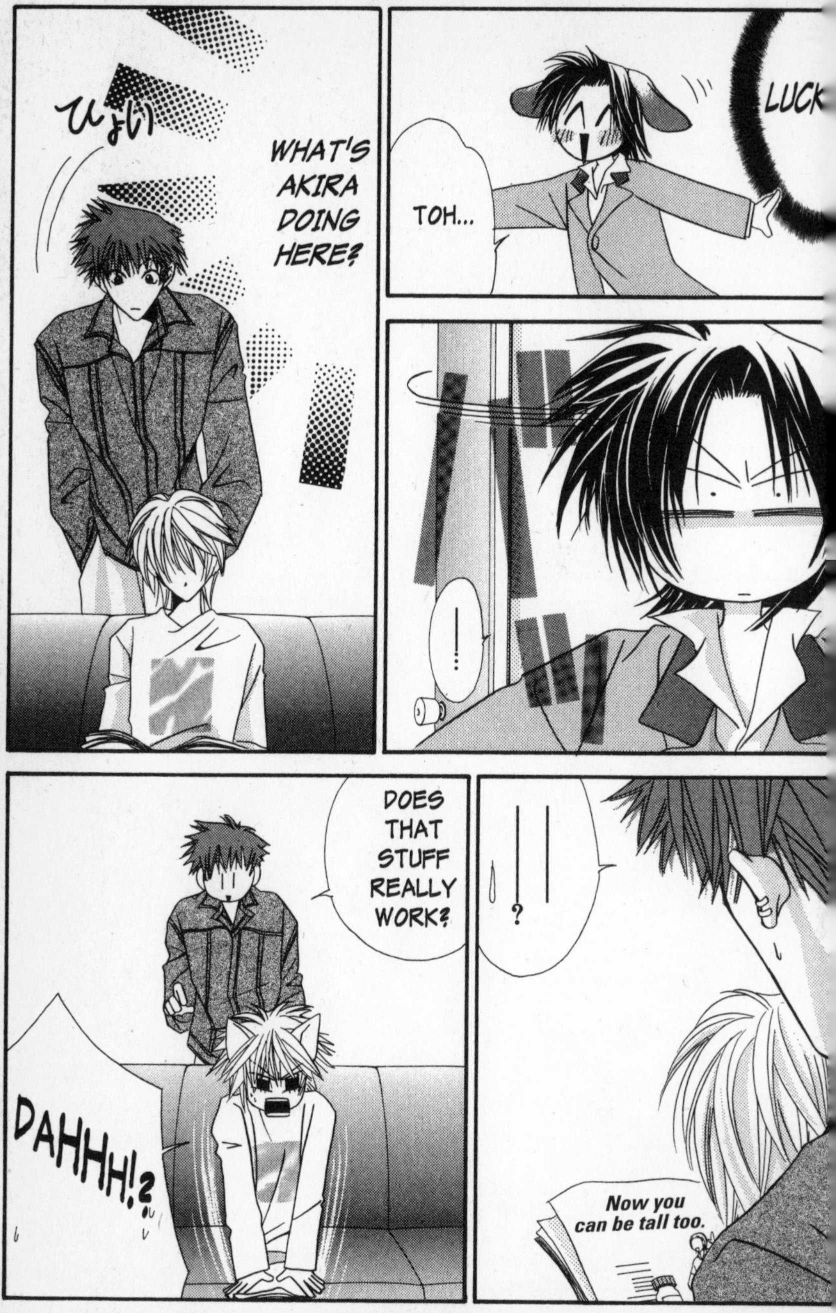

LUCK
TOH...
!...
ひょい
WHAT'S AKIRA DOING HERE?
?
Now you can be tall too.
DOES THAT STUFF REALLY WORK?
DAHHH!?

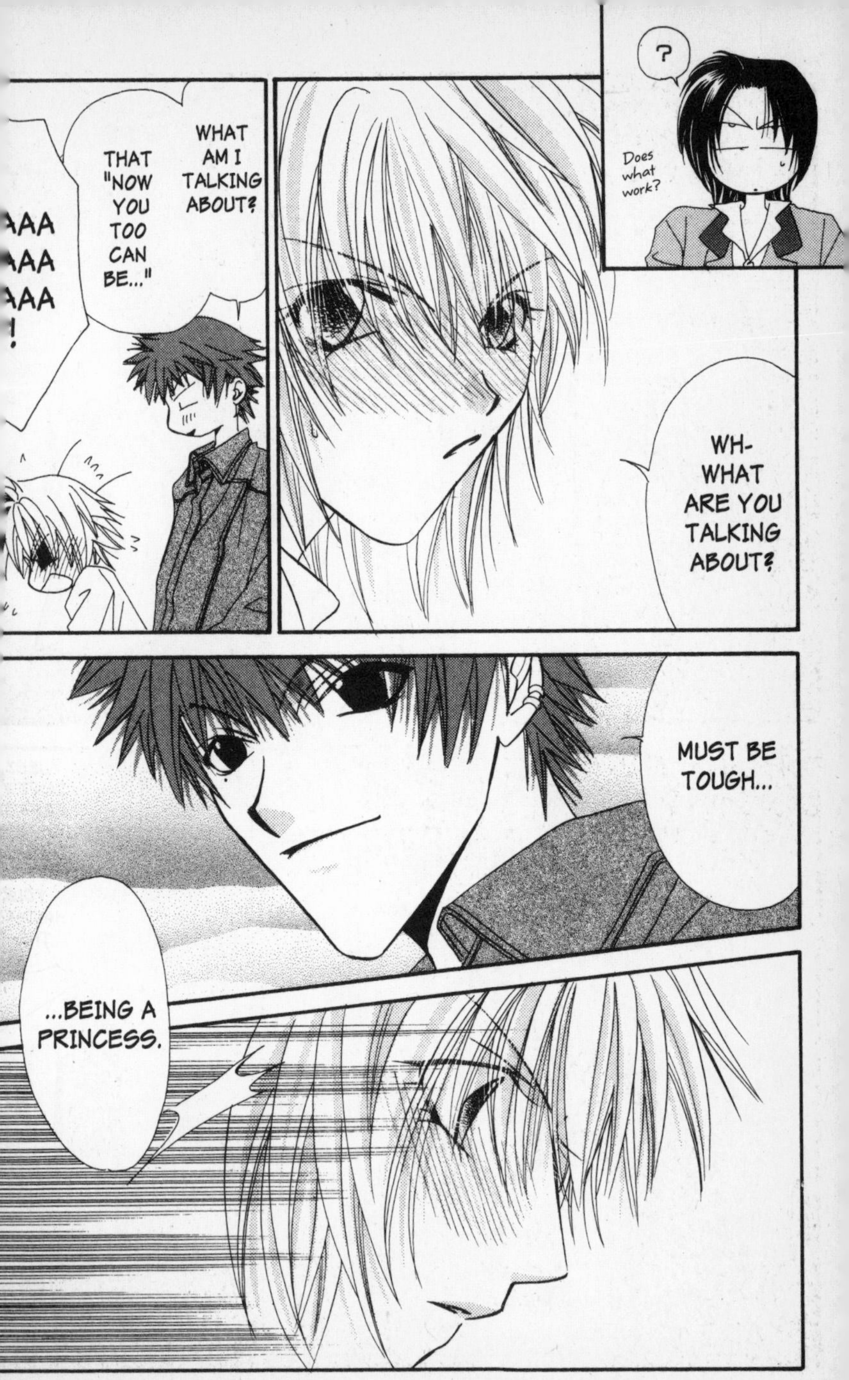
?
Does what work?
WH- WHAT ARE YOU TALKING ABOUT?
WHAT AM I TALKING ABOUT?
THAT "NOW YOU TOO CAN BE..."
AAAAAAAAA!
MUST BE TOUGH...
...BEING A PRINCESS.

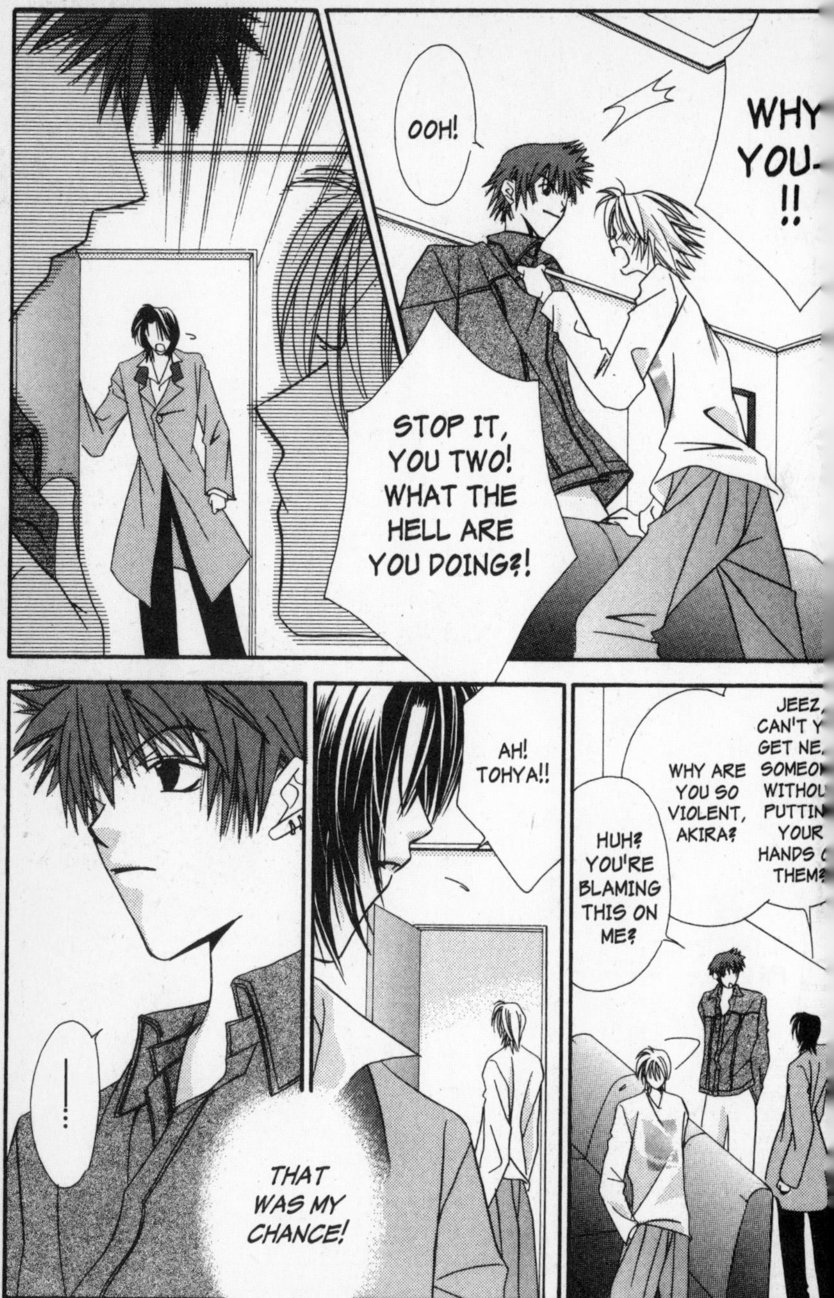
WHY YOU-!!
OOH!
STOP IT, YOU TWO! WHAT THE HELL ARE YOU DOING?!
JEEZ, CAN'T Y GET NE. SOMEO WITHOU PUTTIN YOUR HANDS O THEM?
WHY ARE YOU SO VIOLENT, AKIRA?
HUH? YOU'RE BLAMING THIS ON ME?
AH! TOHYA!!
...!
THAT WAS MY CHANCE!

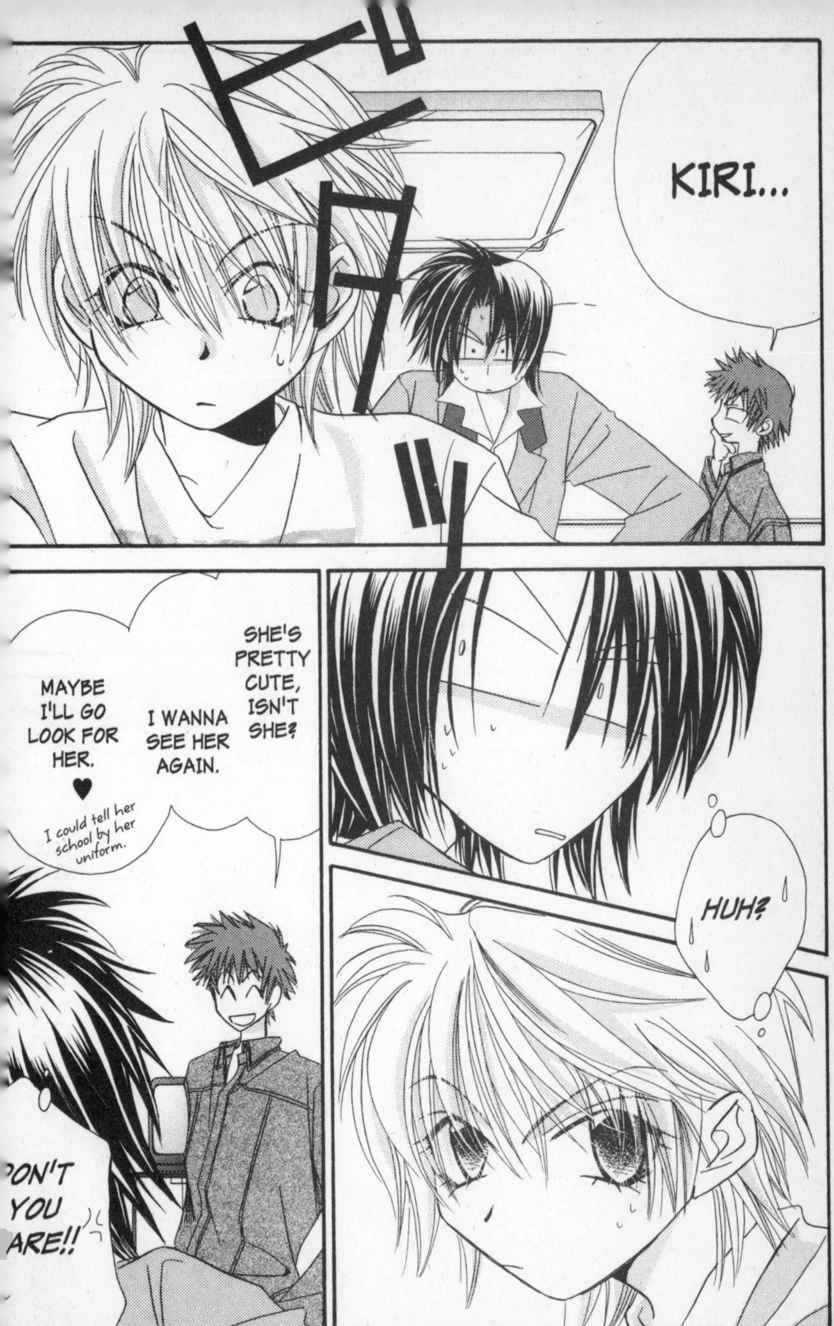
KIRI...
HUH?
SHE'S PRETTY CUTE, ISN'T SHE?
I WANNA SEE HER AGAIN.
MAYBE I'LL GO LOOK FOR HER. ♥
I could tell her school by her uniform.
ON'T YOU ARE!!

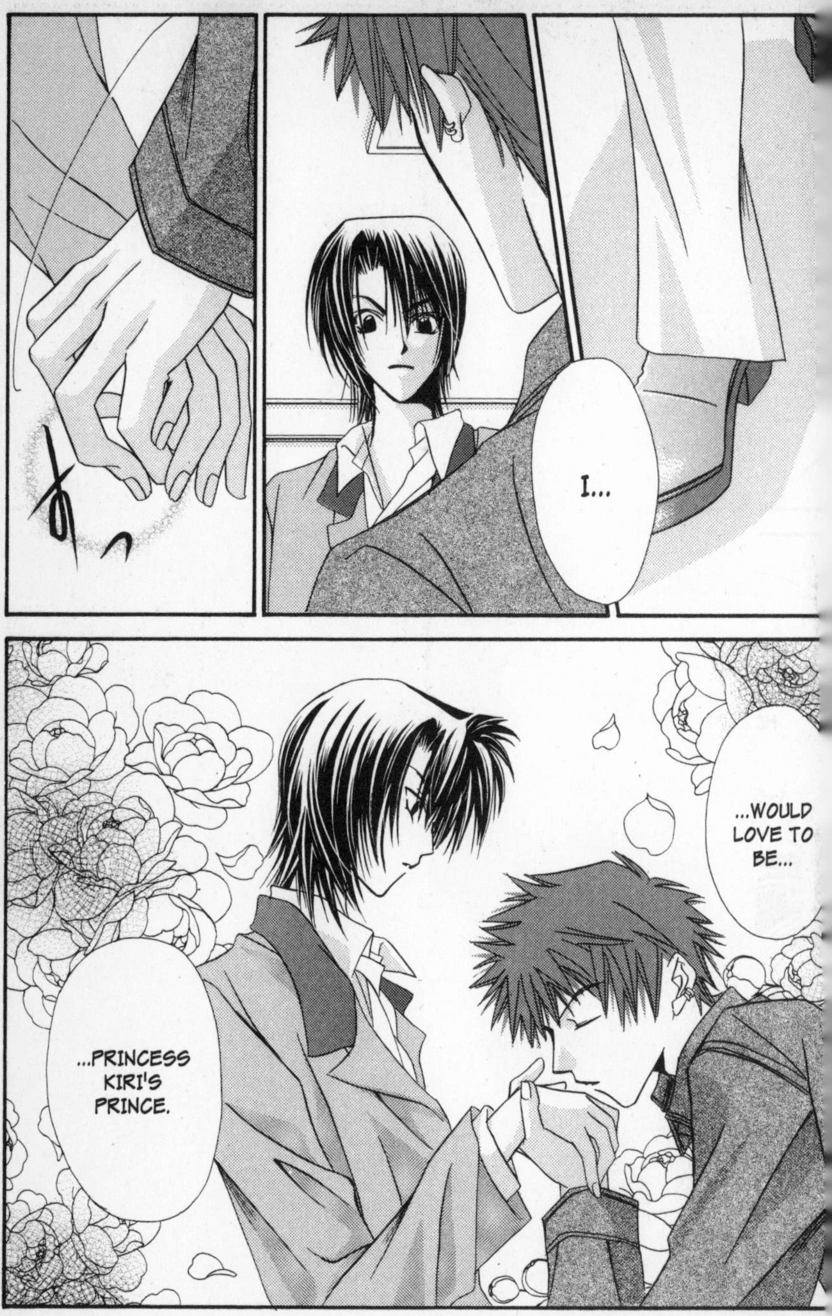
I...
...WOULD LOVE TO BE...
...PRINCESS KIRI'S PRINCE.

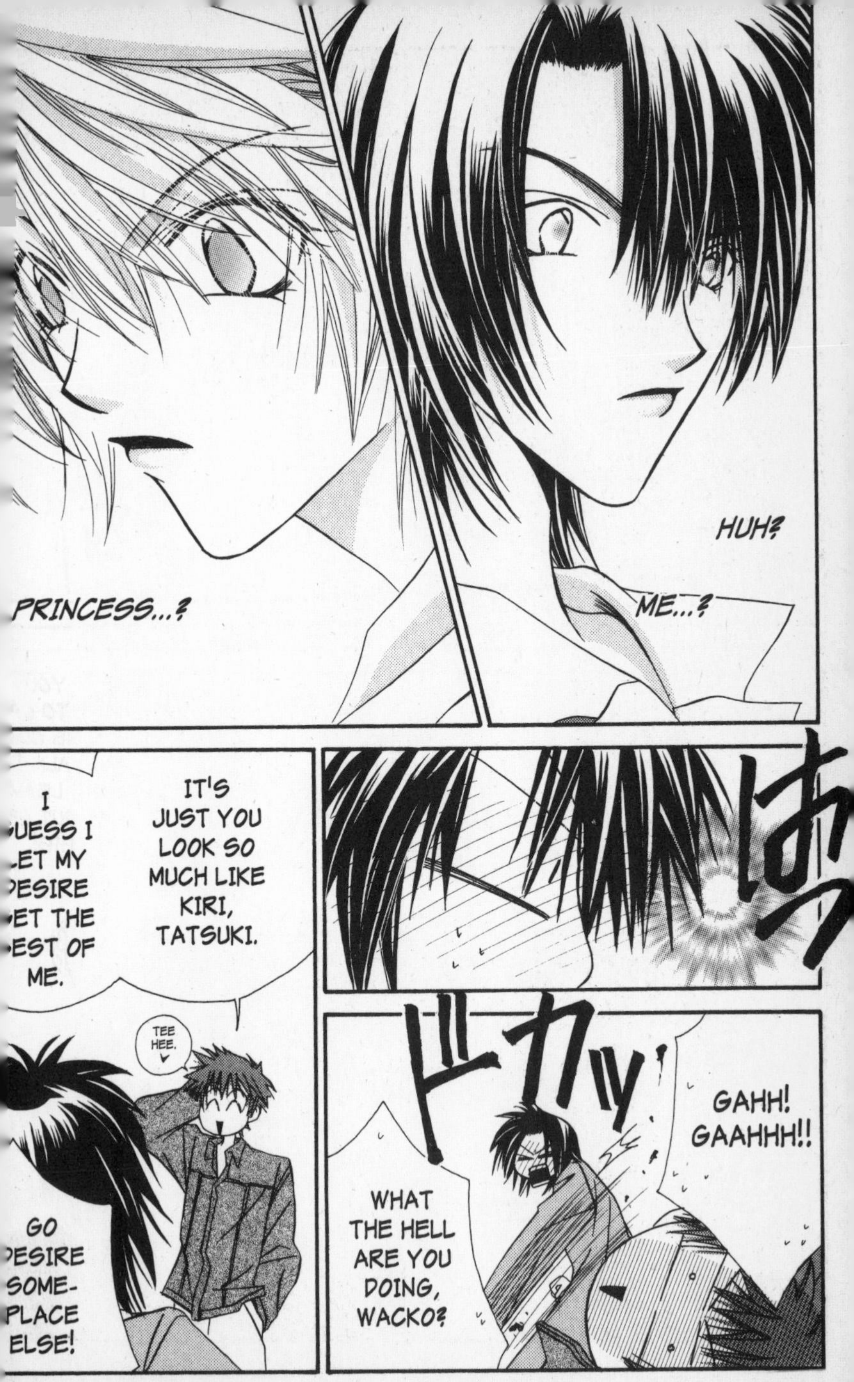
HUH?
ME...?
PRINCESS...?
はっ
IT'S JUST YOU LOOK SO MUCH LIKE KIRI, TATSUKI.
I GUESS I LET MY DESIRE GET THE BEST OF ME.
ドカッ
GAHH! GAAHHH!!
WHAT THE HELL ARE YOU DOING, WACKO?
TEE HEE.
GO DESIRE SOME-PLACE ELSE!

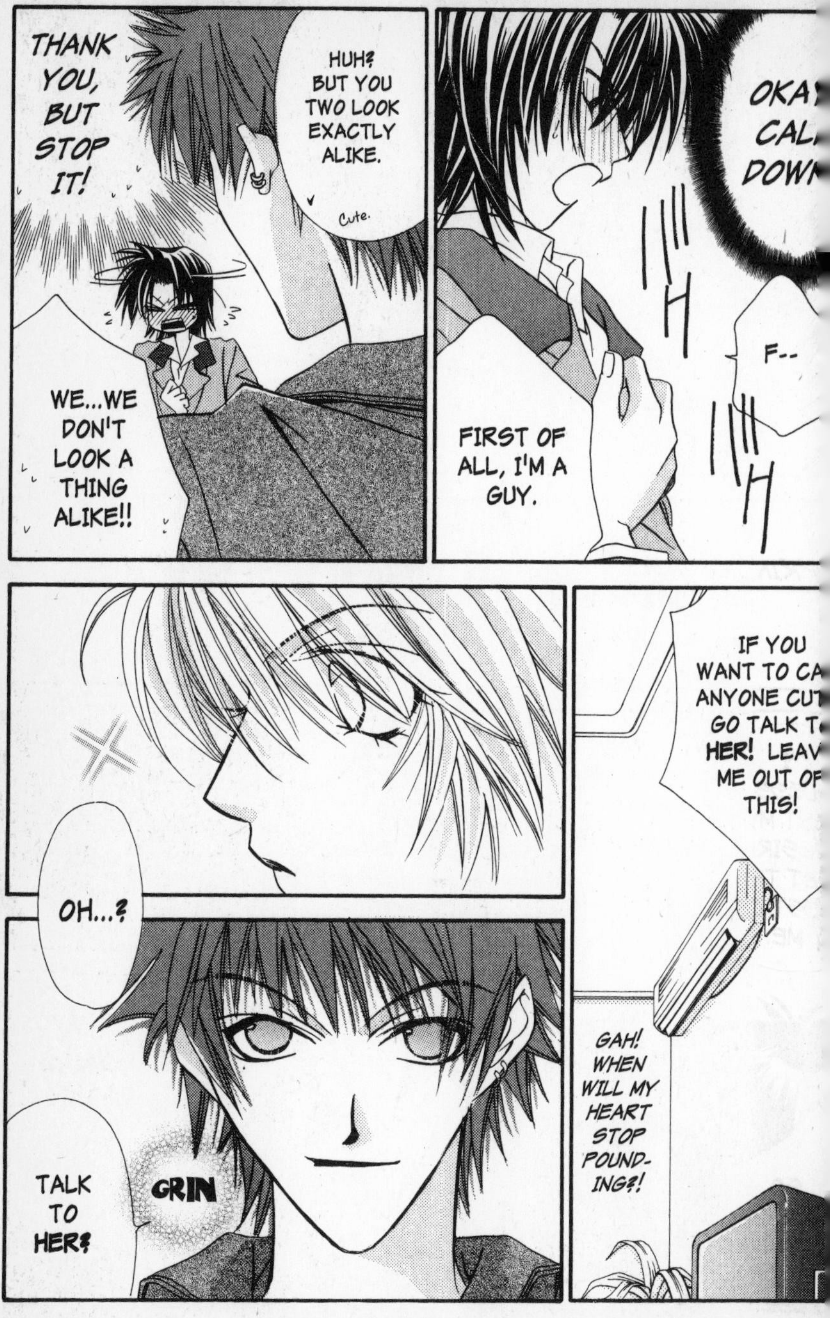
OKA CAL DOW
F--
FIRST OF ALL, I'M A GUY.
HUH? BUT YOU TWO LOOK EXACTLY ALIKE.
Cute.
THANK YOU, BUT STOP IT!
WE...WE DON'T LOOK A THING ALIKE!!
IF YOU WANT TO CA ANYONE CUT GO TALK T HER! LEAV ME OUT OF THIS!
GAH! WHEN WILL MY HEART STOP POUND-ING?!
OH...?
GRIN
TALK TO HER?

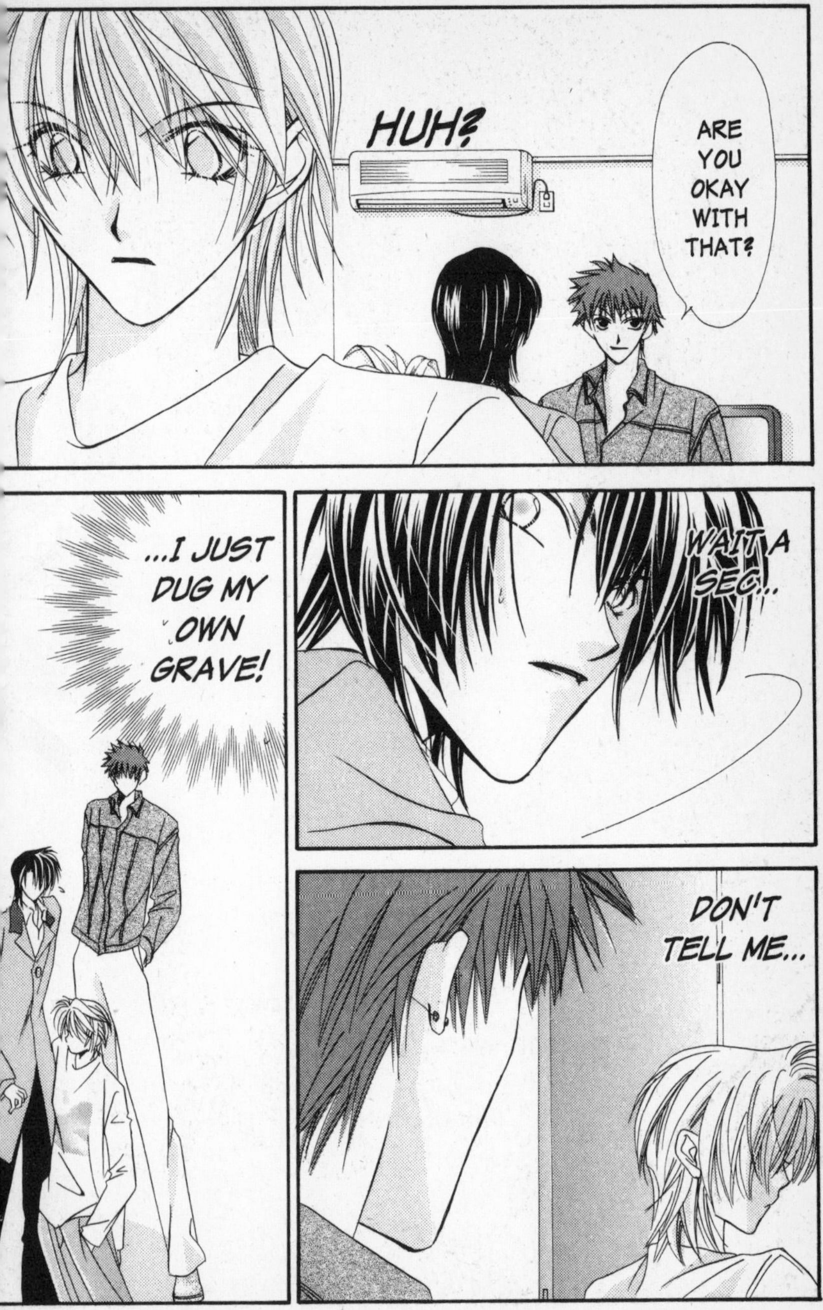
ARE YOU OKAY WITH THAT?
HUH?
WAIT A SEC...
DON'T TELL ME...
...I JUST DUG MY OWN GRAVE!

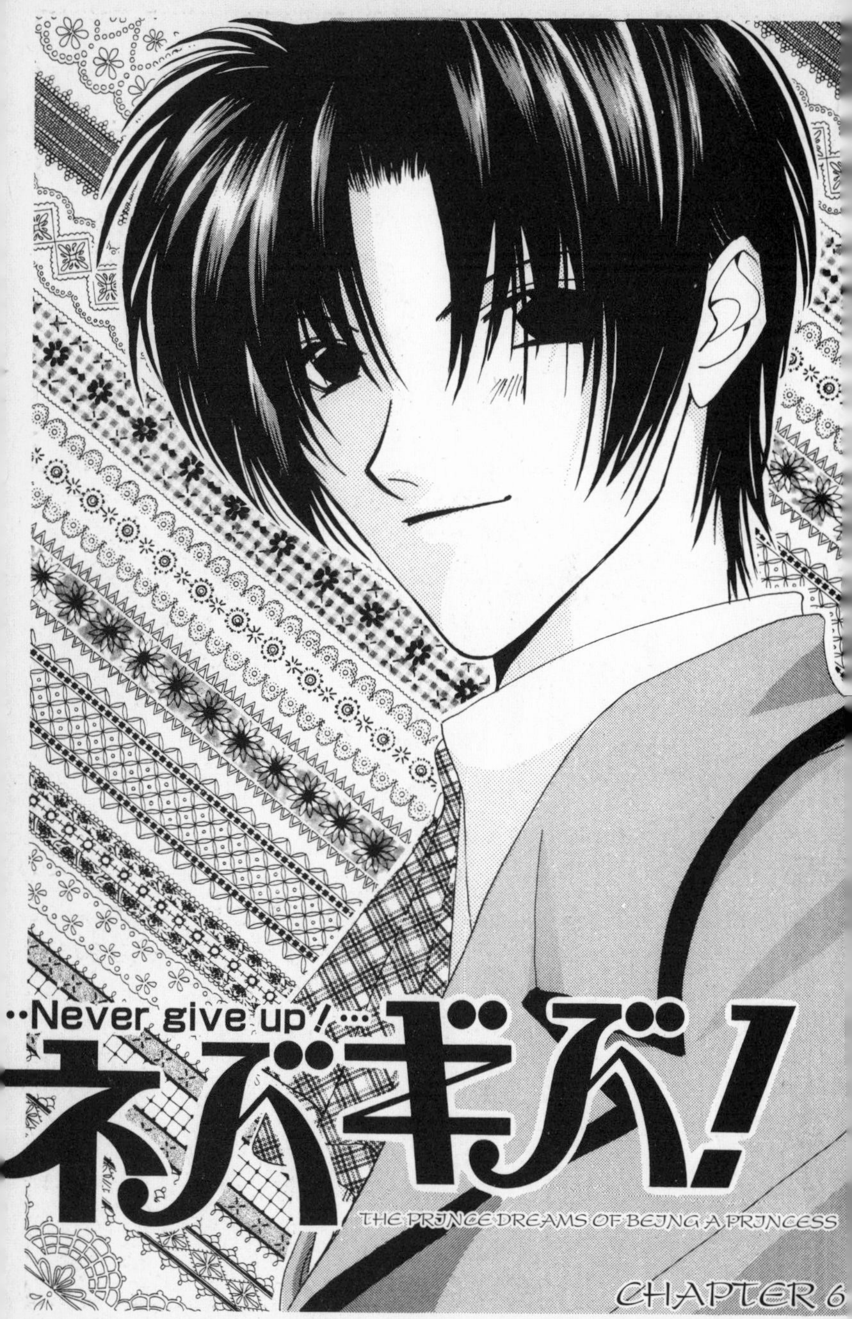

··Never give up!···
ネバギバ!
THE PRINCE DREAMS OF BEING A PRINCESS
CHAPTER 6

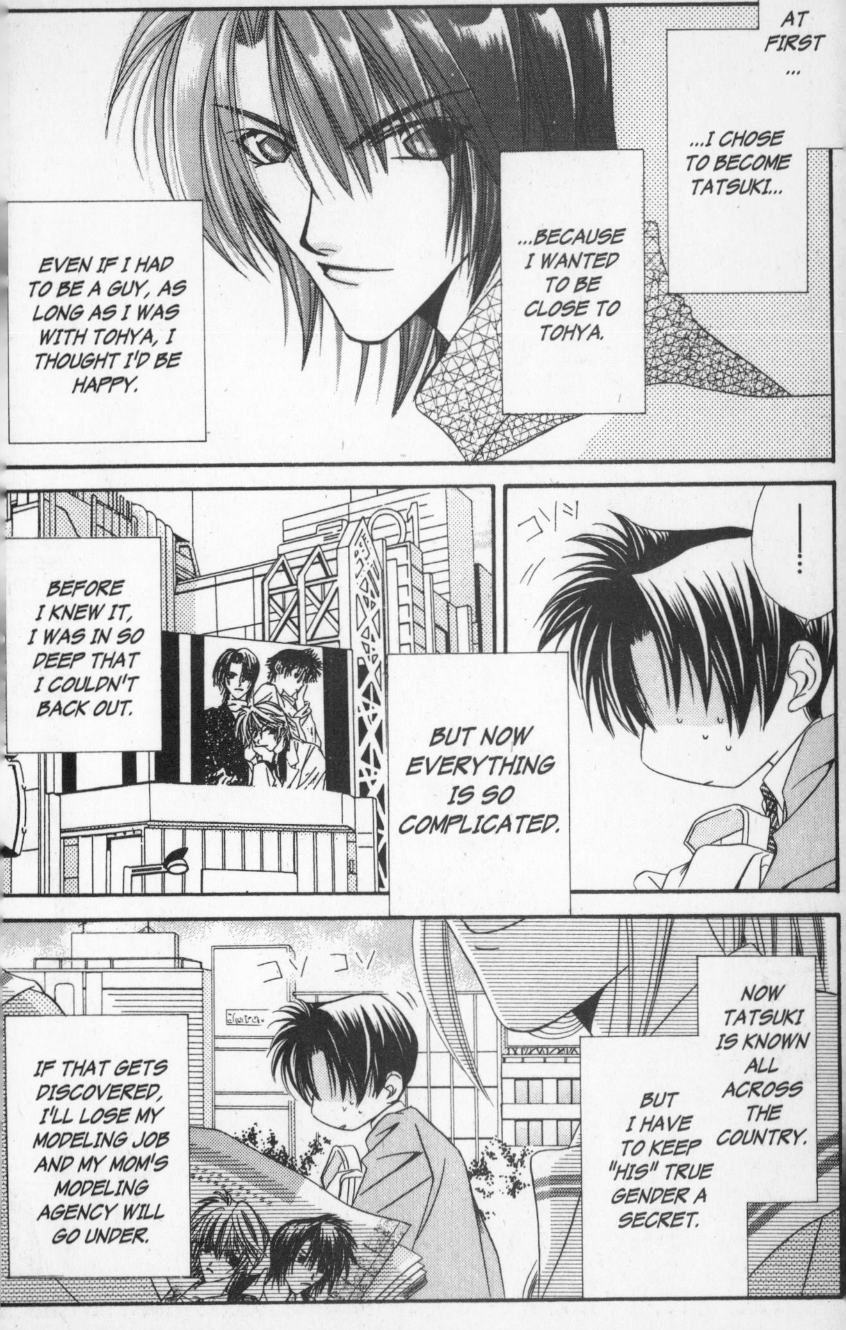
AT FIRST ...
...I CHOSE TO BECOME TATSUKI...
...BECAUSE I WANTED TO BE CLOSE TO TOHYA.
EVEN IF I HAD TO BE A GUY, AS LONG AS I WAS WITH TOHYA, I THOUGHT I'D BE HAPPY.
コソ
!...
BEFORE I KNEW IT, I WAS IN SO DEEP THAT I COULDN'T BACK OUT.
BUT NOW EVERYTHING IS SO COMPLICATED.
コソ コソ
NOW TATSUKI IS KNOWN ALL ACROSS THE COUNTRY.
BUT I HAVE TO KEEP "HIS" TRUE GENDER A SECRET.
IF THAT GETS DISCOVERED, I'LL LOSE MY MODELING JOB AND MY MOM'S MODELING AGENCY WILL GO UNDER.

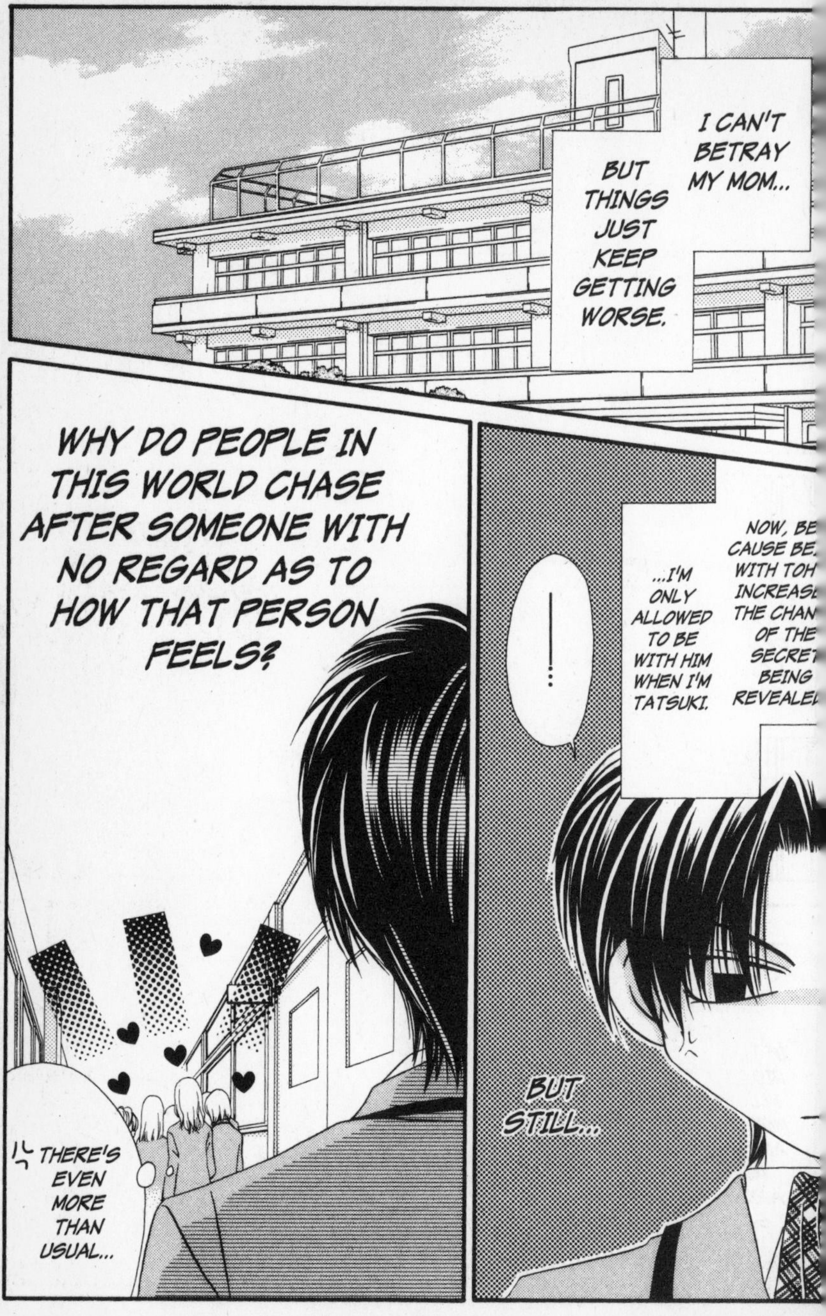
I CAN'T BETRAY MY MOM...
BUT THINGS JUST KEEP GETTING WORSE.
NOW, BE CAUSE BE WITH TOH INCREASE THE CHAN OF THE SECRE BEING REVEALE
...I'M ONLY ALLOWED TO BE WITH HIM WHEN I'M TATSUKI.
!
BUT STILL...
WHY DO PEOPLE IN THIS WORLD CHASE AFTER SOMEONE WITH NO REGARD AS TO HOW THAT PERSON FEELS?
THERE'S EVEN MORE THAN USUAL...

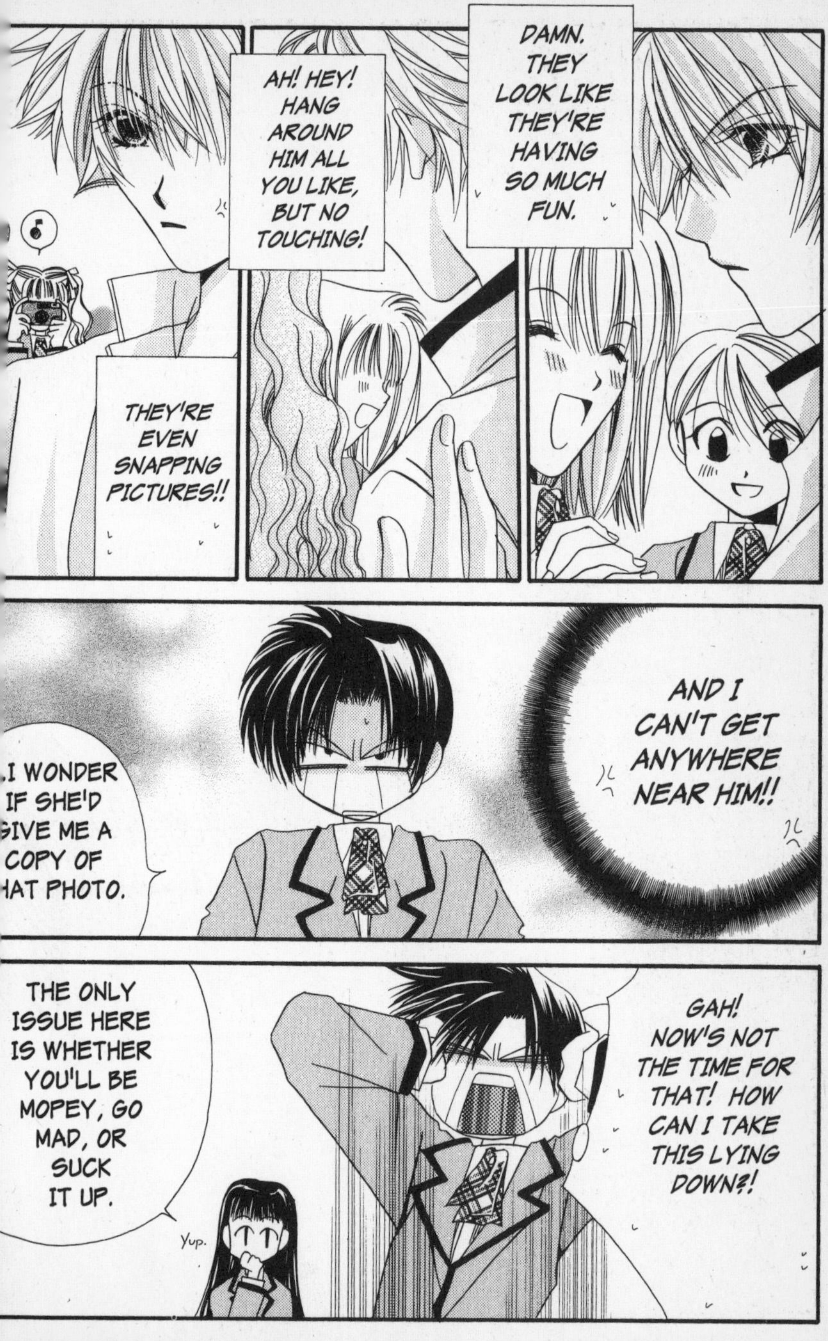
DAMN. THEY LOOK LIKE THEY'RE HAVING SO MUCH FUN.
AH! HEY! HANG AROUND HIM ALL YOU LIKE, BUT NO TOUCHING!
THEY'RE EVEN SNAPPING PICTURES!!
AND I CAN'T GET ANYWHERE NEAR HIM!!
I WONDER IF SHE'D GIVE ME A COPY OF HAT PHOTO.
GAH! NOW'S NOT THE TIME FOR THAT! HOW CAN I TAKE THIS LYING DOWN?!
THE ONLY ISSUE HERE IS WHETHER YOU'LL BE MOPEY, GO MAD, OR SUCK IT UP.
Yup.

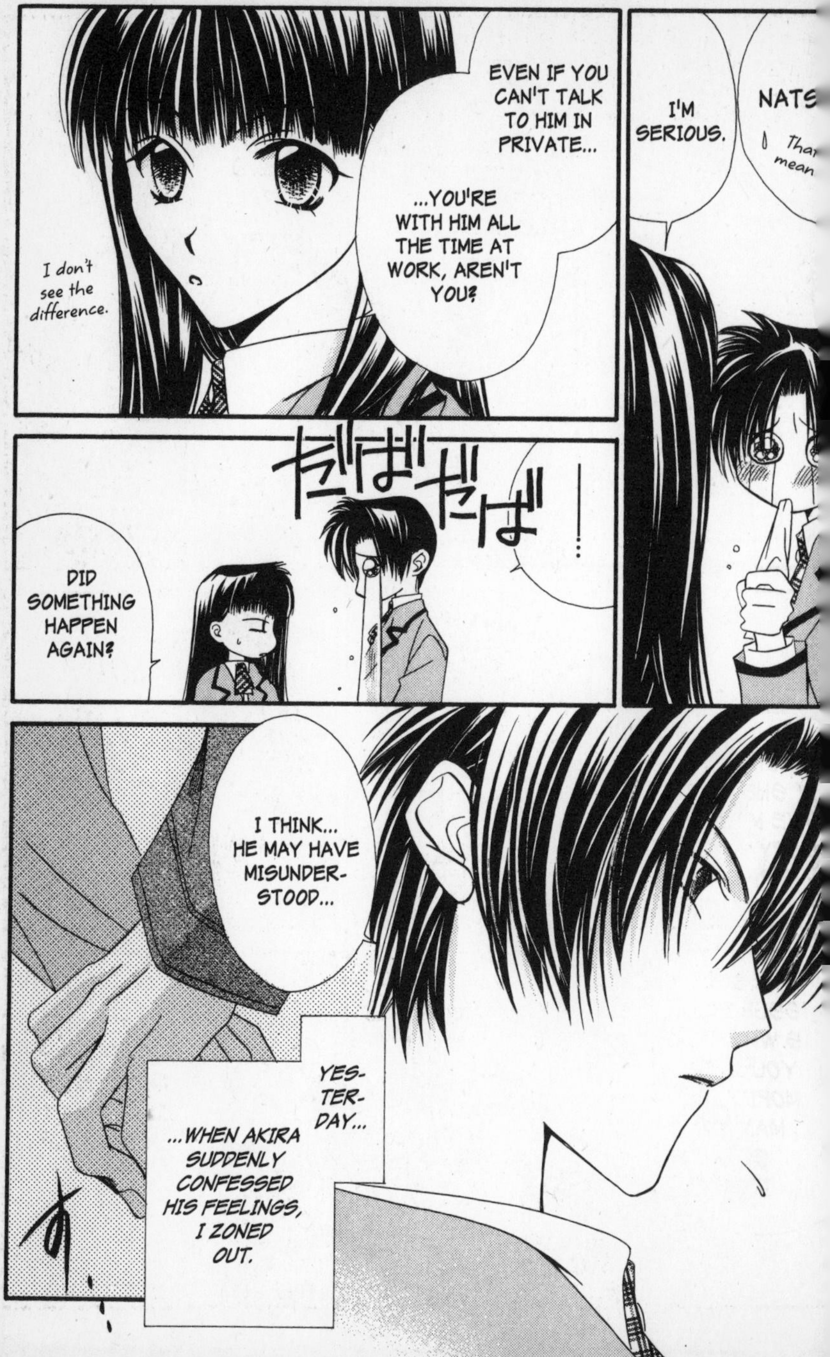
NATS
I'M SERIOUS.
EVEN IF YOU CAN'T TALK TO HIM IN PRIVATE...
...YOU'RE WITH HIM ALL THE TIME AT WORK, AREN'T YOU?
I don't see the difference.
だばだば
...!
DID SOMETHING HAPPEN AGAIN?
I THINK... HE MAY HAVE MISUNDER-STOOD...
YES-TER-DAY...
...WHEN AKIRA SUDDENLY CONFESSED HIS FEELINGS, I ZONED OUT.

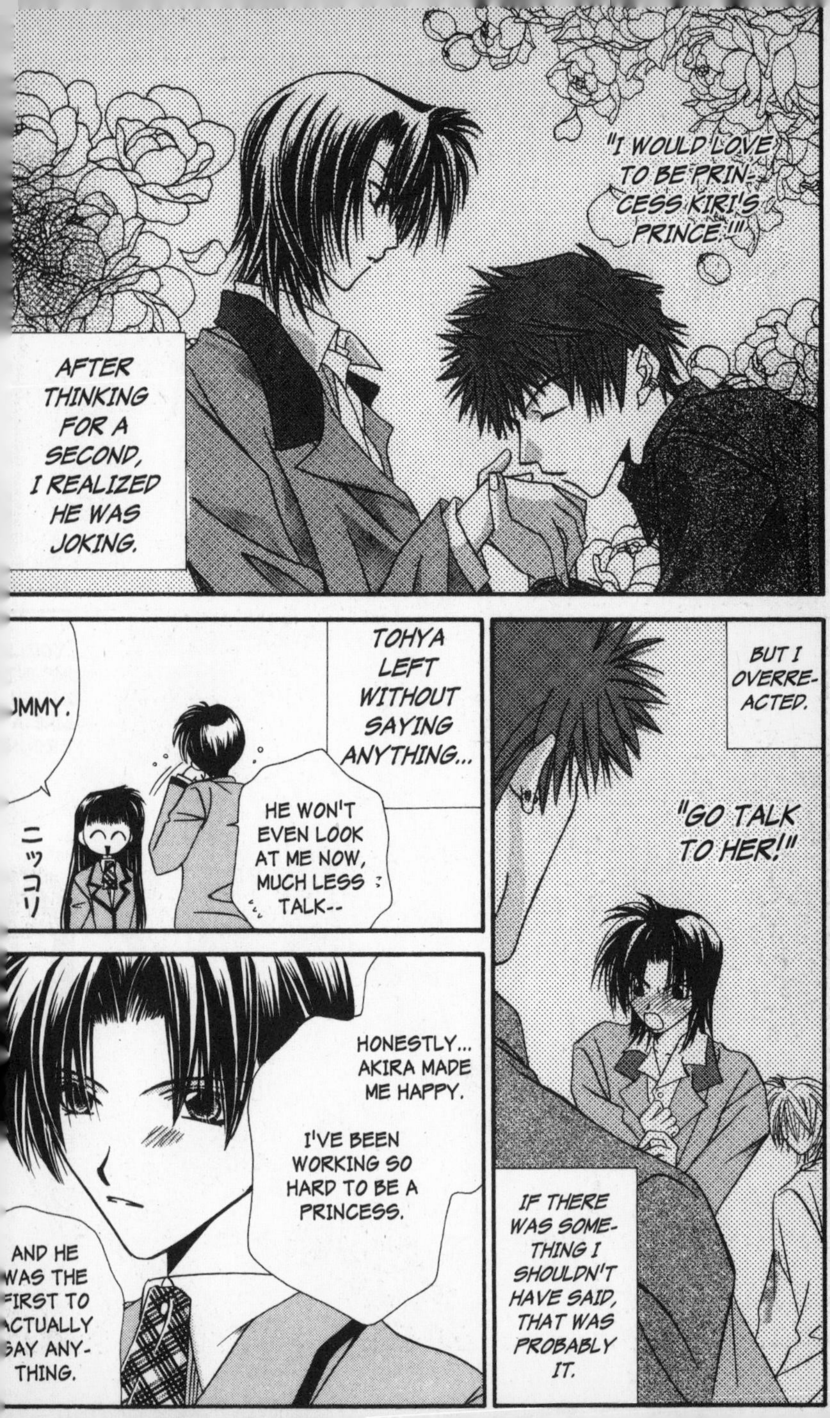
"I WOULD LOVE TO BE PRIN-CESS KIRI'S PRINCE!!!"
AFTER THINKING FOR A SECOND, I REALIZED HE WAS JOKING.
BUT I OVERRE-ACTED.
"GO TALK TO HER!"
IF THERE WAS SOME-THING I SHOULDN'T HAVE SAID, THAT WAS PROBABLY IT.
TOHYA LEFT WITHOUT SAYING ANYTHING...
HE WON'T EVEN LOOK AT ME NOW, MUCH LESS TALK--
UMMY.
ニッコリ
HONESTLY... AKIRA MADE ME HAPPY.
I'VE BEEN WORKING SO HARD TO BE A PRINCESS.
AND HE WAS THE FIRST TO ACTUALLY SAY ANY-THING.

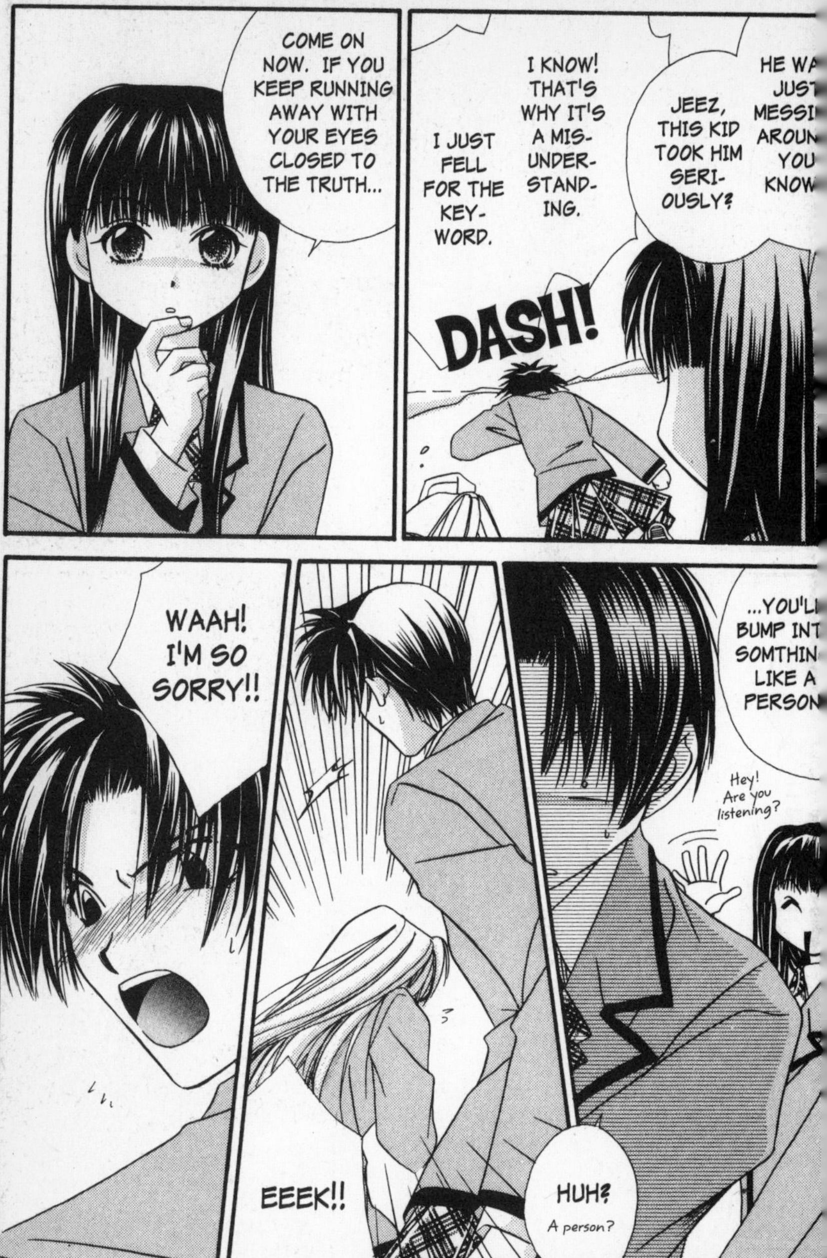
HE WA JUST MESSI AROUN YOU KNOW
JEEZ, THIS KID TOOK HIM SERIOUSLY?
I KNOW! THAT'S WHY IT'S A MISUNDERSTANDING.
I JUST FELL FOR THE KEYWORD.
DASH!
COME ON NOW. IF YOU KEEP RUNNING AWAY WITH YOUR EYES CLOSED TO THE TRUTH...
...YOU'L BUMP INT SOMTHIN LIKE A PERSON
Hey! Are you listening?
HUH?
A person?
EEEK!!
WAAH! I'M SO SORRY!!

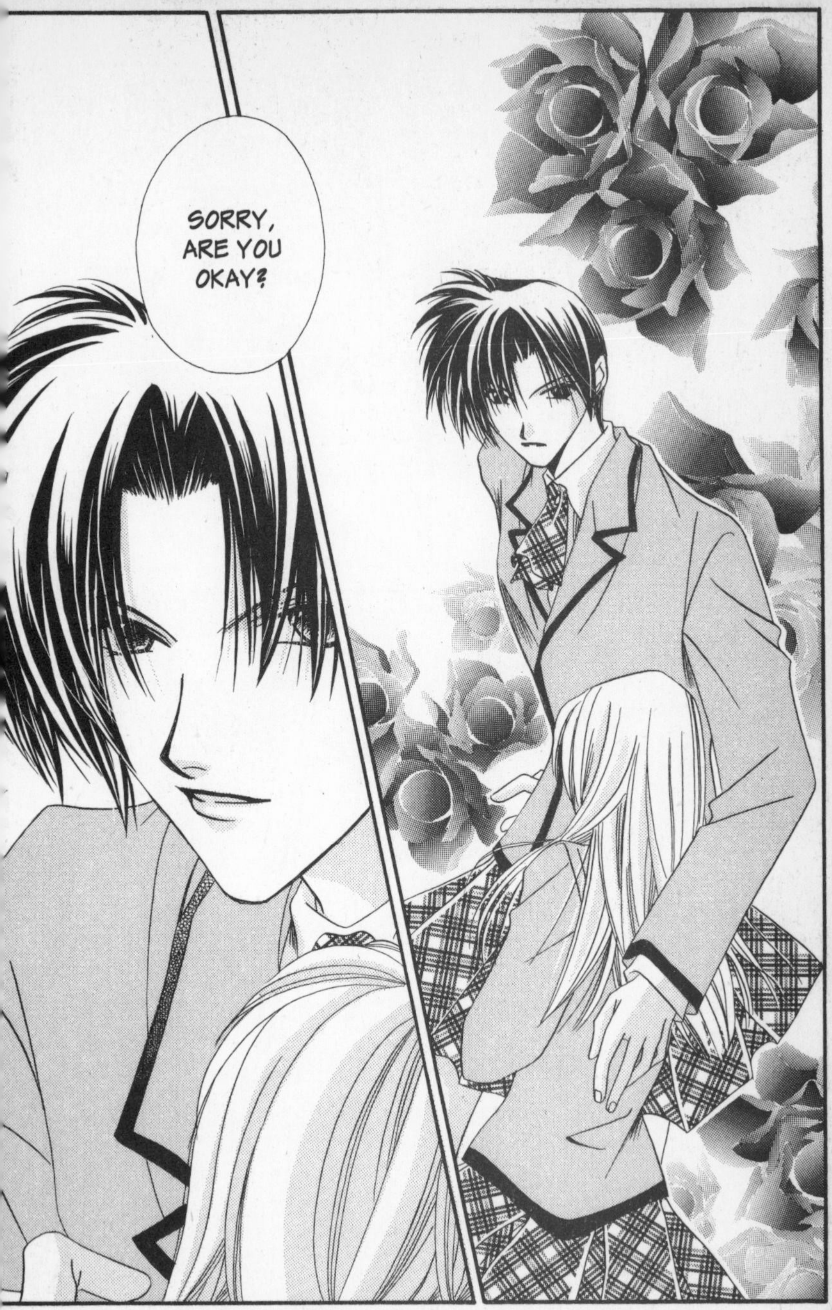
SORRY, ARE YOU OKAY?

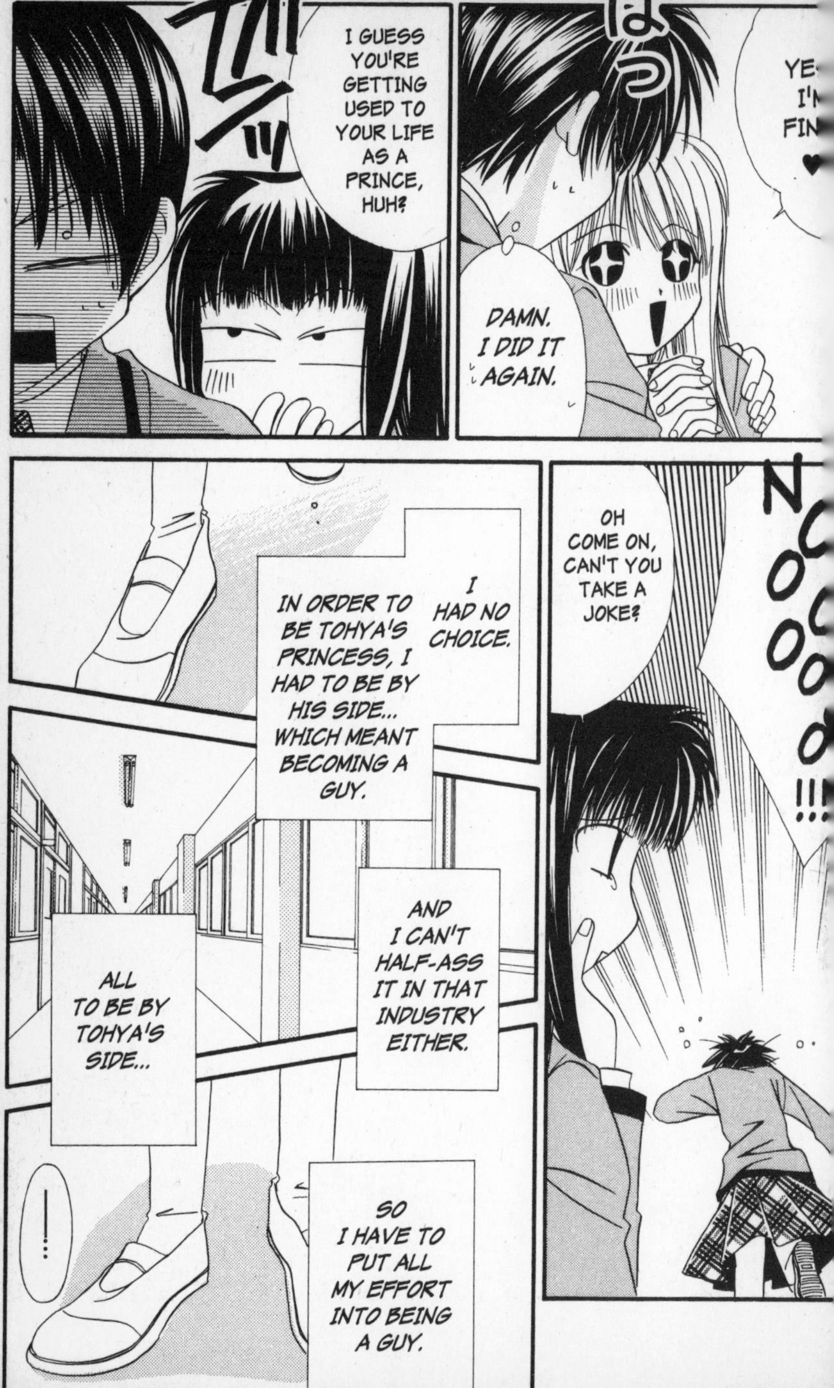
はっ
YE I'M FIN ♥
DAMN. I DID IT AGAIN.
I GUESS YOU'RE GETTING USED TO YOUR LIFE AS A PRINCE, HUH?
OH COME ON, CAN'T YOU TAKE A JOKE?
NOOOOOOO!!!
I HAD NO CHOICE.
IN ORDER TO BE TOHYA'S PRINCESS, I HAD TO BE BY HIS SIDE... WHICH MEANT BECOMING A GUY.
AND I CAN'T HALF-ASS IT IN THAT INDUSTRY EITHER.
ALL TO BE BY TOHYA'S SIDE...
!......
SO I HAVE TO PUT ALL MY EFFORT INTO BEING A GUY.

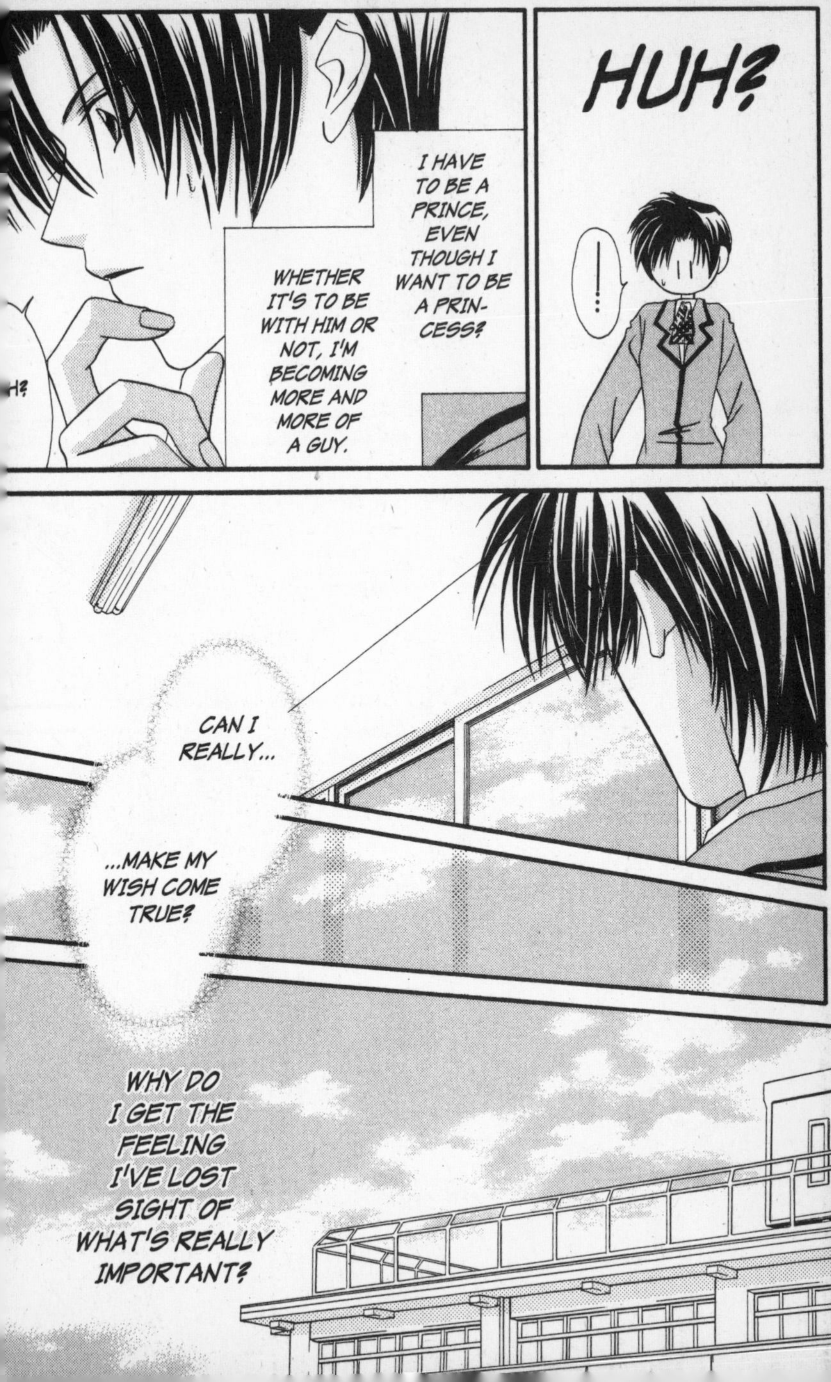
HUH?
...!
I HAVE TO BE A PRINCE, EVEN THOUGH I WANT TO BE A PRIN-CESS?
WHETHER IT'S TO BE WITH HIM OR NOT, I'M BECOMING MORE AND MORE OF A GUY.
CAN I REALLY...
...MAKE MY WISH COME TRUE?
WHY DO I GET THE FEELING I'VE LOST SIGHT OF WHAT'S REALLY IMPORTANT?

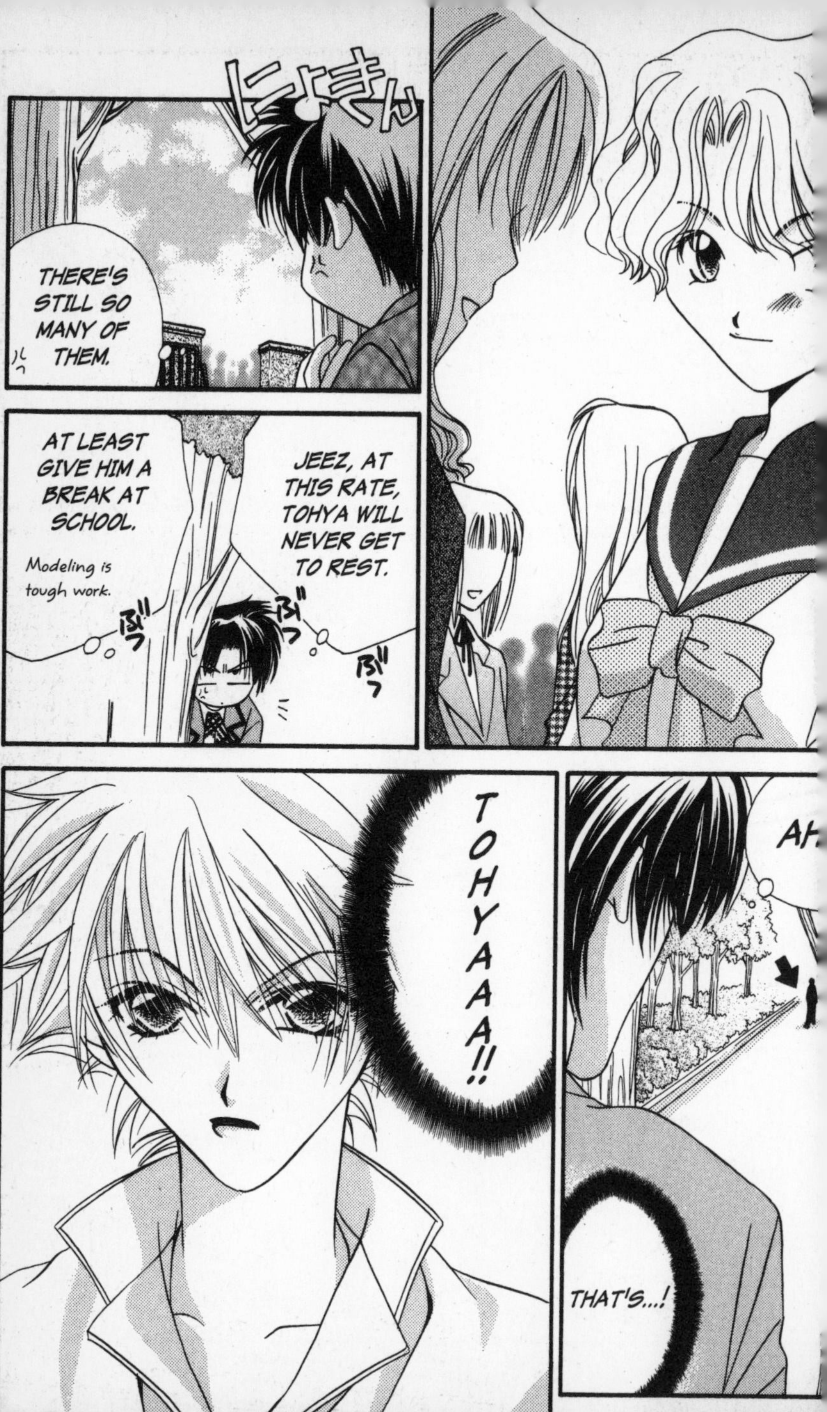
にょきん
THERE'S STILL SO MANY OF THEM.
JEEZ, AT THIS RATE, TOHYA WILL NEVER GET TO REST.
AT LEAST GIVE HIM A BREAK AT SCHOOL.
Modeling is tough work.
AH
THAT'S...!
TOHYAAAA!!

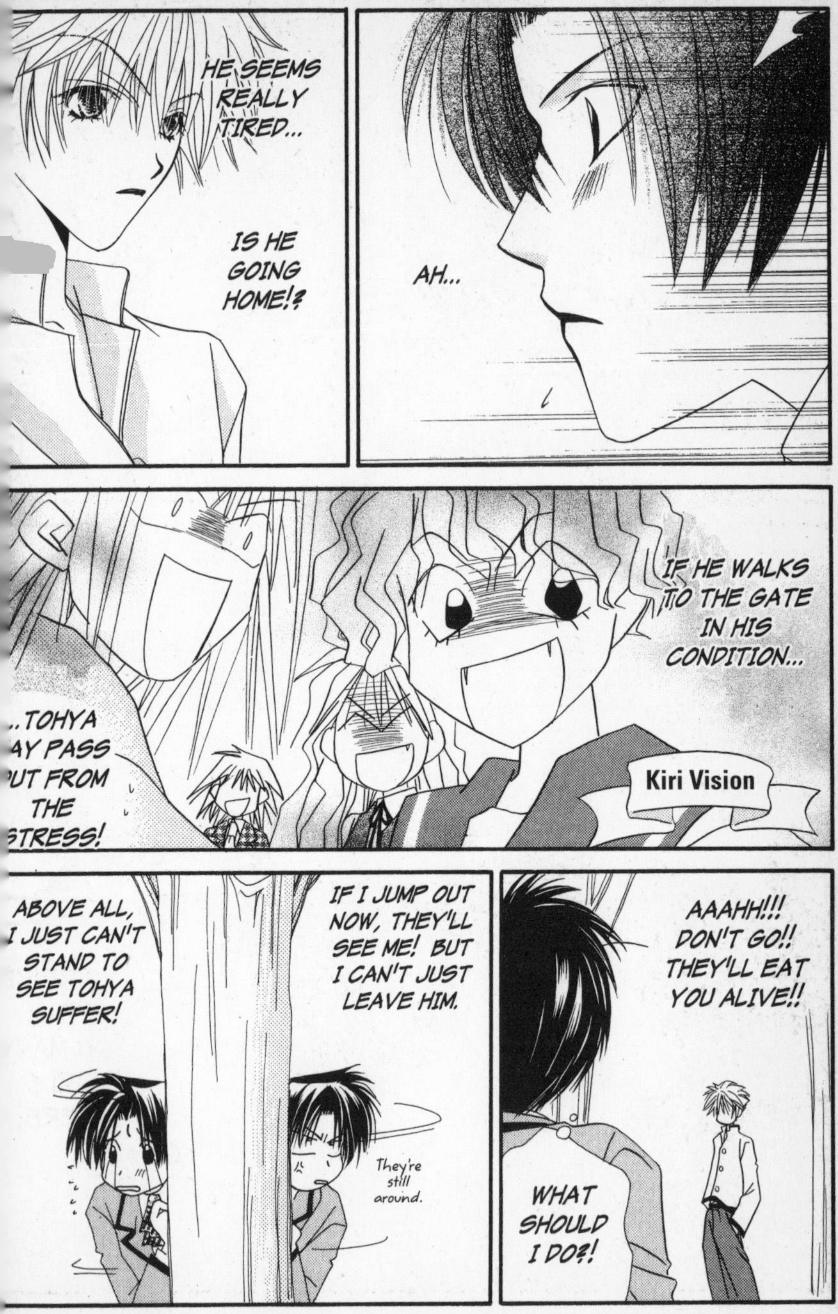
AH...
HE SEEMS REALLY TIRED...
IS HE GOING HOME!?
IF HE WALKS TO THE GATE IN HIS CONDITION...
Kiri Vision
..TOHYA AY PASS UT FROM THE STRESS!
AAAHH!!! DON'T GO!! THEY'LL EAT YOU ALIVE!!
WHAT SHOULD I DO?!
IF I JUMP OUT NOW, THEY'LL SEE ME! BUT I CAN'T JUST LEAVE HIM.
They're still around.
ABOVE ALL, I JUST CAN'T STAND TO SEE TOHYA SUFFER!

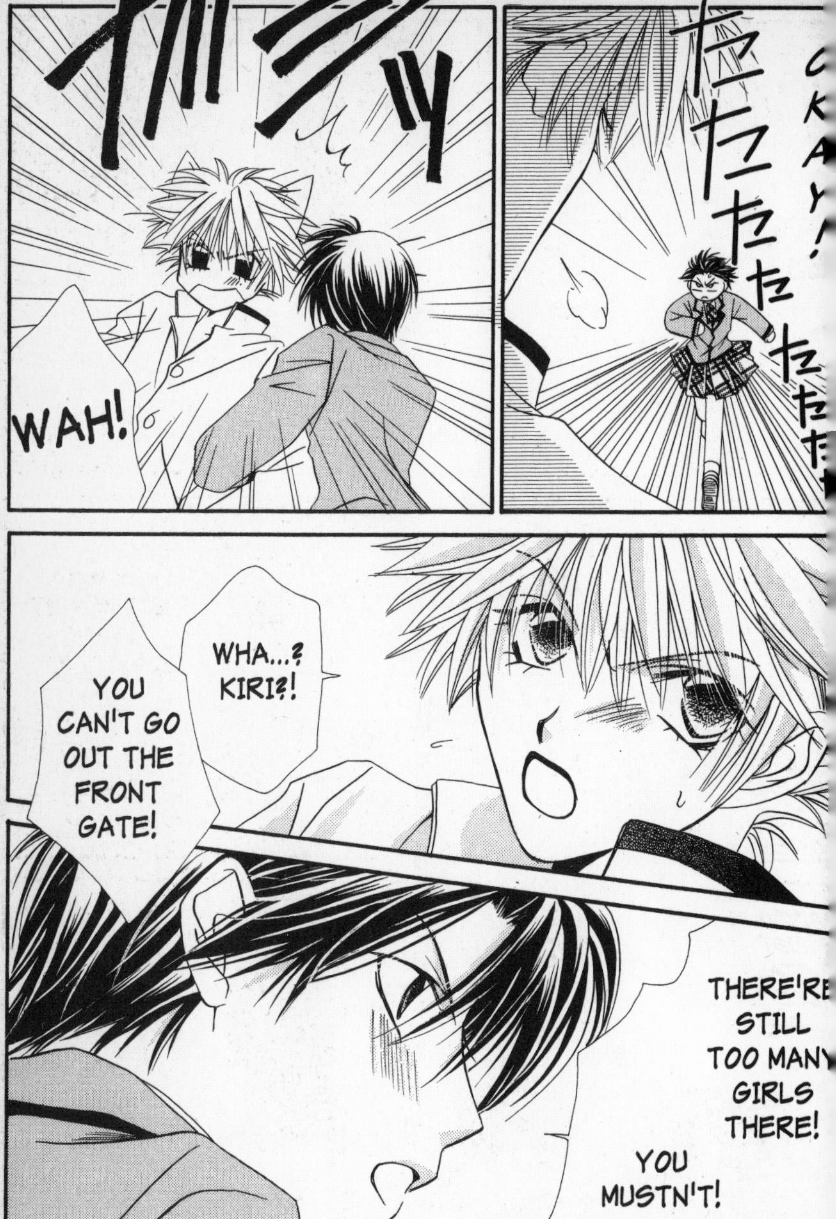

OKAY!
たーたたたたた
ガシッ
WAH!
WHA...? KIRI?!
YOU CAN'T GO OUT THE FRONT GATE!
THERE'RE STILL TOO MANY GIRLS THERE!
YOU MUSTN'T!

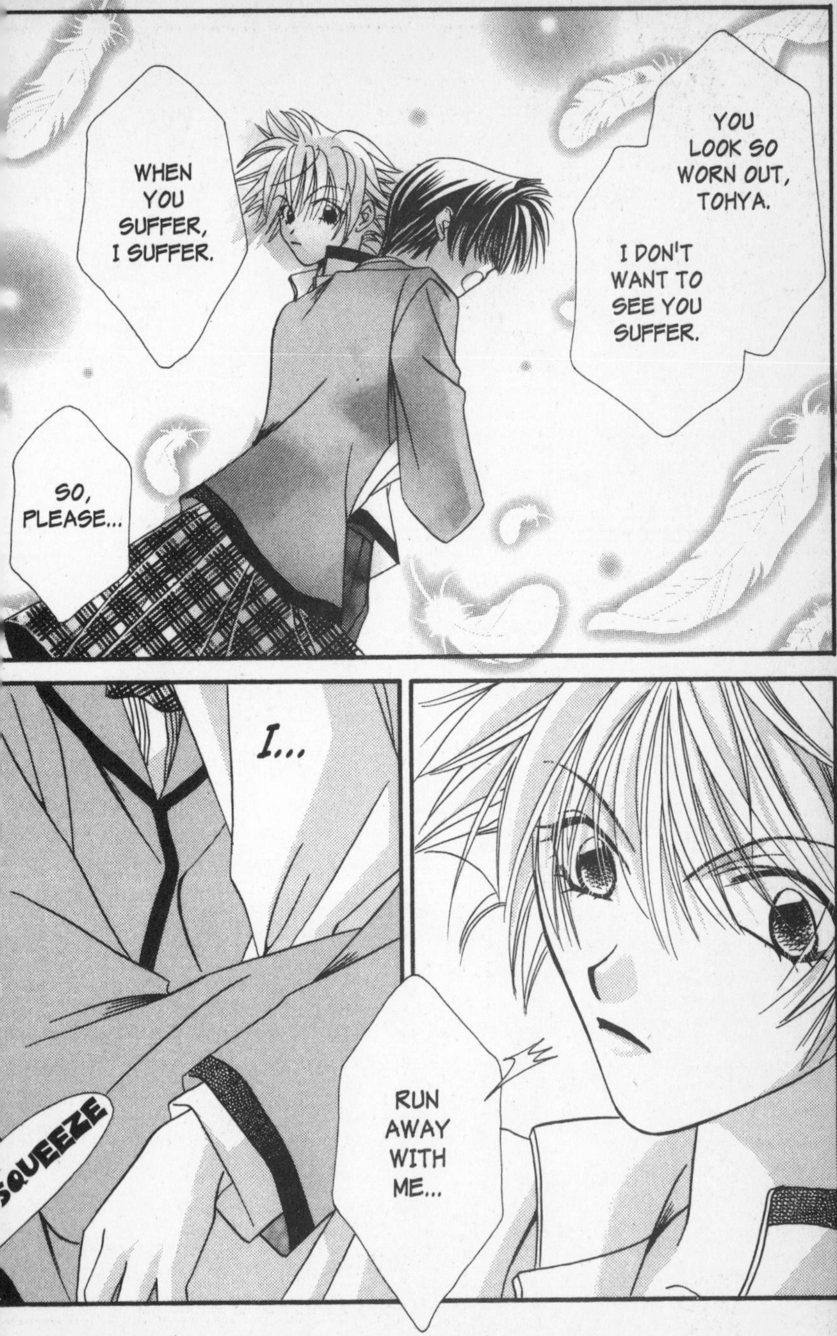
YOU LOOK SO WORN OUT, TOHYA.
I DON'T WANT TO SEE YOU SUFFER.
WHEN YOU SUFFER, I SUFFER.
SO, PLEASE...
RUN AWAY WITH ME...
I...
SQUEEZE

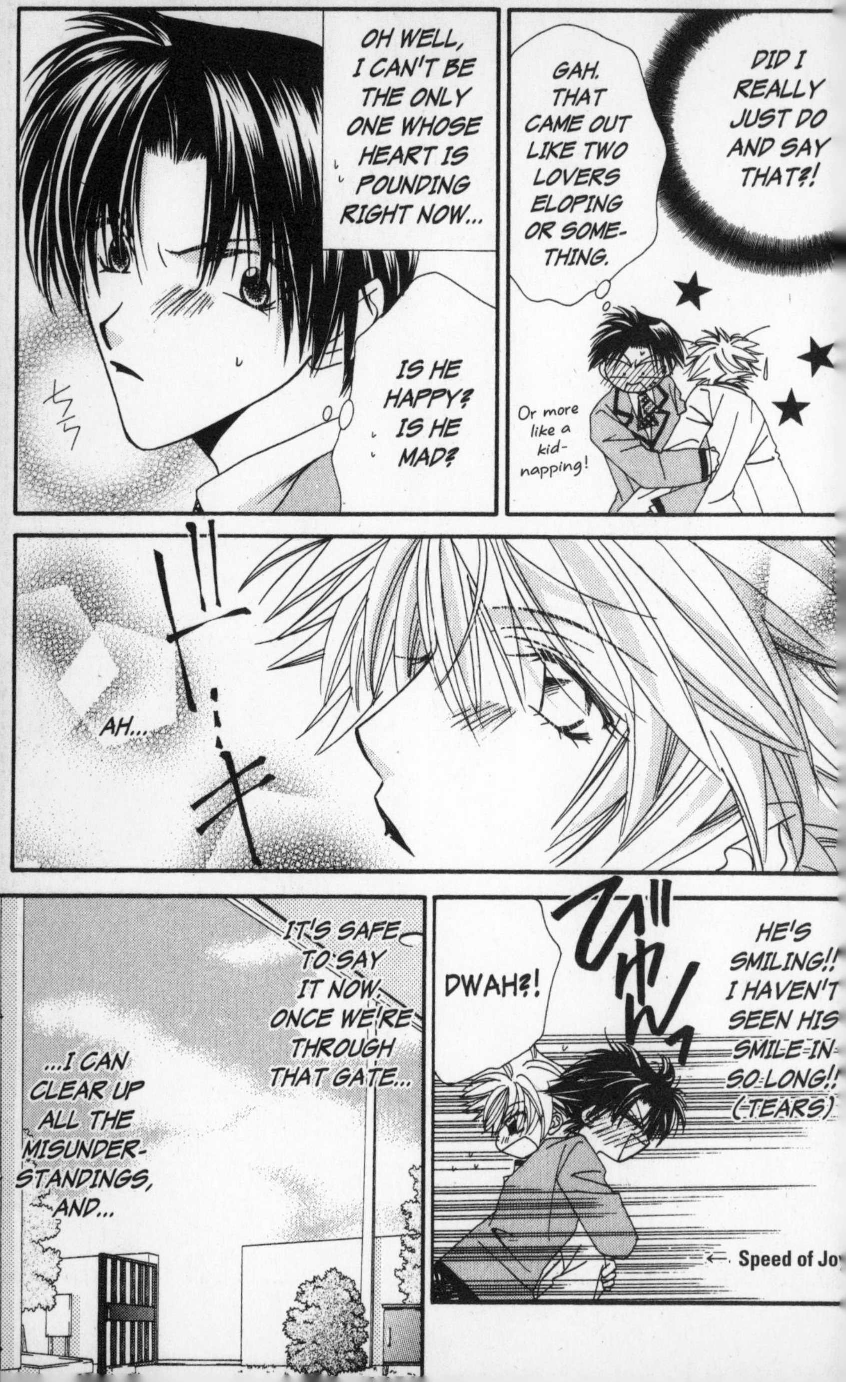
DID I REALLY JUST DO AND SAY THAT?!
GAH. THAT CAME OUT LIKE TWO LOVERS ELOPING OR SOME-THING.
Or more like a kid-napping!
OH WELL, I CAN'T BE THE ONLY ONE WHOSE HEART IS POUNDING RIGHT NOW...
IS HE HAPPY? IS HE MAD?
AH...
HE'S SMILING!! I HAVEN'T SEEN HIS SMILE IN SO LONG!! (TEARS)
DWAH?!
Speed of Jo
IT'S SAFE TO SAY IT NOW. ONCE WE'RE THROUGH THAT GATE...
...I CAN CLEAR UP ALL THE MISUNDER-STANDINGS, AND...

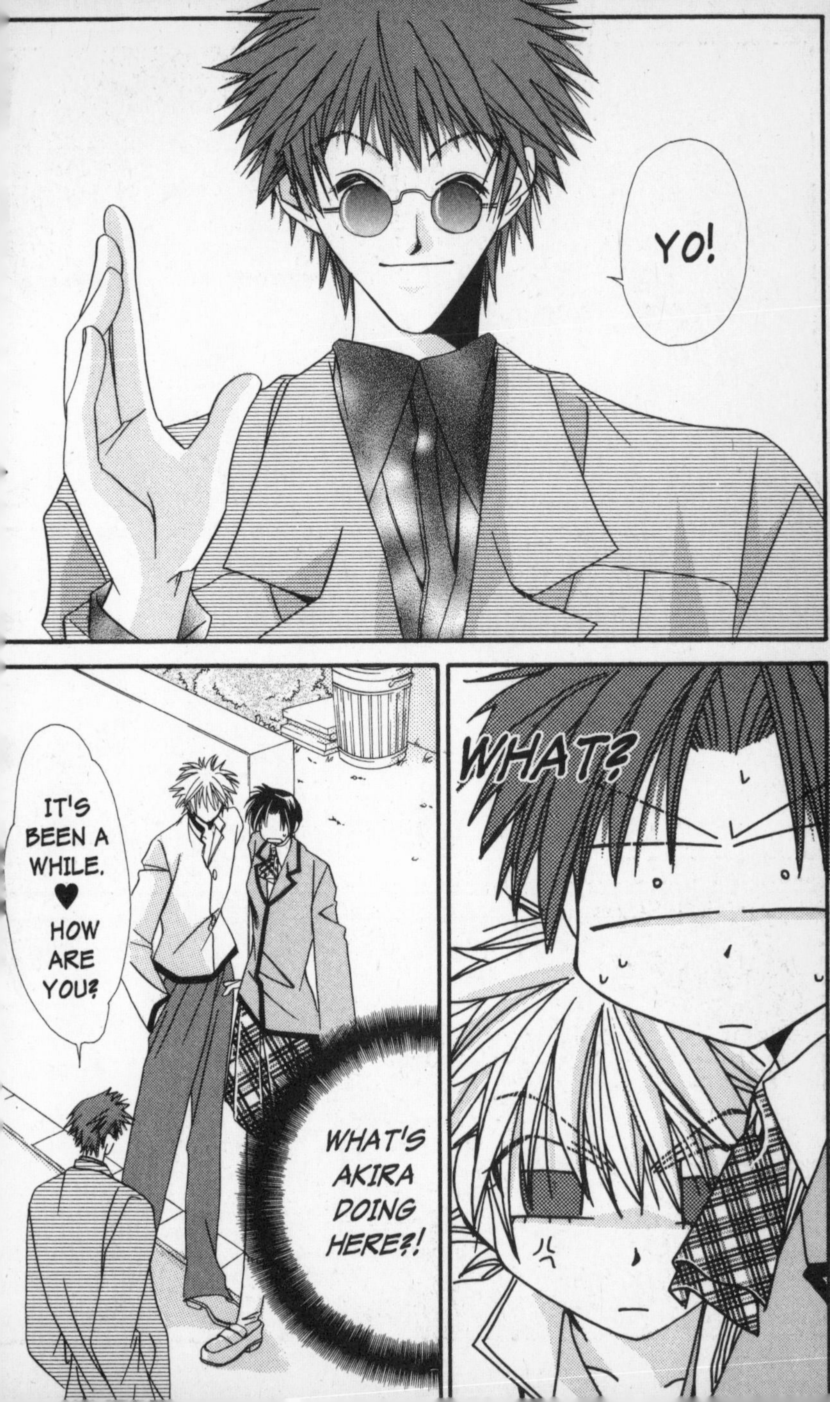
YO!
WHAT?
IT'S BEEN A WHILE. ♥ HOW ARE YOU?
WHAT'S AKIRA DOING HERE?!

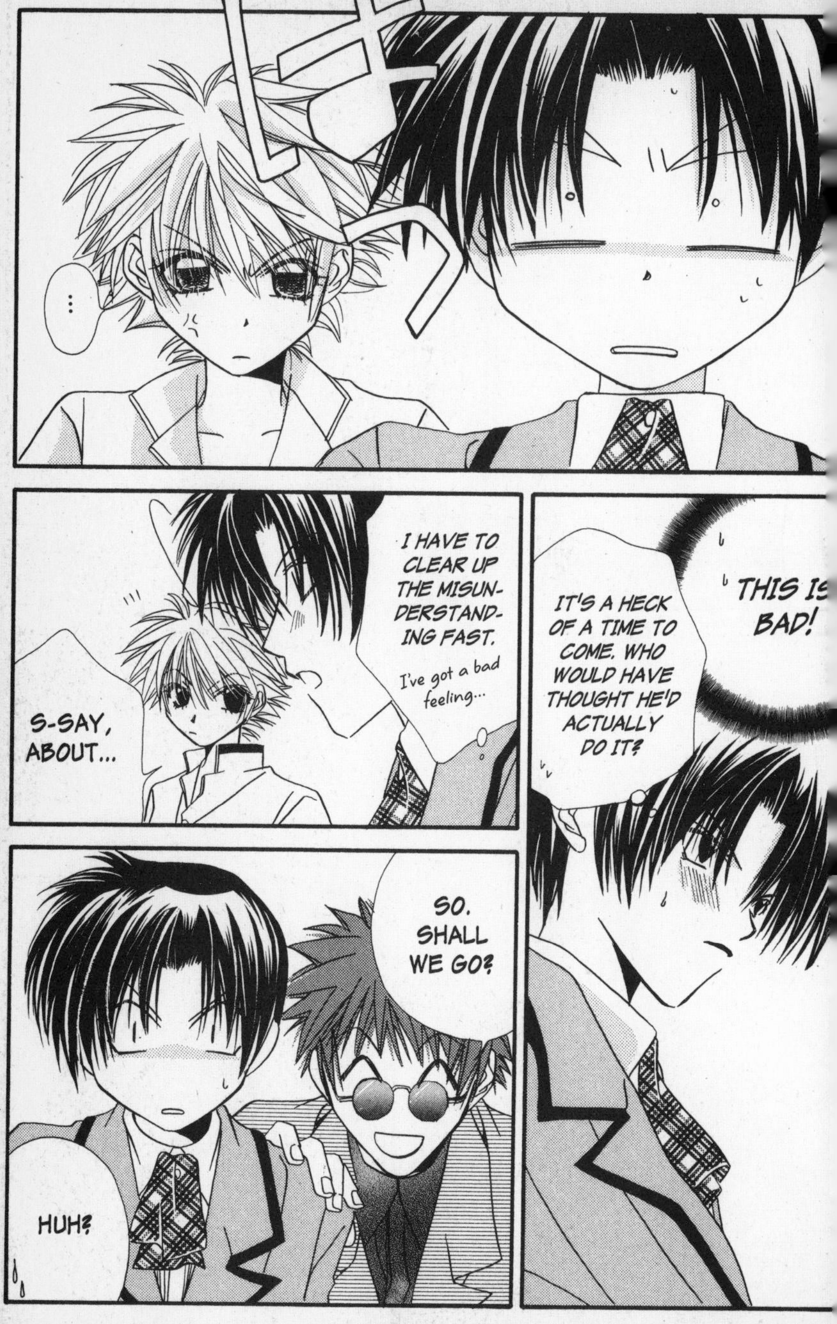

...
THIS IS BAD!
IT'S A HECK OF A TIME TO COME. WHO WOULD HAVE THOUGHT HE'D ACTUALLY DO IT?
I HAVE TO CLEAR UP THE MISUNDERSTANDING FAST.
I've got a bad feeling...
S-SAY, ABOUT...
SO. SHALL WE GO?
HUH?

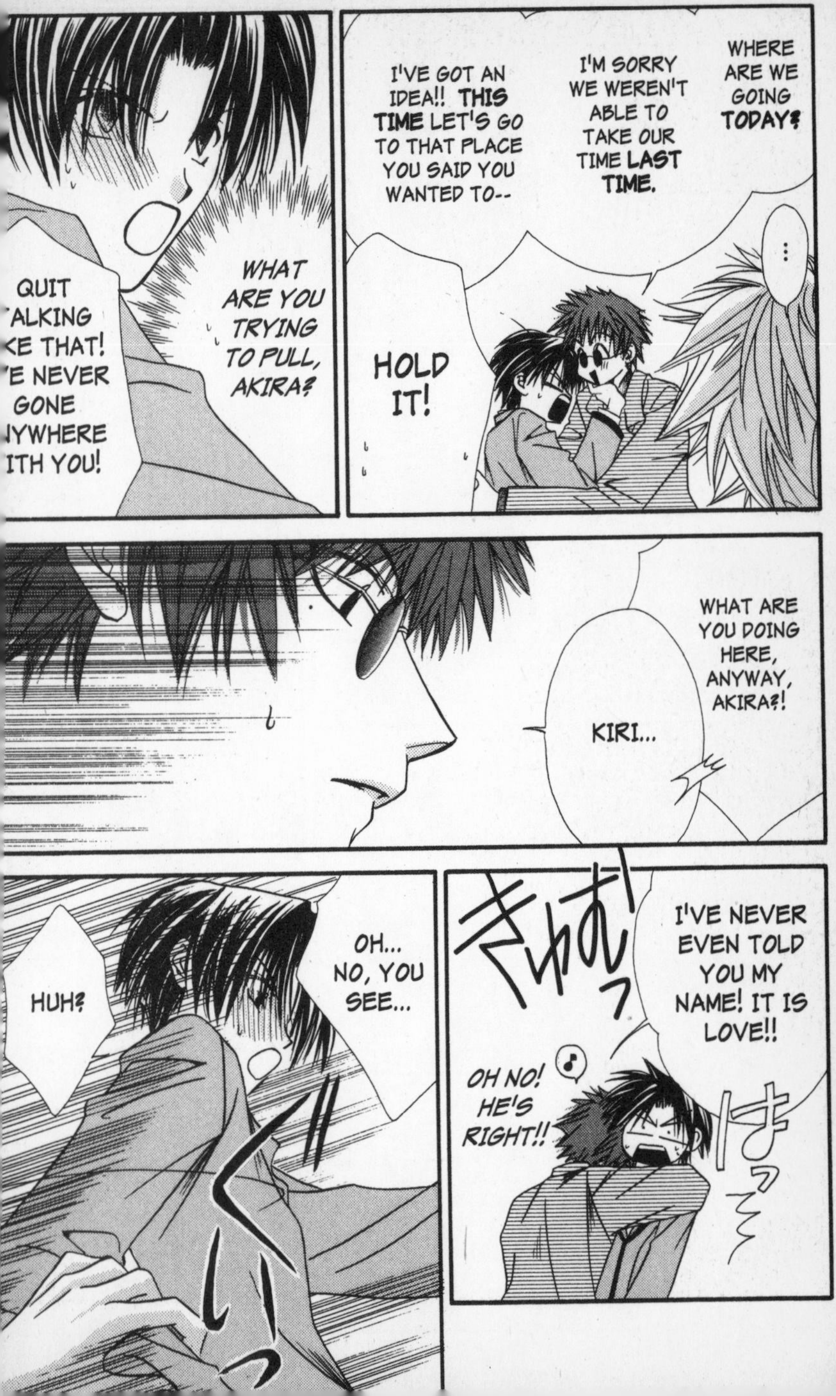
WHERE ARE WE GOING TODAY?
I'M SORRY WE WEREN'T ABLE TO TAKE OUR TIME LAST TIME.
I'VE GOT AN IDEA!! THIS TIME LET'S GO TO THAT PLACE YOU SAID YOU WANTED TO--
...
HOLD IT!
WHAT ARE YOU TRYING TO PULL, AKIRA?
QUIT ALKING KE THAT! 'E NEVER GONE NYWHERE ITH YOU!
WHAT ARE YOU DOING HERE, ANYWAY, AKIRA?!
KIRI...
I'VE NEVER EVEN TOLD YOU MY NAME! IT IS LOVE!!
OH NO! HE'S RIGHT!!
はっ
OH... NO, YOU SEE...
HUH?
くいっ

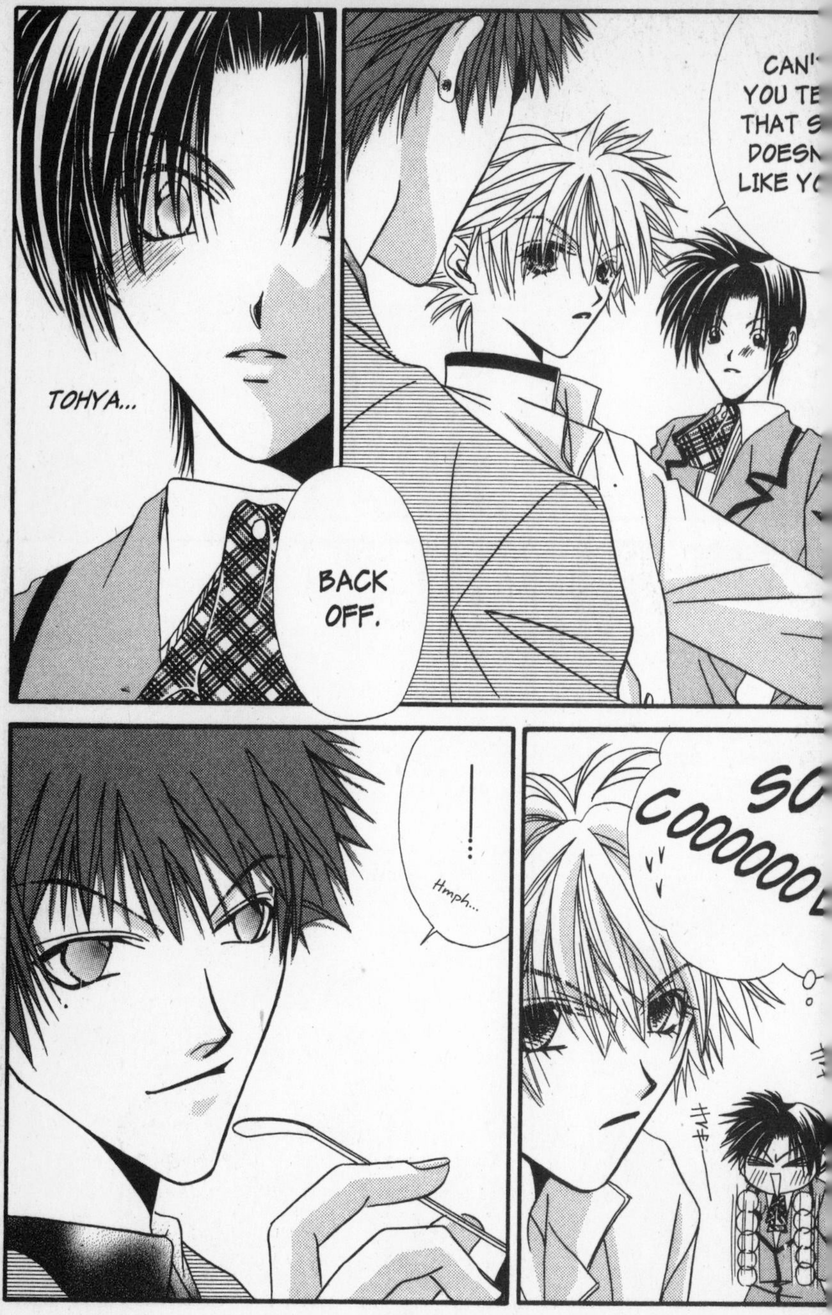

CAN'
YOU TE
THAT S
DOESN
LIKE YO
TOHYA...
BACK OFF.
SO
COOOOOOO
キャ
キャ
Hmph...

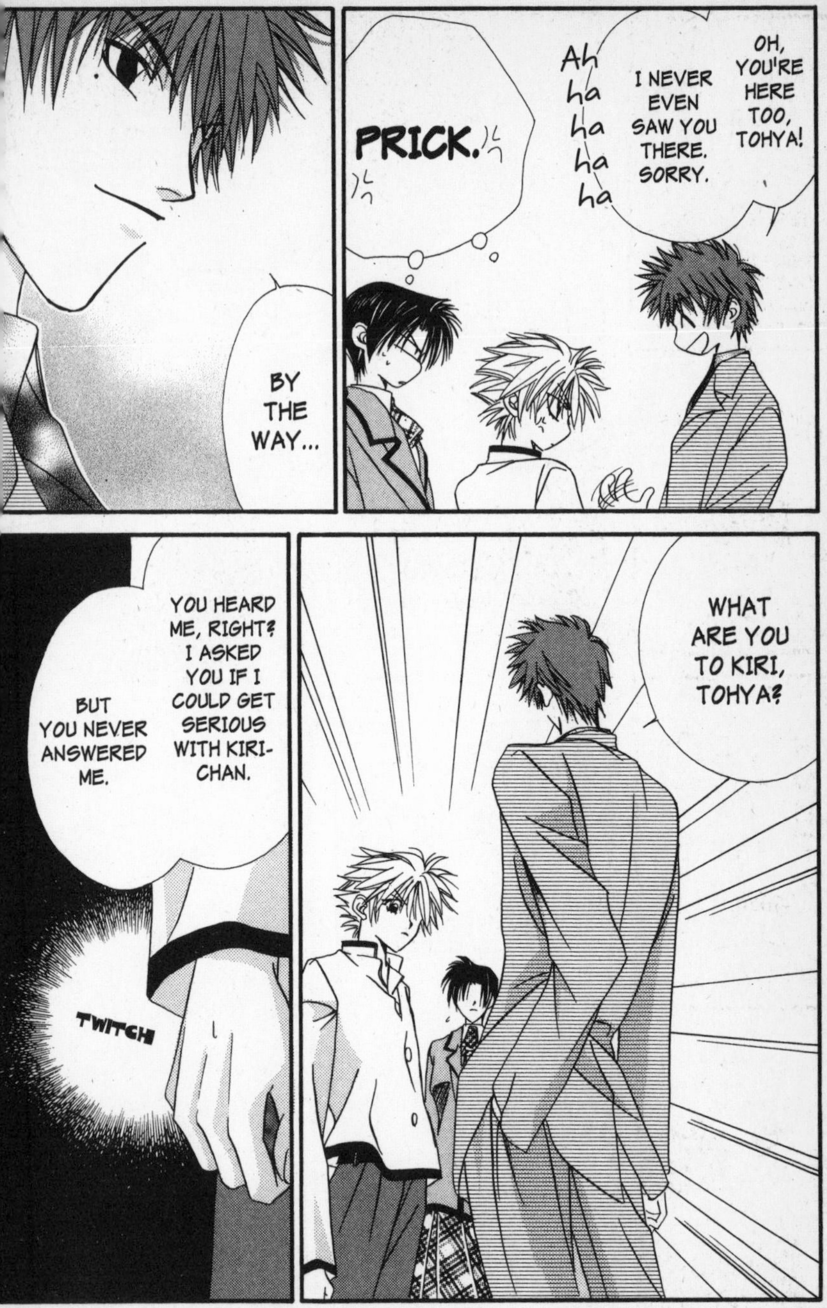
OH, YOU'RE HERE TOO, TOHYA!
I NEVER EVEN SAW YOU THERE. SORRY.
Ah ha ha ha ha
PRICK.
BY THE WAY...
WHAT ARE YOU TO KIRI, TOHYA?
YOU HEARD ME, RIGHT? I ASKED YOU IF I COULD GET SERIOUS WITH KIRI-CHAN.
BUT YOU NEVER ANSWERED ME.
TWITCH

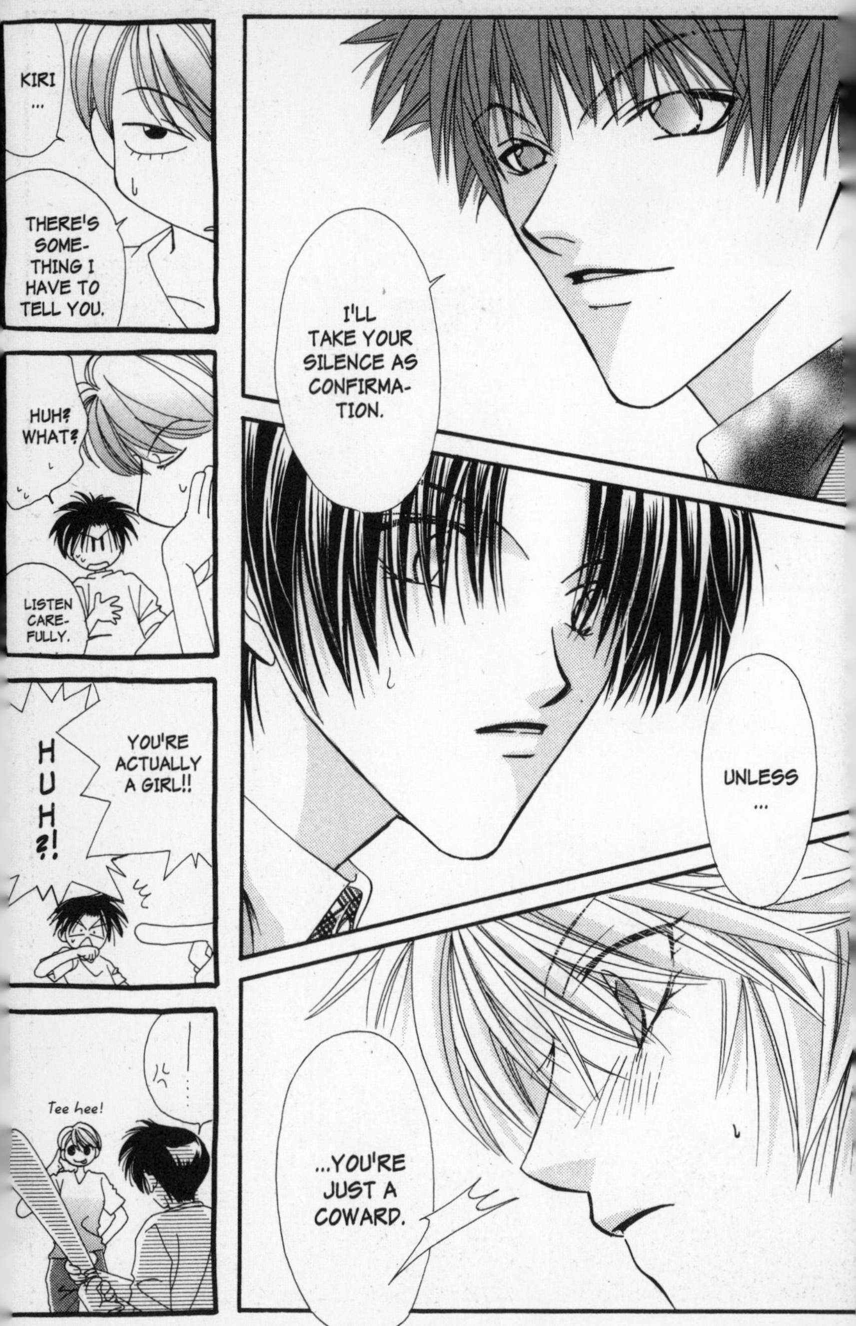
I'LL TAKE YOUR SILENCE AS CONFIRMATION.
UNLESS ...
...YOU'RE JUST A COWARD.
KIRI ...
THERE'S SOMETHING I HAVE TO TELL YOU.
HUH? WHAT?
LISTEN CAREFULLY.
YOU'RE ACTUALLY A GIRL!!
HUH?!
Tee hee!

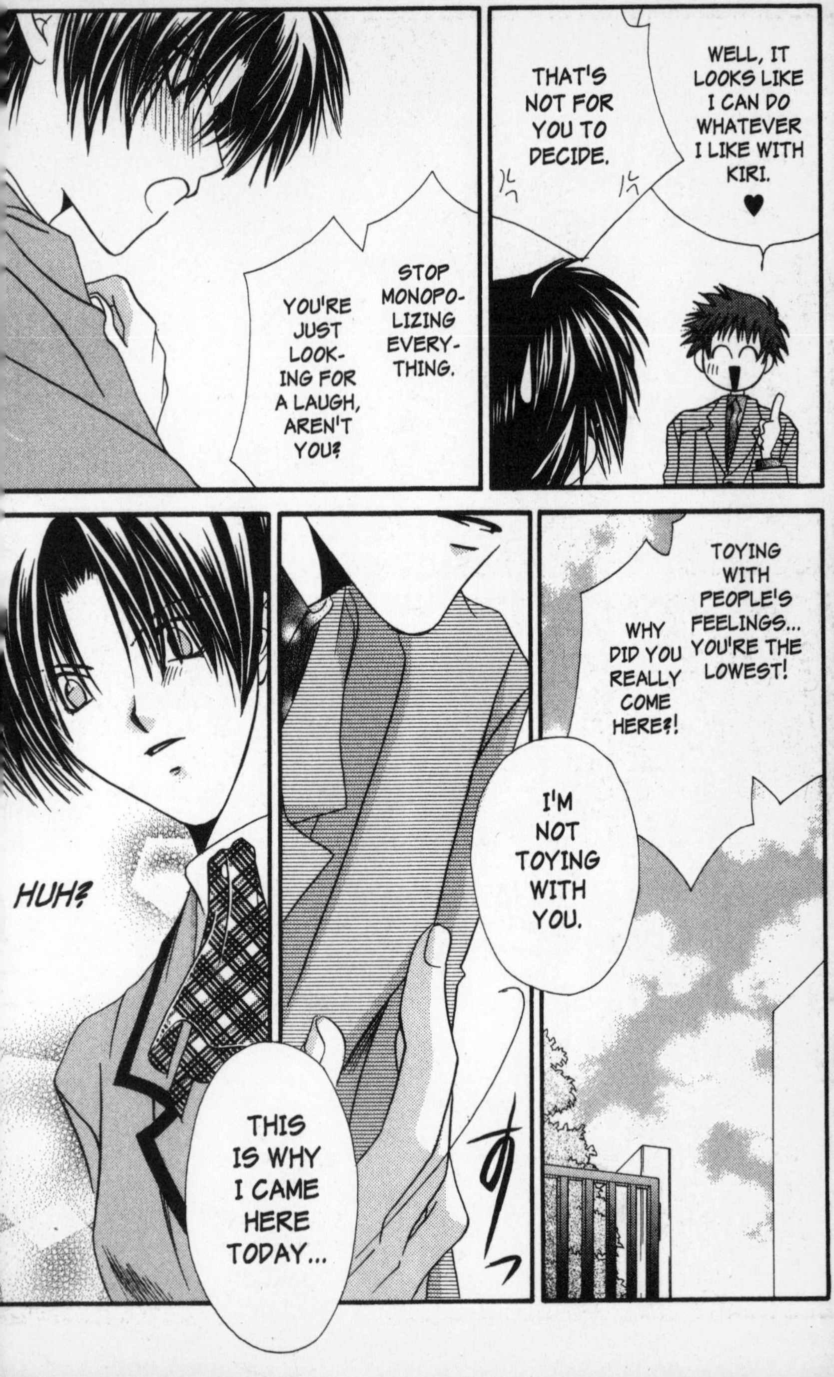
WELL, IT LOOKS LIKE I CAN DO WHATEVER I LIKE WITH KIRI. ♥
THAT'S NOT FOR YOU TO DECIDE.
STOP MONOPO-LIZING EVERY-THING.
YOU'RE JUST LOOK-ING FOR A LAUGH, AREN'T YOU?
TOYING WITH PEOPLE'S FEELINGS... YOU'RE THE LOWEST!
WHY DID YOU REALLY COME HERE?!
I'M NOT TOYING WITH YOU.
THIS IS WHY I CAME HERE TODAY...
HUH?

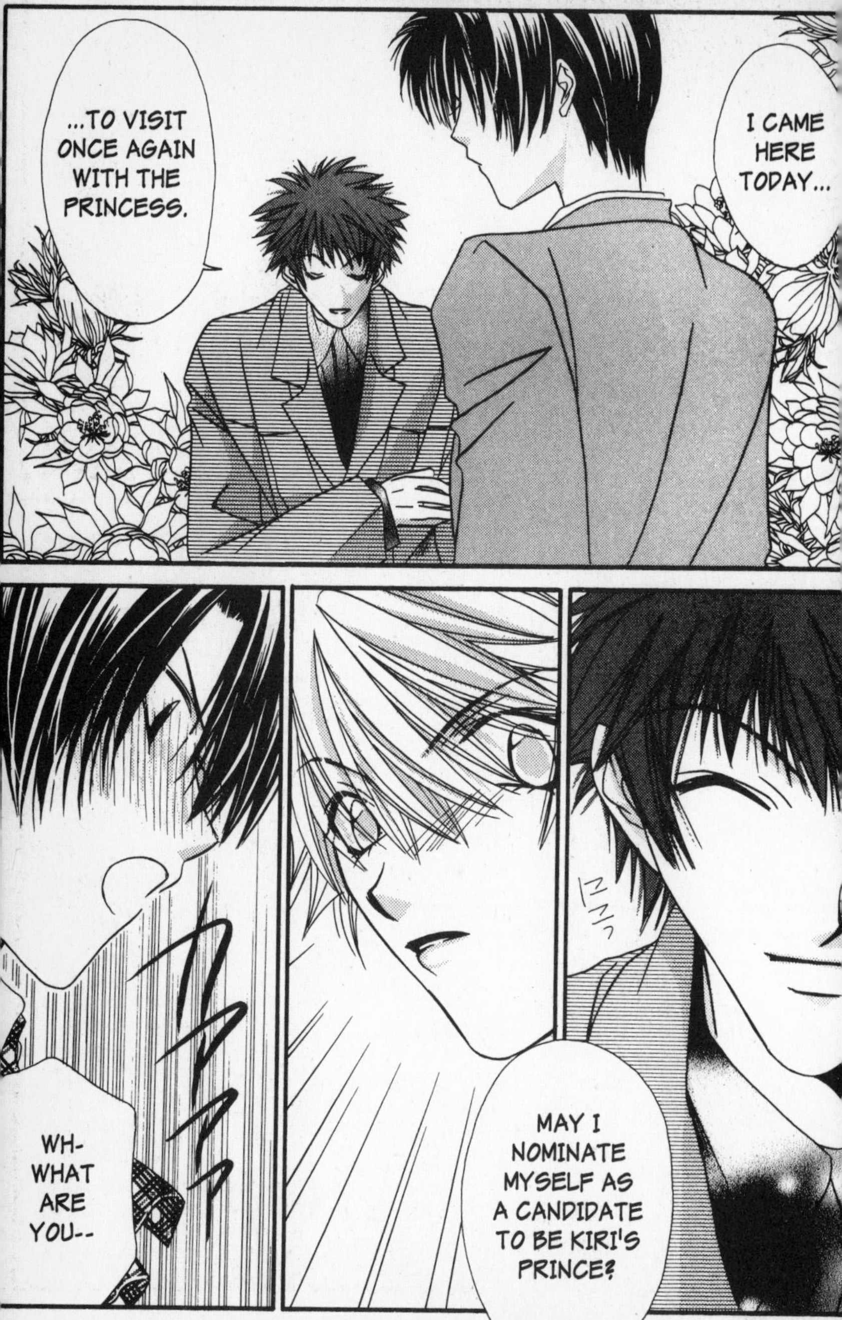
I CAME HERE TODAY...
...TO VISIT ONCE AGAIN WITH THE PRINCESS.
MAY I NOMINATE MYSELF AS A CANDIDATE TO BE KIRI'S PRINCE?
WH- WHAT ARE YOU--

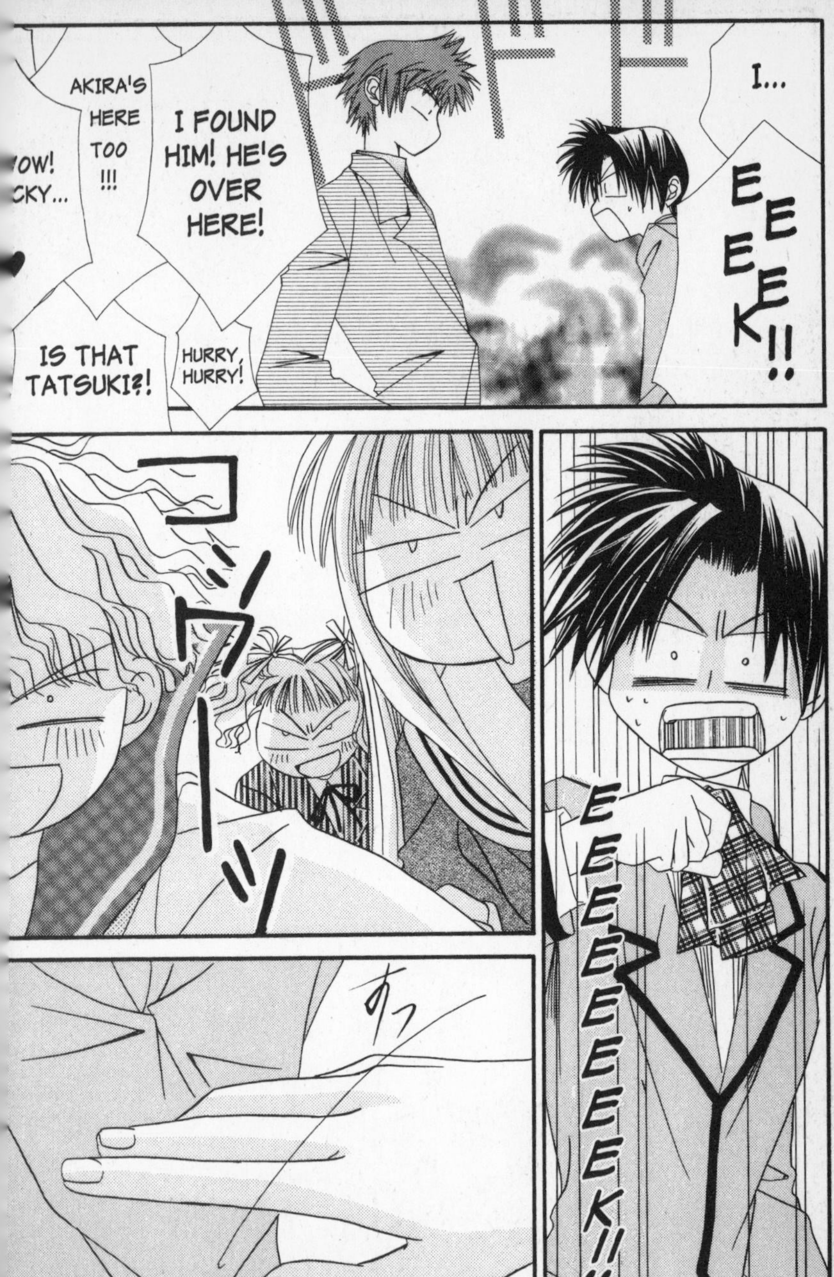

I...
EEEEK!!
I FOUND HIM! HE'S OVER HERE!
AKIRA'S HERE TOO !!!
OW! CKY...
HURRY, HURRY!
IS THAT TATSUKI?!
EEEEEEEEK!!

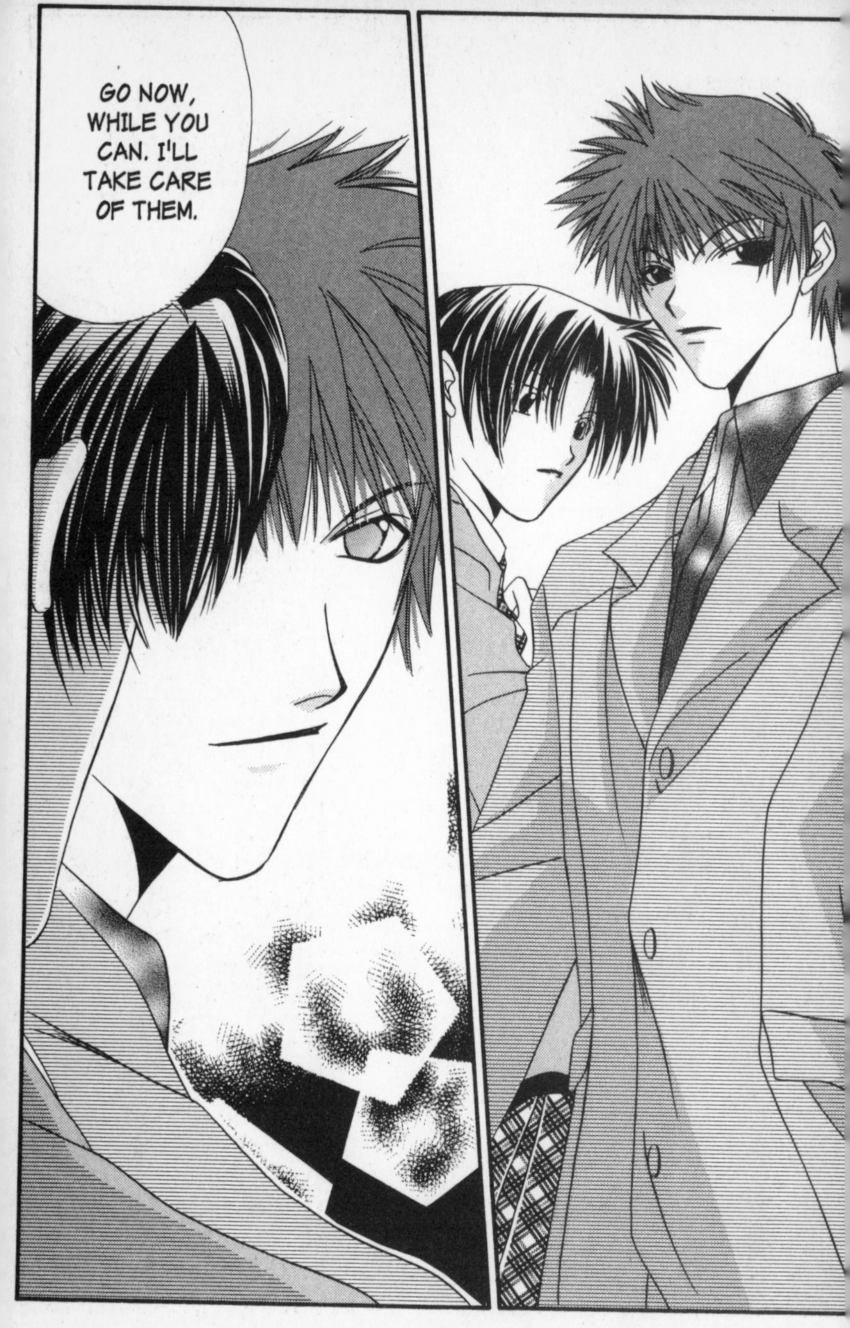
GO NOW, WHILE YOU CAN. I'LL TAKE CARE OF THEM.

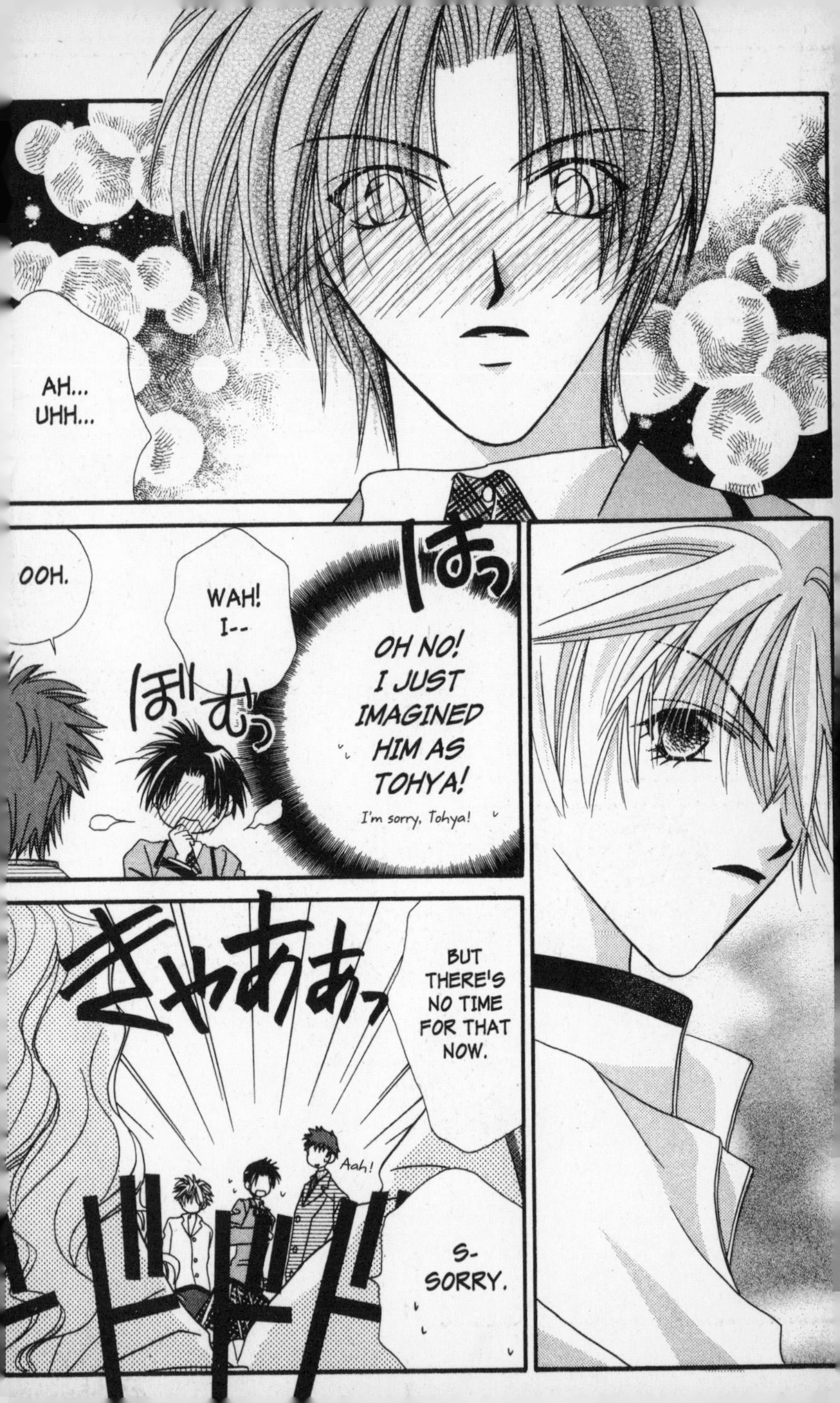
AH... UHH...
はっ
OH NO! I JUST IMAGINED HIM AS TOHYA!
I'm sorry, Tohya!
WAH! I--
ぼむっ
OOH.
BUT THERE'S NO TIME FOR THAT NOW.
きゃあああっ
Aah!
S- SORRY.

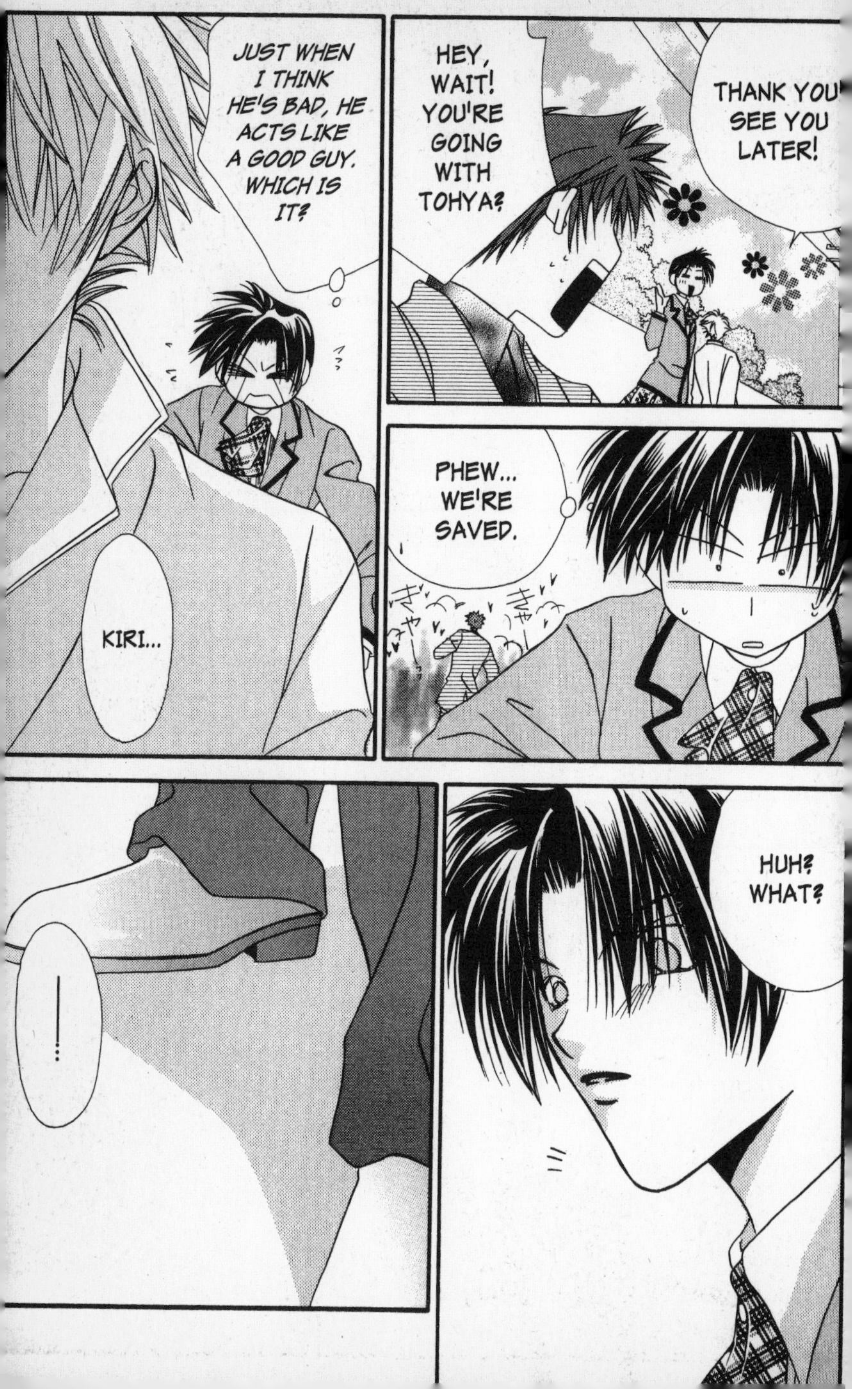
THANK YOU SEE YOU LATER!
HEY, WAIT! YOU'RE GOING WITH TOHYA?
PHEW... WE'RE SAVED.
JUST WHEN I THINK HE'S BAD, HE ACTS LIKE A GOOD GUY. WHICH IS IT?
KIRI...
HUH? WHAT?
......

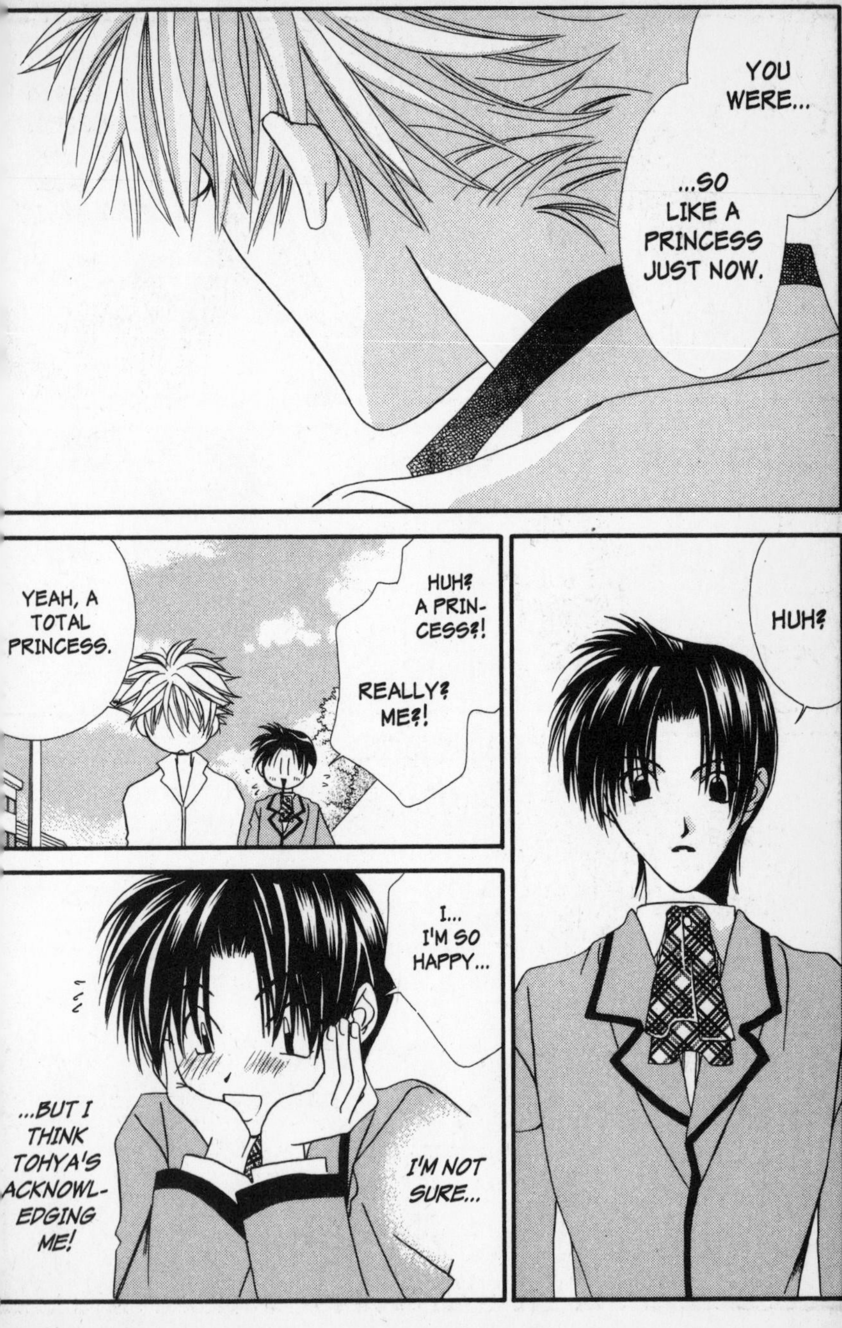
YOU WERE...
...SO LIKE A PRINCESS JUST NOW.
HUH?
HUH? A PRIN-CESS?!
REALLY? ME?!
YEAH, A TOTAL PRINCESS.
I... I'M SO HAPPY...
I'M NOT SURE...
...BUT I THINK TOHYA'S ACKNOWL-EDGING ME!

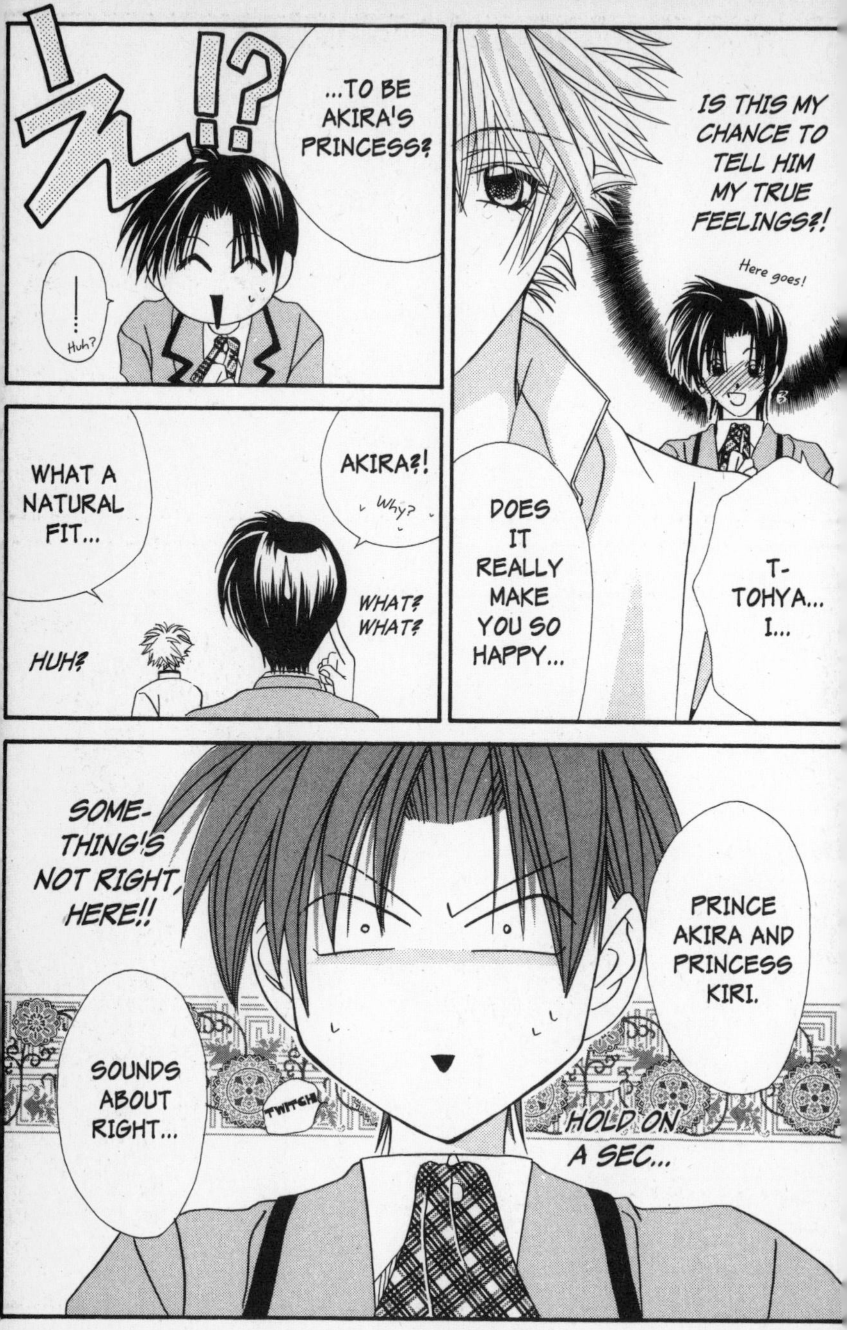
IS THIS MY CHANCE TO TELL HIM MY TRUE FEELINGS?!
Here goes!
T-TOHYA... I...
DOES IT REALLY MAKE YOU SO HAPPY...
...TO BE AKIRA'S PRINCESS?
え!?
!... Huh?
AKIRA?!
Why?
WHAT? WHAT?
WHAT A NATURAL FIT...
HUH?
PRINCE AKIRA AND PRINCESS KIRI.
HOLD ON A SEC...
SOMETHING'S NOT RIGHT, HERE!!
TWITCH
SOUNDS ABOUT RIGHT...

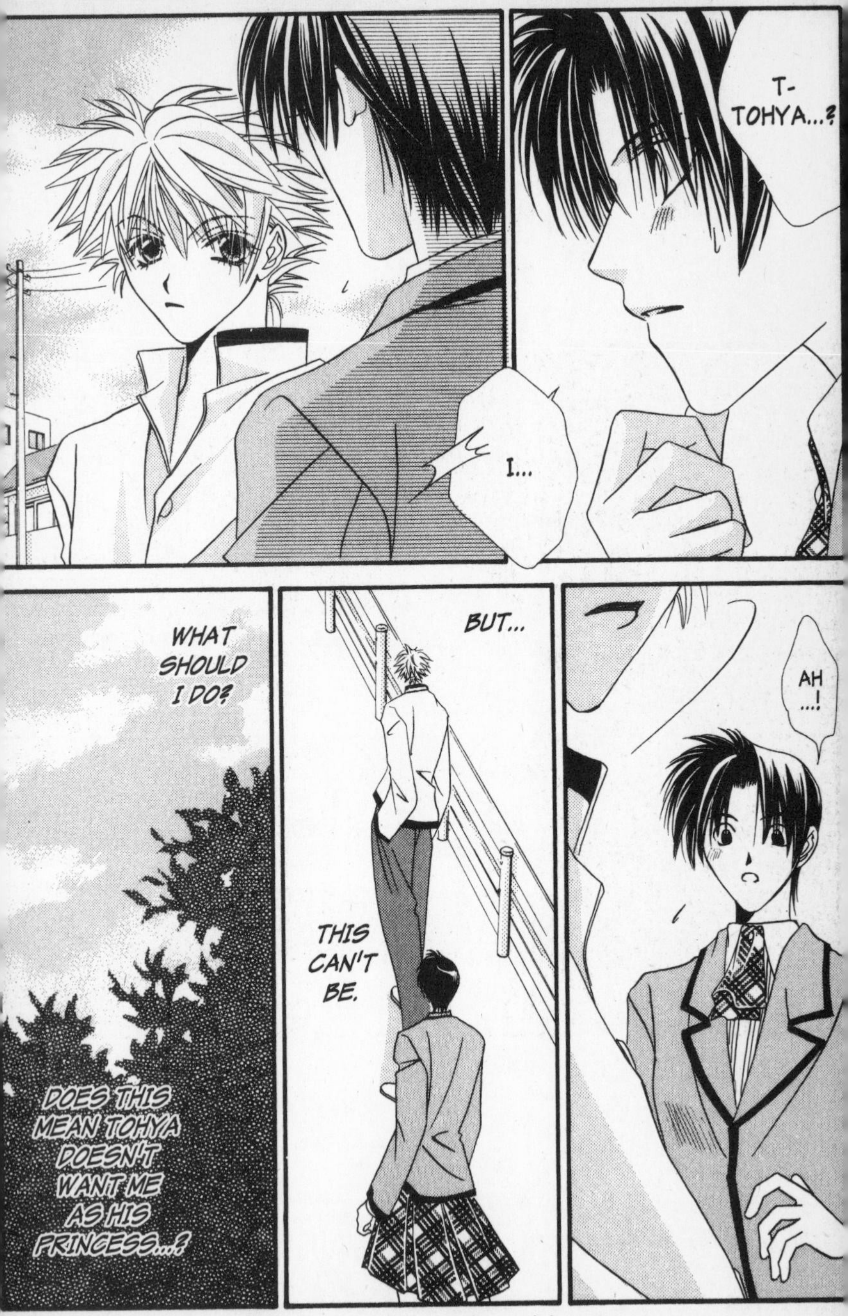
T- TOHYA...?
I...
AH ...!
BUT...
THIS CAN'T BE.
WHAT SHOULD I DO?
DOES THIS MEAN TOHYA DOESN'T WANT ME AS HIS PRINCESS...?

To Be Continued in Vol. 2!

Secrets of the Muto Household

--Neither Sea nor Sky-- by Shinoyu

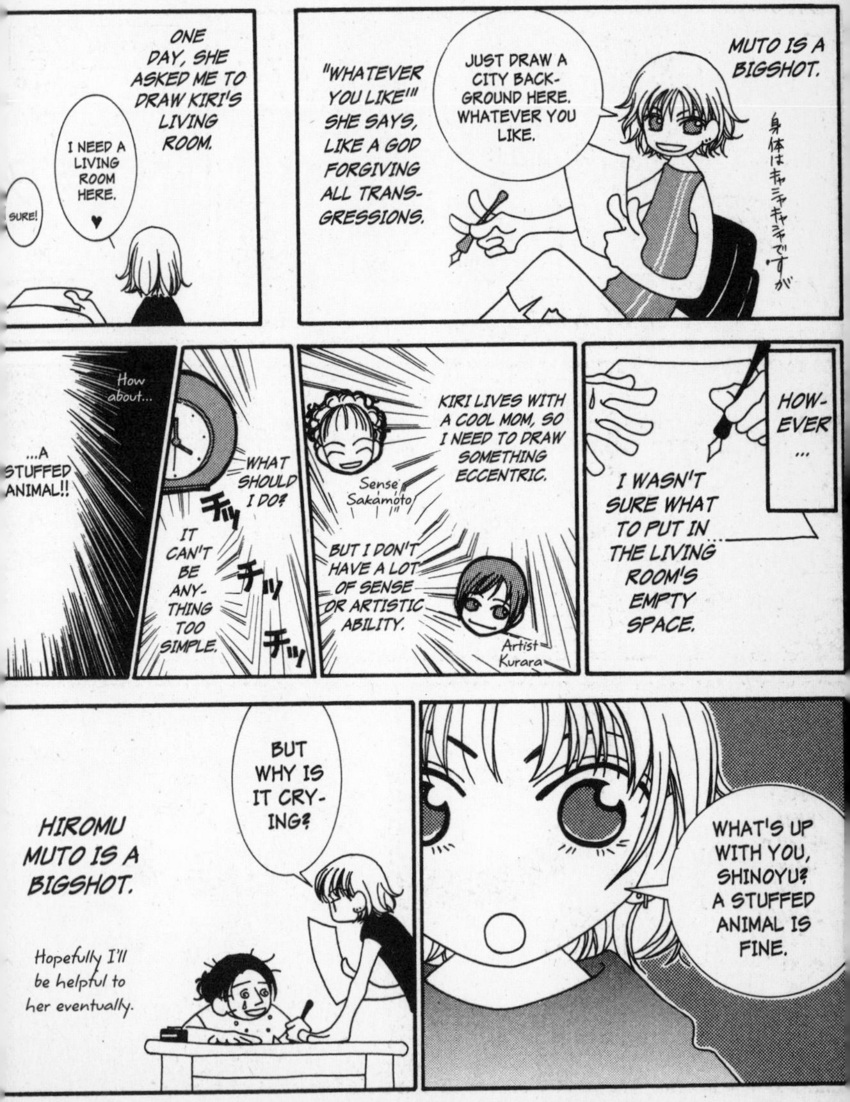
MUTO IS A BIGSHOT.
身体はキャシャキャシャですが
JUST DRAW A CITY BACK-GROUND HERE. WHATEVER YOU LIKE.
"WHATEVER YOU LIKE!" SHE SAYS, LIKE A GOD FORGIVING ALL TRANS-GRESSIONS.
ONE DAY, SHE ASKED ME TO DRAW KIRI'S LIVING ROOM.
I NEED A LIVING ROOM HERE. ♥
SURE!
HOW-EVER...
I WASN'T SURE WHAT TO PUT IN THE LIVING ROOM'S EMPTY SPACE.
KIRI LIVES WITH A COOL MOM, SO I NEED TO DRAW SOMETHING ECCENTRIC.
Sense Sakamoto
BUT I DON'T HAVE A LOT OF SENSE OR ARTISTIC ABILITY.
Artist Kurara
WHAT SHOULD I DO?
チッ
IT CAN'T BE ANYTHING TOO SIMPLE.
チッ
チッ
How about...
...A STUFFED ANIMAL!!
WHAT'S UP WITH YOU, SHINOYU? A STUFFED ANIMAL IS FINE.
BUT WHY IS IT CRYING?
HIROMU MUTO IS A BIGSHOT.
Hopefully I'll be helpful to her eventually.

Secrets of the Muto Household

--Muto in the Morning-- by Kurara

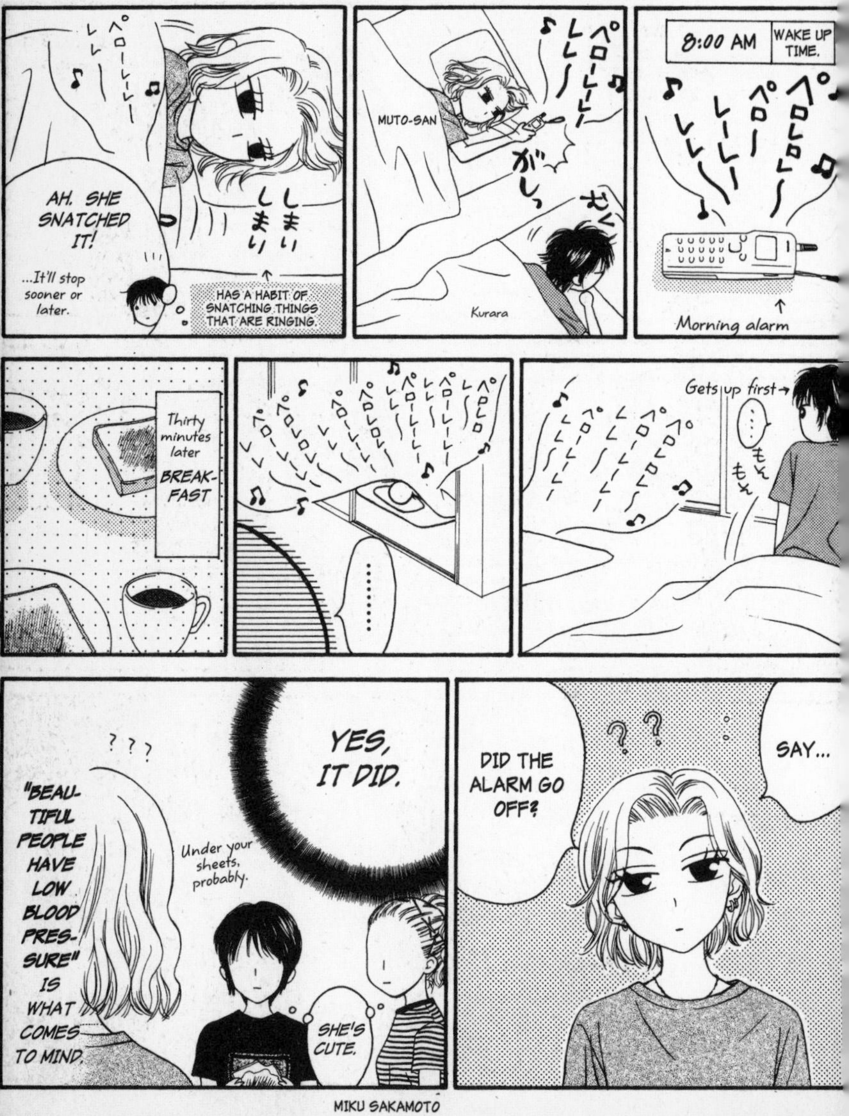
8:00 AM
WAKE UP TIME.
Morning alarm
MUTO-SAN
がしっ
むく
Kurara
AH. SHE SNATCHED IT!
しまい しまい
...It'll stop sooner or later.
HAS A HABIT OF SNATCHING THINGS THAT ARE RINGING.
Gets up first
...
もそ もそ
......
Thirty minutes later
BREAKFAST
SAY...
DID THE ALARM GO OFF?
??
YES, IT DID.
???
Under your sheets, probably.
SHE'S CUTE.
"BEAUTIFUL PEOPLE HAVE LOW BLOOD PRESSURE" IS WHAT COMES TO MIND.

MIKU SAKAMOTO

Secrets of the Muto Household

--Muto Counts-- by Sakamoto

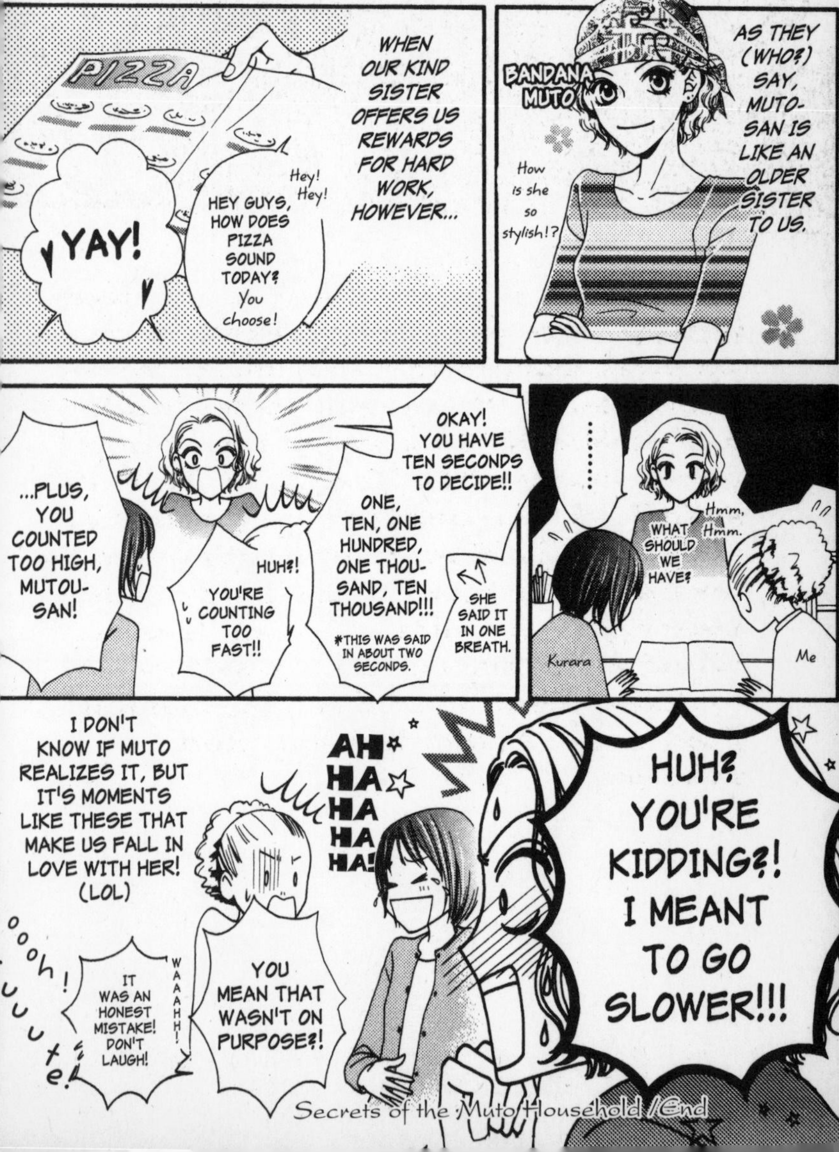

BANDANA MUTO
AS THEY (WHO?) SAY, MUTO-SAN IS LIKE AN OLDER SISTER TO US.
How is she so stylish!?
WHEN OUR KIND SISTER OFFERS US REWARDS FOR HARD WORK, HOWEVER...
Hey! Hey!
HEY GUYS, HOW DOES PIZZA SOUND TODAY? You choose!
PIZZA
YAY!
......
Hmm, Hmm.
WHAT SHOULD WE HAVE?
Kurara
Me
OKAY! YOU HAVE TEN SECONDS TO DECIDE!!
SHE SAID IT IN ONE BREATH.
ONE, TEN, ONE HUNDRED, ONE THOU-SAND, TEN THOUSAND!!!
*THIS WAS SAID IN ABOUT TWO SECONDS.
HUH?!
YOU'RE COUNTING TOO FAST!!
...PLUS, YOU COUNTED TOO HIGH, MUTOU-SAN!
HUH? YOU'RE KIDDING?! I MEANT TO GO SLOWER!!!
AH HA HA HA HA!
YOU MEAN THAT WASN'T ON PURPOSE?!
WAAAHH!
IT WAS AN HONEST MISTAKE! DON'T LAUGH!
oooh! cuuute!
I DON'T KNOW IF MUTO REALIZES IT, BUT IT'S MOMENTS LIKE THESE THAT MAKE US FALL IN LOVE WITH HER! (LOL)
Secrets of the Muto Household /End

In the next volume of...

NEVER GIVE UP ™

Just when Kiri is about to confess her feelings for Tohya, Akira shows up and sabotages her plan. When she gets up the nerve to try again, her romantic moment is interrupted once again--this time, by Tohya's sister! Then another girl sets her sights on Tohya, complicating matters even further. When Tohya goes missing, even more drama ensues. What will happen next in this world of high fashion and high passion? Find out in this action-packed volume!

TOKYOPOP SHOP

Ayumu struggles with her studies, and the all-important high school entrance exams are approaching. Fortunately, she has help from her best bud Shii-chan, who is at the top of the class. But when the test results come back, the friends are surprised: Ayumu surpasses Shii-chan's scores and gets into the school of her choice—without Shii-chan! Losing her friend is so painful for Ayumu that she starts cutting herself to ease her sorrow. Finally, Ayumu seeks comfort in a new friend, Manami. But will Manami prove to be the friend that Ayumu truly needs? Or will Ayumu continue down a dark path?

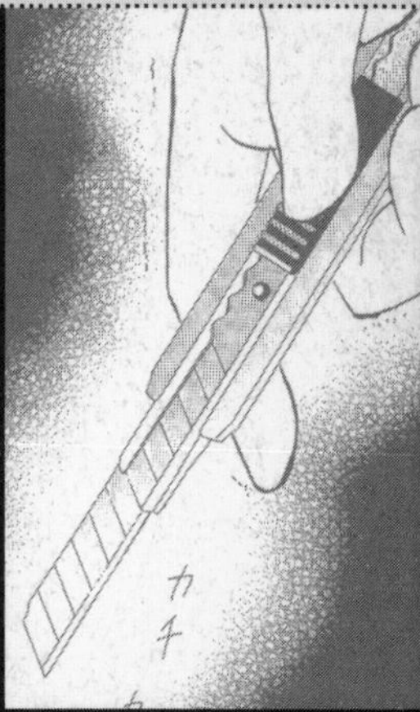
カチ

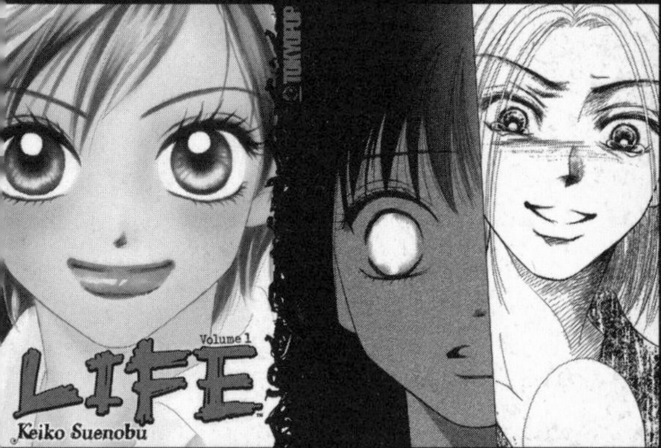
TOKYOPOP
Volume 1
LIFE
Keiko Suenobu

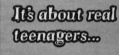

It's about real teenagers...

It's about real high school...

It's about real life.

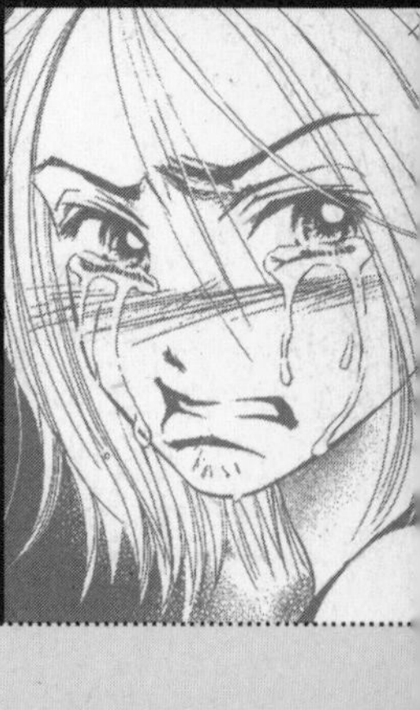

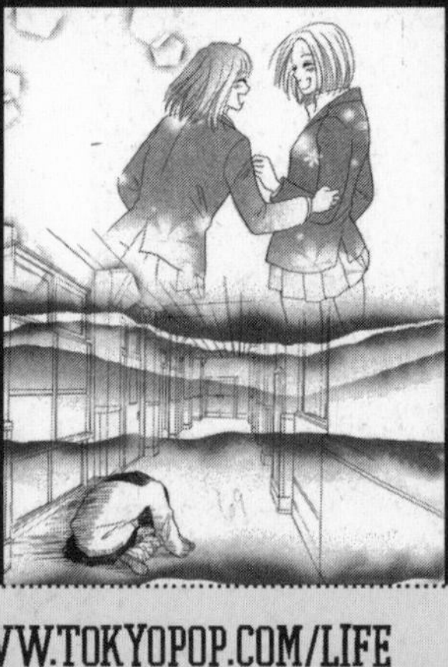

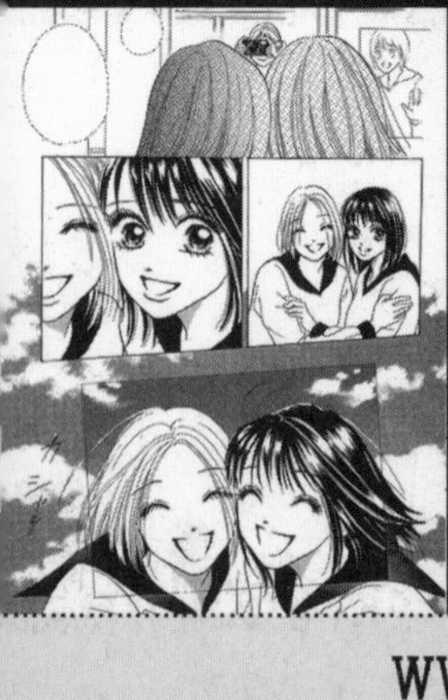

WWW.TOKYOPOP.COM/LIFE

LIFE
BY KEIKO SUENOBU

Ordinary high school teenagers...
Except that they're not.

OT
OLDER TEEN
AGE 16+

© Keiko Suenobu

STOP!

This is the back of the book.
You wouldn't want to spoil a great ending!

This book is printed "manga-style," in the authentic Japanese right-to-left format. Since none of the artwork has been flipped or altered, readers get to experience the story just as the creator intended. You've been asking for it, so TOKYOPOP® delivered: authentic, hot-off-the-press, and far more fun!

DIRECTIONS

If this is your first time reading manga-style, here's a quick guide to help you understand how it works.

It's easy... just start in the top right panel and follow the numbers. Have fun, and look for more 100% authentic manga from TOKYOPOP®!